DRIFTING DRAGONS

Taku Kuwabara

4

DRIFTING DRAGONS

Table of Contents

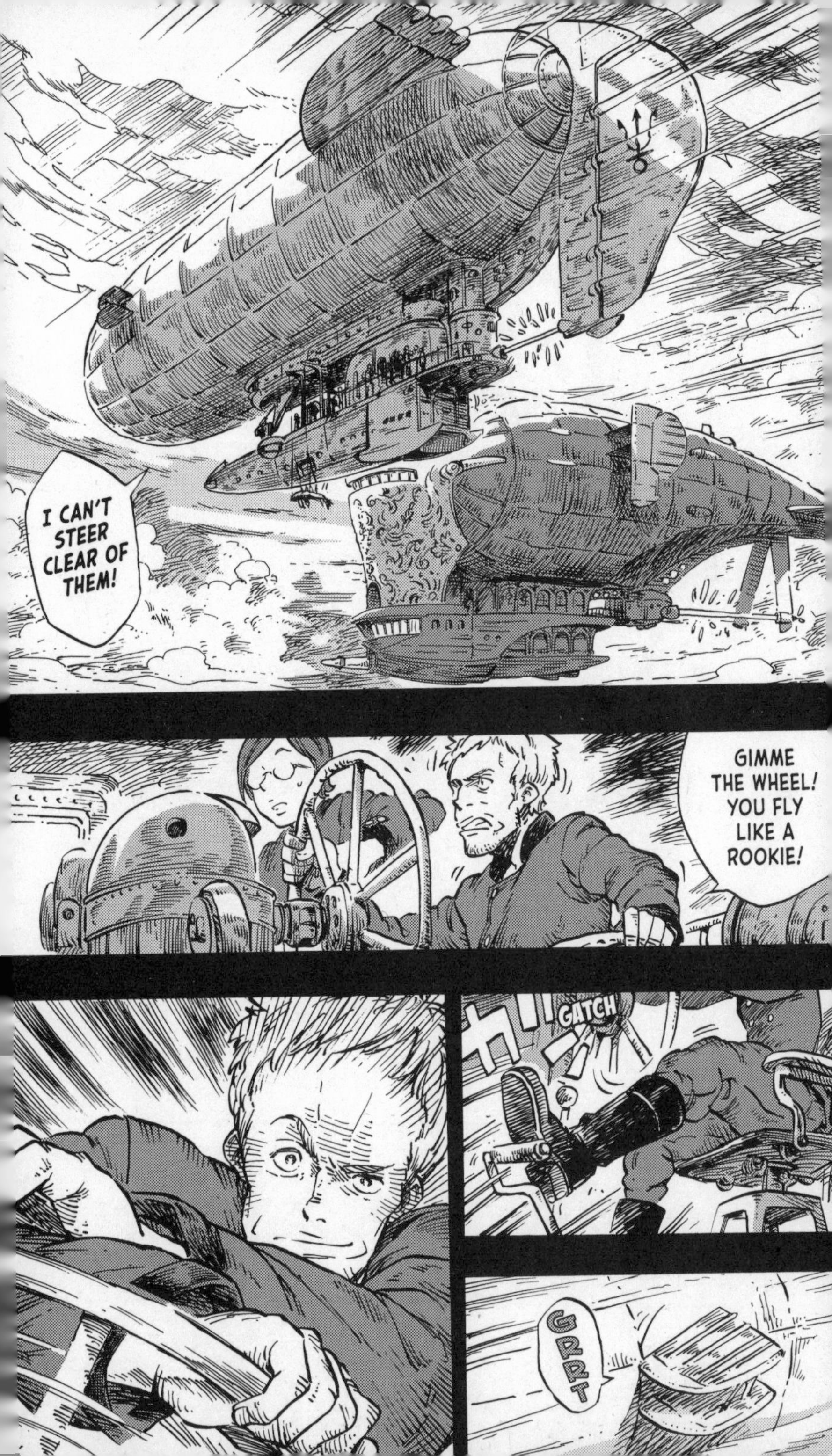
I CAN'T STEER CLEAR OF THEM!
GIMME THE WHEEL! YOU FLY LIKE A ROOKIE!
GATCH
GRRT

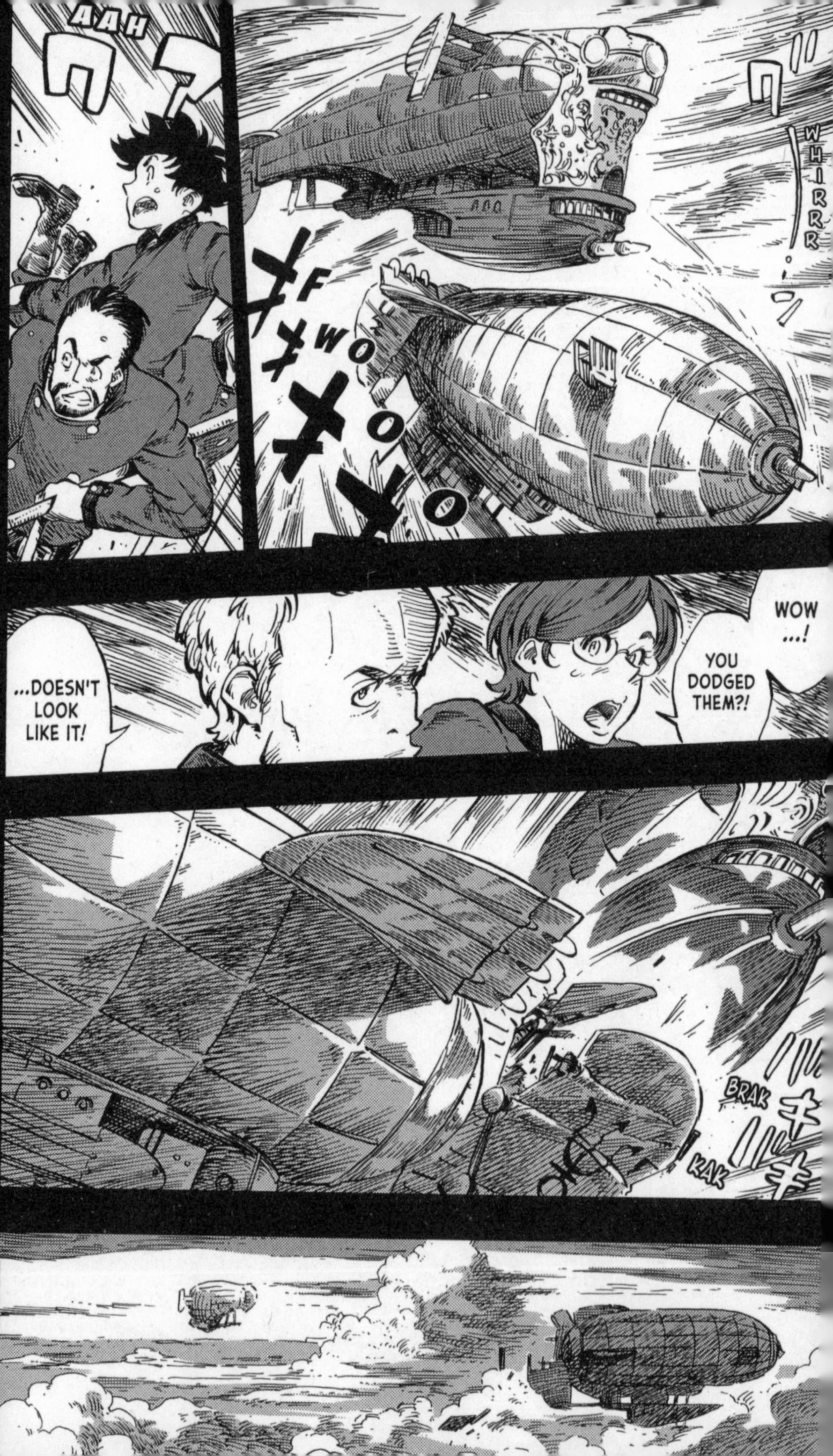
WHIRRR
FWOOO
AAH
WOW ...!
YOU DODGED THEM?!
...DOESN'T LOOK LIKE IT!
BRAK
KAK

Flight 18 Luxury Liner & Cafeteria Cheeseburgers

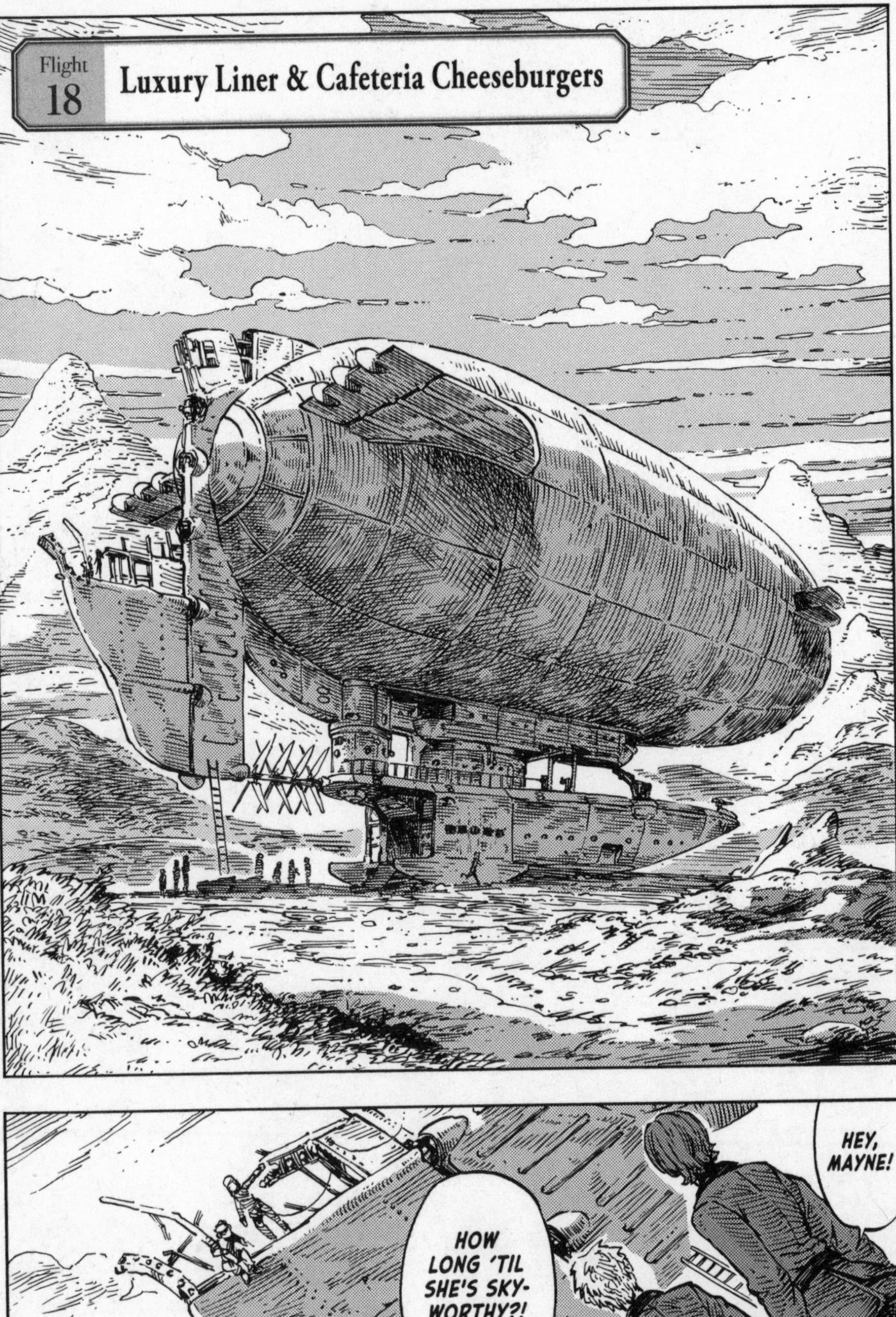
HEY, MAYNE!
HOW LONG 'TIL SHE'S SKY-WORTHY?!

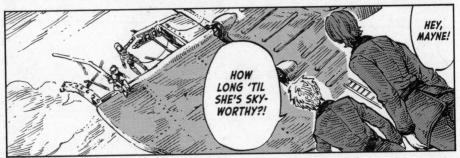

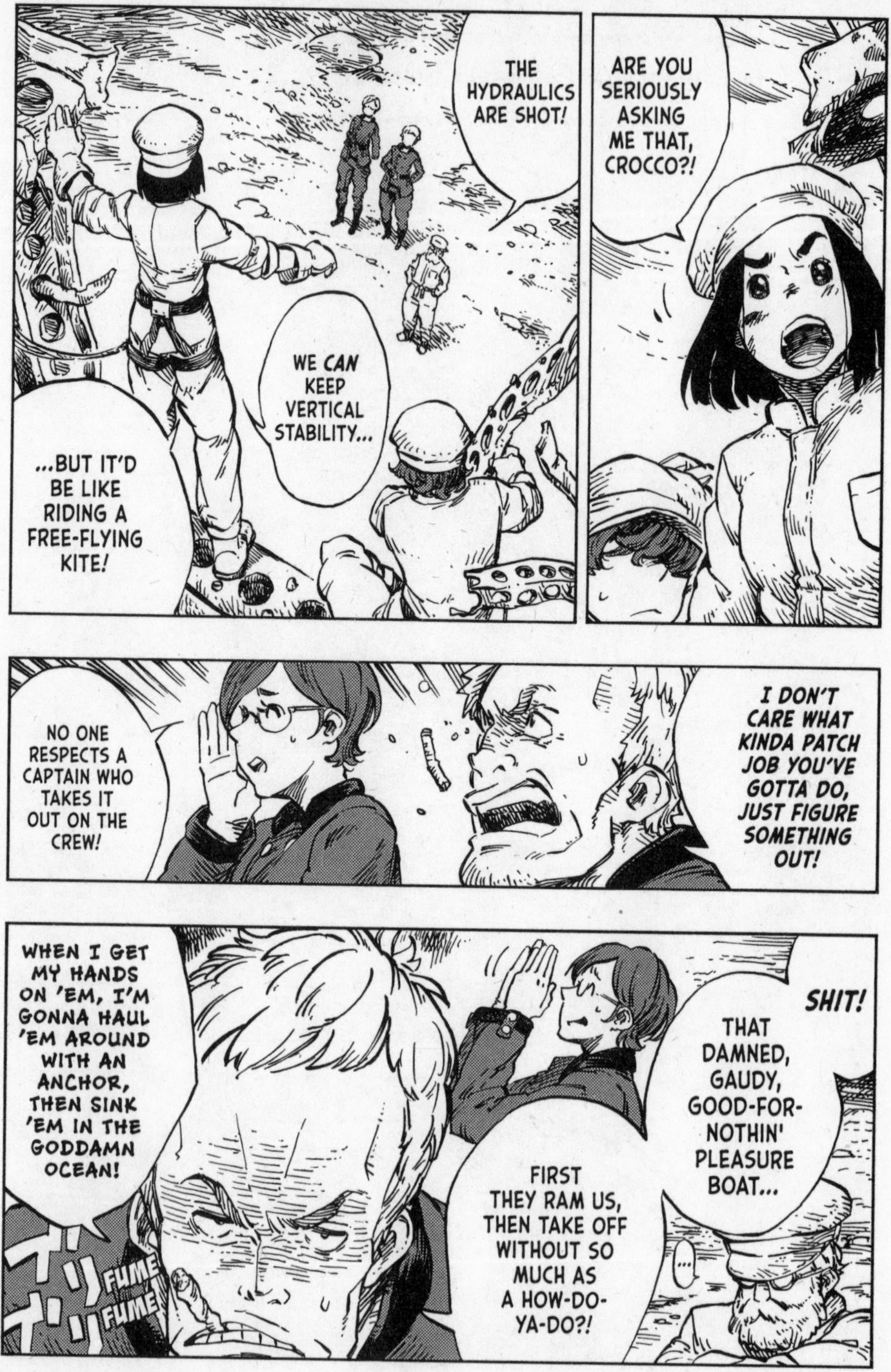
ARE YOU SERIOUSLY ASKING ME THAT, CROCCO?!
THE HYDRAULICS ARE SHOT!
WE CAN KEEP VERTICAL STABILITY...
...BUT IT'D BE LIKE RIDING A FREE-FLYING KITE!
I DON'T CARE WHAT KINDA PATCH JOB YOU'VE GOTTA DO, JUST FIGURE SOMETHING OUT!
NO ONE RESPECTS A CAPTAIN WHO TAKES IT OUT ON THE CREW!
SHIT!
THAT DAMNED, GAUDY, GOOD-FOR-NOTHIN' PLEASURE BOAT...
...
FIRST THEY RAM US, THEN TAKE OFF WITHOUT SO MUCH AS A HOW-DO-YA-DO?!
WHEN I GET MY HANDS ON 'EM, I'M GONNA HAUL 'EM AROUND WITH AN ANCHOR, THEN SINK 'EM IN THE GODDAMN OCEAN!
FUME FUME

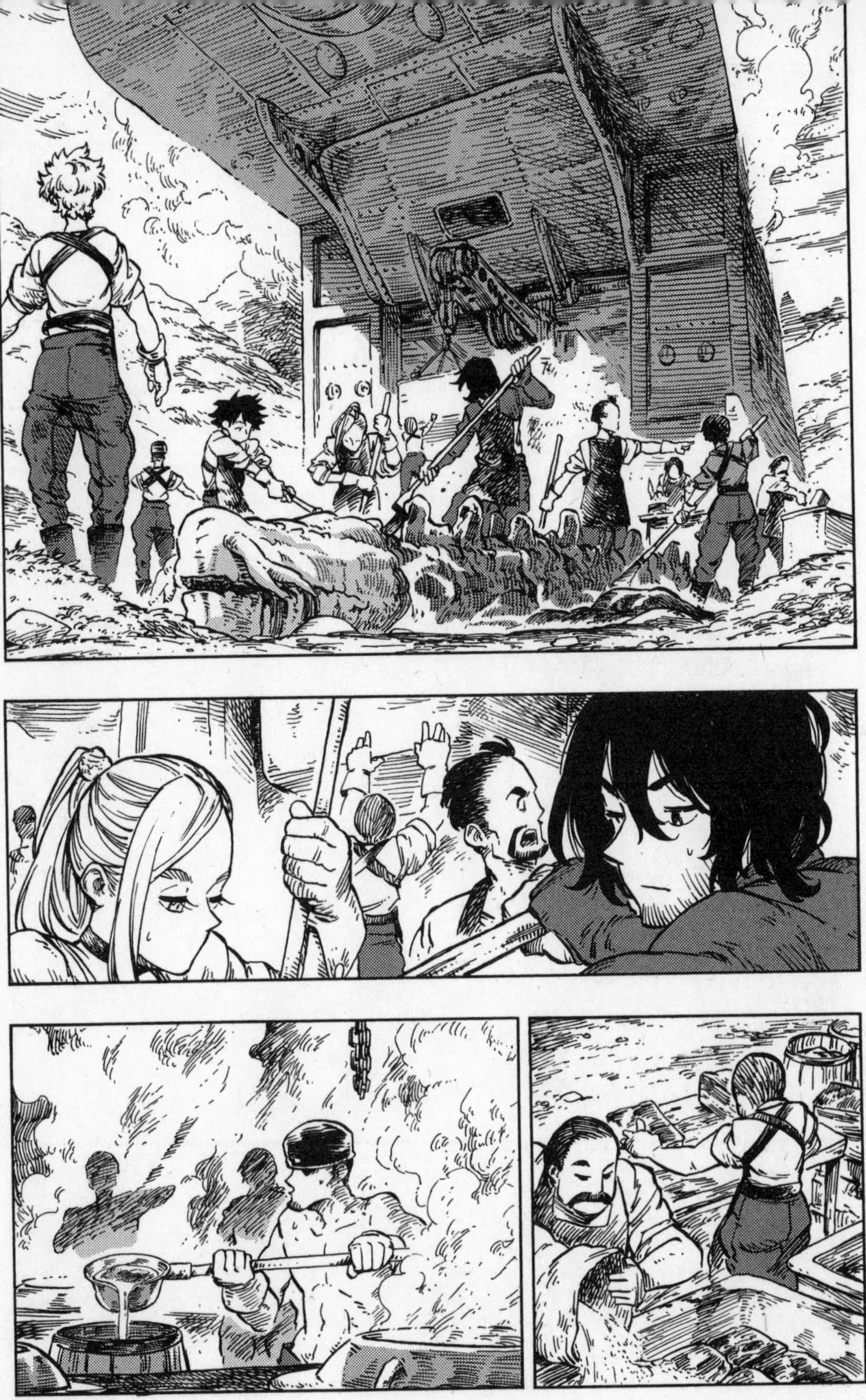

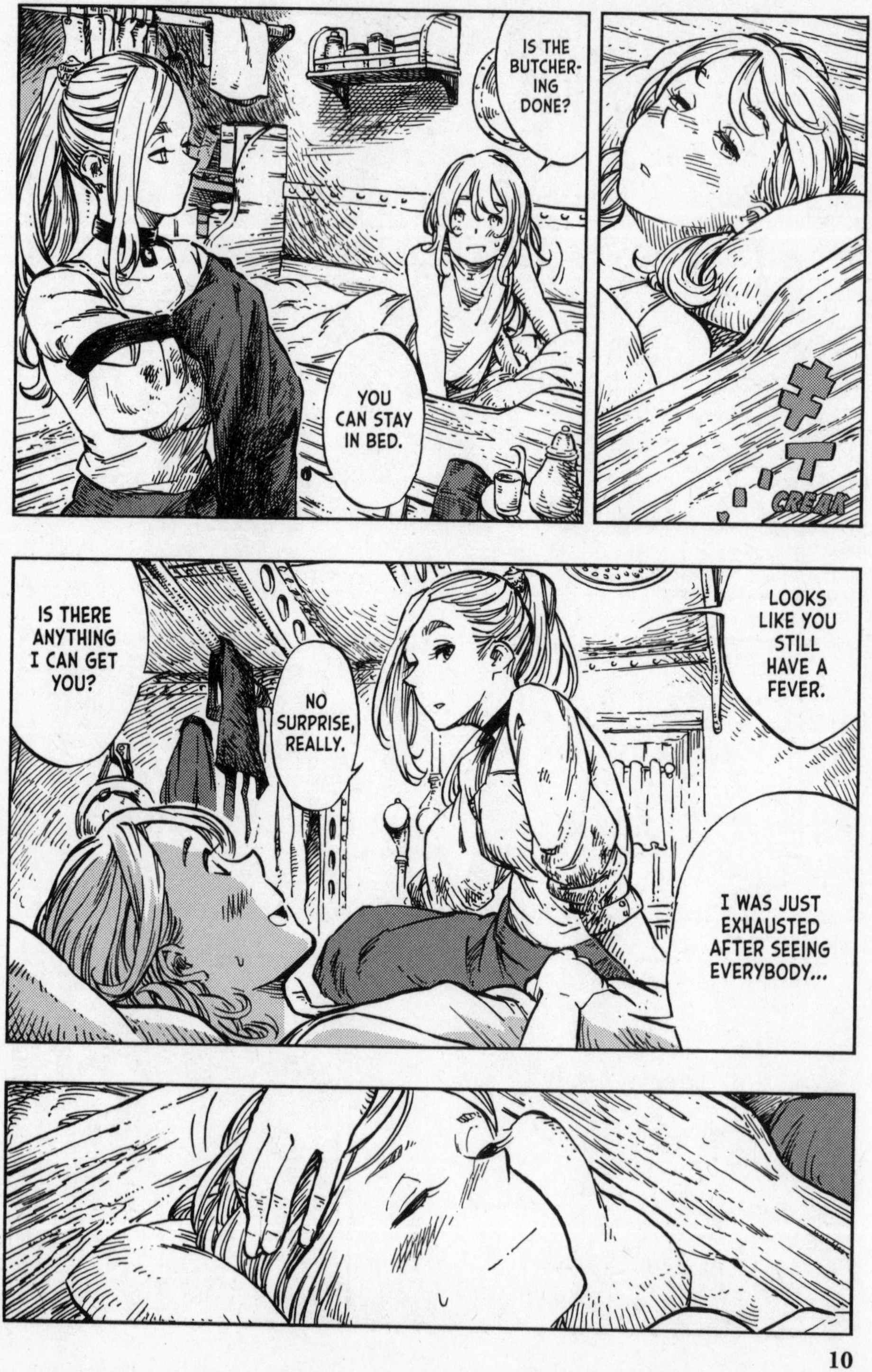
CREAK
IS THE BUTCHER-ING DONE?
YOU CAN STAY IN BED.
LOOKS LIKE YOU STILL HAVE A FEVER.
I WAS JUST EXHAUSTED AFTER SEEING EVERYBODY...
NO SURPRISE, REALLY.
IS THERE ANYTHING I CAN GET YOU?

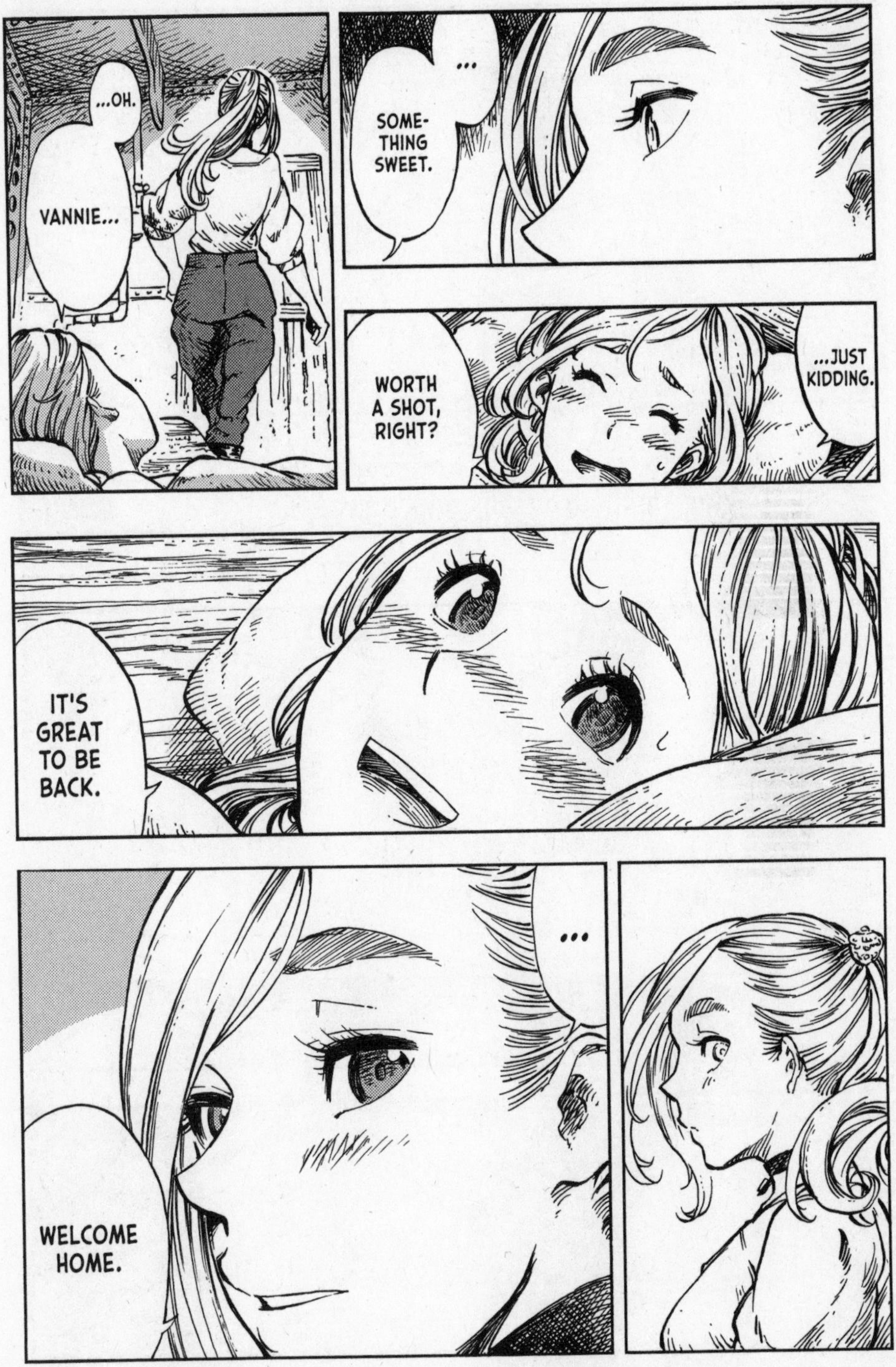
...
SOMETHING SWEET.
...JUST KIDDING.
WORTH A SHOT, RIGHT?
...OH.
VANNIE...
IT'S GREAT TO BE BACK.
...
WELCOME HOME.

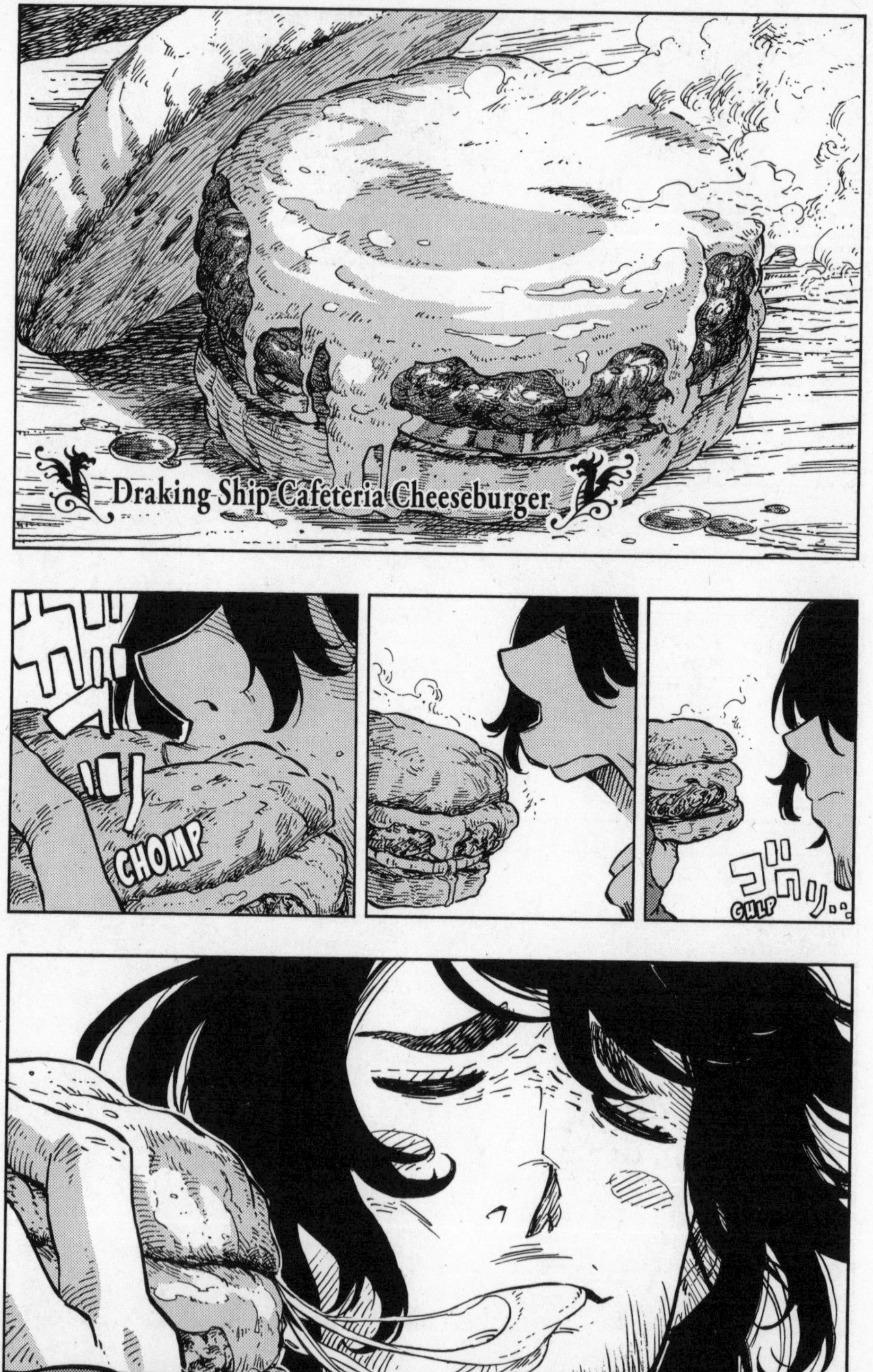
Draking Ship Cafeteria Cheeseburger
GULP
CHOMP

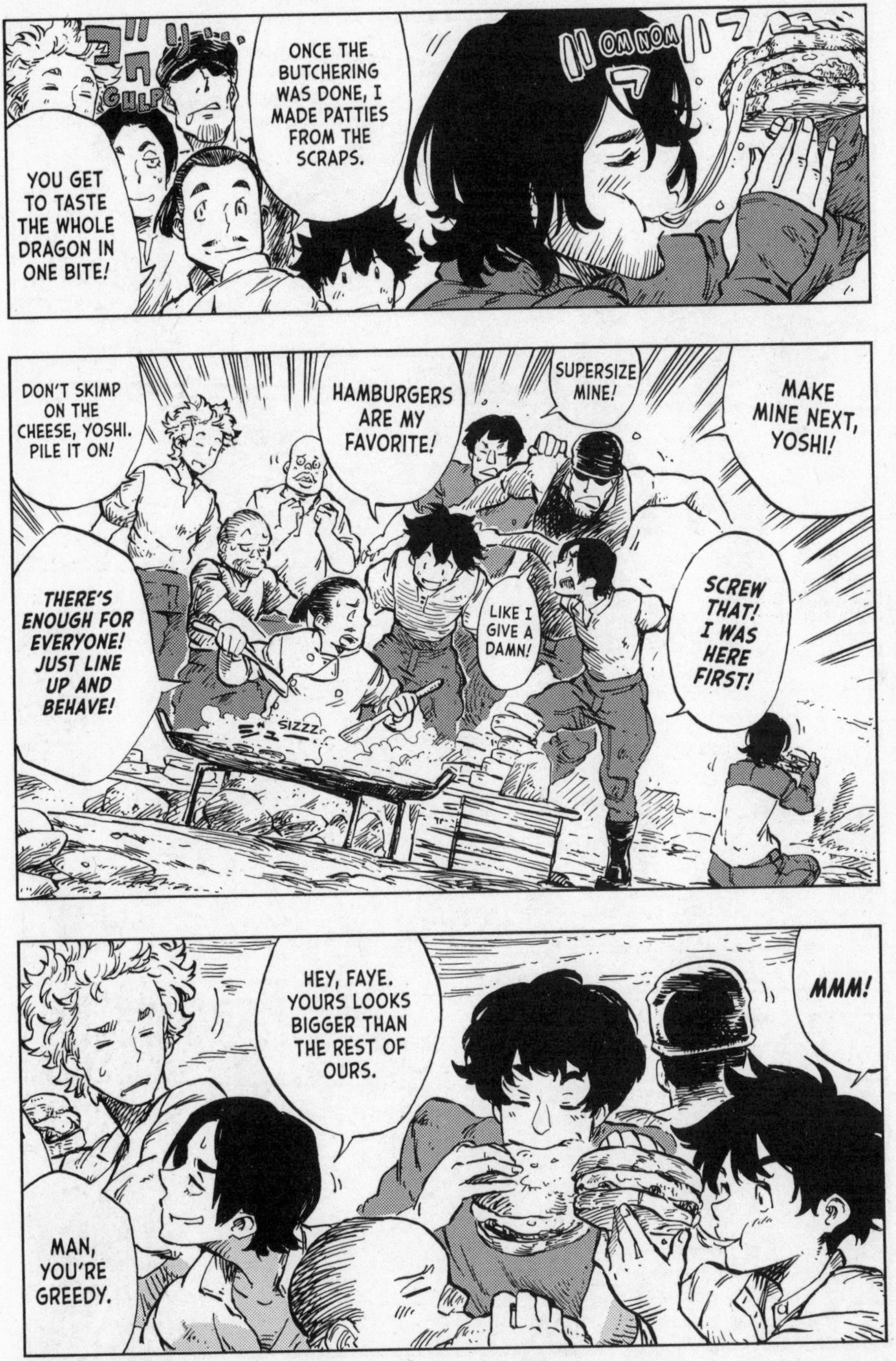
OM NOM
ONCE THE BUTCHERING WAS DONE, I MADE PATTIES FROM THE SCRAPS.
GULP
YOU GET TO TASTE THE WHOLE DRAGON IN ONE BITE!
MAKE MINE NEXT, YOSHI!
SUPERSIZE MINE!
HAMBURGERS ARE MY FAVORITE!
DON'T SKIMP ON THE CHEESE, YOSHI. PILE IT ON!
SCREW THAT! I WAS HERE FIRST!
LIKE I GIVE A DAMN!
THERE'S ENOUGH FOR EVERYONE! JUST LINE UP AND BEHAVE!
SIZZZ
MMM!
HEY, FAYE. YOURS LOOKS BIGGER THAN THE REST OF OURS.
MAN, YOU'RE GREEDY.

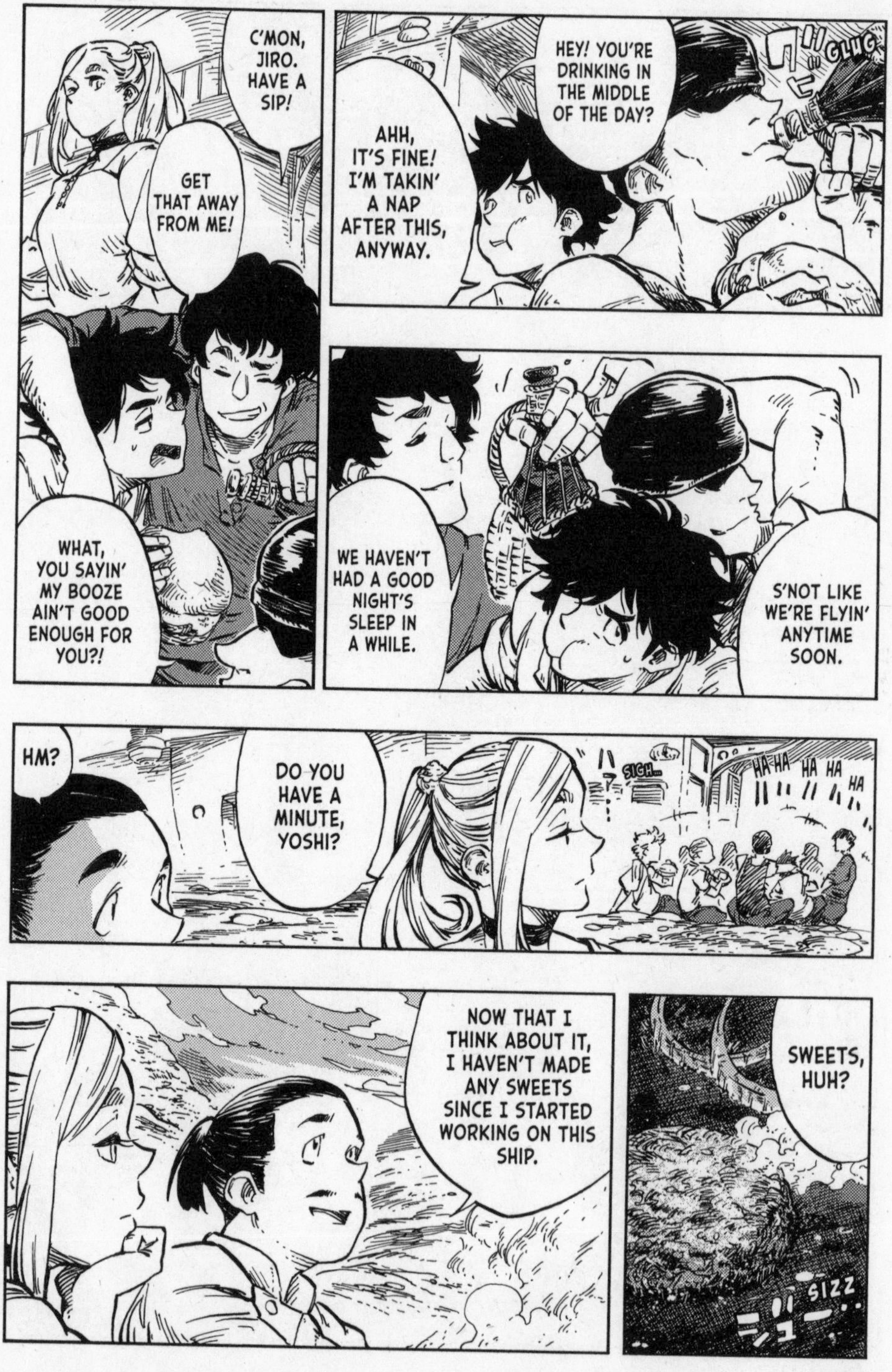
GLUG
HEY! YOU'RE DRINKING IN THE MIDDLE OF THE DAY?
AHH, IT'S FINE! I'M TAKIN' A NAP AFTER THIS, ANYWAY.
S'NOT LIKE WE'RE FLYIN' ANYTIME SOON.
WE HAVEN'T HAD A GOOD NIGHT'S SLEEP IN A WHILE.
C'MON, JIRO. HAVE A SIP!
GET THAT AWAY FROM ME!
WHAT, YOU SAYIN' MY BOOZE AIN'T GOOD ENOUGH FOR YOU?!
HA HA HA HA HA
SIGH...
DO YOU HAVE A MINUTE, YOSHI?
HM?
SWEETS, HUH?
SIZZ...
NOW THAT I THINK ABOUT IT, I HAVEN'T MADE ANY SWEETS SINCE I STARTED WORKING ON THIS SHIP.

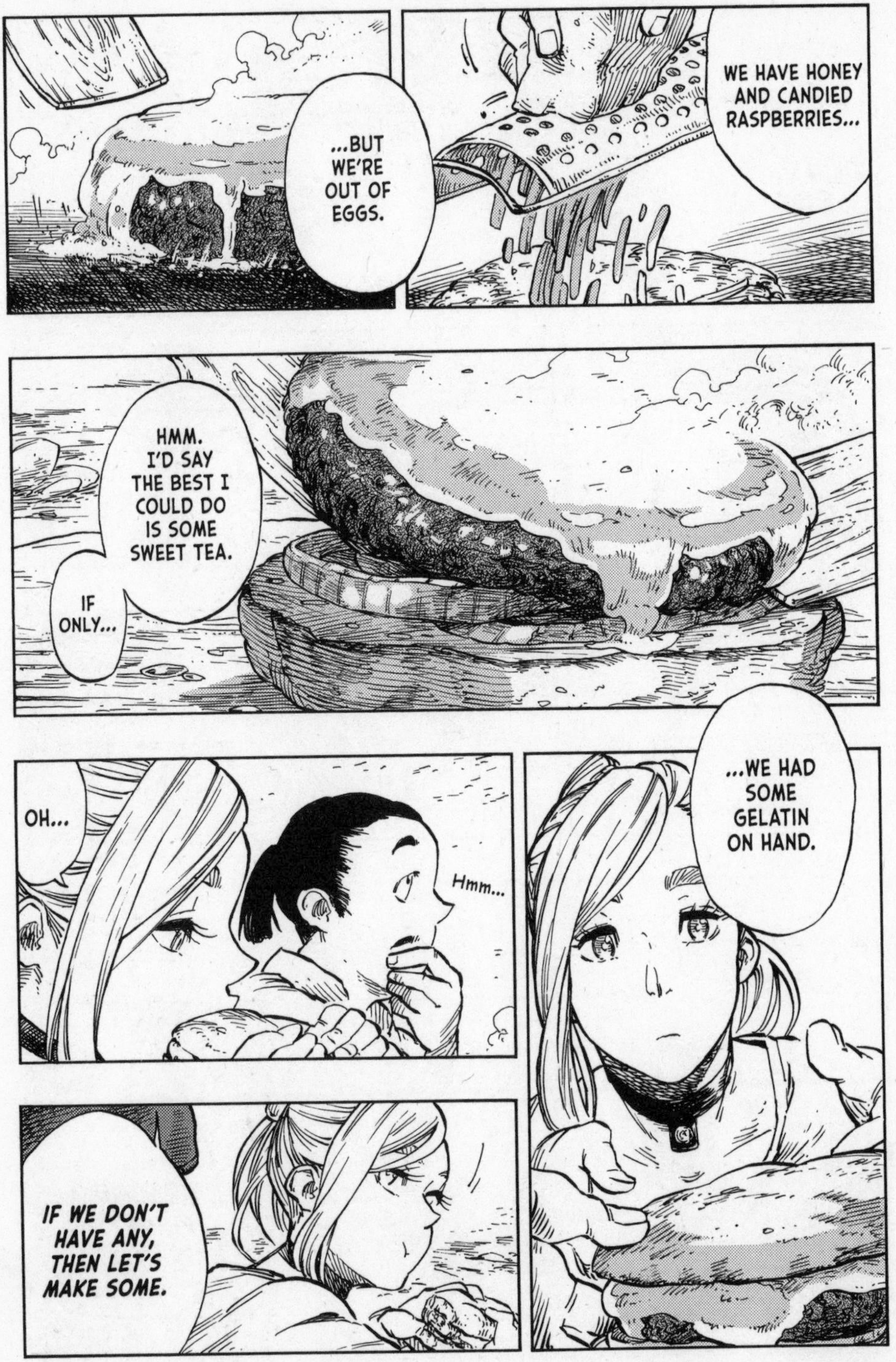
WE HAVE HONEY AND CANDIED RASPBERRIES...
...BUT WE'RE OUT OF EGGS.
HMM. I'D SAY THE BEST I COULD DO IS SOME SWEET TEA.
IF ONLY...
...WE HAD SOME GELATIN ON HAND.
OH...
Hmm...
IF WE DON'T HAVE ANY, THEN LET'S MAKE SOME.

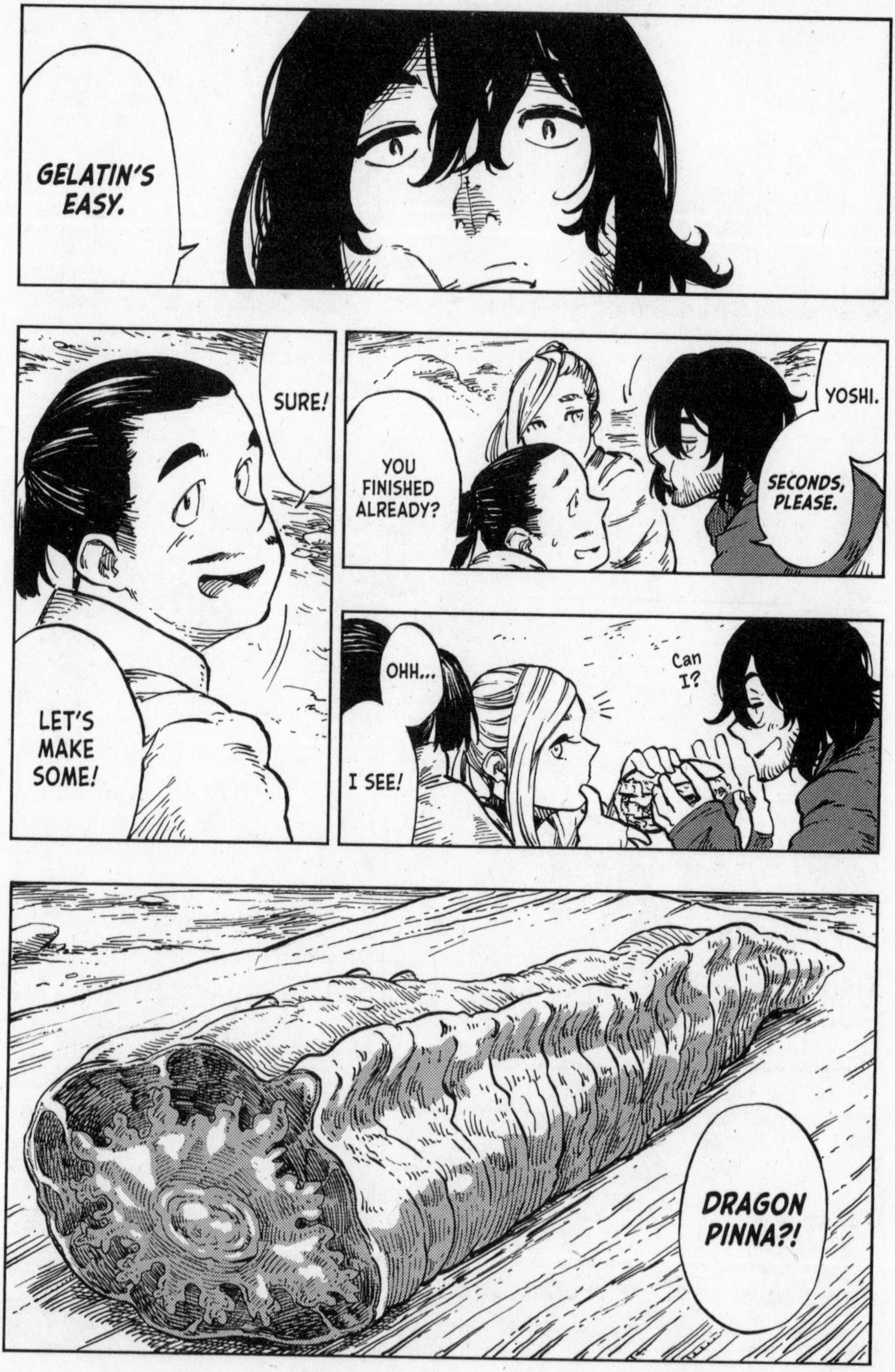
GELATIN'S EASY.
YOSHI.
SECONDS, PLEASE.
YOU FINISHED ALREADY?
Can I?
OHH...
I SEE!
SURE!
LET'S MAKE SOME!
DRAGON PINNA?!

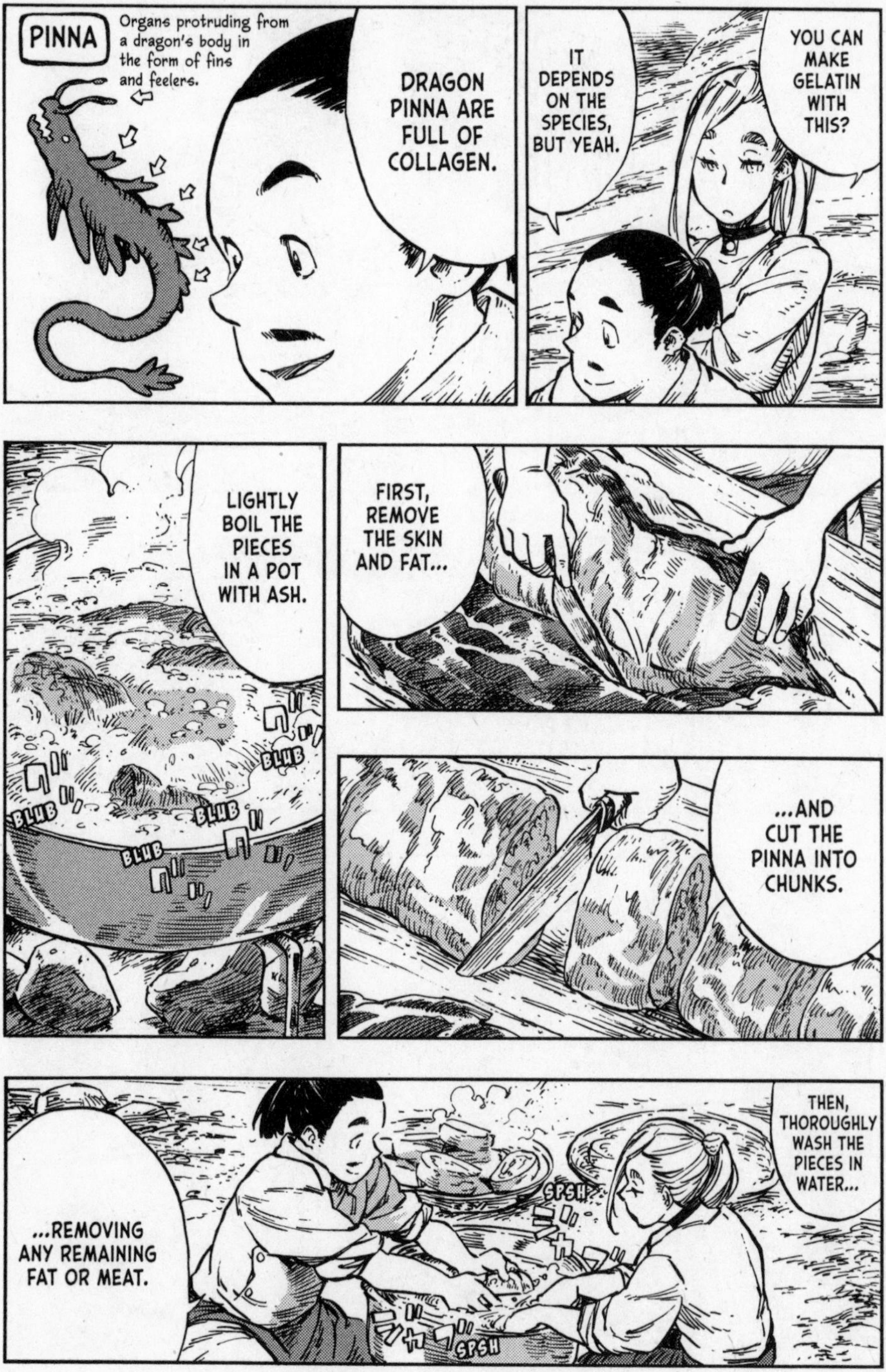
YOU CAN MAKE GELATIN WITH THIS?
IT DEPENDS ON THE SPECIES, BUT YEAH.
DRAGON PINNA ARE FULL OF COLLAGEN.
PINNA
Organs protruding from a dragon's body in the form of fins and feelers.
FIRST, REMOVE THE SKIN AND FAT...
...AND CUT THE PINNA INTO CHUNKS.
LIGHTLY BOIL THE PIECES IN A POT WITH ASH.
BLUB
BLUB
BLUB
BLUB
THEN, THOROUGHLY WASH THE PIECES IN WATER...
SPSH
...REMOVING ANY REMAINING FAT OR MEAT.
SPSH

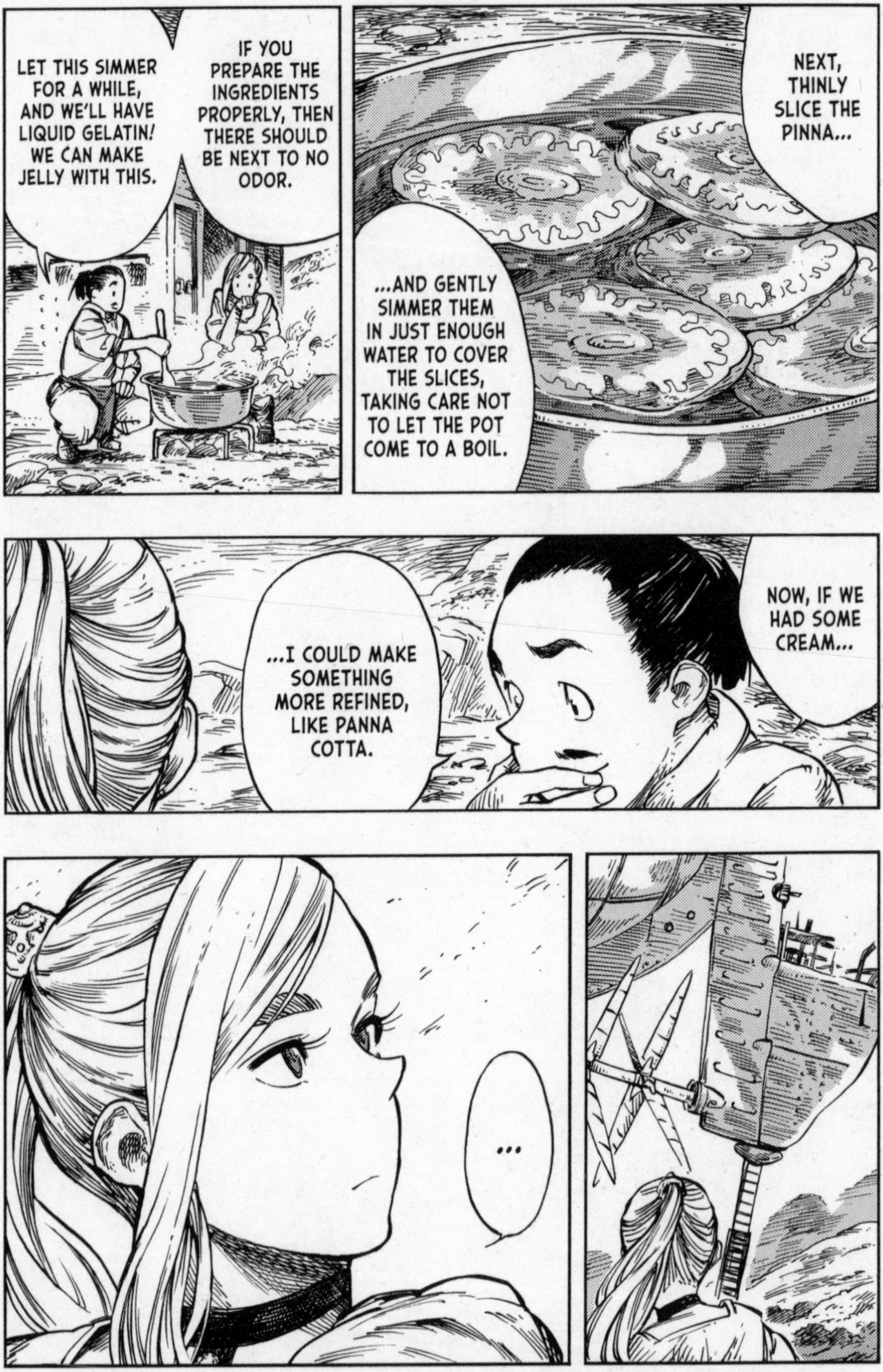
NEXT, THINLY SLICE THE PINNA...
...AND GENTLY SIMMER THEM IN JUST ENOUGH WATER TO COVER THE SLICES, TAKING CARE NOT TO LET THE POT COME TO A BOIL.
IF YOU PREPARE THE INGREDIENTS PROPERLY, THEN THERE SHOULD BE NEXT TO NO ODOR.
LET THIS SIMMER FOR A WHILE, AND WE'LL HAVE LIQUID GELATIN! WE CAN MAKE JELLY WITH THIS.
NOW, IF WE HAD SOME CREAM...
...I COULD MAKE SOMETHING MORE REFINED, LIKE PANNA COTTA.
...

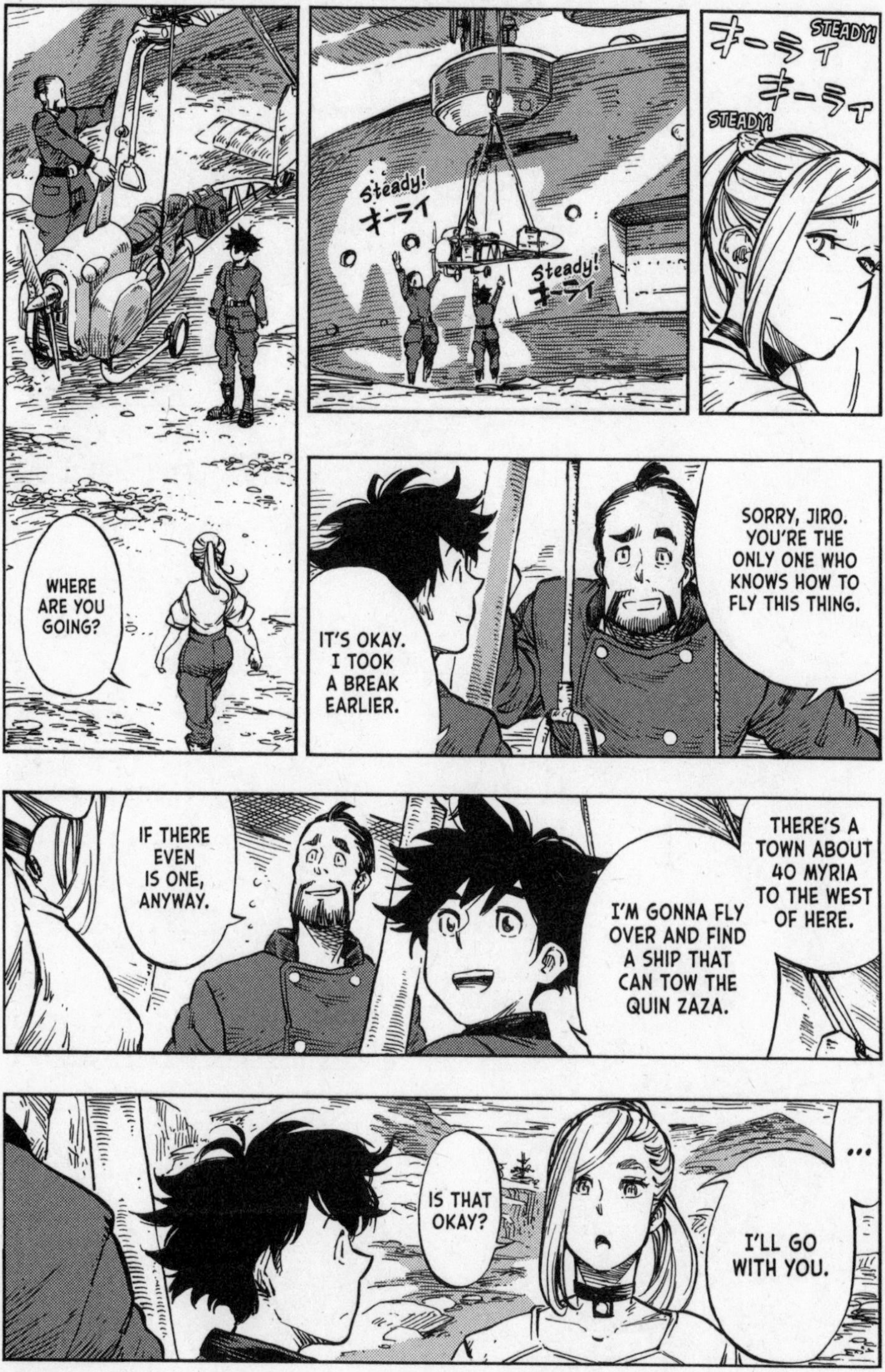
STEADY!
オーライ
オーライ
STEADY!
Steady!
オーライ
Steady!
オーライ
SORRY, JIRO. YOU'RE THE ONLY ONE WHO KNOWS HOW TO FLY THIS THING.
IT'S OKAY. I TOOK A BREAK EARLIER.
WHERE ARE YOU GOING?
THERE'S A TOWN ABOUT 40 MYRIA TO THE WEST OF HERE.
I'M GONNA FLY OVER AND FIND A SHIP THAT CAN TOW THE QUIN ZAZA.
IF THERE EVEN IS ONE, ANYWAY.
...
I'LL GO WITH YOU.
IS THAT OKAY?

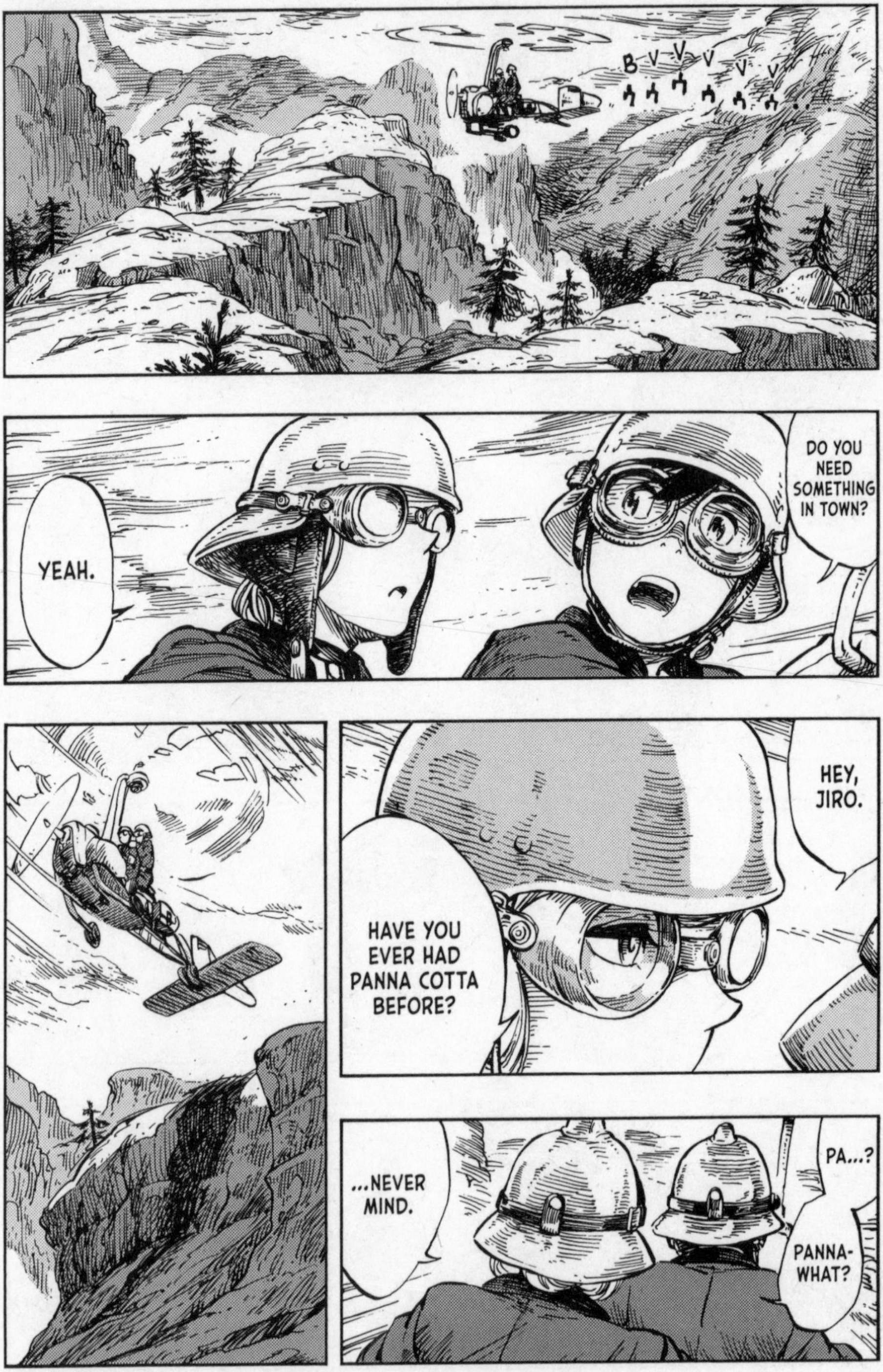
BVVVVV...
DO YOU NEED SOMETHING IN TOWN?
YEAH.
HEY, JIRO.
HAVE YOU EVER HAD PANNA COTTA BEFORE?
PA...?
PANNA-WHAT?
...NEVER MIND.

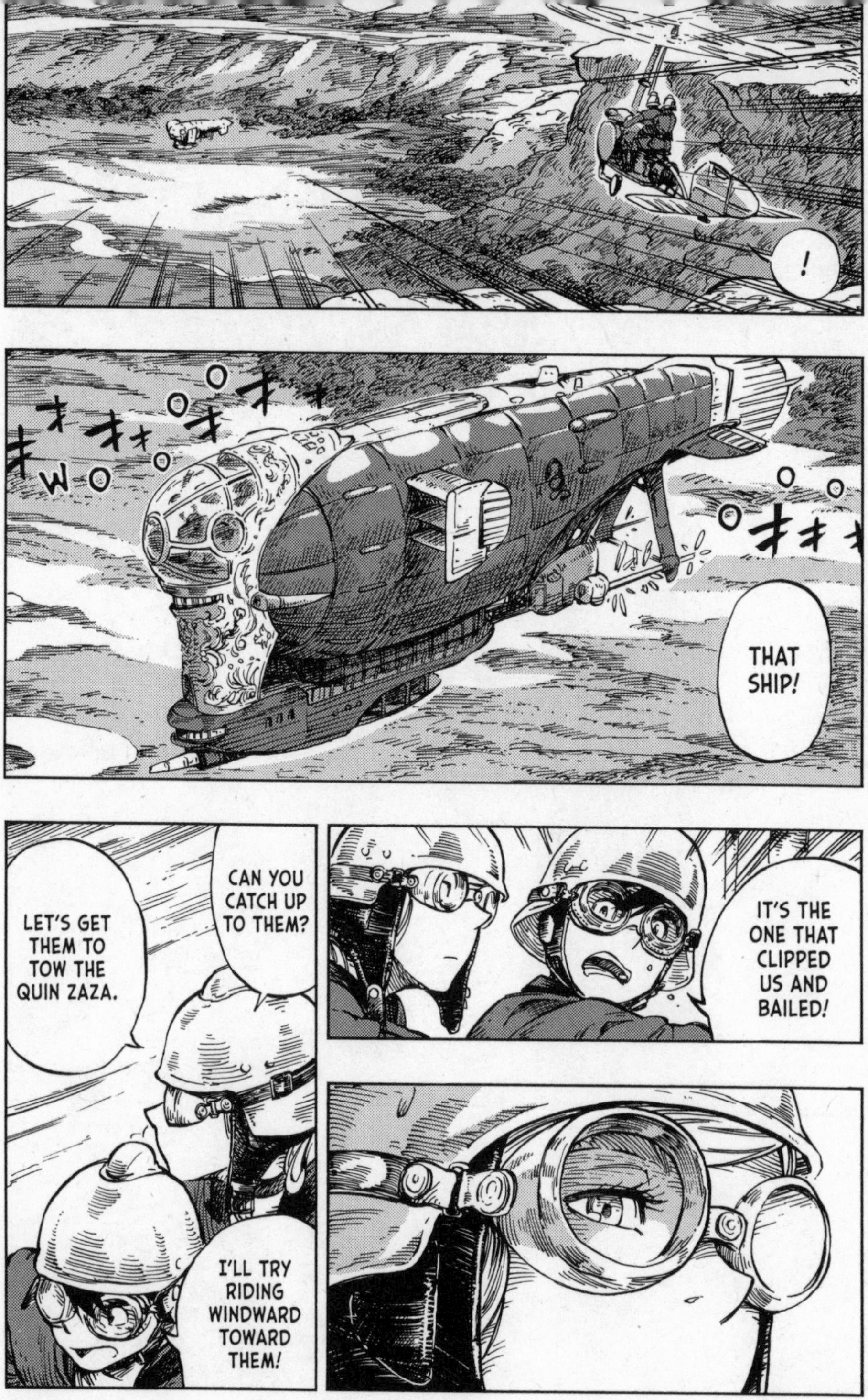
!
THAT SHIP!
IT'S THE ONE THAT CLIPPED US AND BAILED!
CAN YOU CATCH UP TO THEM?
LET'S GET THEM TO TOW THE QUIN ZAZA.
I'LL TRY RIDING WINDWARD TOWARD THEM!

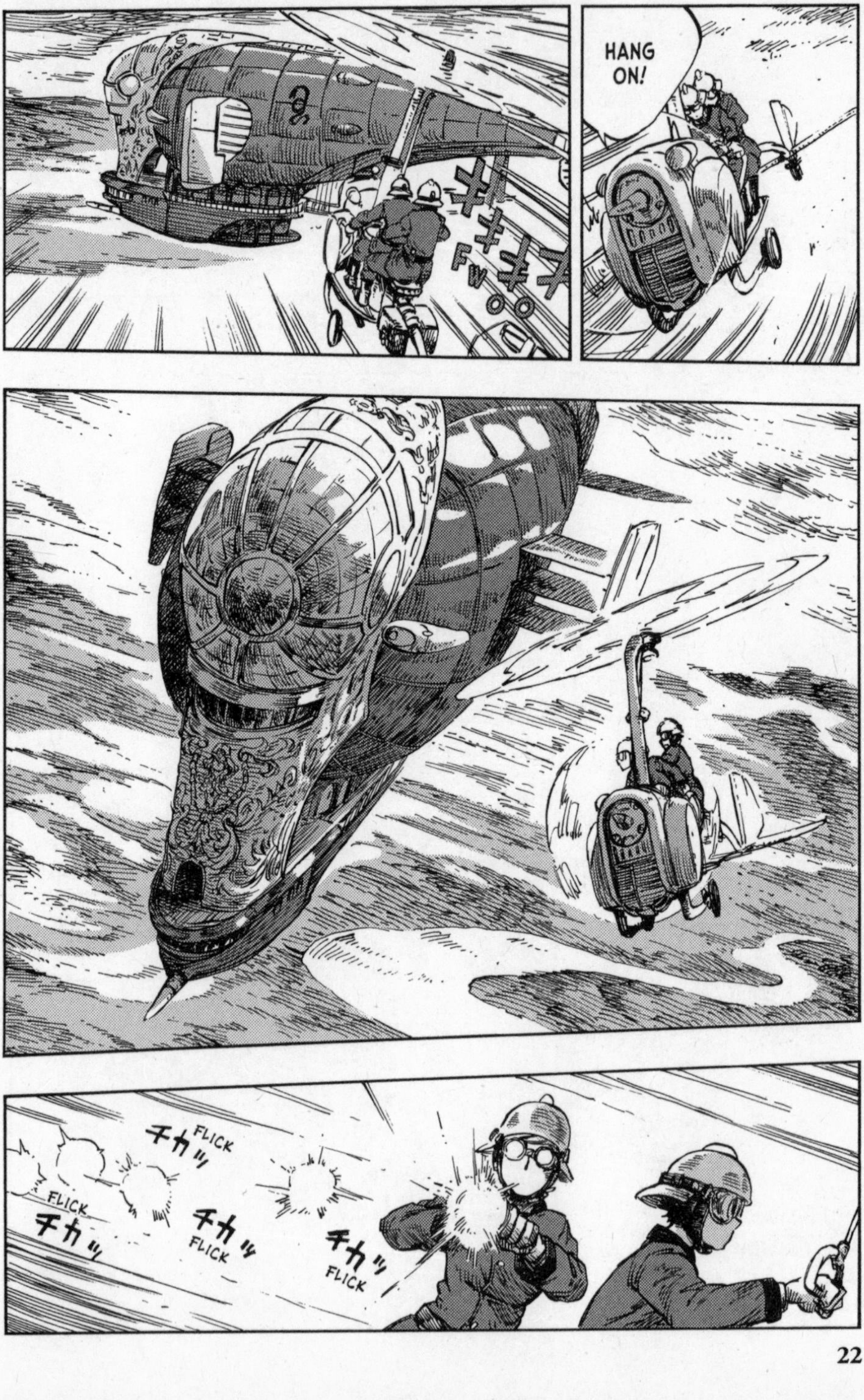
HANG ON!
FWOO
チカッ FLICK
チカッ FLICK
チカッ FLICK
チカッ FLICK
チカッ FLICK

THEY AREN'T RESPONDING TO THE SIGNAL.

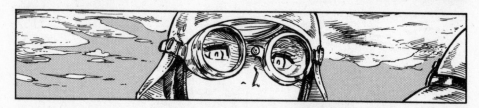

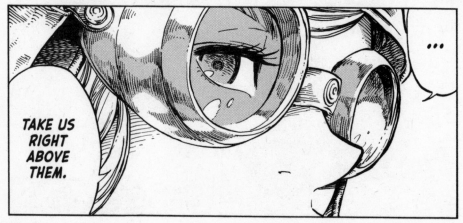

TAKE US RIGHT ABOVE THEM.

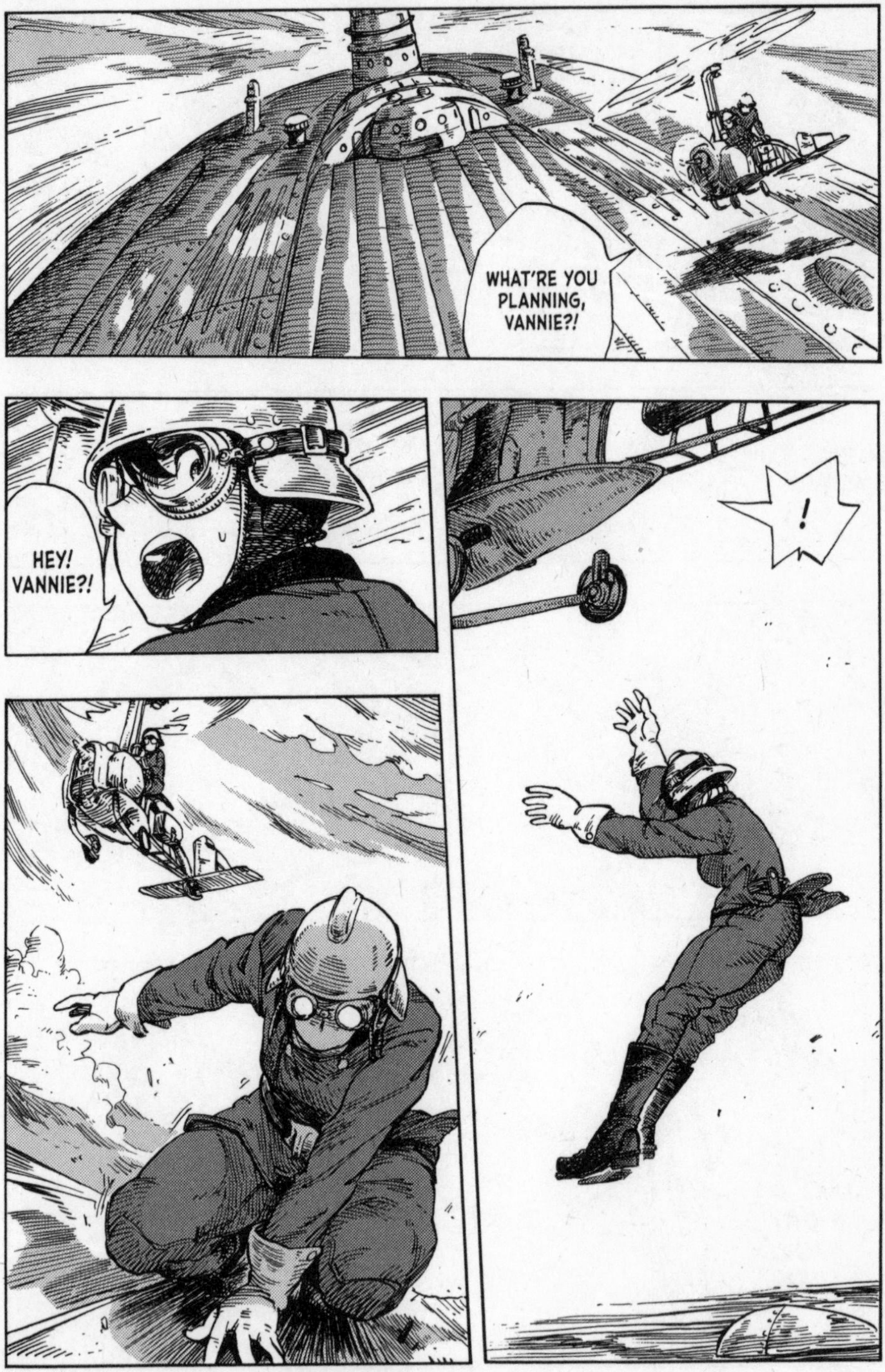
WHAT'RE YOU PLANNING, VANNIE?!
!
HEY! VANNIE?!

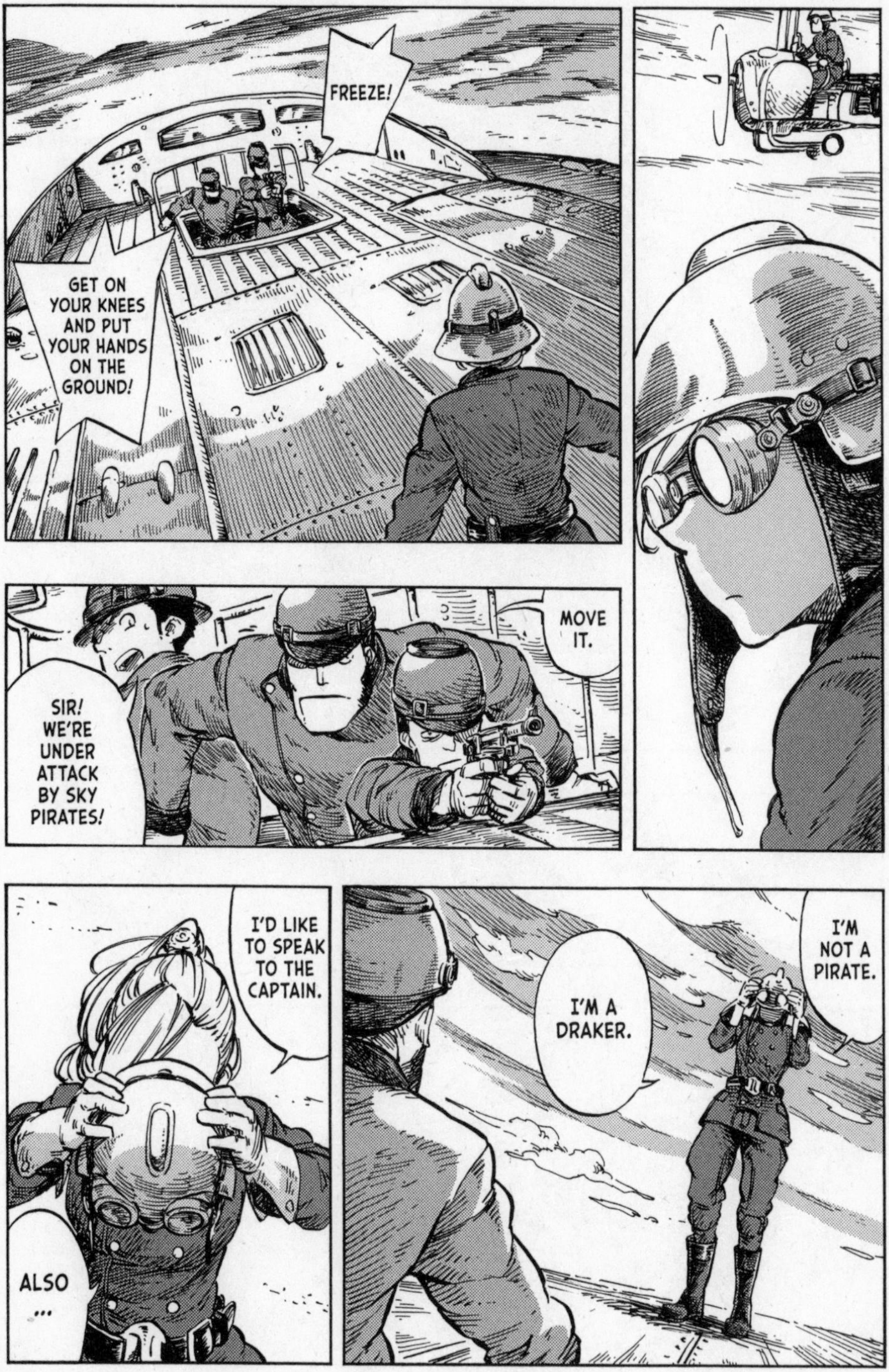
FREEZE!
GET ON YOUR KNEES AND PUT YOUR HANDS ON THE GROUND!
MOVE IT.
SIR! WE'RE UNDER ATTACK BY SKY PIRATES!
I'M NOT A PIRATE.
I'M A DRAKER.
I'D LIKE TO SPEAK TO THE CAPTAIN.
ALSO ...

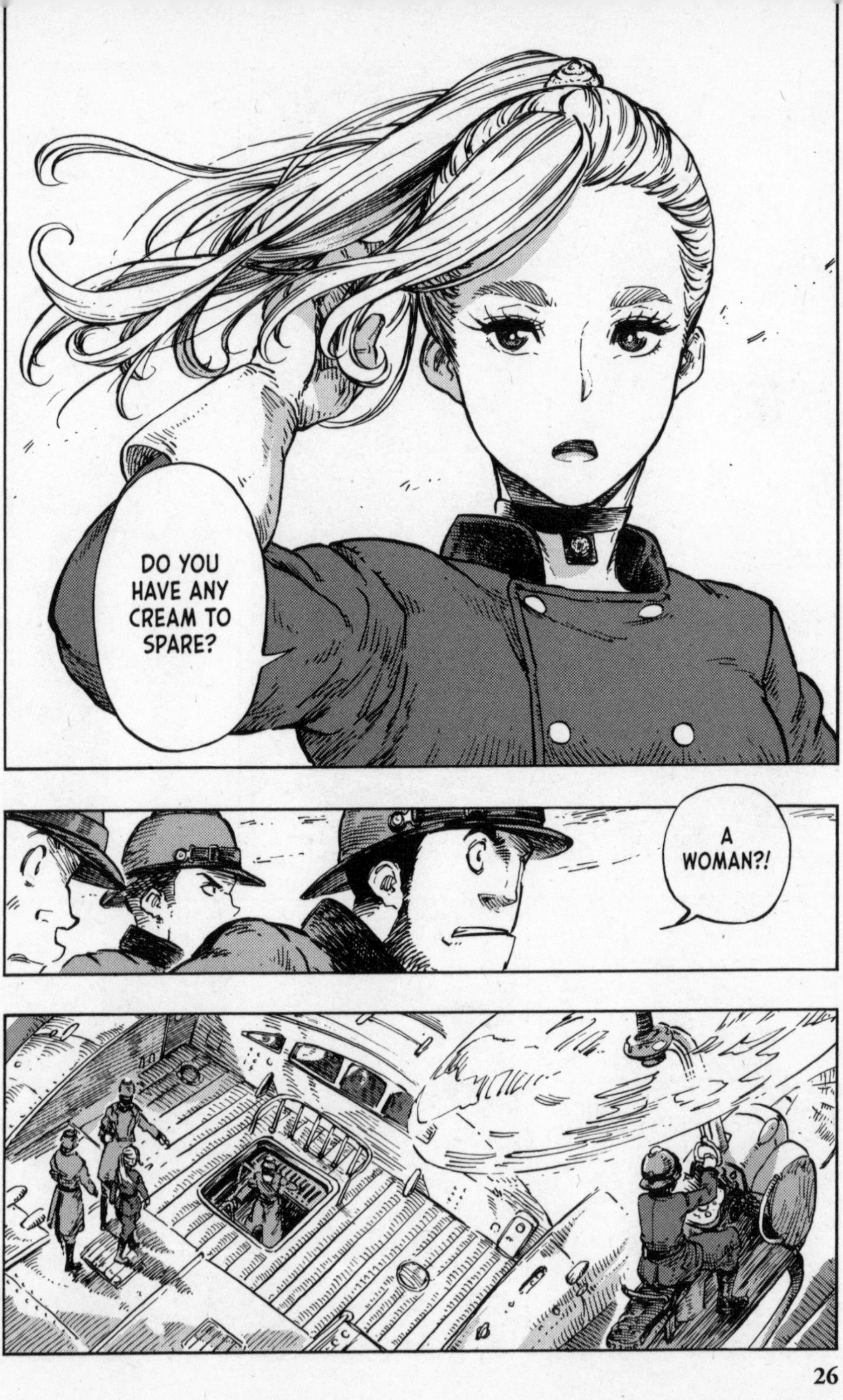
DO YOU HAVE ANY CREAM TO SPARE?
A WOMAN?!

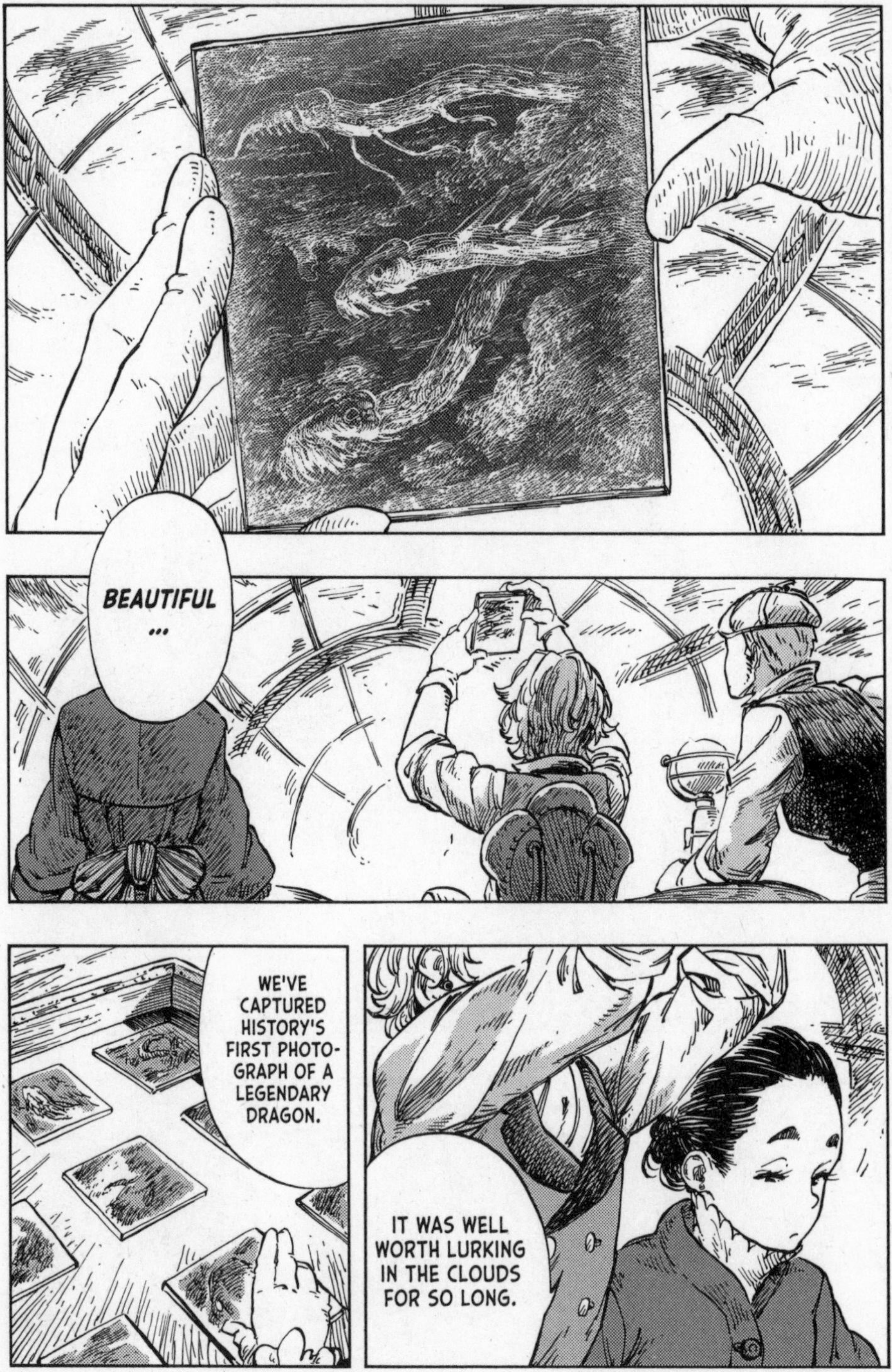
BEAUTIFUL ...
IT WAS WELL WORTH LURKING IN THE CLOUDS FOR SO LONG.
WE'VE CAPTURED HISTORY'S FIRST PHOTOGRAPH OF A LEGENDARY DRAGON.

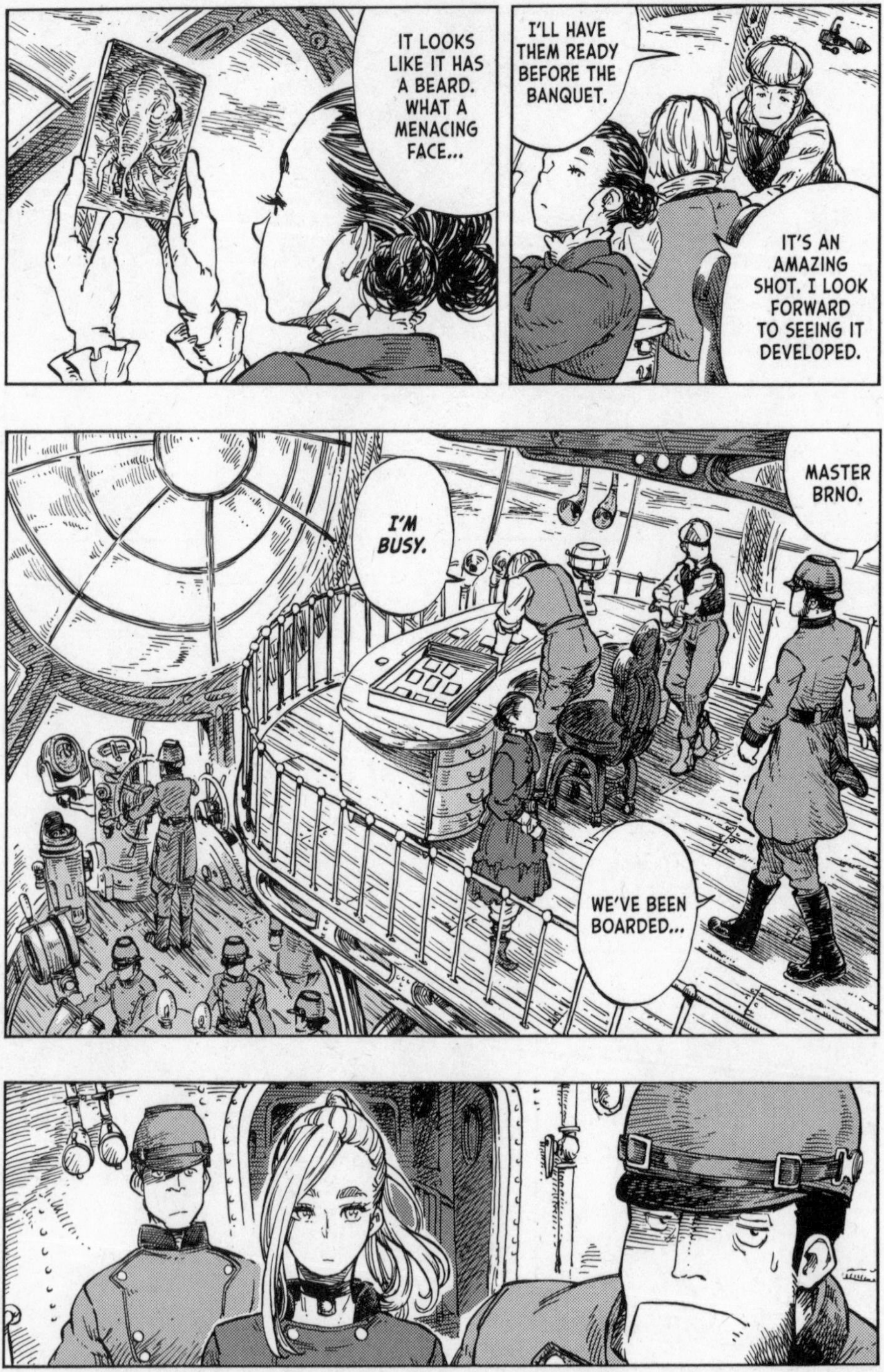
I'LL HAVE THEM READY BEFORE THE BANQUET.
IT'S AN AMAZING SHOT. I LOOK FORWARD TO SEEING IT DEVELOPED.
IT LOOKS LIKE IT HAS A BEARD. WHAT A MENACING FACE...
MASTER BRNO.
I'M BUSY.
WE'VE BEEN BOARDED...

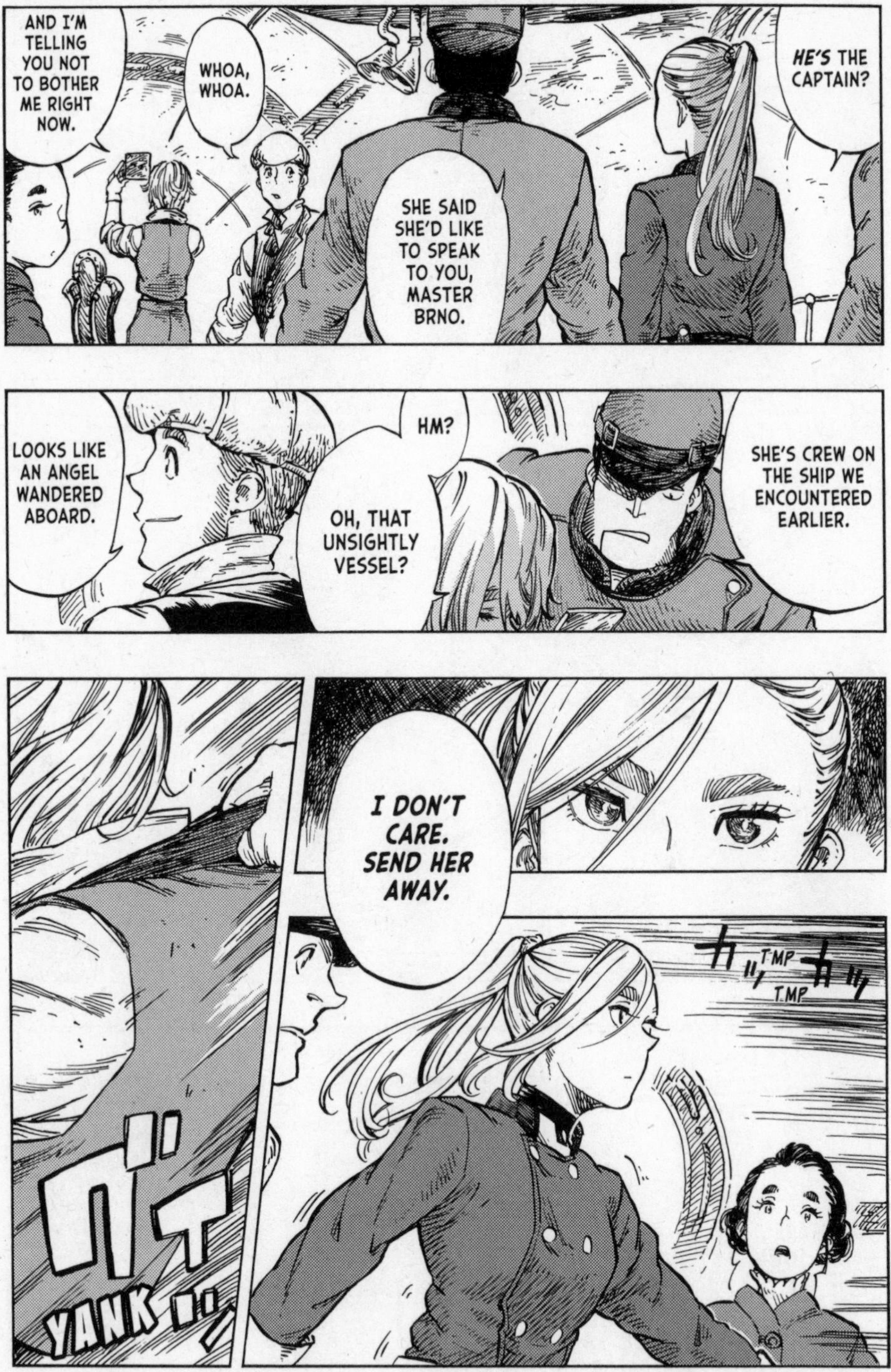
HE'S THE CAPTAIN?
SHE SAID SHE'D LIKE TO SPEAK TO YOU, MASTER BRNO.
WHOA, WHOA.
AND I'M TELLING YOU NOT TO BOTHER ME RIGHT NOW.
SHE'S CREW ON THE SHIP WE ENCOUNTERED EARLIER.
HM?
OH, THAT UNSIGHTLY VESSEL?
LOOKS LIKE AN ANGEL WANDERED ABOARD.
I DON'T CARE. SEND HER AWAY.
TMP
TMP
YANK

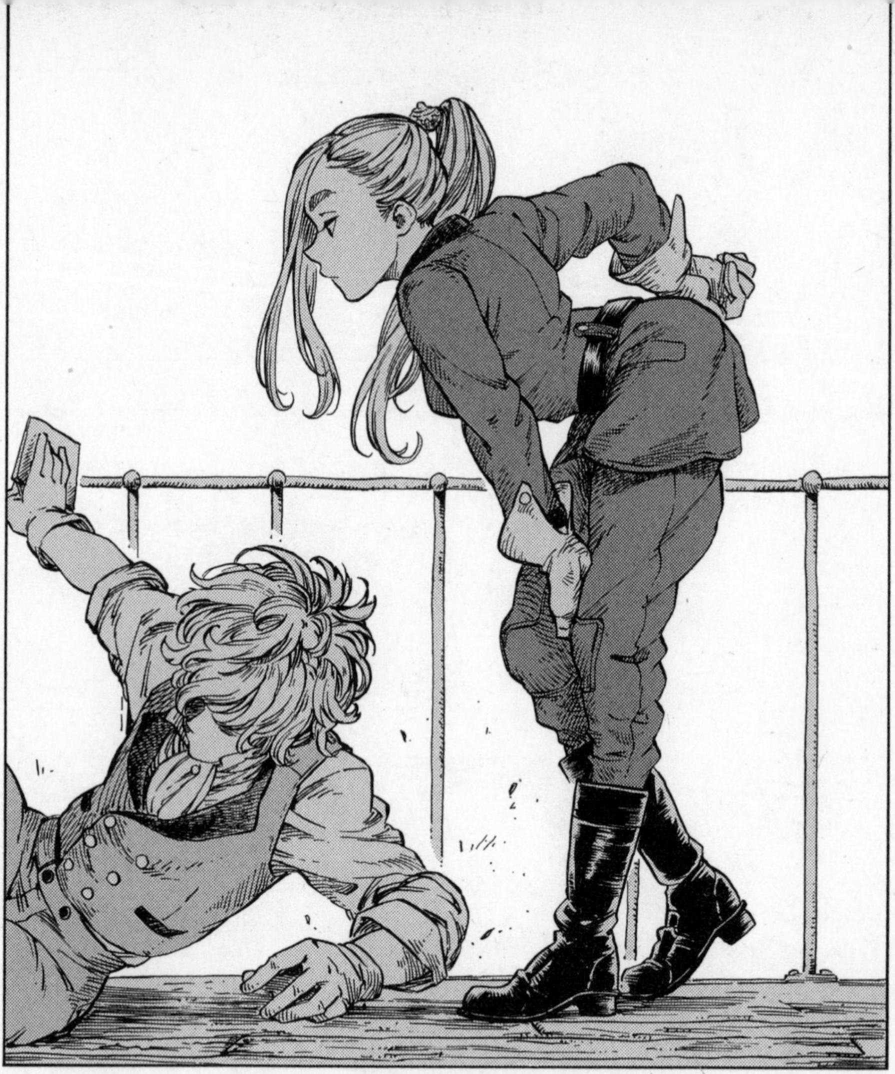

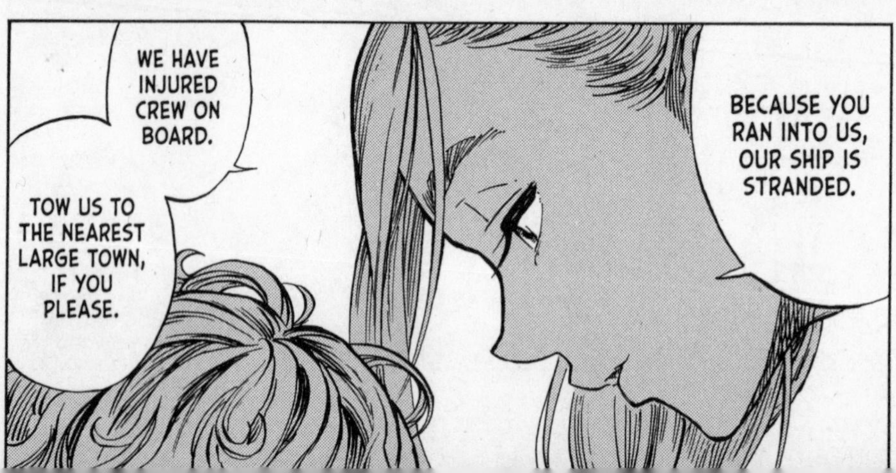
BECAUSE YOU RAN INTO US, OUR SHIP IS STRANDED.
WE HAVE INJURED CREW ON BOARD.
TOW US TO THE NEAREST LARGE TOWN, IF YOU PLEASE.

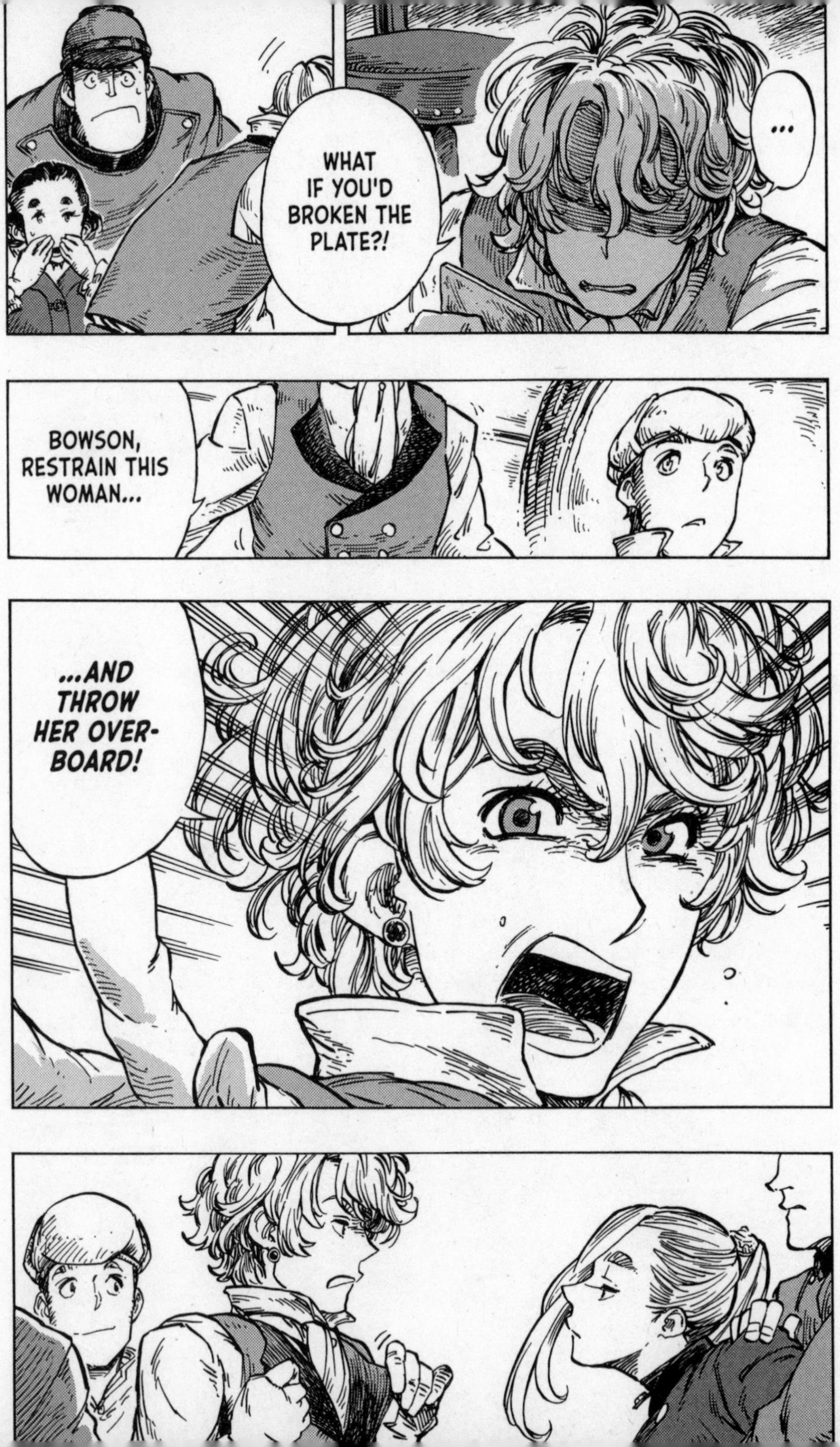
...
WHAT IF YOU'D BROKEN THE PLATE?!
BOWSON, RESTRAIN THIS WOMAN...
...AND THROW HER OVER-BOARD!

Draking Ship Cafeteria Cheeseburger

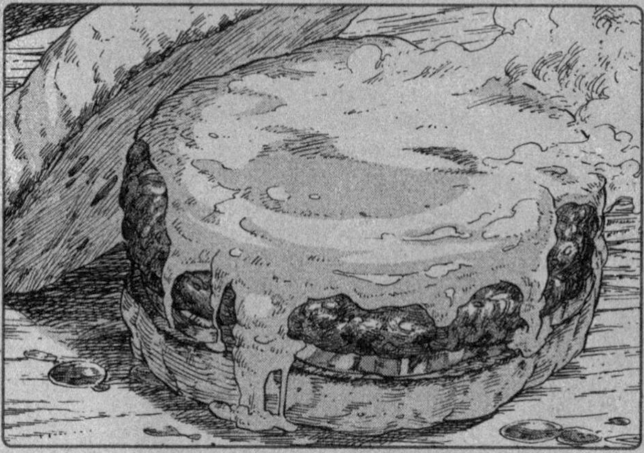

Ingredients (Serves 1)

- ✦ 200 g of dragon-meat scraps
- ✦ 1 tsp of salt
- ✦ Pepper to taste
- ✦ A pinch of dried mint
- ✦ 1-2 rings of sliced onion
- ✦ 1 set of buns
- ✦ Chedder cheese as desired

01
Tenderize meat scraps with the spine of a kitchen knife and finely mince.

02
Salt minced meat and knead with a wooden spatula until the mixture is slightly sticky. Add pepper and crushed dried mint, and mix until well incorporated.

03
Form the meat into a patty and fry in an oiled pan on one side for about four minutes. Meanwhile, fry the onion slices in the same pan with the meat patty.

04
Flip the patty, top with grated cheddar cheese to preference, and let the patty cook for another four to five minutes.

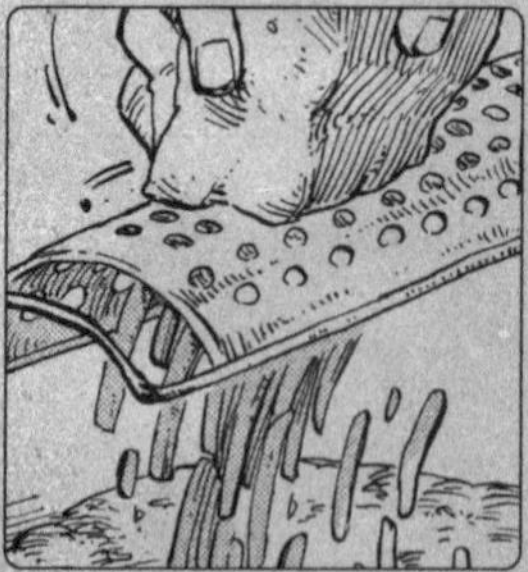

05
Lay the cooked onion slices on the bottom bun, followed by the patty, and finish it off with the top bun.

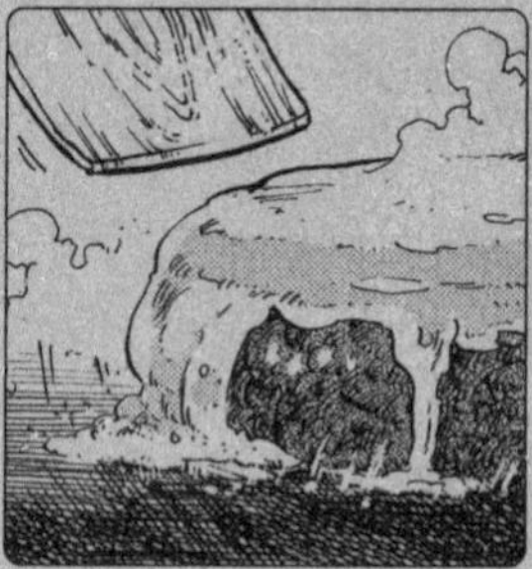

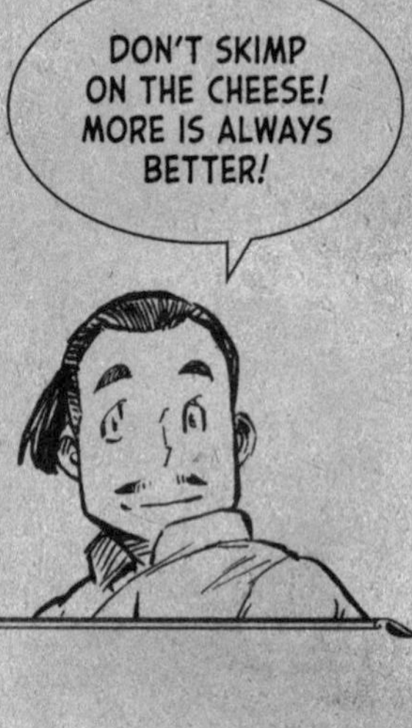
DON'T SKIMP ON THE CHEESE! MORE IS ALWAYS BETTER!

Flight 19 The Oboro Casca & Brno Massinga

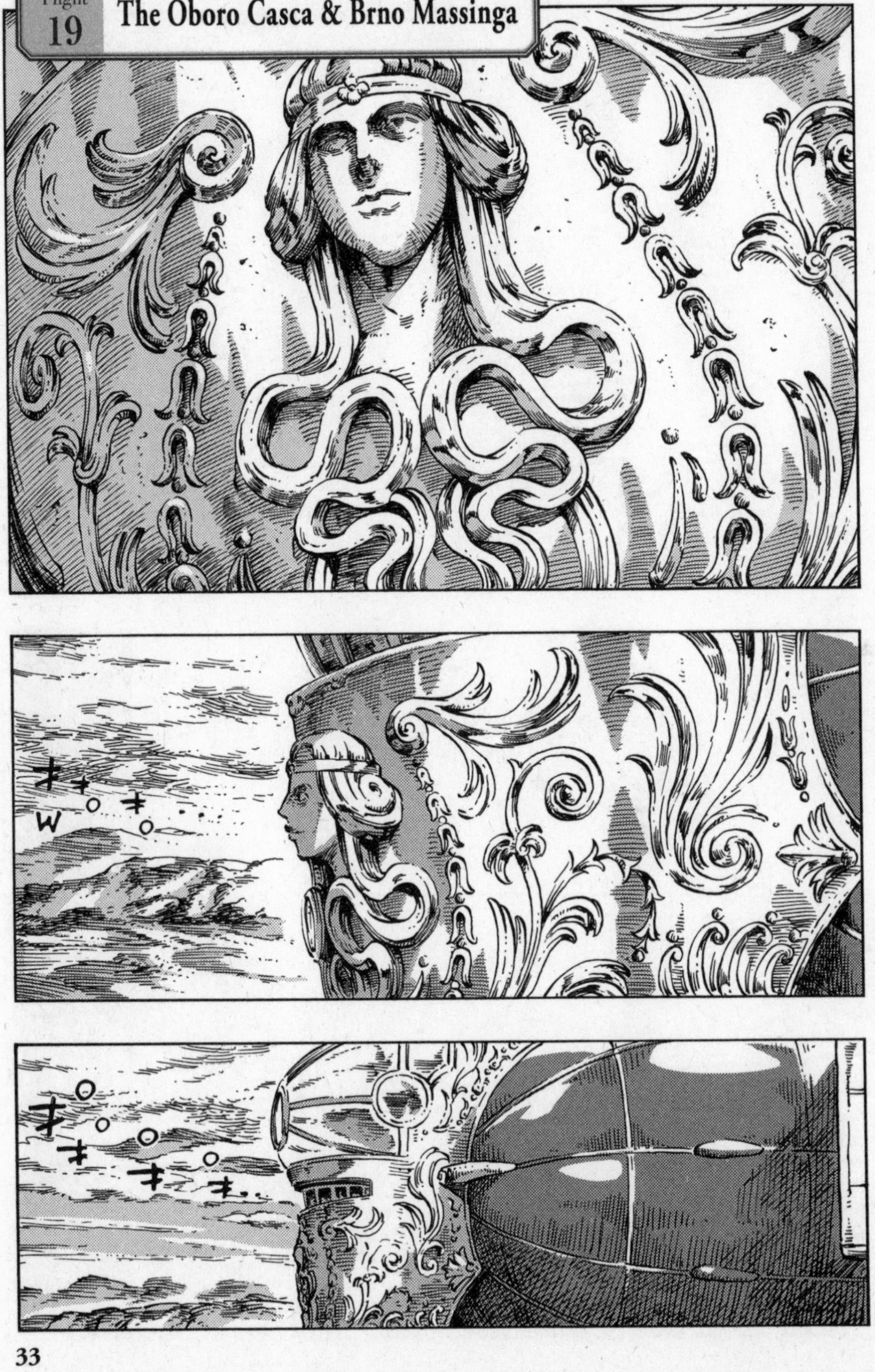

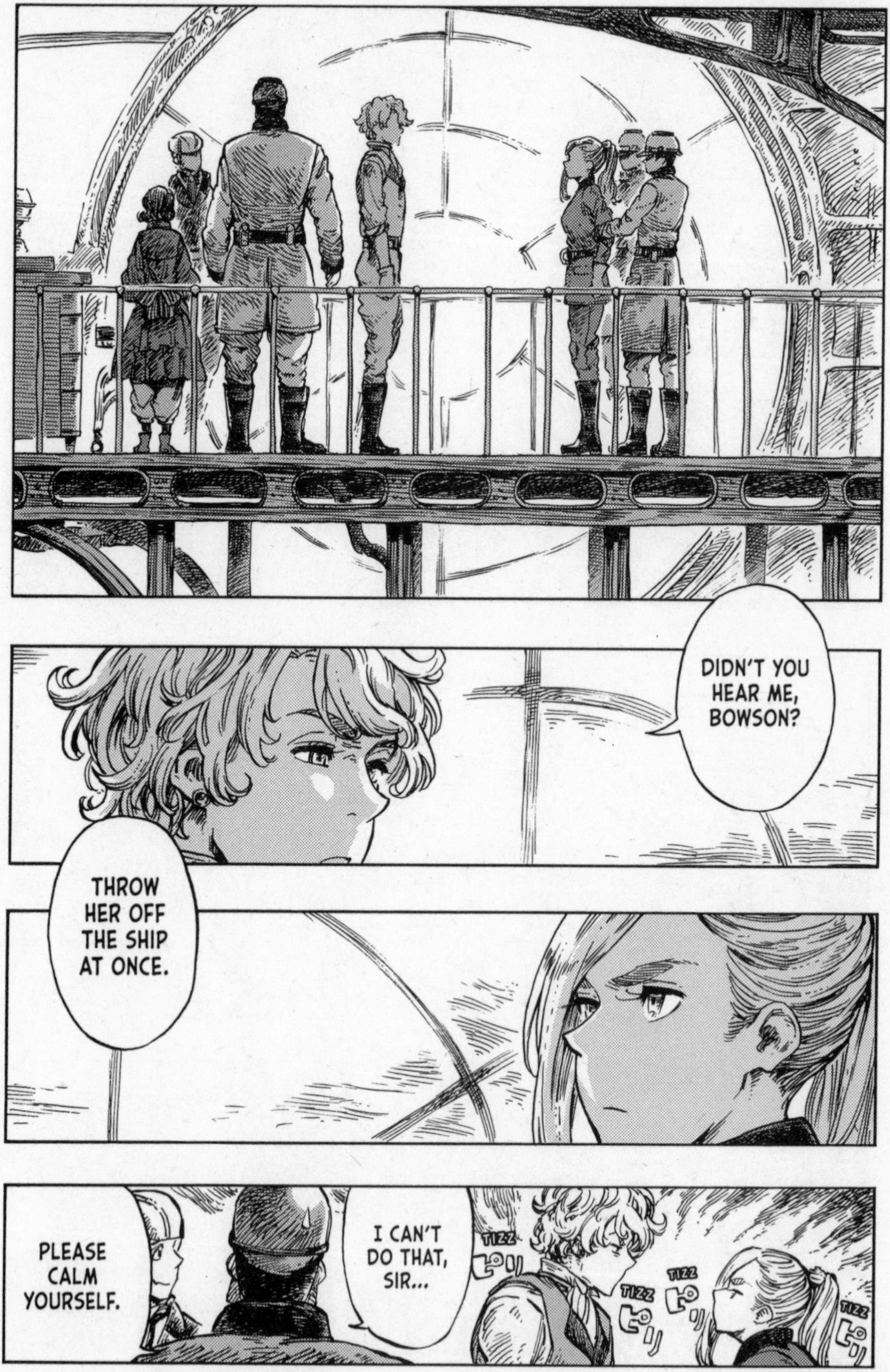
DIDN'T YOU HEAR ME, BOWSON?
THROW HER OFF THE SHIP AT ONCE.
TIZZ
TIZZ
TIZZ
TIZZ
I CAN'T DO THAT, SIR...
PLEASE CALM YOURSELF.

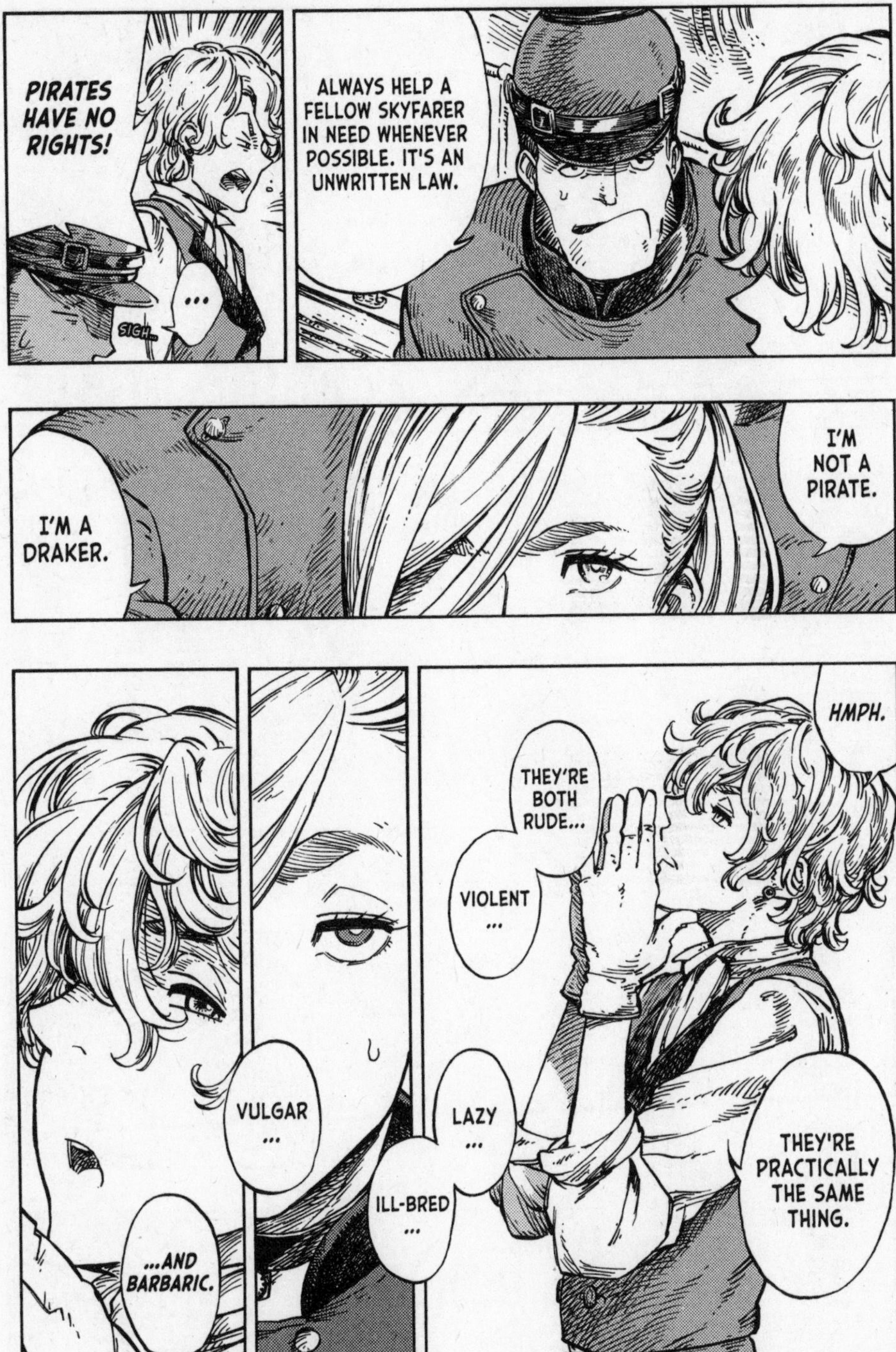
ALWAYS HELP A FELLOW SKYFARER IN NEED WHENEVER POSSIBLE. IT'S AN UNWRITTEN LAW.
PIRATES HAVE NO RIGHTS!
...
SIGH...
I'M NOT A PIRATE.
I'M A DRAKER.
HMPH.
THEY'RE BOTH RUDE...
VIOLENT ...
THEY'RE PRACTICALLY THE SAME THING.
LAZY ...
ILL-BRED ...
VULGAR ...
...AND BARBARIC.

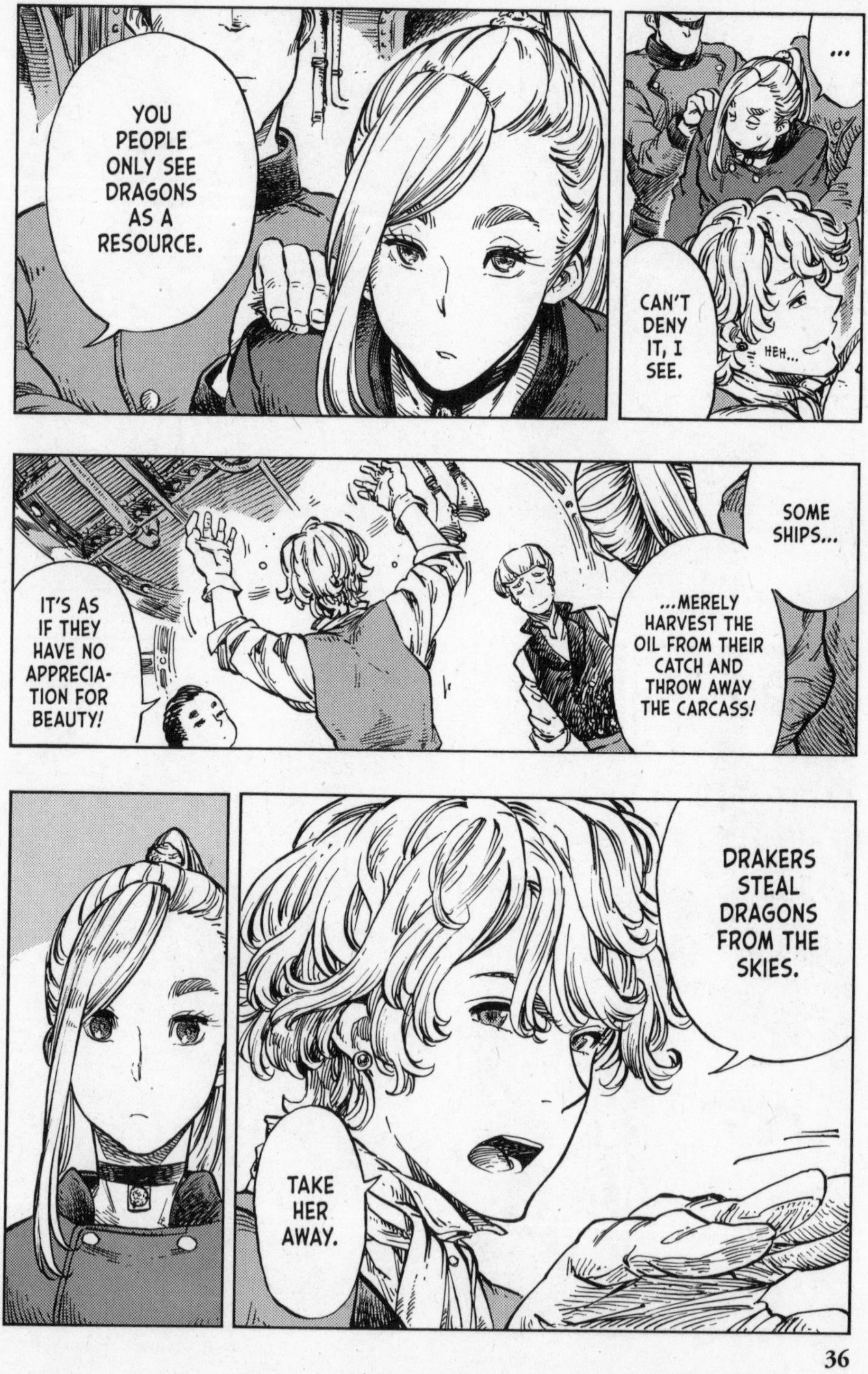
...
CAN'T DENY IT, I SEE.
HEH...
YOU PEOPLE ONLY SEE DRAGONS AS A RESOURCE.
SOME SHIPS...
...MERELY HARVEST THE OIL FROM THEIR CATCH AND THROW AWAY THE CARCASS!
IT'S AS IF THEY HAVE NO APPRECIATION FOR BEAUTY!
DRAKERS STEAL DRAGONS FROM THE SKIES.
TAKE HER AWAY.

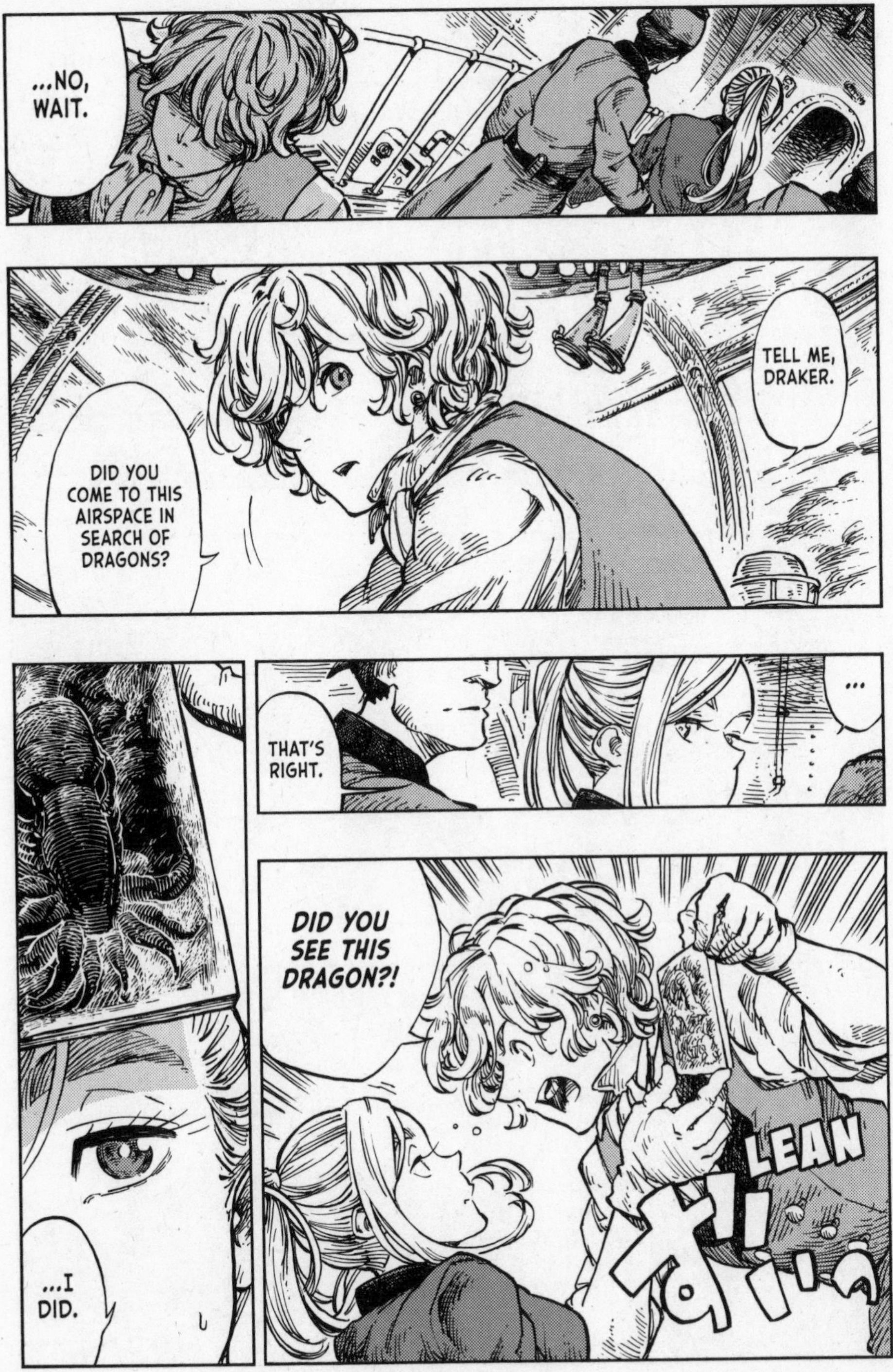
...NO, WAIT.
TELL ME, DRAKER.
DID YOU COME TO THIS AIRSPACE IN SEARCH OF DRAGONS?
...
THAT'S RIGHT.
DID YOU SEE THIS DRAGON?!
LEAN
...I DID.

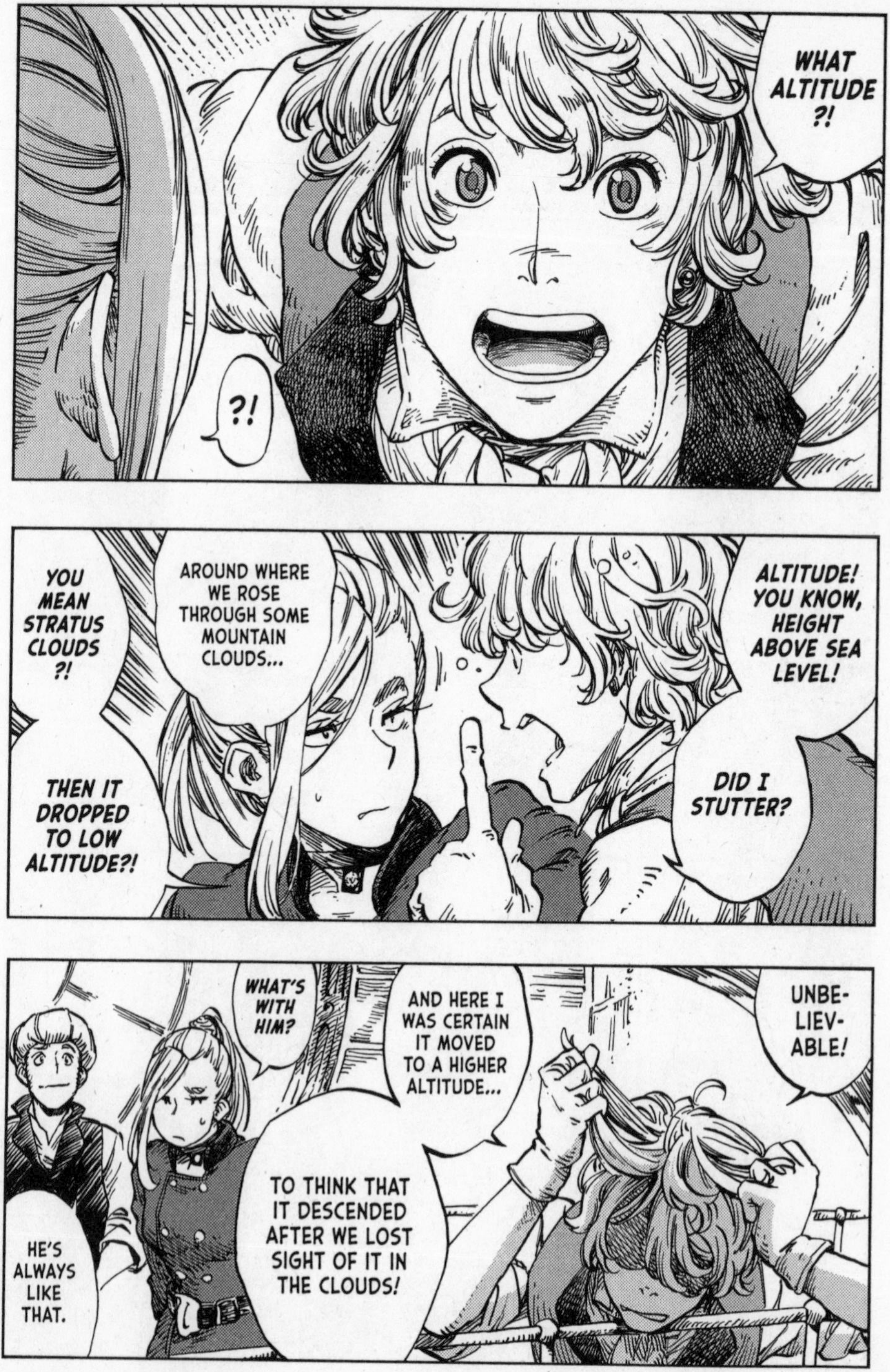
WHAT ALTITUDE ?!
?!
ALTITUDE! YOU KNOW, HEIGHT ABOVE SEA LEVEL!
DID I STUTTER?
AROUND WHERE WE ROSE THROUGH SOME MOUNTAIN CLOUDS...
YOU MEAN STRATUS CLOUDS ?!
THEN IT DROPPED TO LOW ALTITUDE?!
UNBE- LIEV- ABLE!
AND HERE I WAS CERTAIN IT MOVED TO A HIGHER ALTITUDE...
TO THINK THAT IT DESCENDED AFTER WE LOST SIGHT OF IT IN THE CLOUDS!
WHAT'S WITH HIM?
HE'S ALWAYS LIKE THAT.

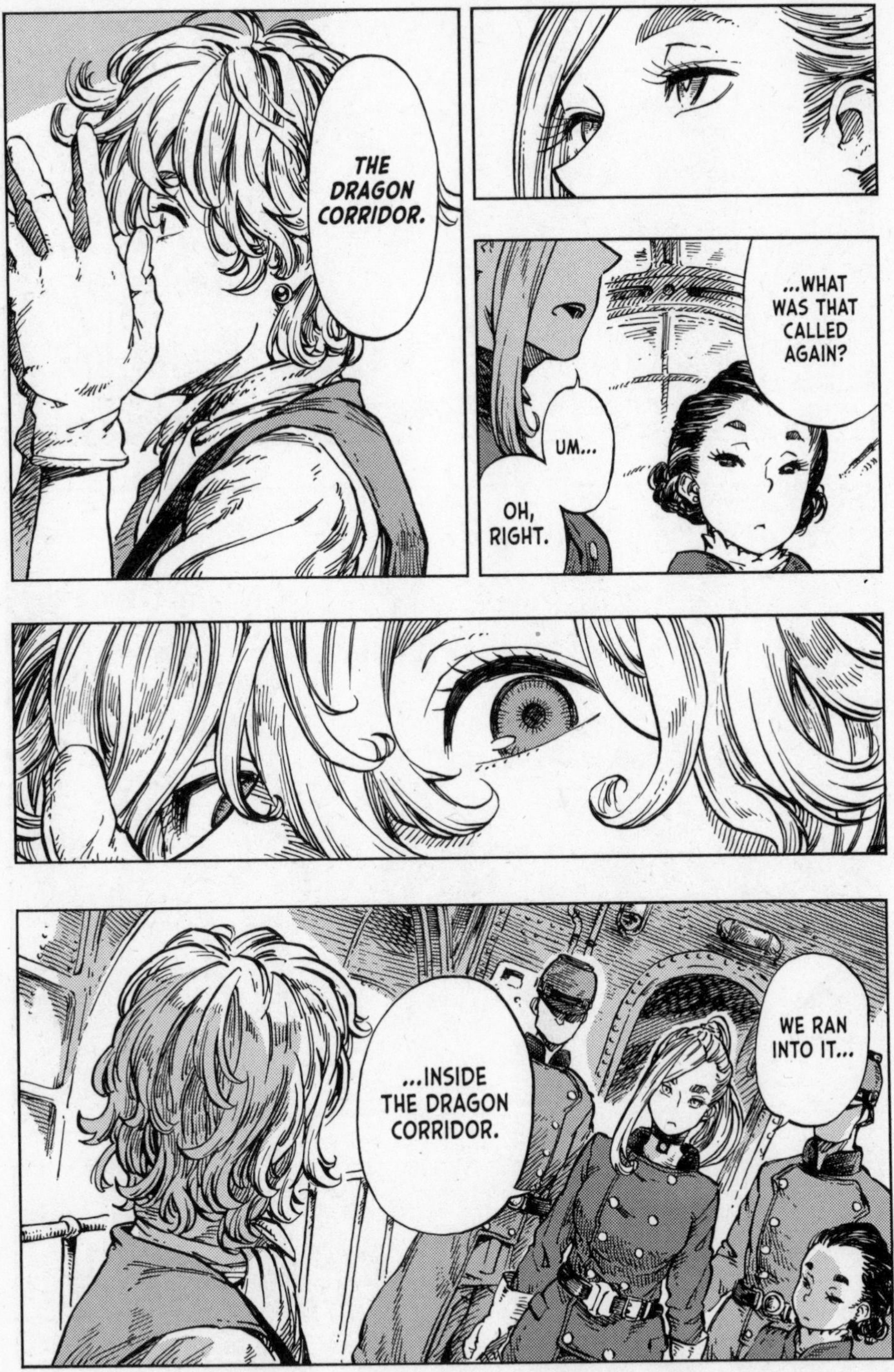
...WHAT WAS THAT CALLED AGAIN?
UM...
OH, RIGHT.
THE DRAGON CORRIDOR.
WE RAN INTO IT...
...INSIDE THE DRAGON CORRIDOR.

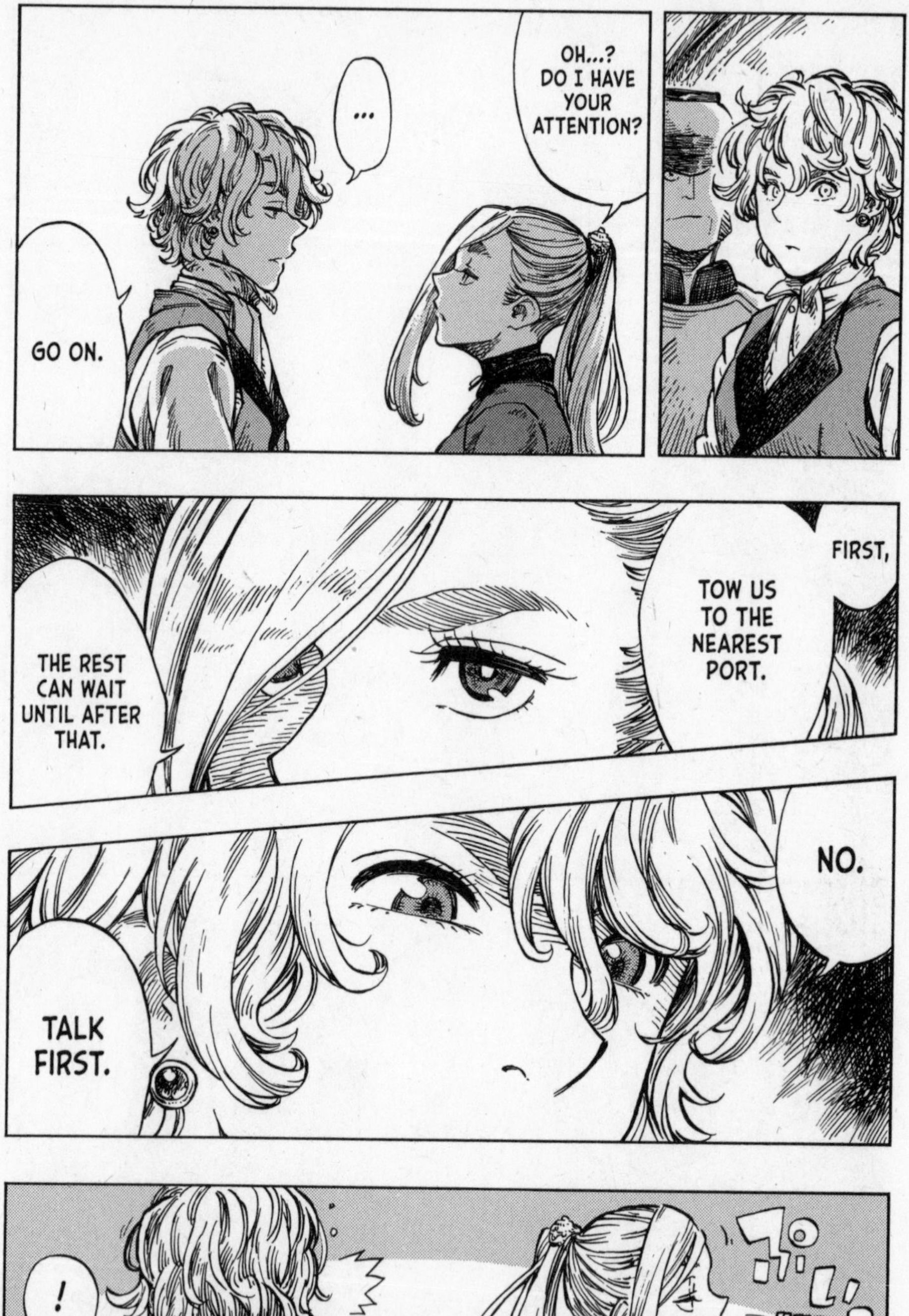
OH...? DO I HAVE YOUR ATTENTION?
...
GO ON.
FIRST,
TOW US TO THE NEAREST PORT.
THE REST CAN WAIT UNTIL AFTER THAT.
NO.
TALK FIRST.
HMPH
!

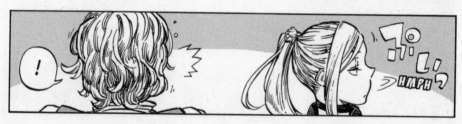

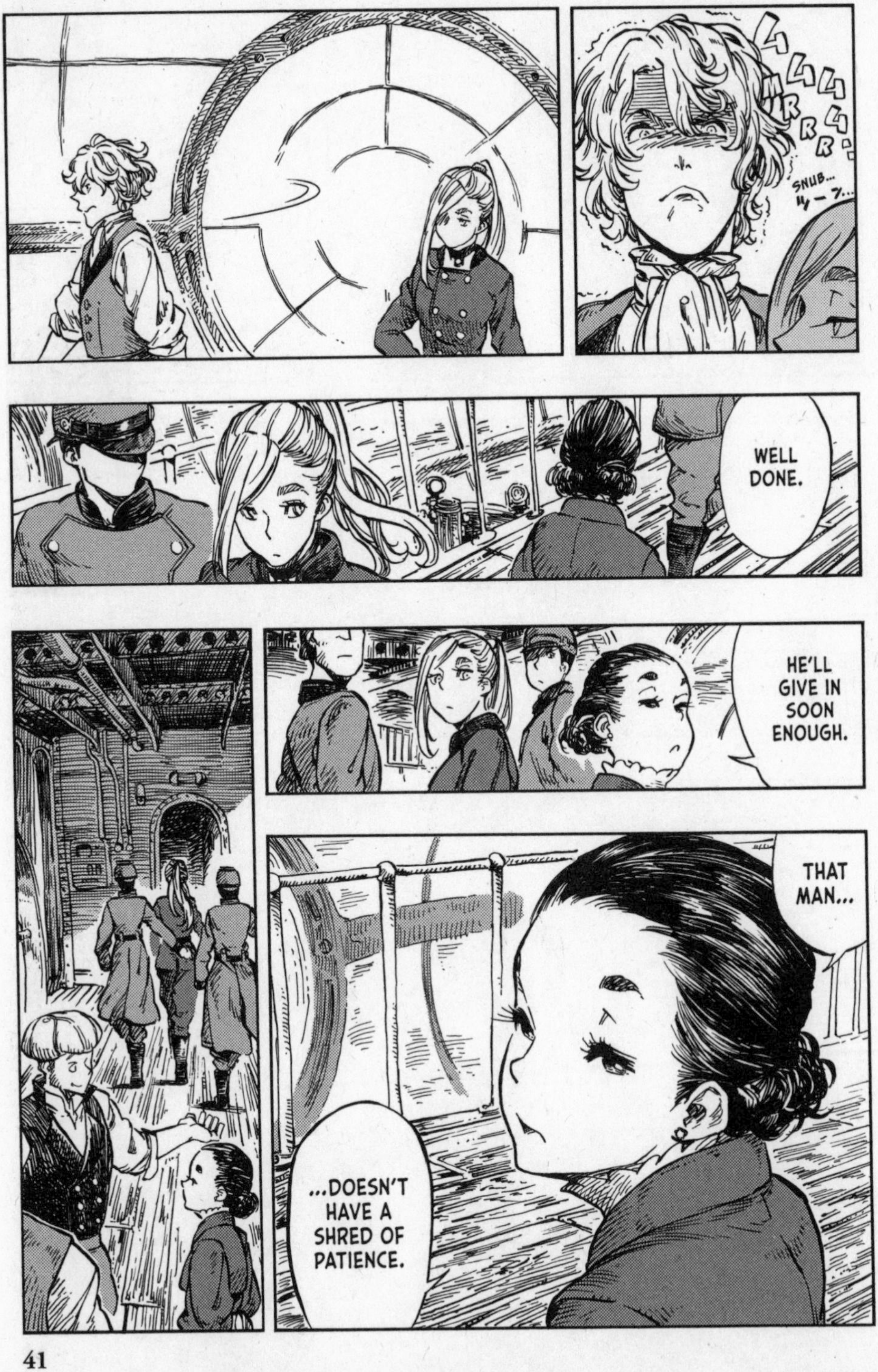
ムムムムム…
MRRR
SNUB...
ツーン...
WELL DONE.
HE'LL GIVE IN SOON ENOUGH.
THAT MAN...
...DOESN'T HAVE A SHRED OF PATIENCE.

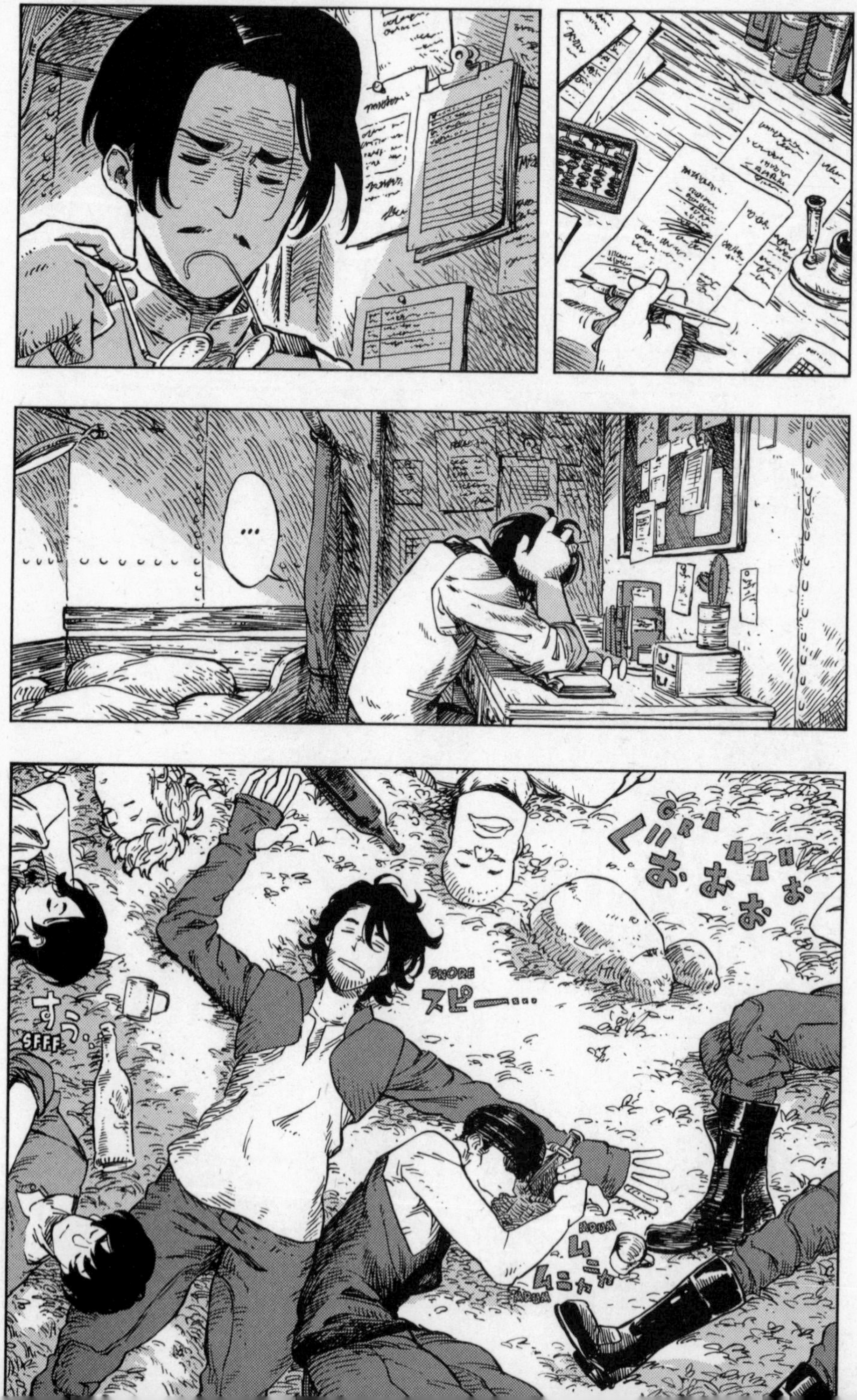
…
ぐぉぉぉぉ
GRAAHH
スピー…
SNORE
MRUM
ムニャ
ムニャ
すぅ…
SFFF

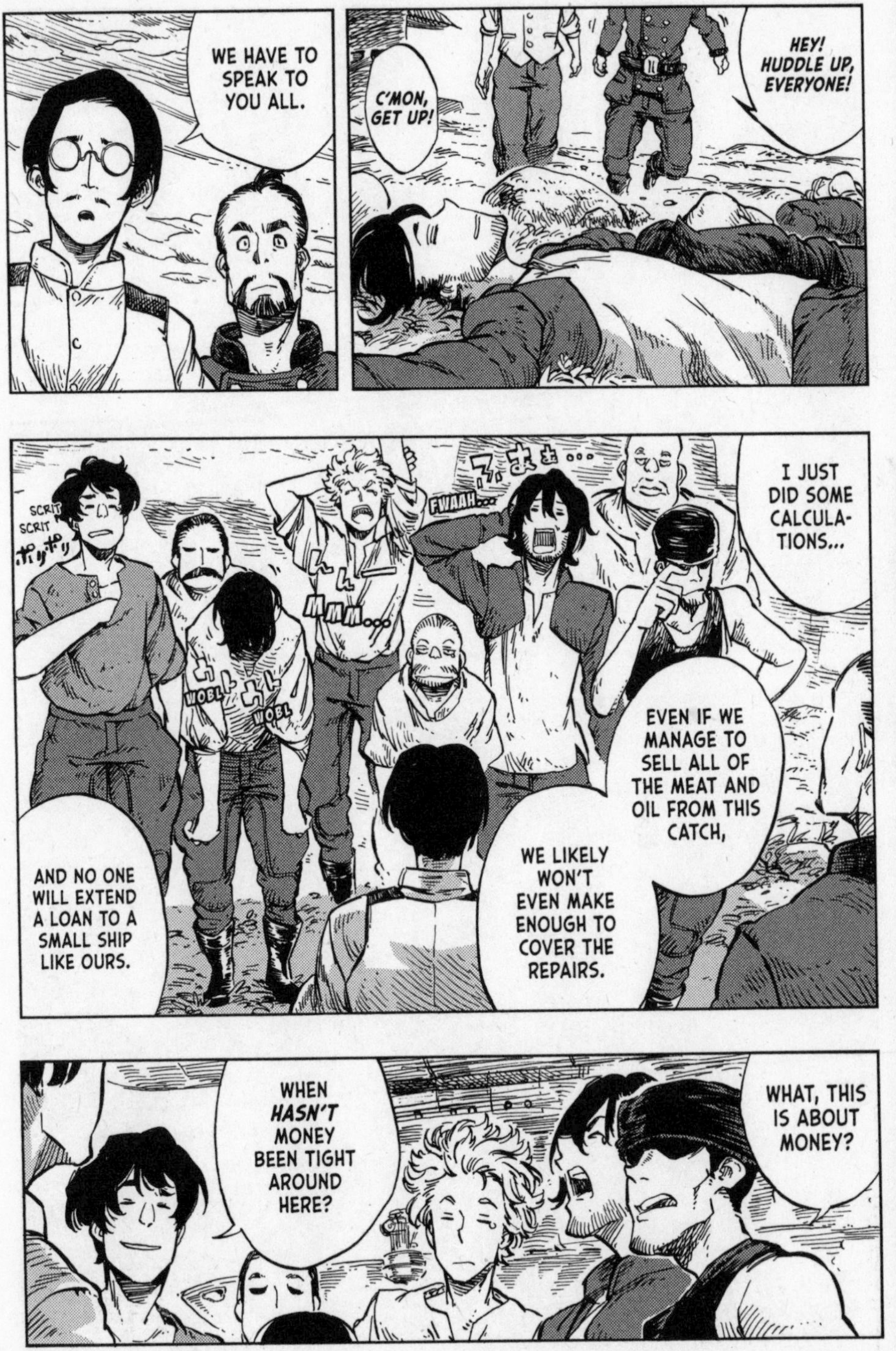
HEY! HUDDLE UP, EVERYONE!
C'MON, GET UP!
WE HAVE TO SPEAK TO YOU ALL.
I JUST DID SOME CALCULATIONS...
FWAAH...
MMM...
SCRIT SCRIT
WOBL WOBL
EVEN IF WE MANAGE TO SELL ALL OF THE MEAT AND OIL FROM THIS CATCH,
WE LIKELY WON'T EVEN MAKE ENOUGH TO COVER THE REPAIRS.
AND NO ONE WILL EXTEND A LOAN TO A SMALL SHIP LIKE OURS.
WHAT, THIS IS ABOUT MONEY?
WHEN *HASN'T* MONEY BEEN TIGHT AROUND HERE?

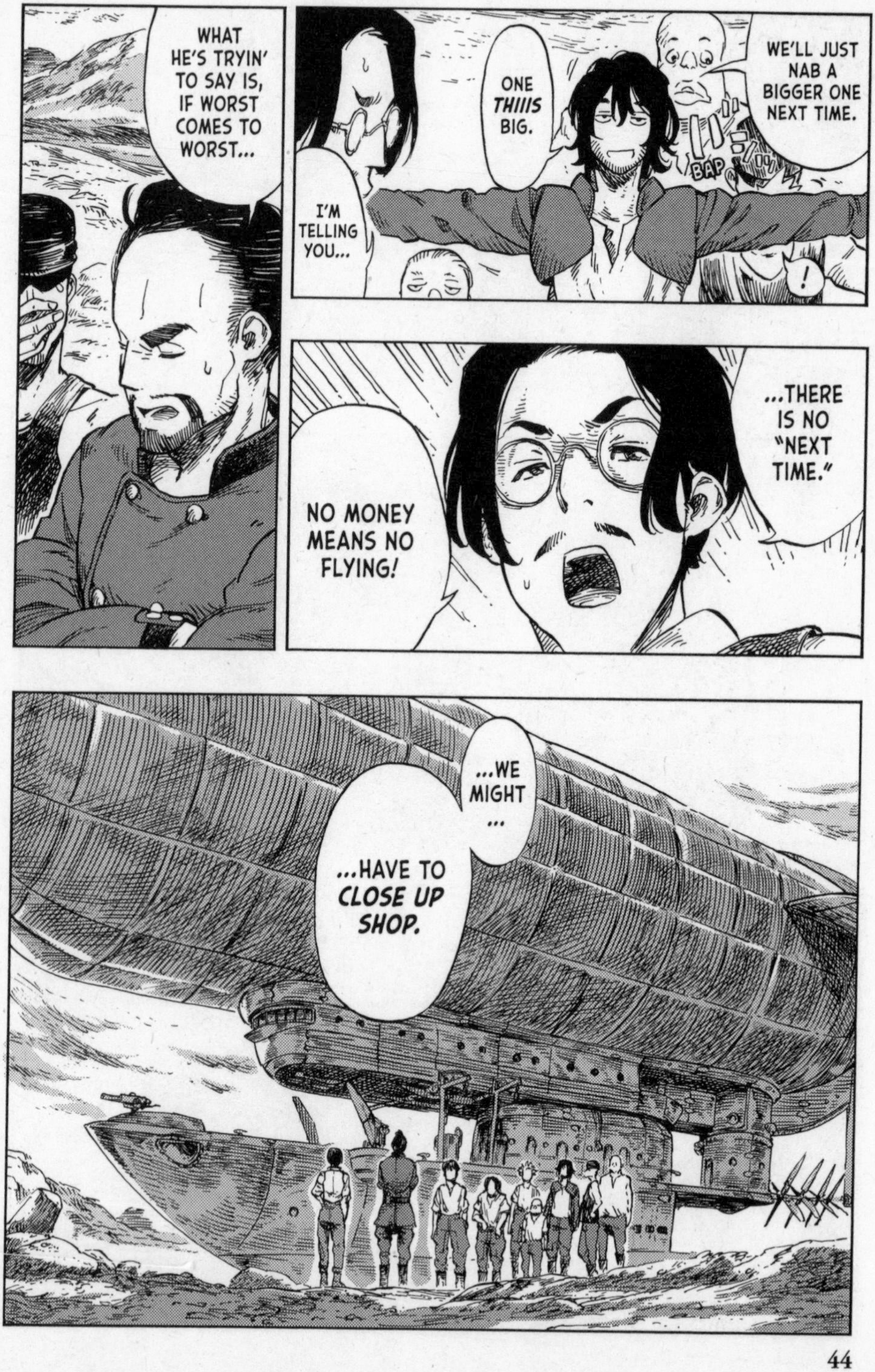
WE'LL JUST NAB A BIGGER ONE NEXT TIME.
BAP
!
ONE *THIIIS* BIG.
I'M TELLING YOU...
...THERE IS NO "NEXT TIME."
NO MONEY MEANS NO FLYING!
WHAT HE'S TRYIN' TO SAY IS, IF WORST COMES TO WORST...
...WE MIGHT ...
...HAVE TO *CLOSE UP SHOP.*

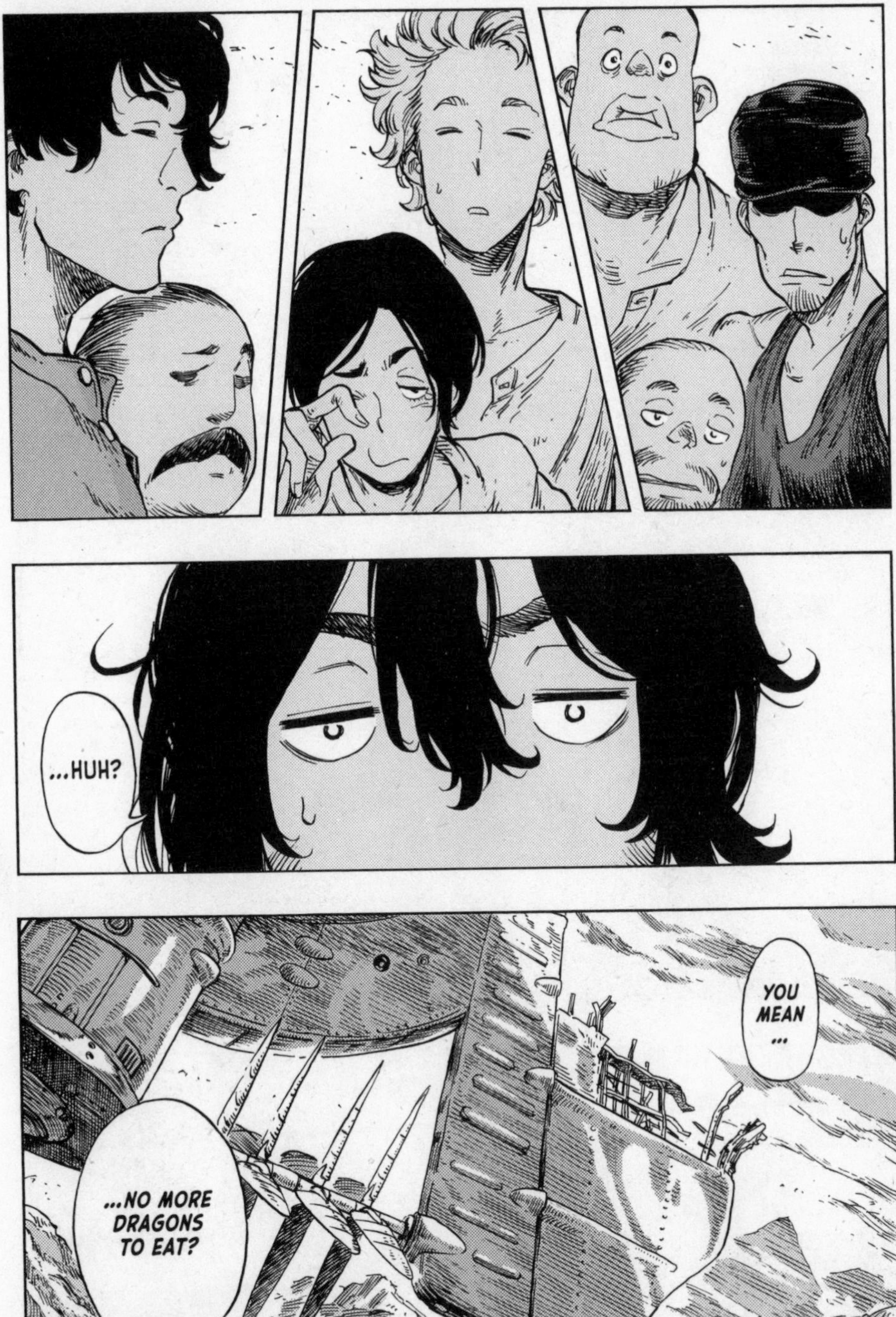
...HUH?
YOU MEAN ...
...NO MORE DRAGONS TO EAT?

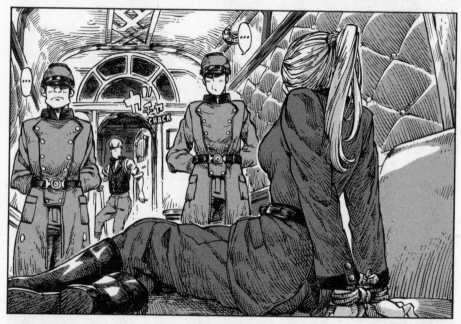

JUST AS I EXPECTED. THIS WILL MAKE FOR QUITE A PICTURE.

PHEW.

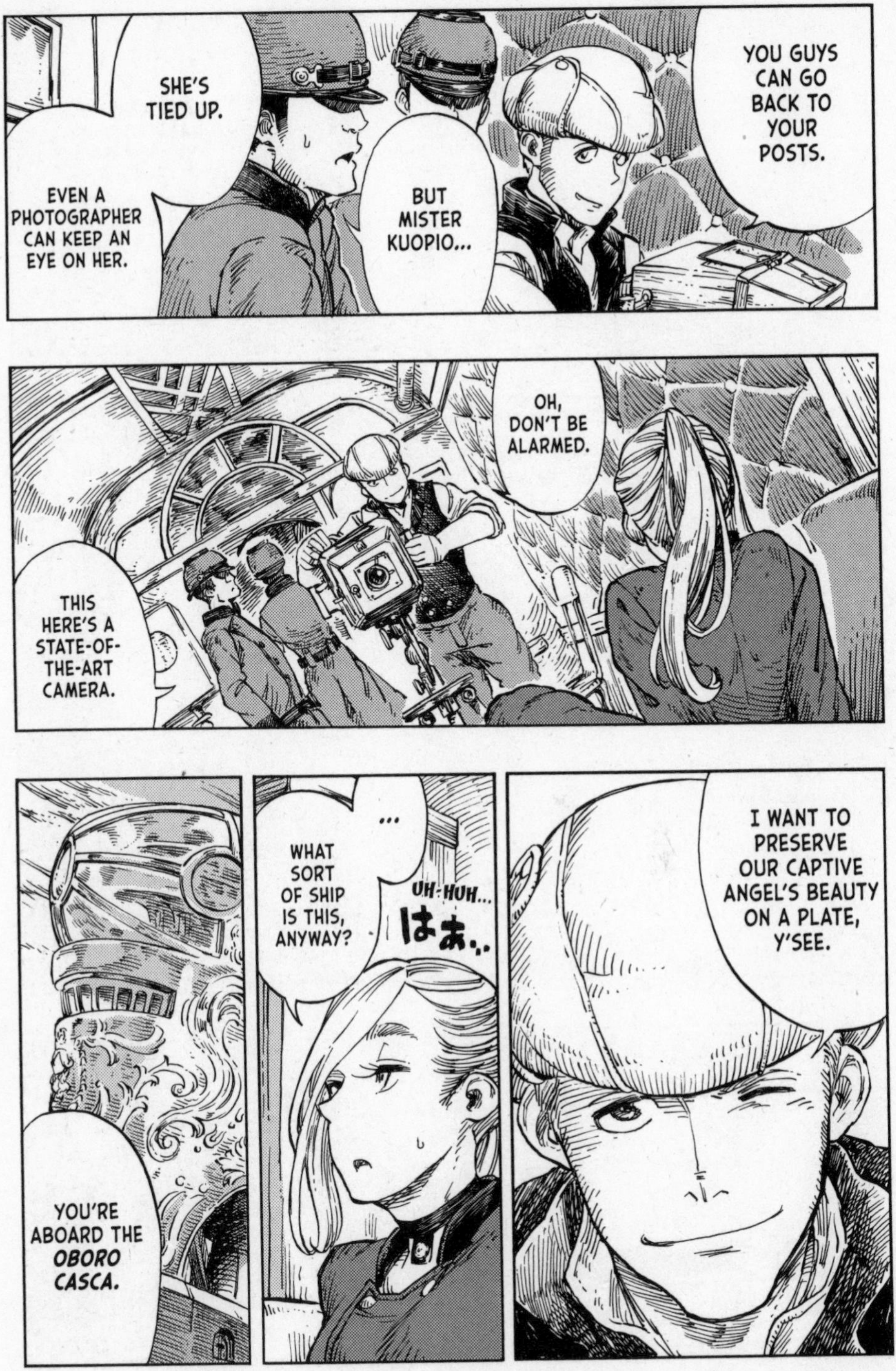
YOU GUYS CAN GO BACK TO YOUR POSTS.
BUT MISTER KUOPIO...
SHE'S TIED UP.
EVEN A PHOTOGRAPHER CAN KEEP AN EYE ON HER.
OH, DON'T BE ALARMED.
THIS HERE'S A STATE-OF-THE-ART CAMERA.
I WANT TO PRESERVE OUR CAPTIVE ANGEL'S BEAUTY ON A PLATE, Y'SEE.
...
UH-HUH...
はぁ..
WHAT SORT OF SHIP IS THIS, ANYWAY?
YOU'RE ABOARD THE *OBORO CASCA.*

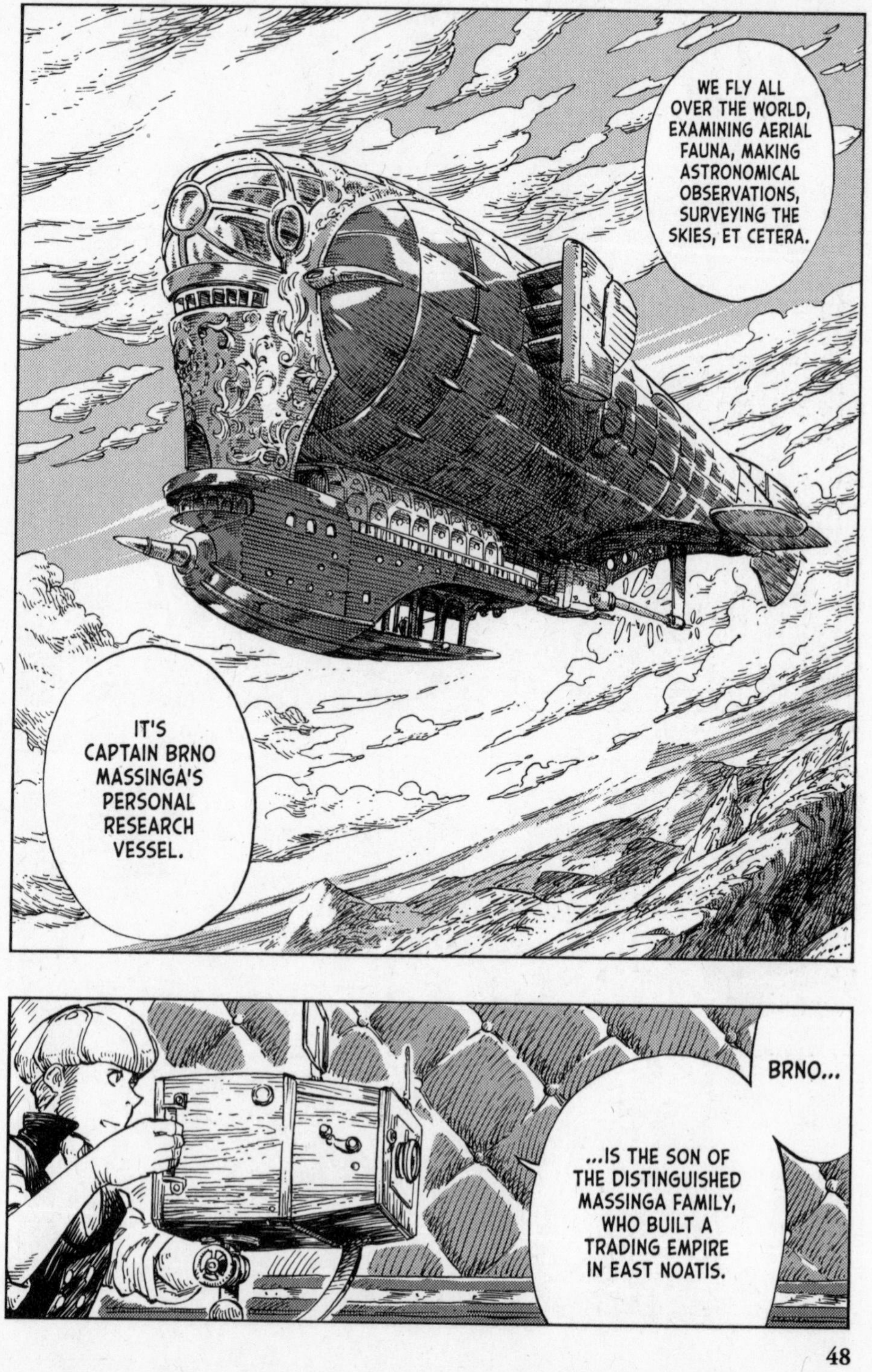
WE FLY ALL OVER THE WORLD, EXAMINING AERIAL FAUNA, MAKING ASTRONOMICAL OBSERVATIONS, SURVEYING THE SKIES, ET CETERA.
IT'S CAPTAIN BRNO MASSINGA'S PERSONAL RESEARCH VESSEL.
BRNO...
...IS THE SON OF THE DISTINGUISHED MASSINGA FAMILY, WHO BUILT A TRADING EMPIRE IN EAST NOATIS.

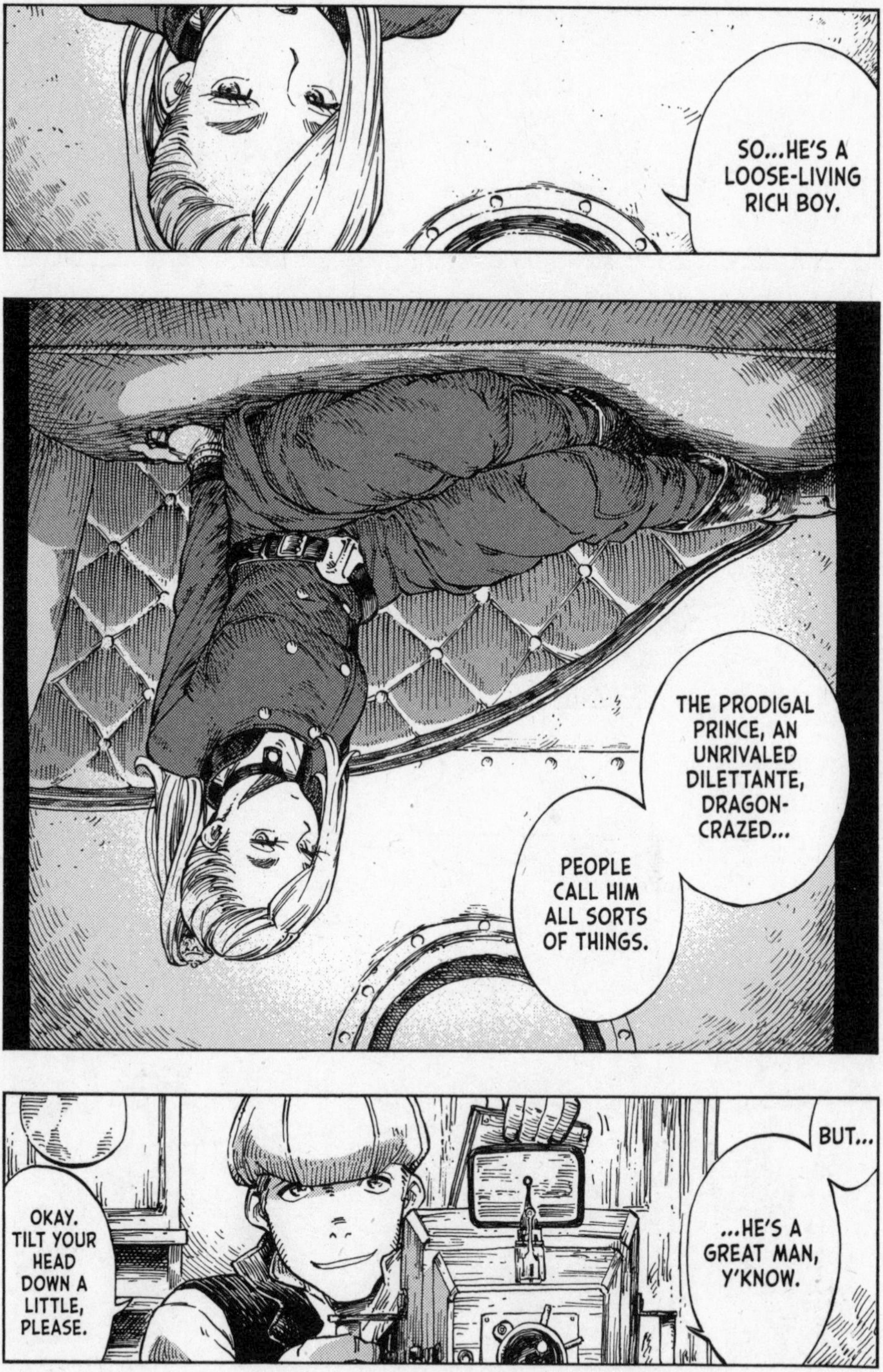
SO...HE'S A LOOSE-LIVING RICH BOY.
THE PRODIGAL PRINCE, AN UNRIVALED DILETTANTE, DRAGON-CRAZED...
PEOPLE CALL HIM ALL SORTS OF THINGS.
BUT...
...HE'S A GREAT MAN, Y'KNOW.
OKAY. TILT YOUR HEAD DOWN A LITTLE, PLEASE.

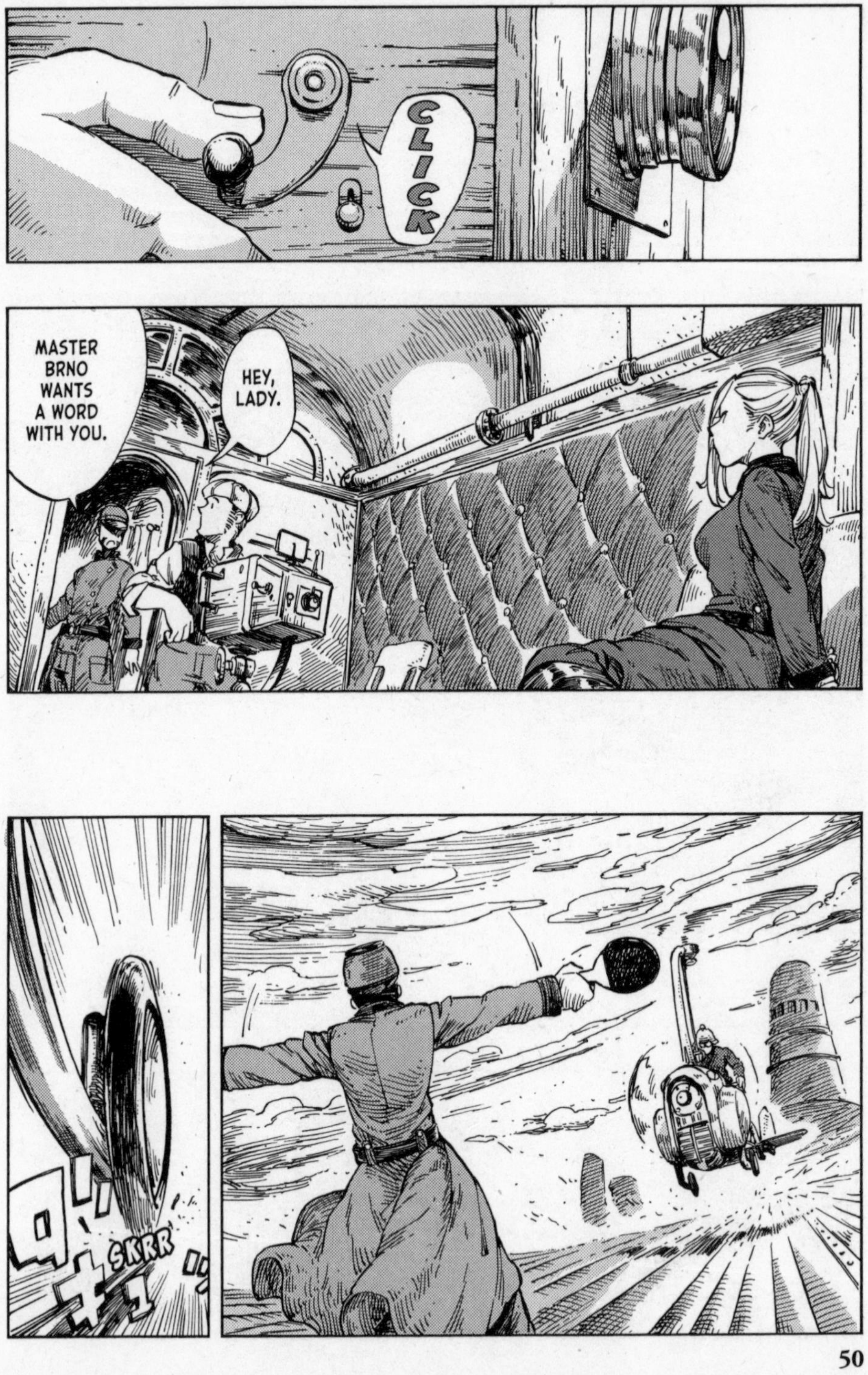
CLICK
HEY, LADY.
MASTER BRNO WANTS A WORD WITH YOU.
SKRR

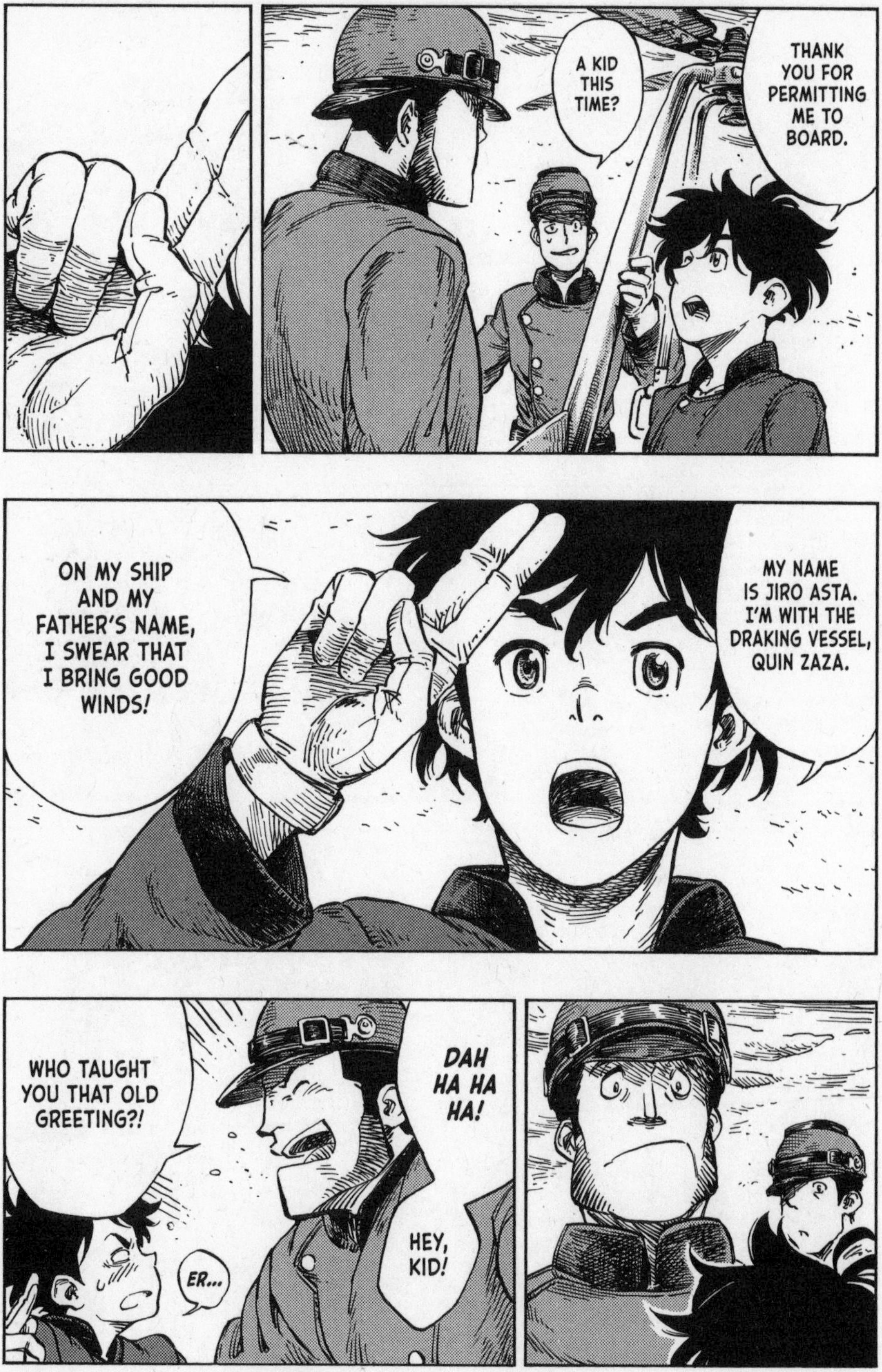
THANK YOU FOR PERMITTING ME TO BOARD.
A KID THIS TIME?
MY NAME IS JIRO ASTA. I'M WITH THE DRAKING VESSEL, QUIN ZAZA.
ON MY SHIP AND MY FATHER'S NAME, I SWEAR THAT I BRING GOOD WINDS!
DAH HA HA HA!
WHO TAUGHT YOU THAT OLD GREETING?!
HEY, KID!
ER...

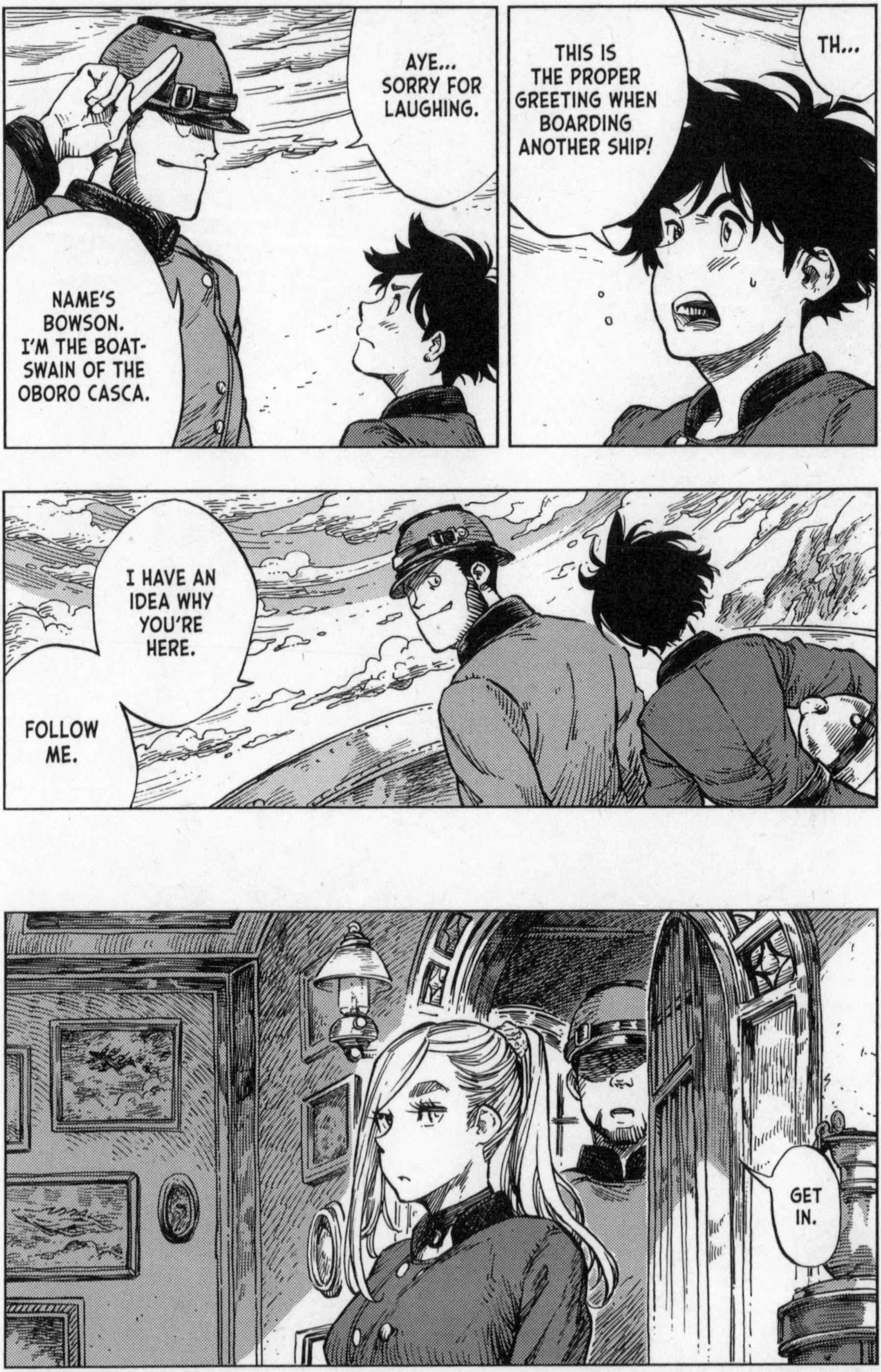
TH...
THIS IS THE PROPER GREETING WHEN BOARDING ANOTHER SHIP!
AYE... SORRY FOR LAUGHING.
NAME'S BOWSON. I'M THE BOAT-SWAIN OF THE OBORO CASCA.
I HAVE AN IDEA WHY YOU'RE HERE.
FOLLOW ME.
GET IN.

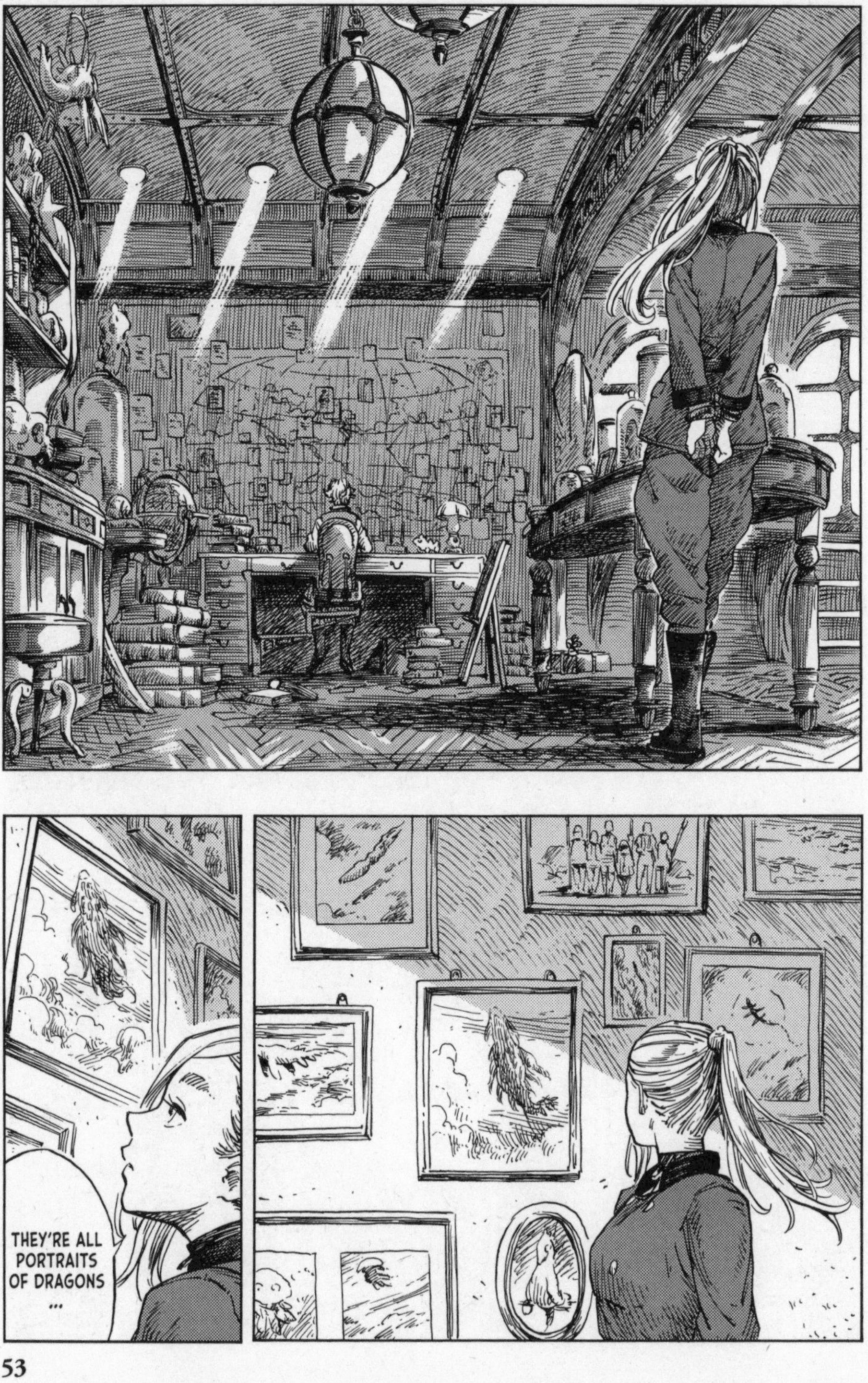
THEY'RE ALL PORTRAITS OF DRAGONS ...

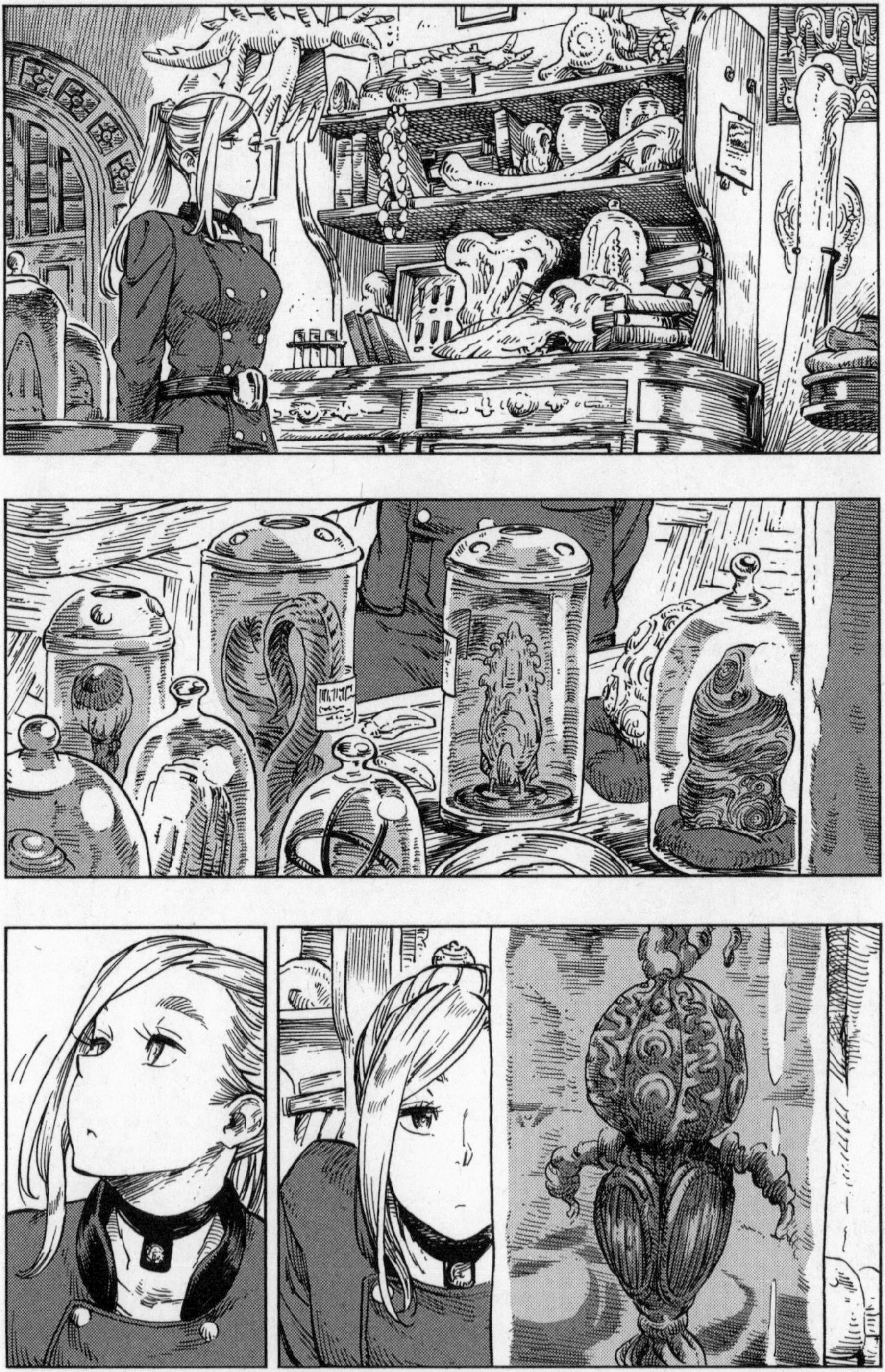

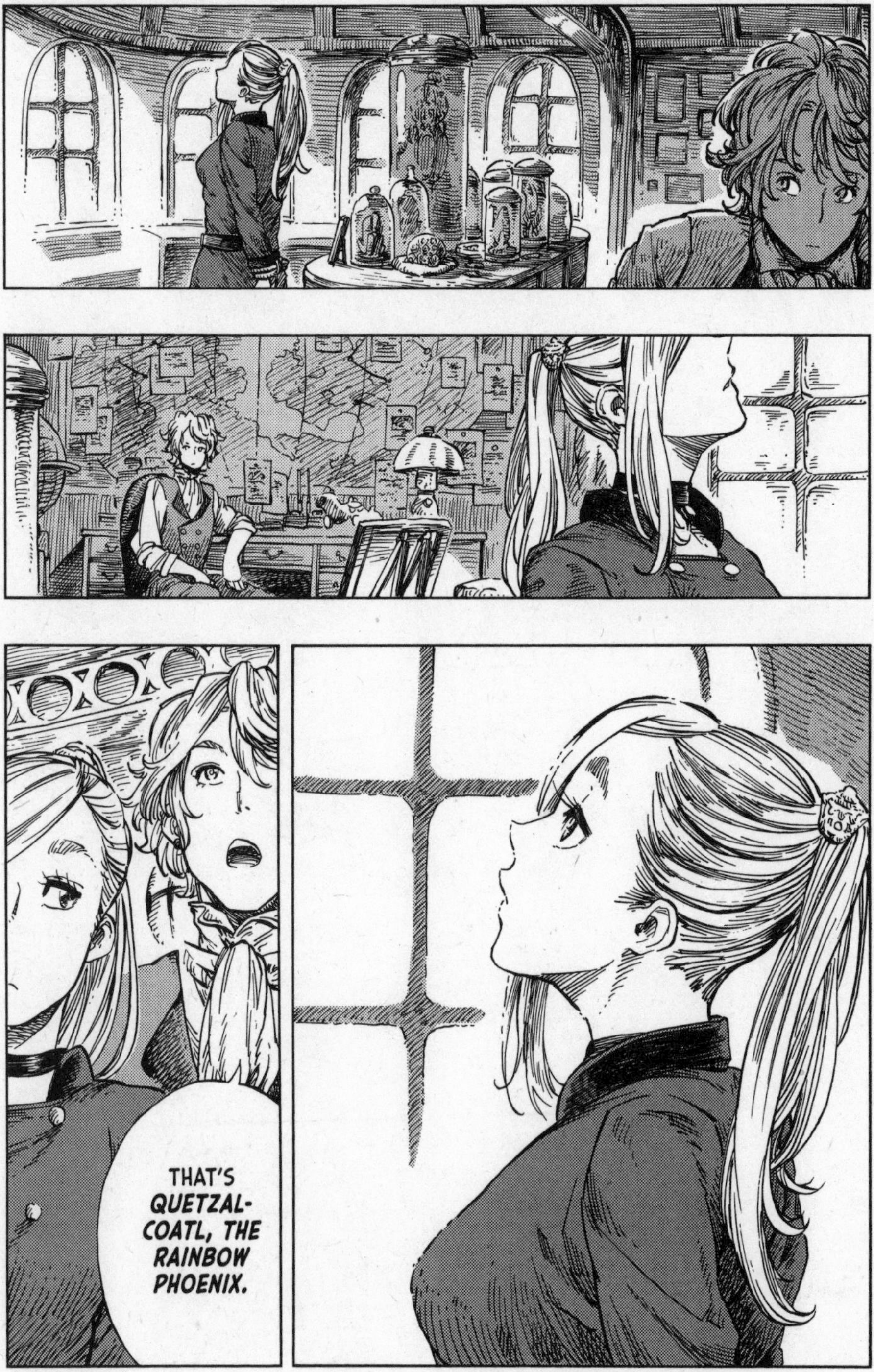
THAT'S QUETZAL-COATL, THE RAINBOW PHOENIX.

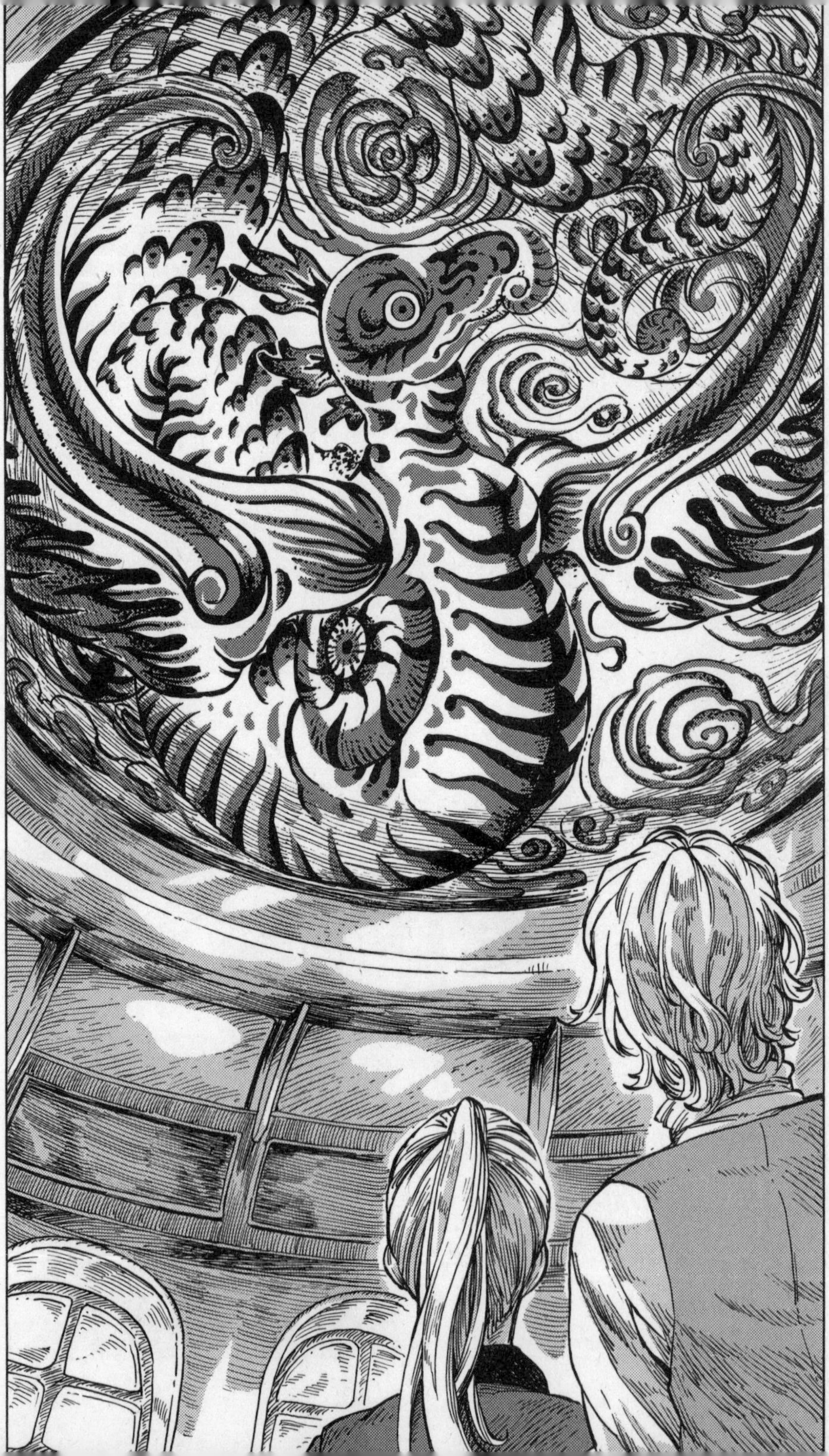

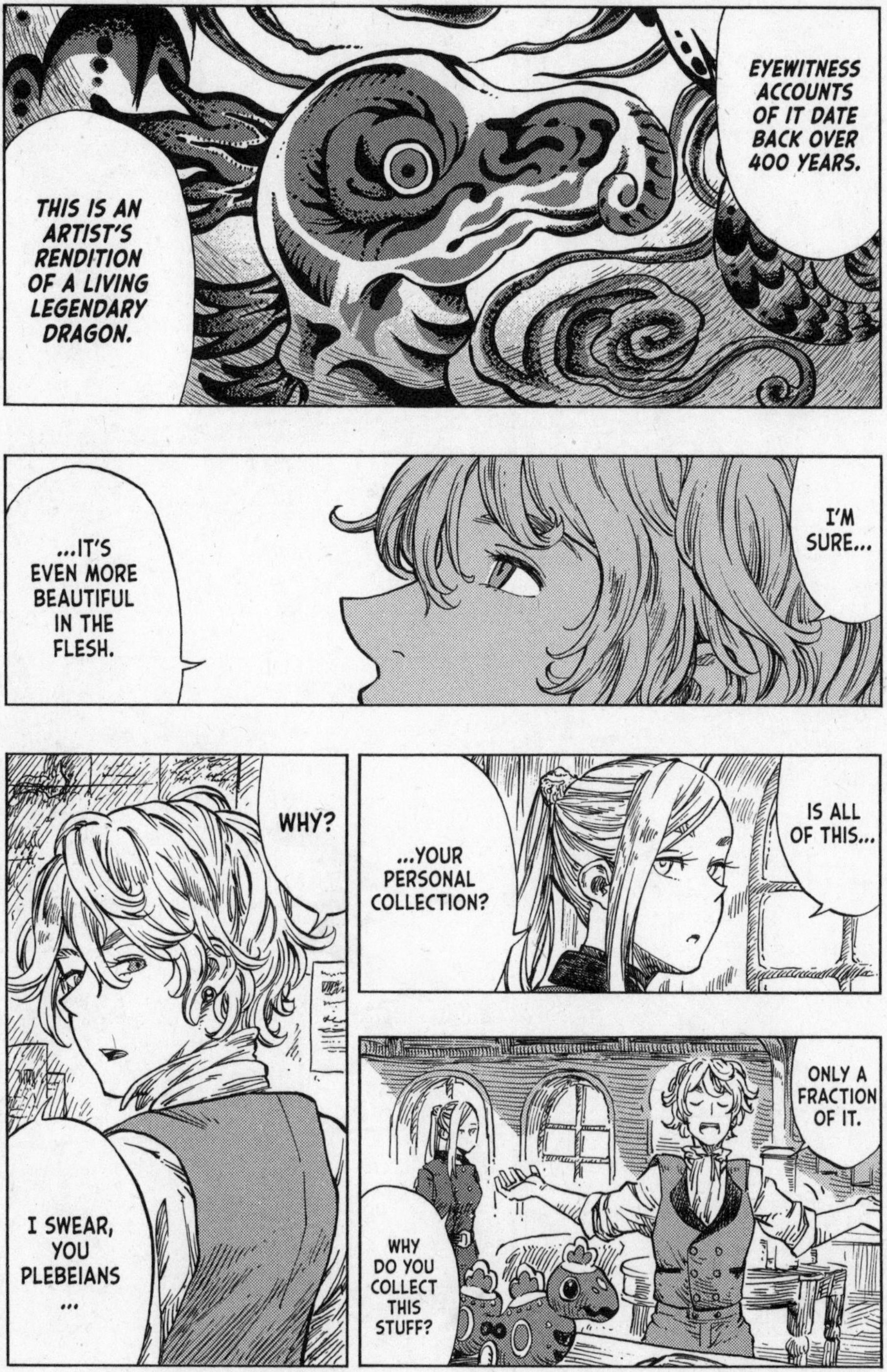
EYEWITNESS ACCOUNTS OF IT DATE BACK OVER 400 YEARS.
THIS IS AN ARTIST'S RENDITION OF A LIVING LEGENDARY DRAGON.
I'M SURE...
...IT'S EVEN MORE BEAUTIFUL IN THE FLESH.
IS ALL OF THIS...
...YOUR PERSONAL COLLECTION?
ONLY A FRACTION OF IT.
WHY DO YOU COLLECT THIS STUFF?
WHY?
I SWEAR, YOU PLEBEIANS ...

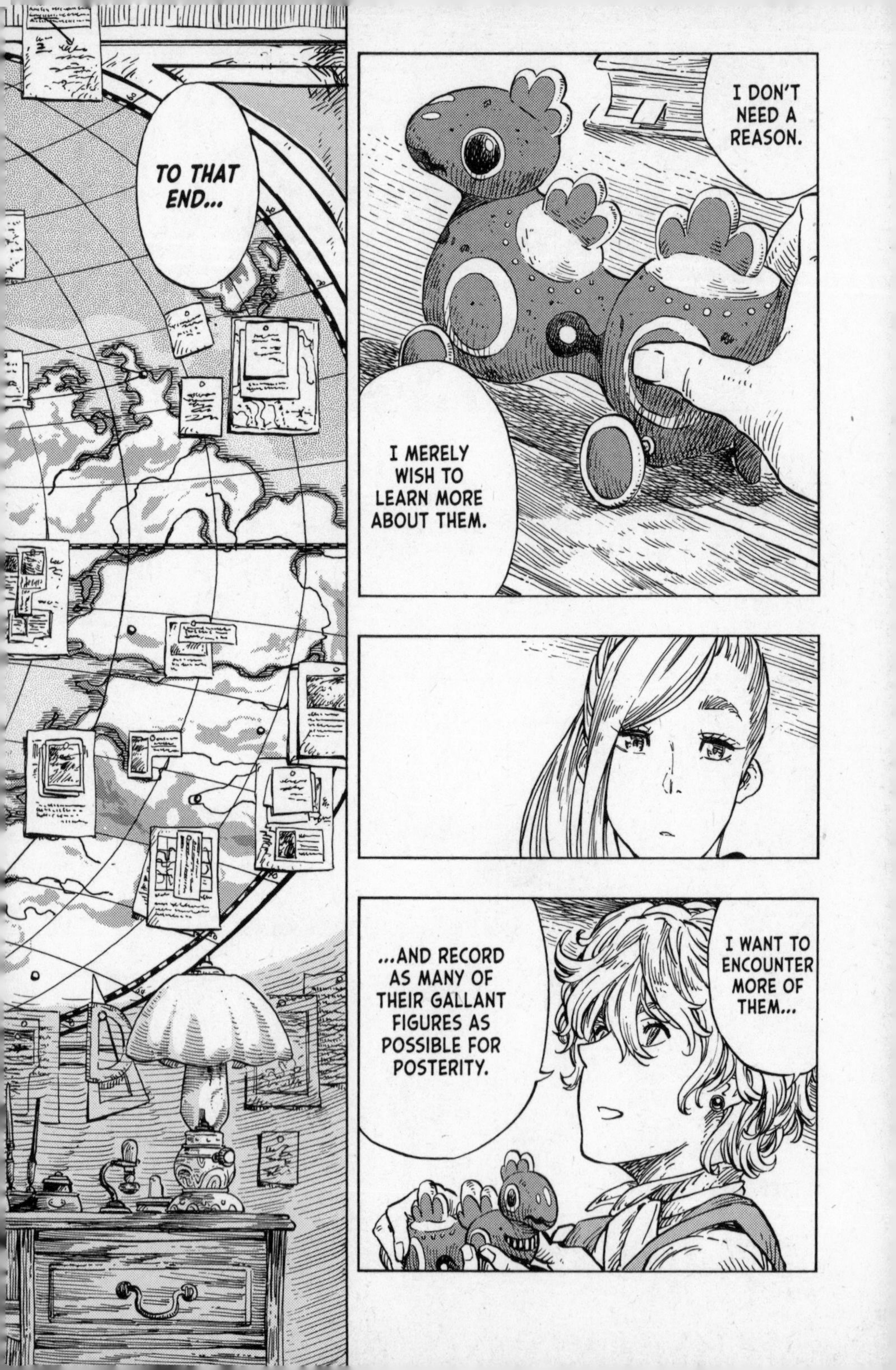
I DON'T NEED A REASON.
I MERELY WISH TO LEARN MORE ABOUT THEM.
I WANT TO ENCOUNTER MORE OF THEM...
...AND RECORD AS MANY OF THEIR GALLANT FIGURES AS POSSIBLE FOR POSTERITY.
TO THAT END...

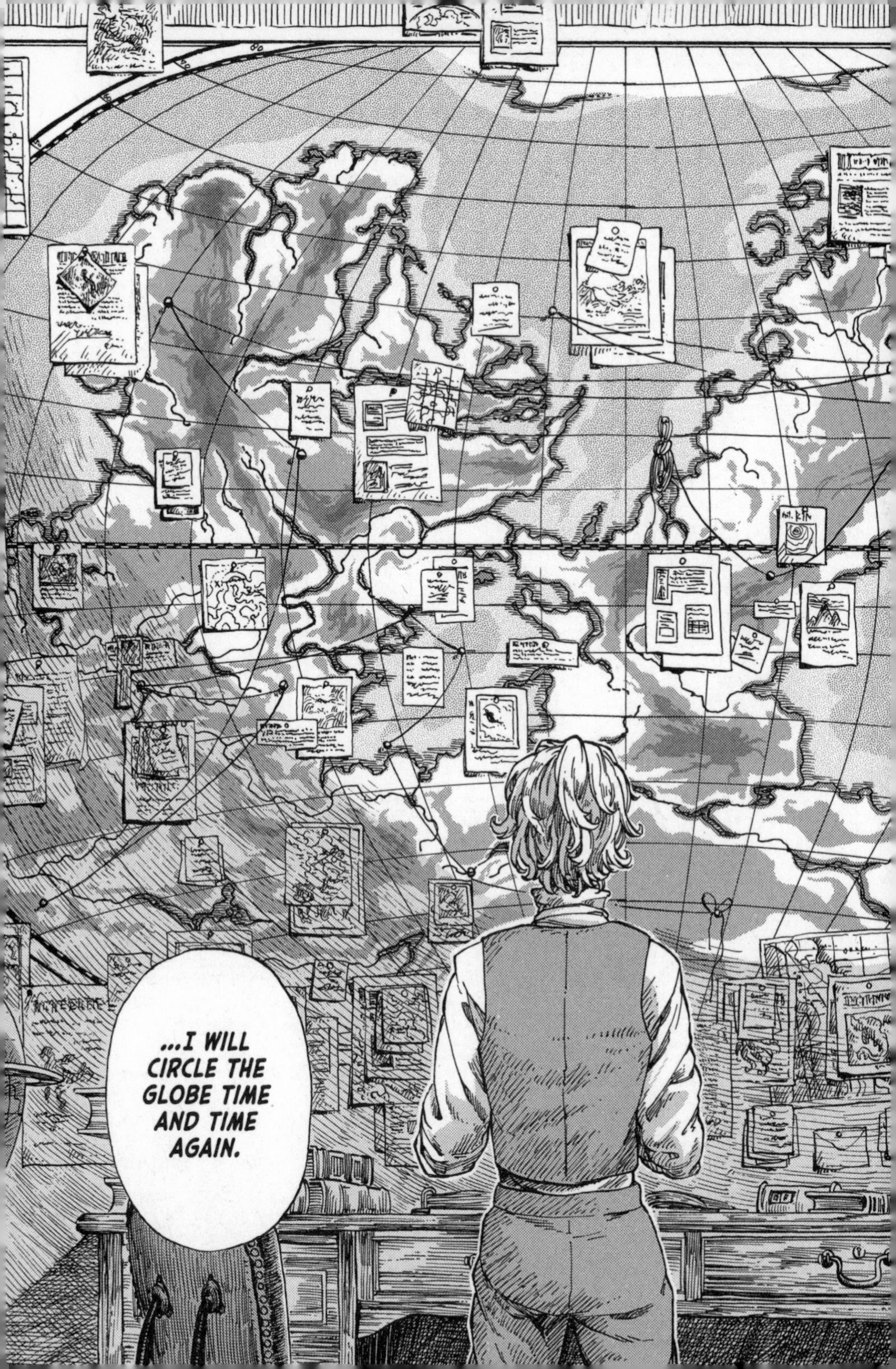
...I WILL CIRCLE THE GLOBE TIME AND TIME AGAIN.

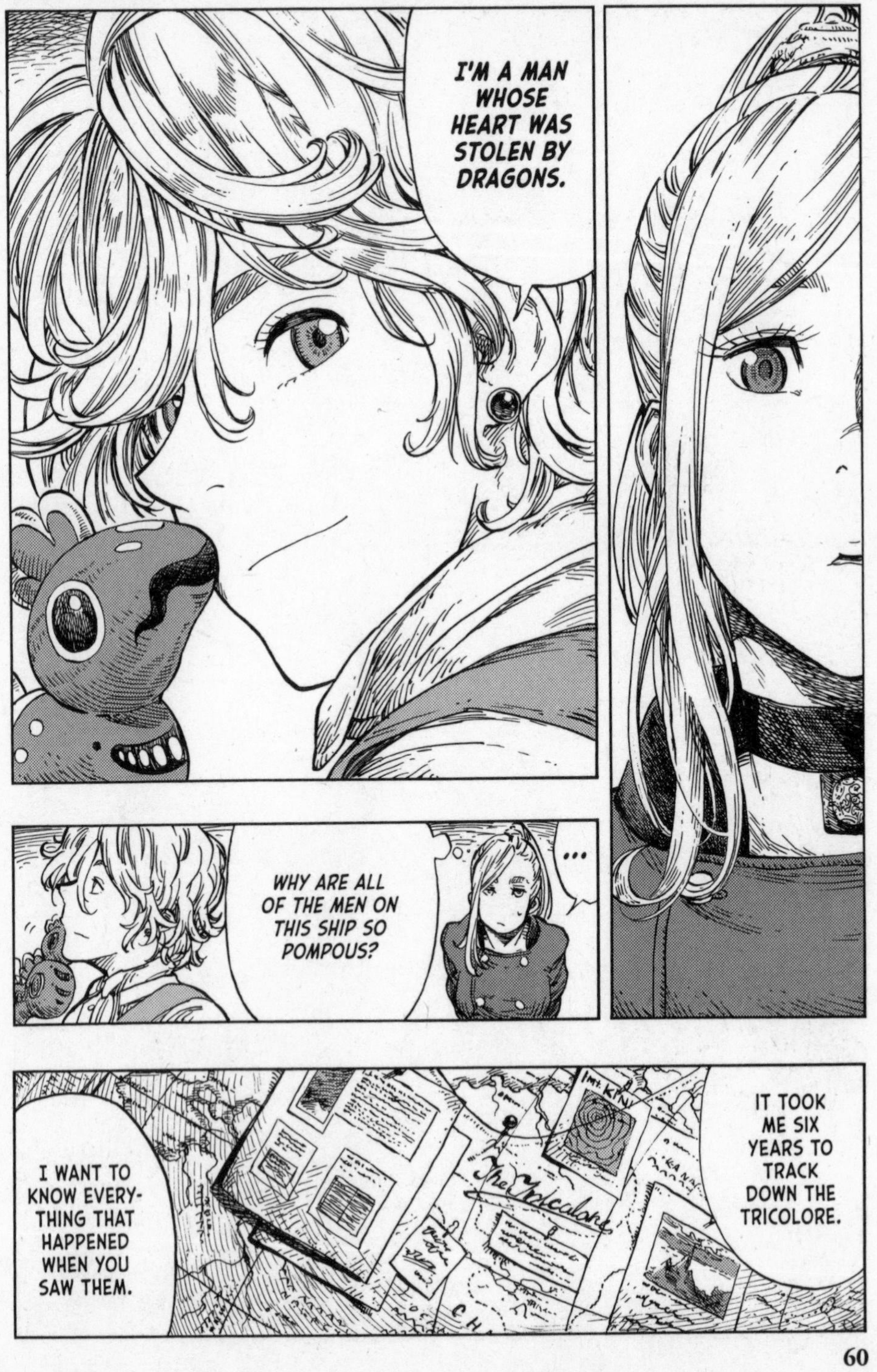
I'M A MAN WHOSE HEART WAS STOLEN BY DRAGONS.
...
WHY ARE ALL OF THE MEN ON THIS SHIP SO POMPOUS?
IT TOOK ME SIX YEARS TO TRACK DOWN THE TRICOLORE.
The Tricolore
I WANT TO KNOW EVERY-THING THAT HAPPENED WHEN YOU SAW THEM.

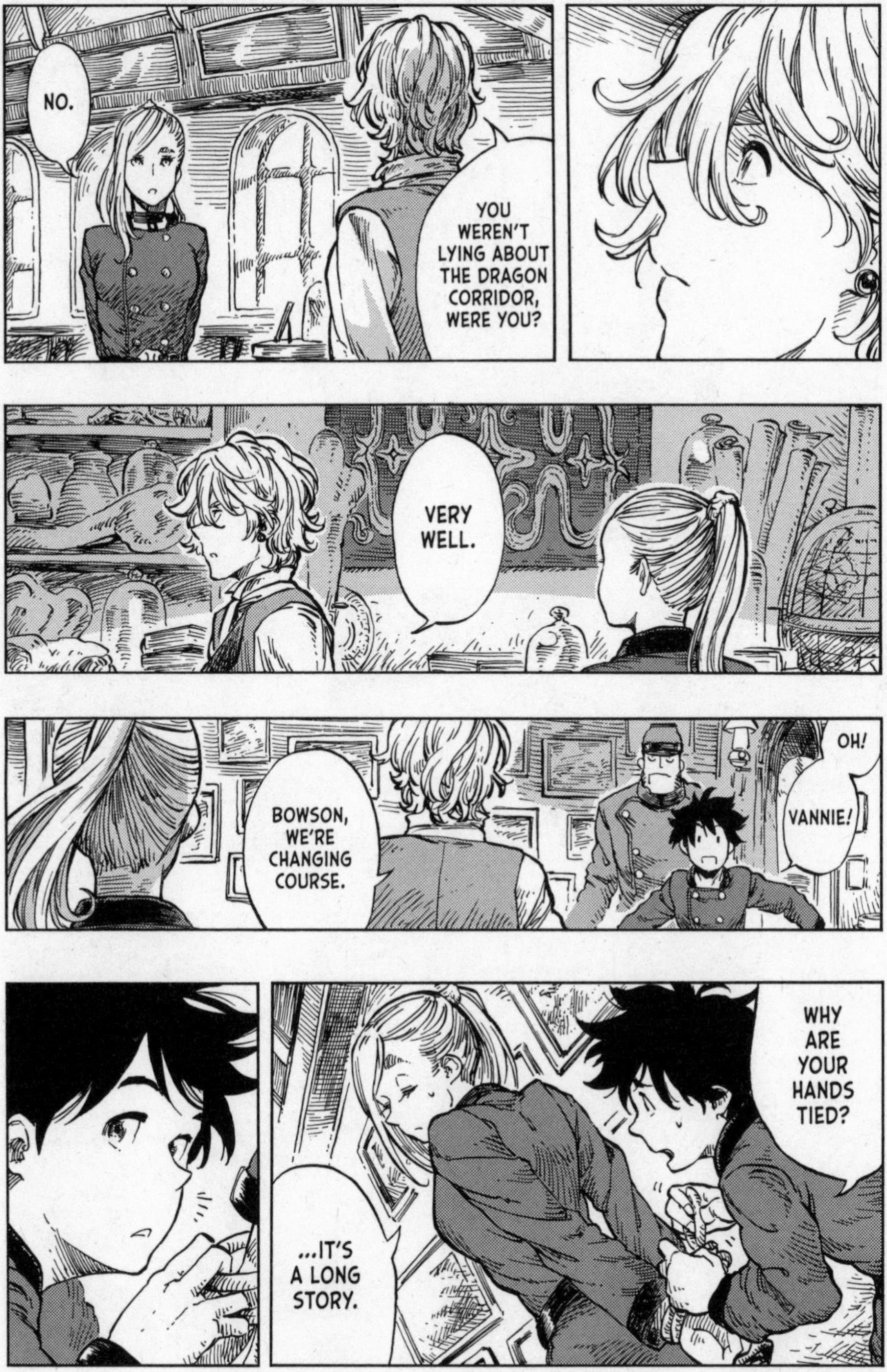
YOU WEREN'T LYING ABOUT THE DRAGON CORRIDOR, WERE YOU?
NO.
VERY WELL.
OH!
VANNIE!
BOWSON, WE'RE CHANGING COURSE.
WHY ARE YOUR HANDS TIED?
...IT'S A LONG STORY.

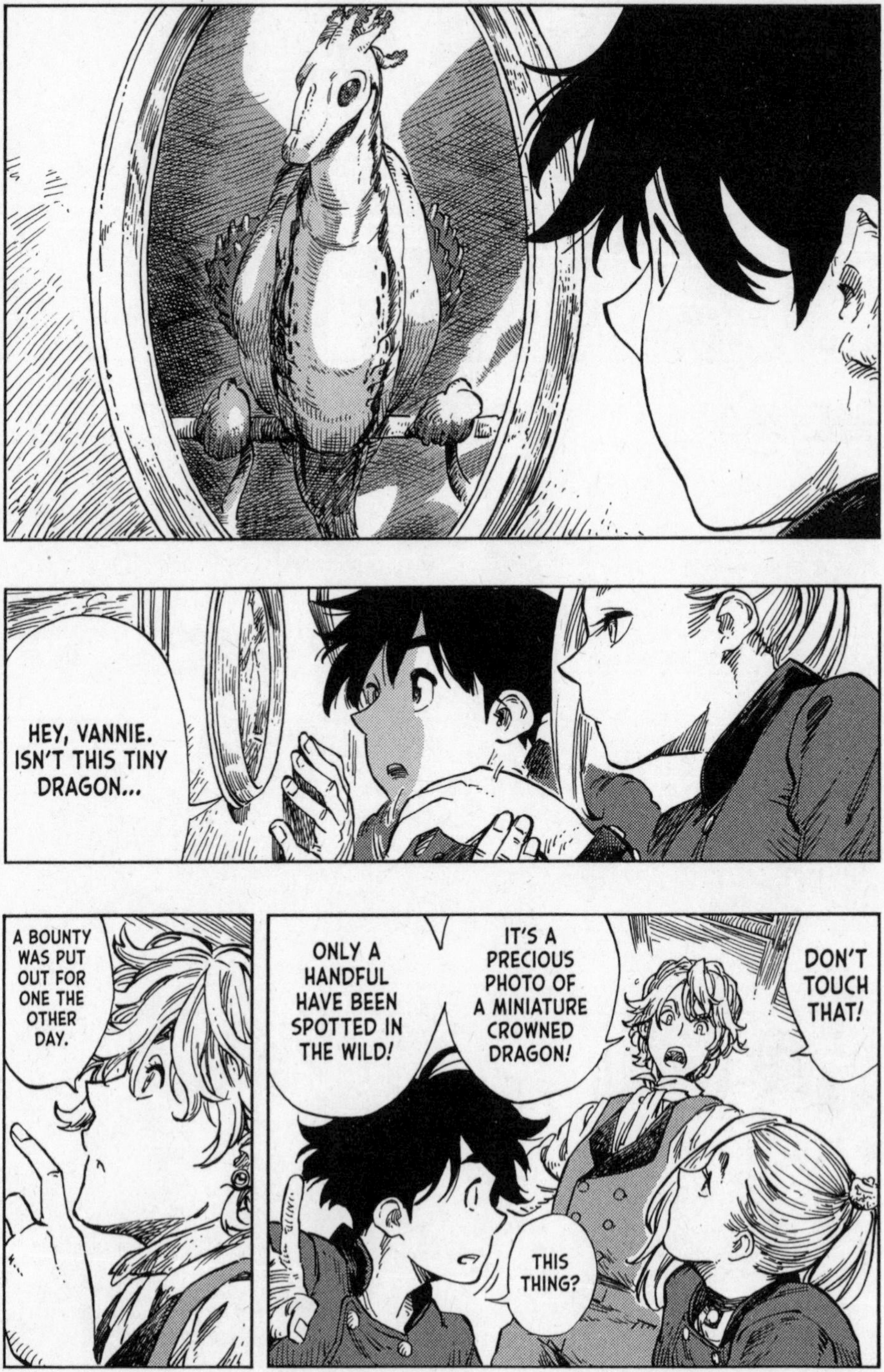
HEY, VANNIE. ISN'T THIS TINY DRAGON...
DON'T TOUCH THAT!
IT'S A PRECIOUS PHOTO OF A MINIATURE CROWNED DRAGON!
ONLY A HANDFUL HAVE BEEN SPOTTED IN THE WILD!
THIS THING?
A BOUNTY WAS PUT OUT FOR ONE THE OTHER DAY.

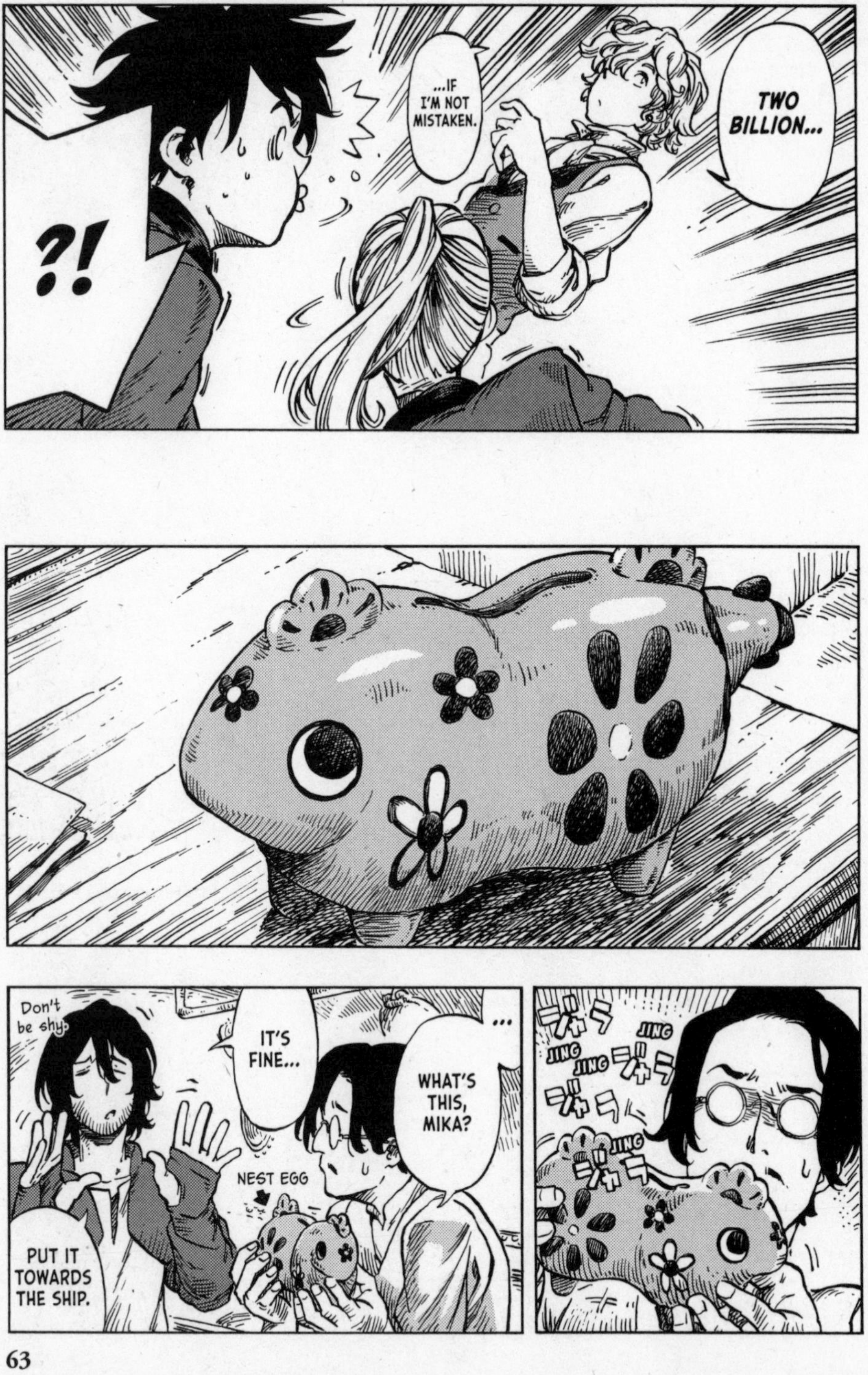
TWO BILLION...
...IF I'M NOT MISTAKEN.
?!
ジャラ
JING
JING
ジャラ
JING
ジャラ
ジャラ
JING
ジャラ
...
WHAT'S THIS, MIKA?
IT'S FINE...
Don't be shy.
NEST EGG
PUT IT TOWARDS THE SHIP.

How to Take Dry-Plate Photos

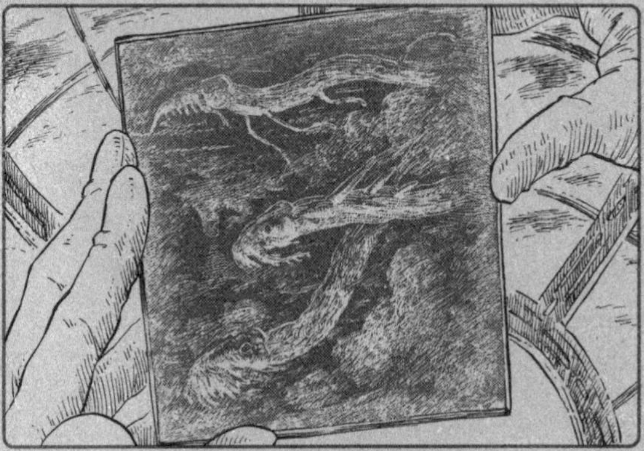

01
In a darkroom, load the glass plate (coated with light-sensitive silver salts) into the film holder.

02
Set the camera on a tripod.

03
Open the lens to its widest aperture and use a loupe to check the subject through the focusing screen (a small window onto which the subject is projected) while adjusting the focus.

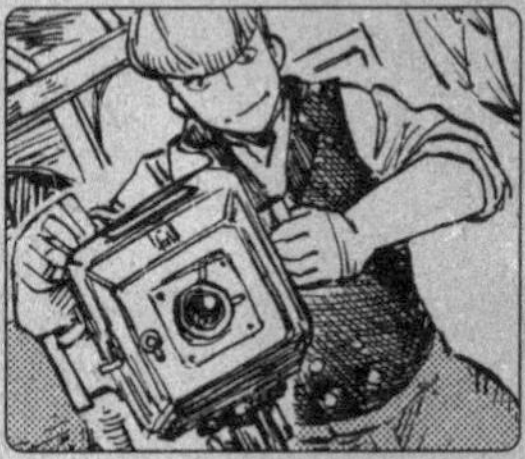

04
Close the shutter and adjust the aperture.

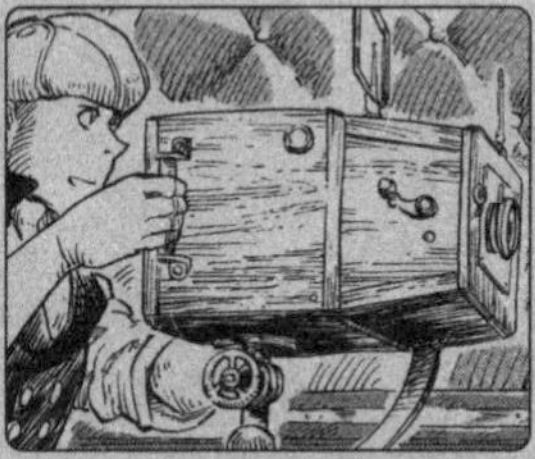

05
Close the focusing screen and slide the film holder into the camera.

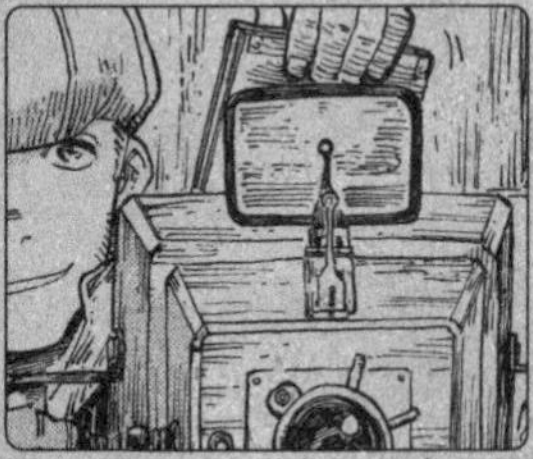

06
Remove the shade from the film holder and release the shutter.

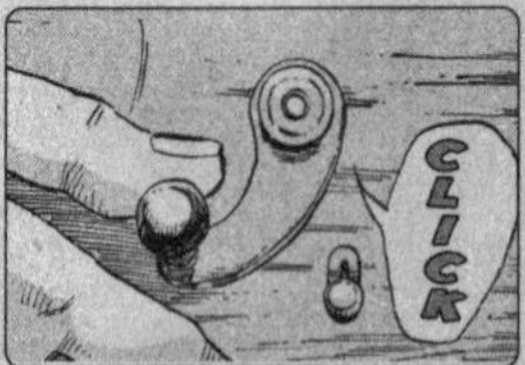
CLICK

07
Place the shade back on and remove the film holder.

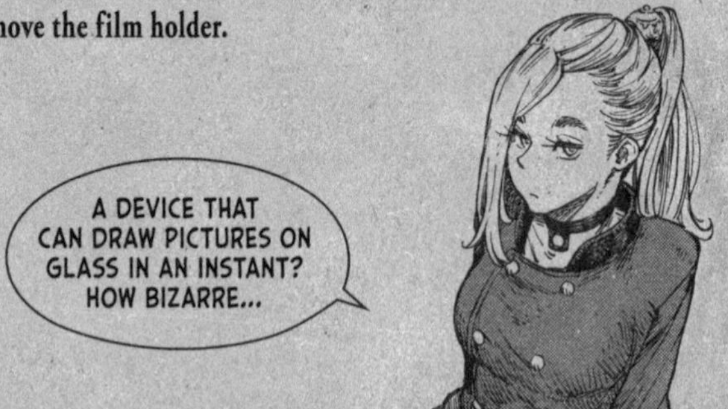
A DEVICE THAT CAN DRAW PICTURES ON GLASS IN AN INSTANT? HOW BIZARRE...

Flight 20 Repair Costs & Dragon Art

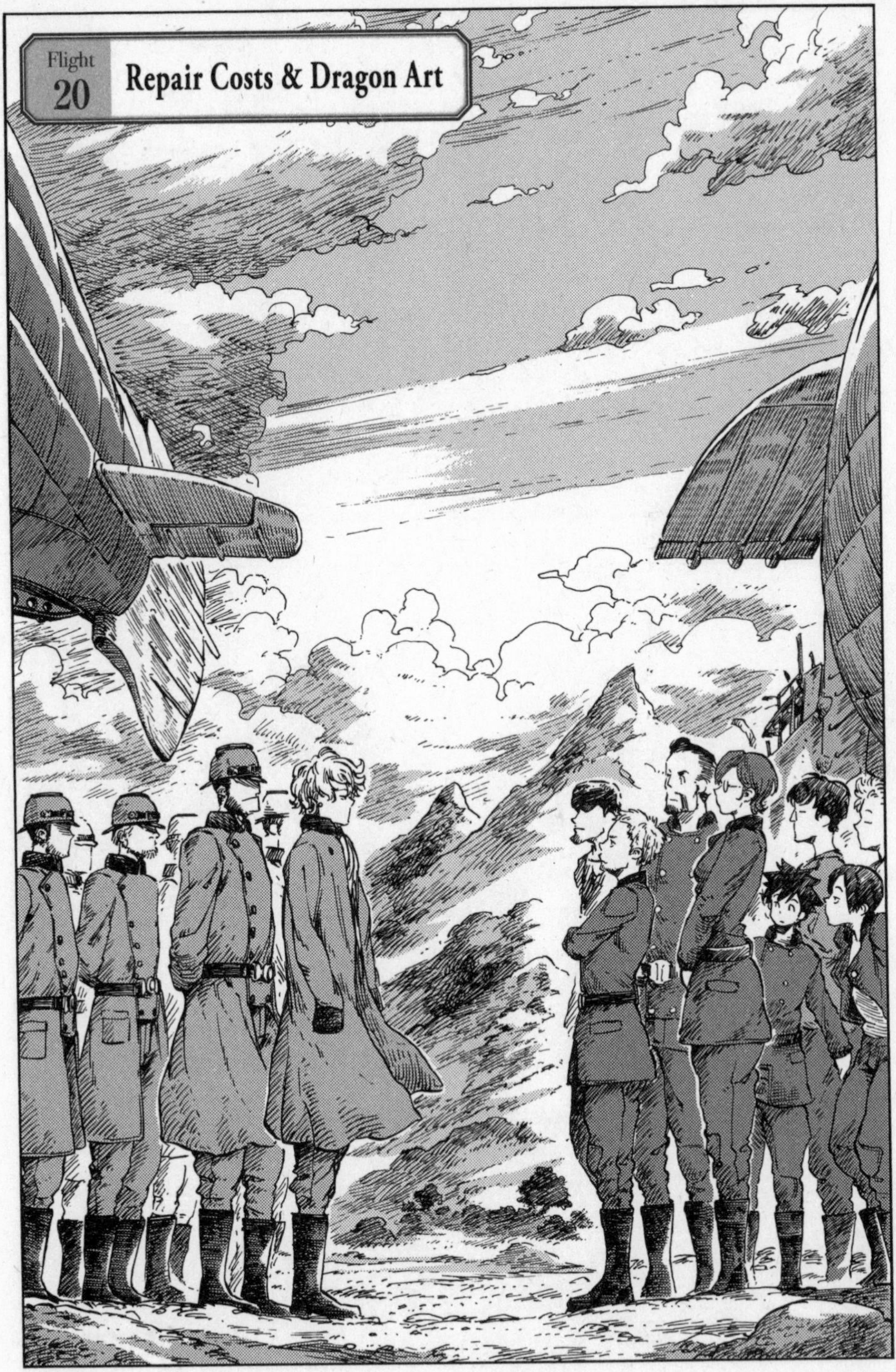

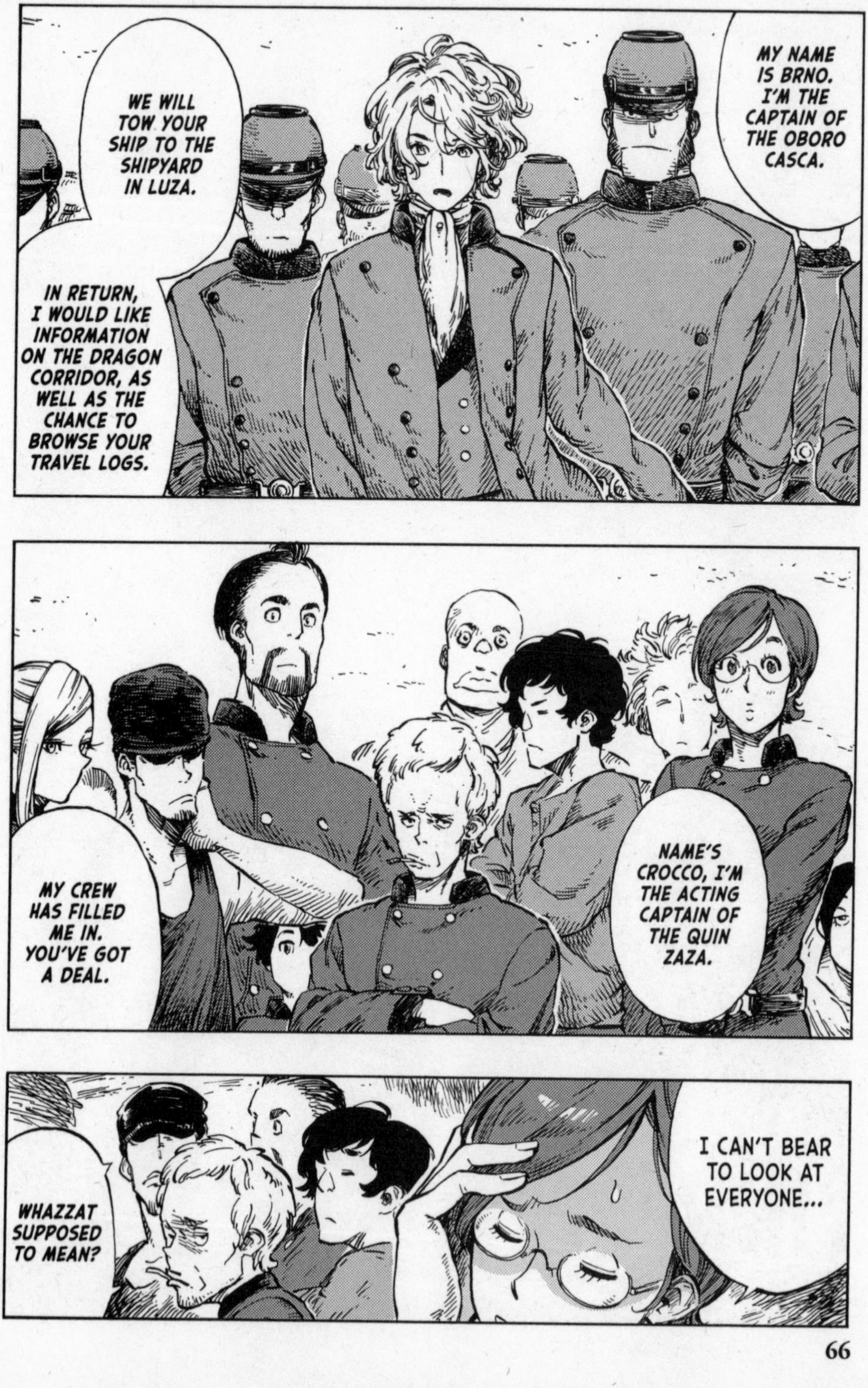
MY NAME IS BRNO. I'M THE CAPTAIN OF THE OBORO CASCA.
WE WILL TOW YOUR SHIP TO THE SHIPYARD IN LUZA.
IN RETURN, I WOULD LIKE INFORMATION ON THE DRAGON CORRIDOR, AS WELL AS THE CHANCE TO BROWSE YOUR TRAVEL LOGS.
NAME'S CROCCO, I'M THE ACTING CAPTAIN OF THE QUIN ZAZA.
MY CREW HAS FILLED ME IN. YOU'VE GOT A DEAL.
I CAN'T BEAR TO LOOK AT EVERYONE...
WHAZZAT SUPPOSED TO MEAN?

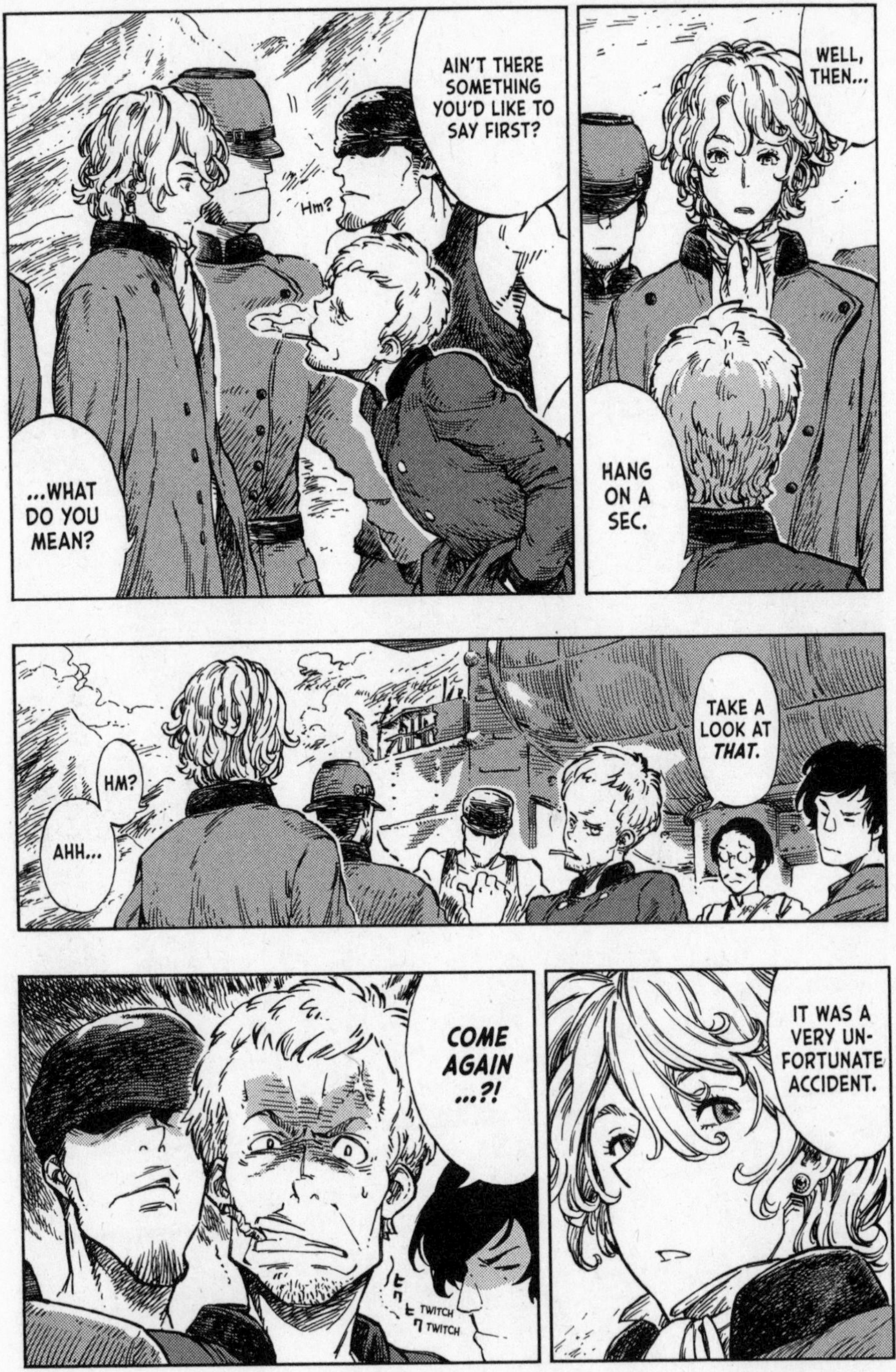
WELL, THEN...
HANG ON A SEC.
AIN'T THERE SOMETHING YOU'D LIKE TO SAY FIRST?
Hm?
...WHAT DO YOU MEAN?
TAKE A LOOK AT *THAT.*
HM?
AHH...
IT WAS A VERY UN-FORTUNATE ACCIDENT.
COME AGAIN ...?!
TWITCH
TWITCH

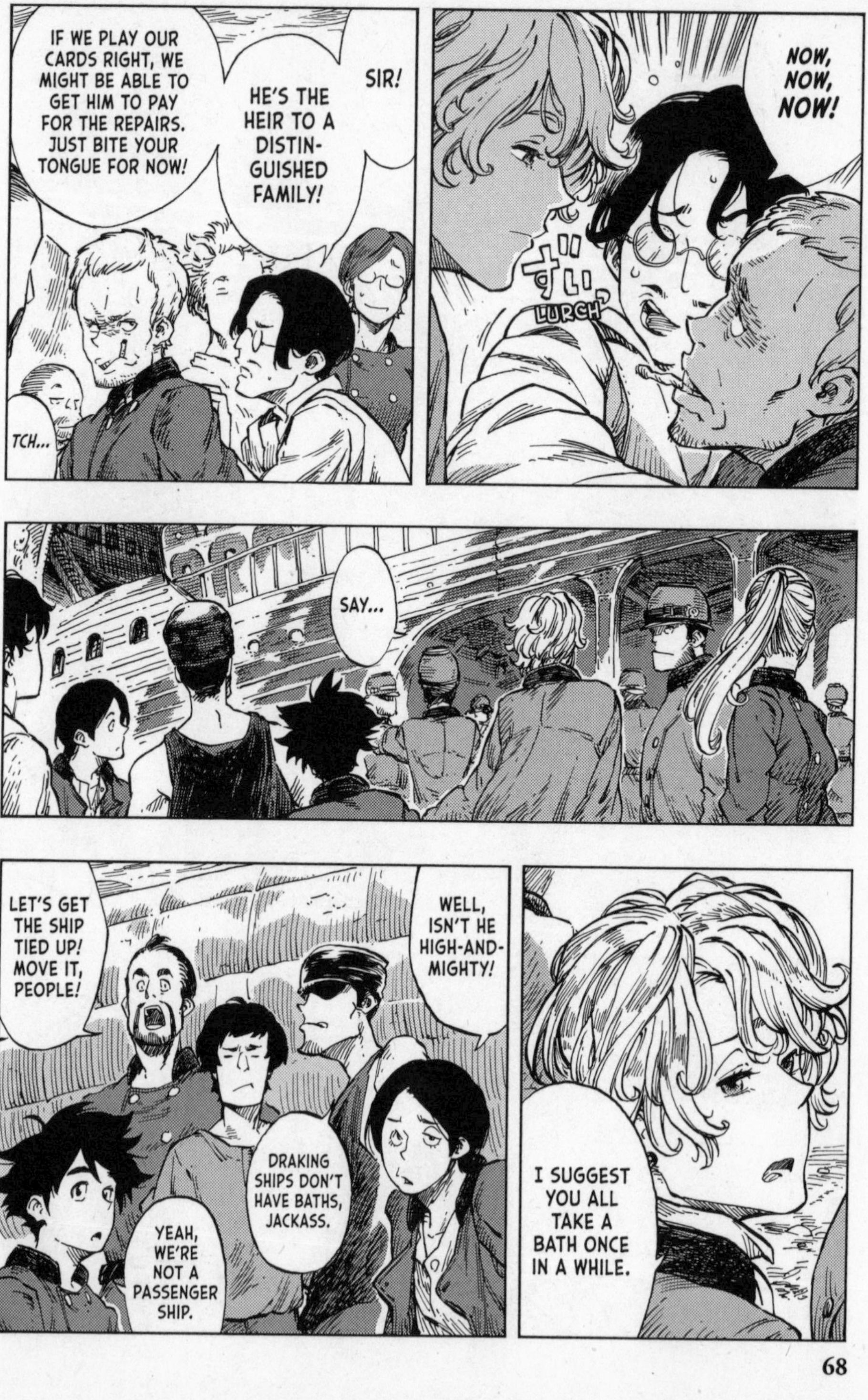
NOW, NOW, NOW!
ずい
LURCH
SIR!
HE'S THE HEIR TO A DISTINGUISHED FAMILY!
IF WE PLAY OUR CARDS RIGHT, WE MIGHT BE ABLE TO GET HIM TO PAY FOR THE REPAIRS. JUST BITE YOUR TONGUE FOR NOW!
TCH...
SAY...
I SUGGEST YOU ALL TAKE A BATH ONCE IN A WHILE.
WELL, ISN'T HE HIGH-AND-MIGHTY!
LET'S GET THE SHIP TIED UP! MOVE IT, PEOPLE!
DRAKING SHIPS DON'T HAVE BATHS, JACKASS.
YEAH, WE'RE NOT A PASSENGER SHIP.

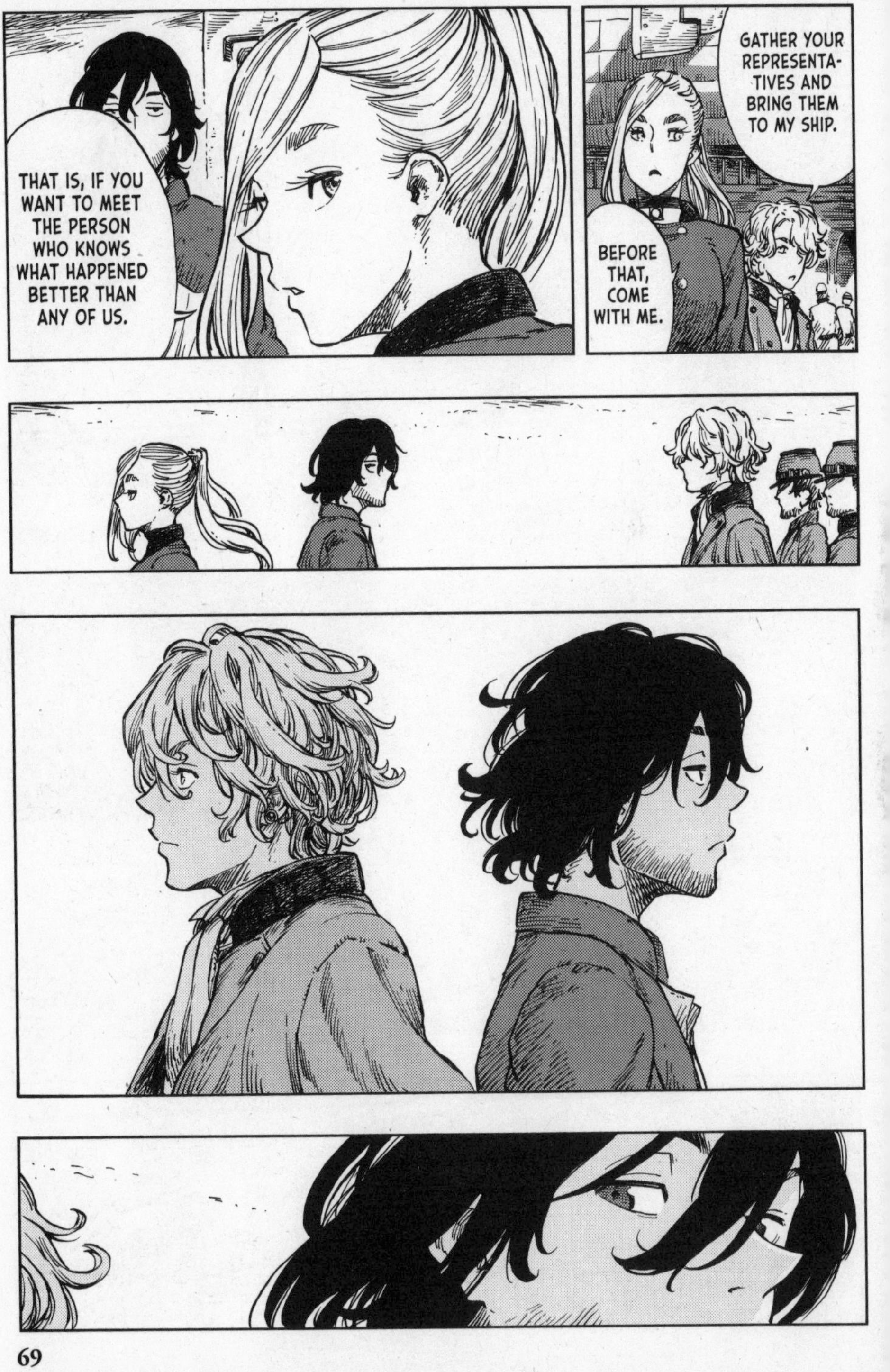
GATHER YOUR REPRESENTA-TIVES AND BRING THEM TO MY SHIP.
BEFORE THAT, COME WITH ME.
THAT IS, IF YOU WANT TO MEET THE PERSON WHO KNOWS WHAT HAPPENED BETTER THAN ANY OF US.

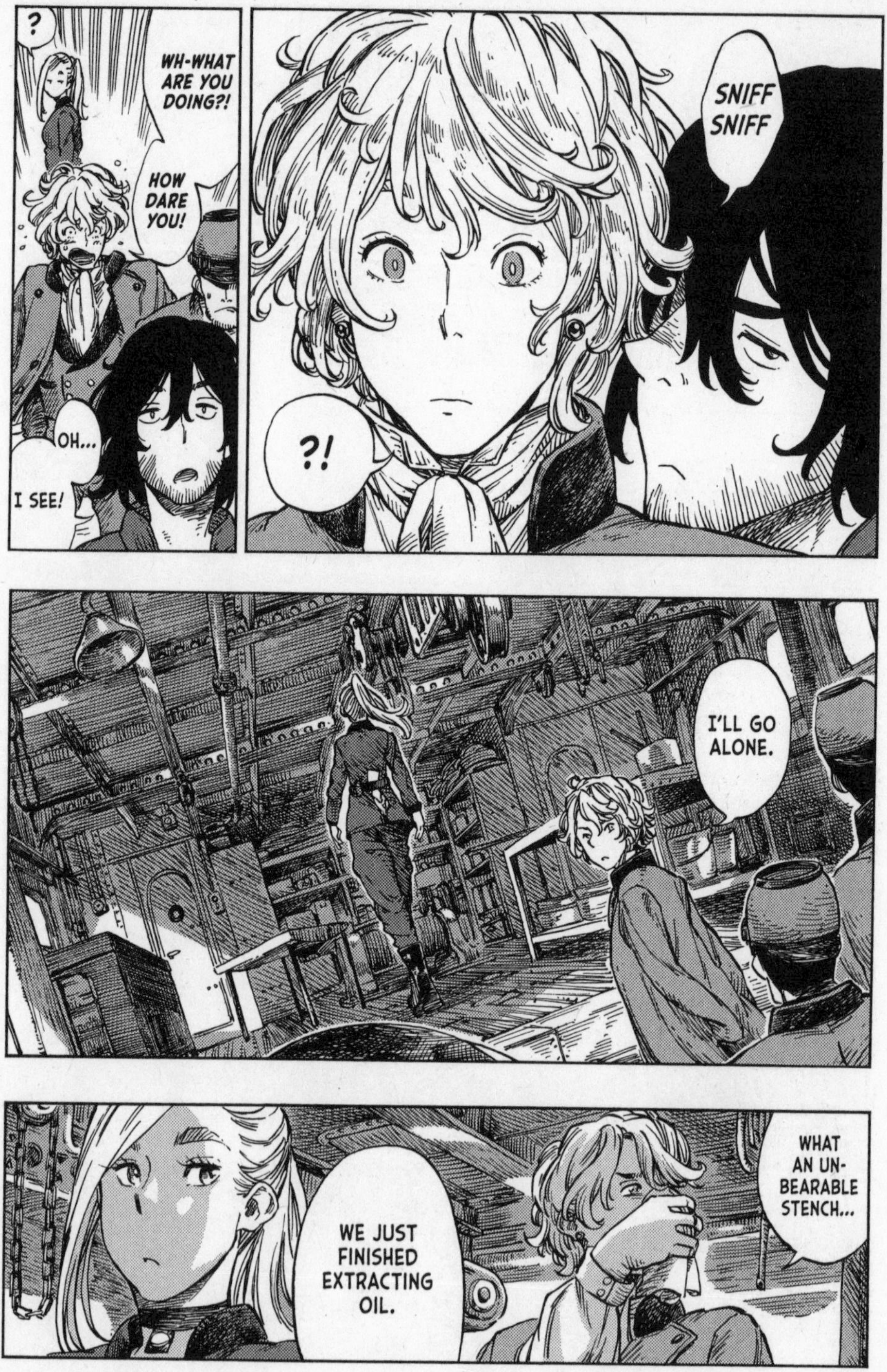
SNIFF SNIFF
?!
?
WH-WHAT ARE YOU DOING?!
HOW DARE YOU!
OH...
I SEE!
I'LL GO ALONE.
WHAT AN UN-BEARABLE STENCH...
WE JUST FINISHED EXTRACTING OIL.

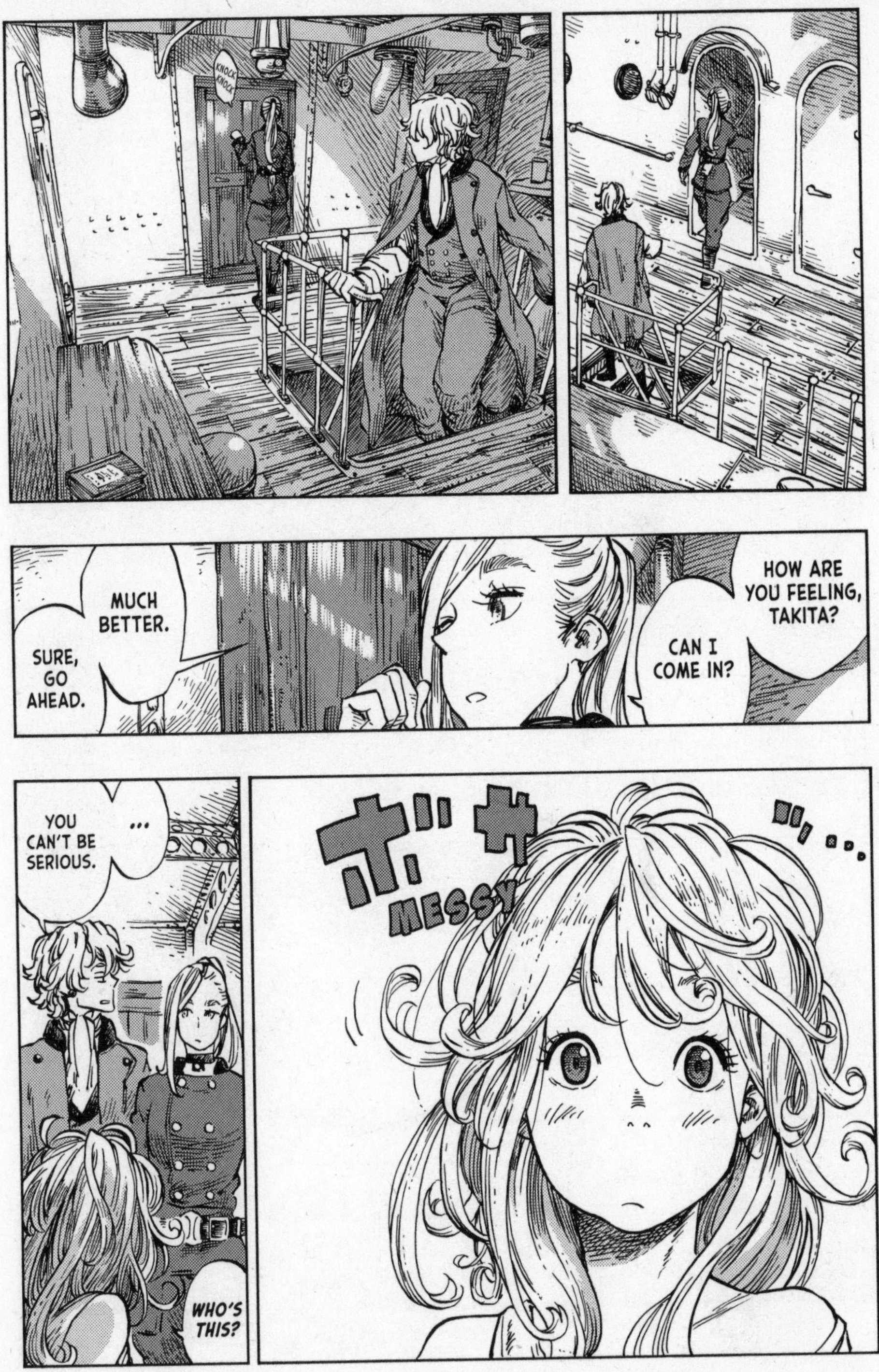
KNOCK KNOCK
HOW ARE YOU FEELING, TAKITA?
CAN I COME IN?
MUCH BETTER.
SURE, GO AHEAD.
MESSY
...
YOU CAN'T BE SERIOUS.
WHO'S THIS?

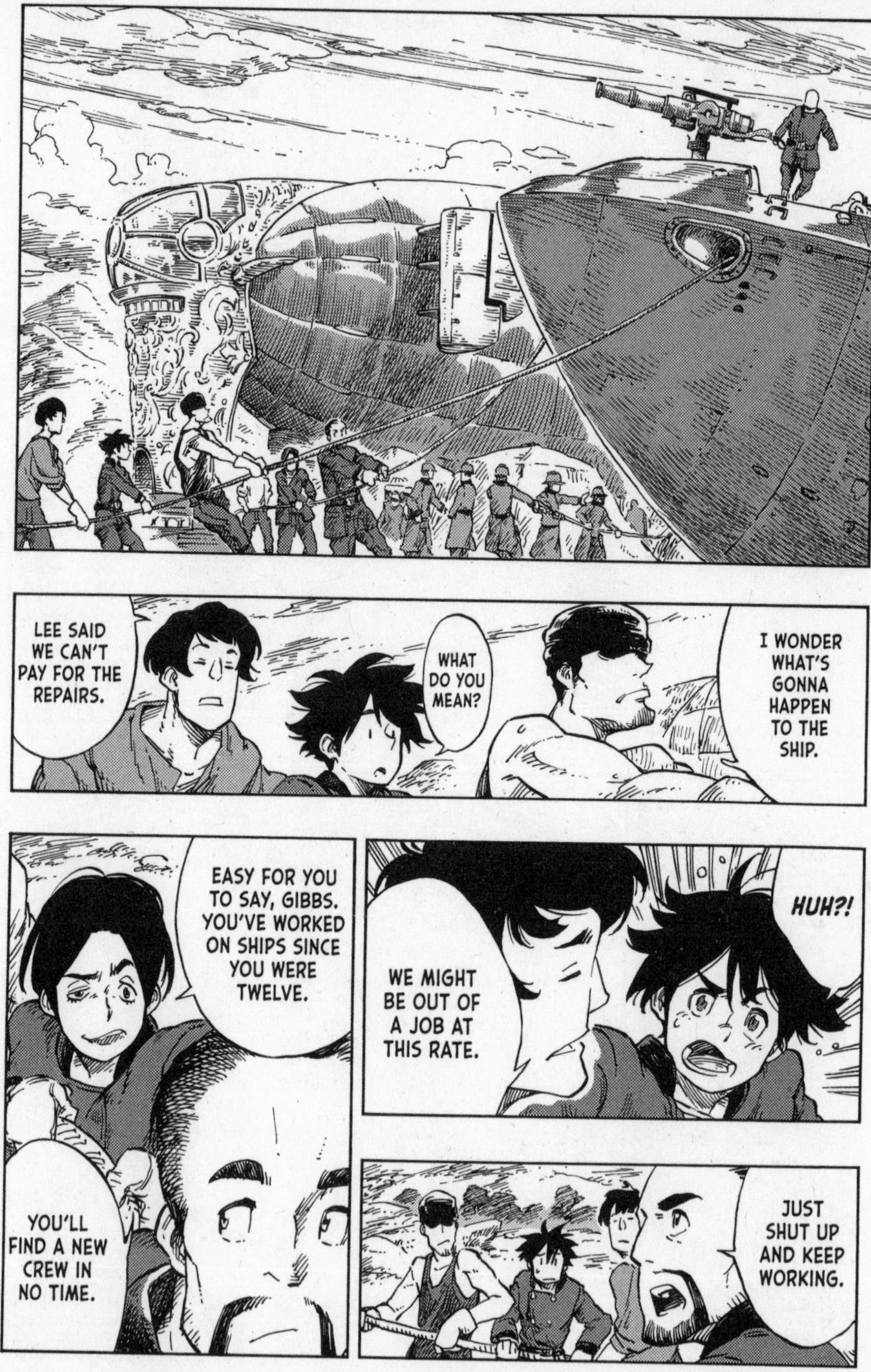
I WONDER WHAT'S GONNA HAPPEN TO THE SHIP.
WHAT DO YOU MEAN?
LEE SAID WE CAN'T PAY FOR THE REPAIRS.
HUH?!
WE MIGHT BE OUT OF A JOB AT THIS RATE.
JUST SHUT UP AND KEEP WORKING.
EASY FOR YOU TO SAY, GIBBS. YOU'VE WORKED ON SHIPS SINCE YOU WERE TWELVE.
YOU'LL FIND A NEW CREW IN NO TIME.

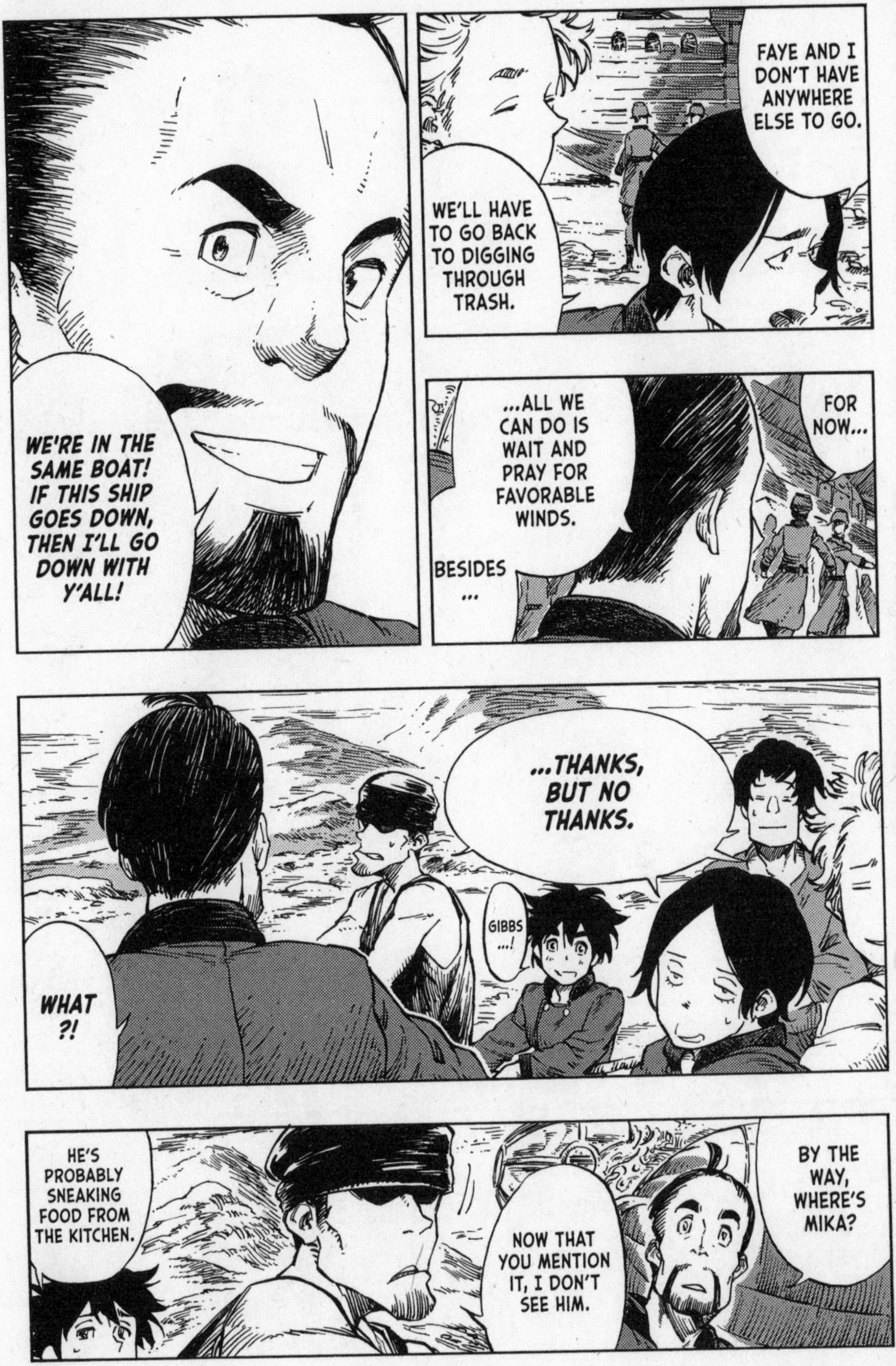
FAYE AND I DON'T HAVE ANYWHERE ELSE TO GO.
WE'LL HAVE TO GO BACK TO DIGGING THROUGH TRASH.
FOR NOW...
...ALL WE CAN DO IS WAIT AND PRAY FOR FAVORABLE WINDS.
BESIDES ...
WE'RE IN THE SAME BOAT! IF THIS SHIP GOES DOWN, THEN I'LL GO DOWN WITH Y'ALL!
...THANKS, BUT NO THANKS.
GIBBS ...!
WHAT ?!
BY THE WAY, WHERE'S MIKA?
NOW THAT YOU MENTION IT, I DON'T SEE HIM.
HE'S PROBABLY SNEAKING FOOD FROM THE KITCHEN.

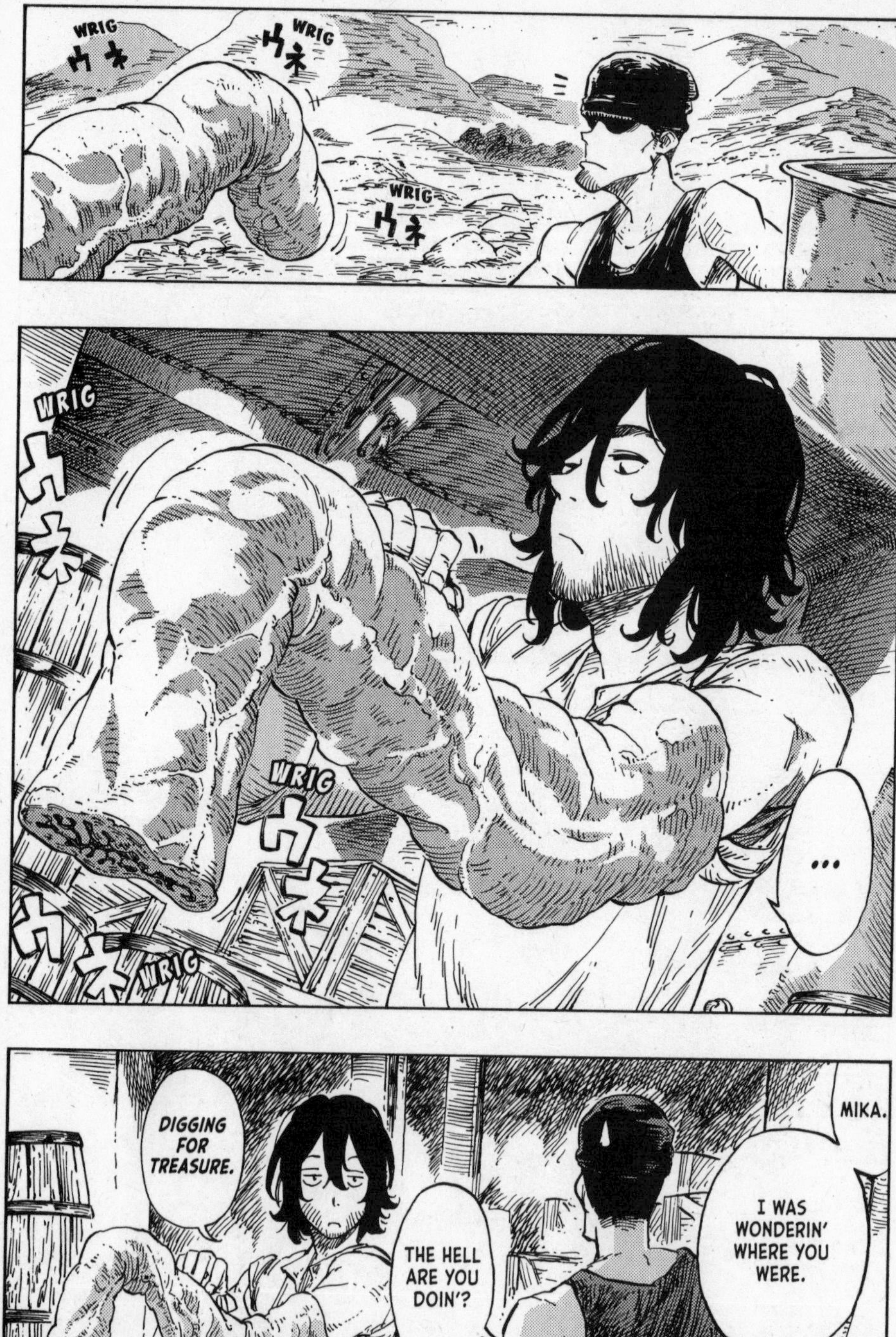
WRIG
ウネ
WRIG
ウネ
WRIG
ウネ
WRIG
ウネ
...
WRIG
ウネ
WRIG
ウネ
MIKA.
I WAS WONDERIN' WHERE YOU WERE.
THE HELL ARE YOU DOIN'?
DIGGING FOR TREASURE.

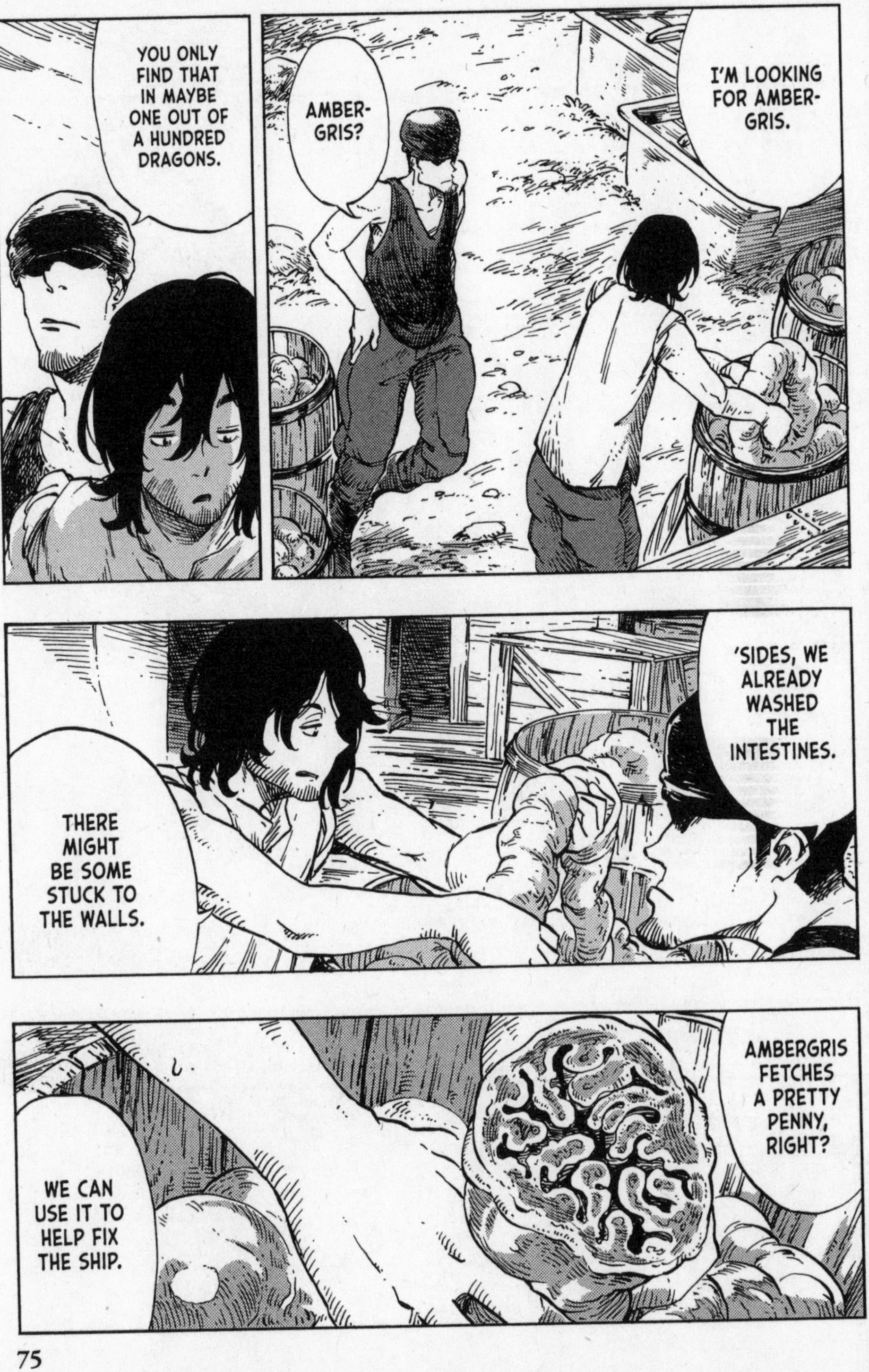
I'M LOOKING FOR AMBER-GRIS.
AMBER-GRIS?
YOU ONLY FIND THAT IN MAYBE ONE OUT OF A HUNDRED DRAGONS.
'SIDES, WE ALREADY WASHED THE INTESTINES.
THERE MIGHT BE SOME STUCK TO THE WALLS.
AMBERGRIS FETCHES A PRETTY PENNY, RIGHT?
WE CAN USE IT TO HELP FIX THE SHIP.

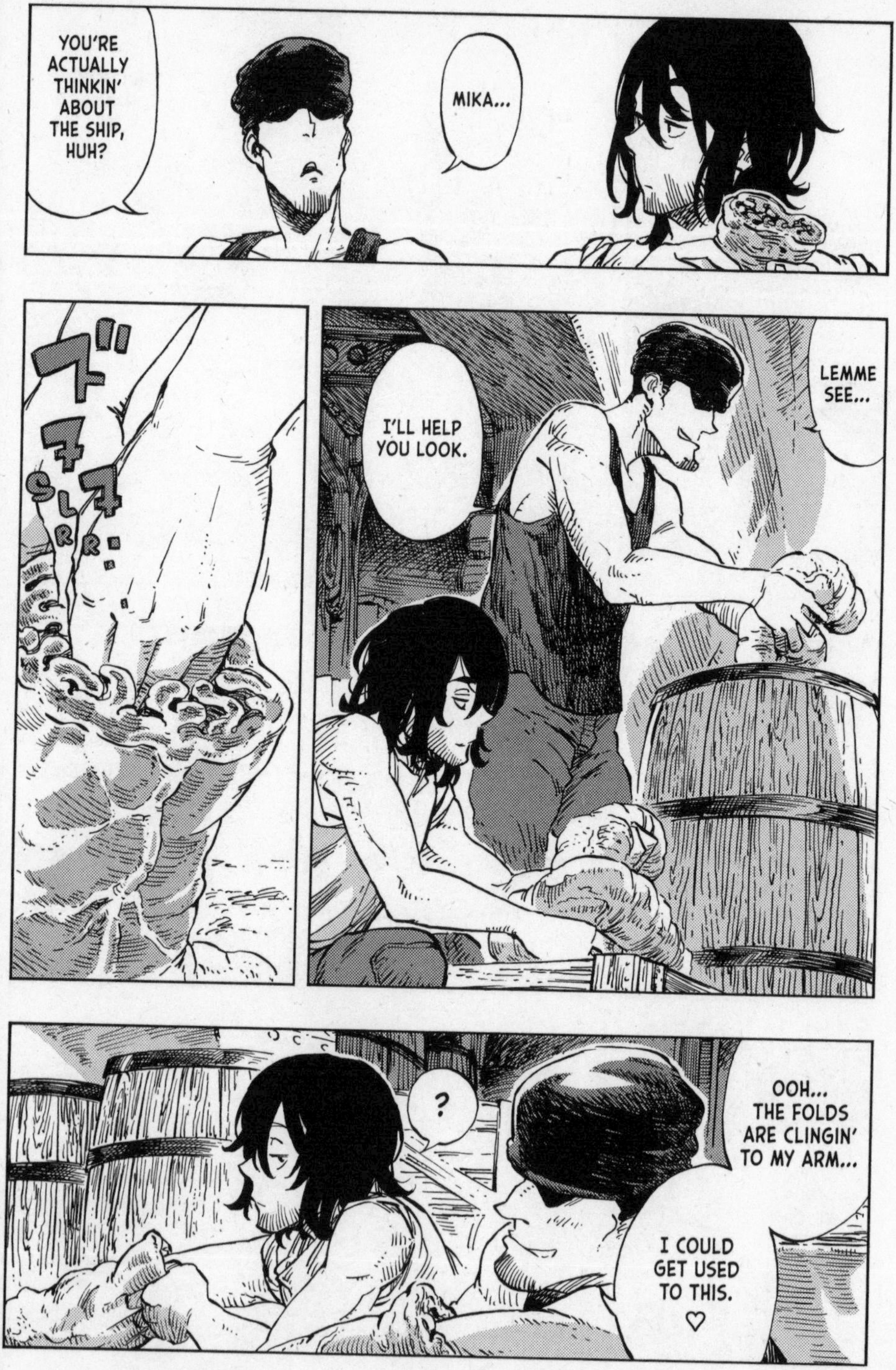
MIKA...
YOU'RE ACTUALLY THINKIN' ABOUT THE SHIP, HUH?
LEMME SEE...
I'LL HELP YOU LOOK.
SLRRR
OOH... THE FOLDS ARE CLINGIN' TO MY ARM...
I COULD GET USED TO THIS. ♡
?

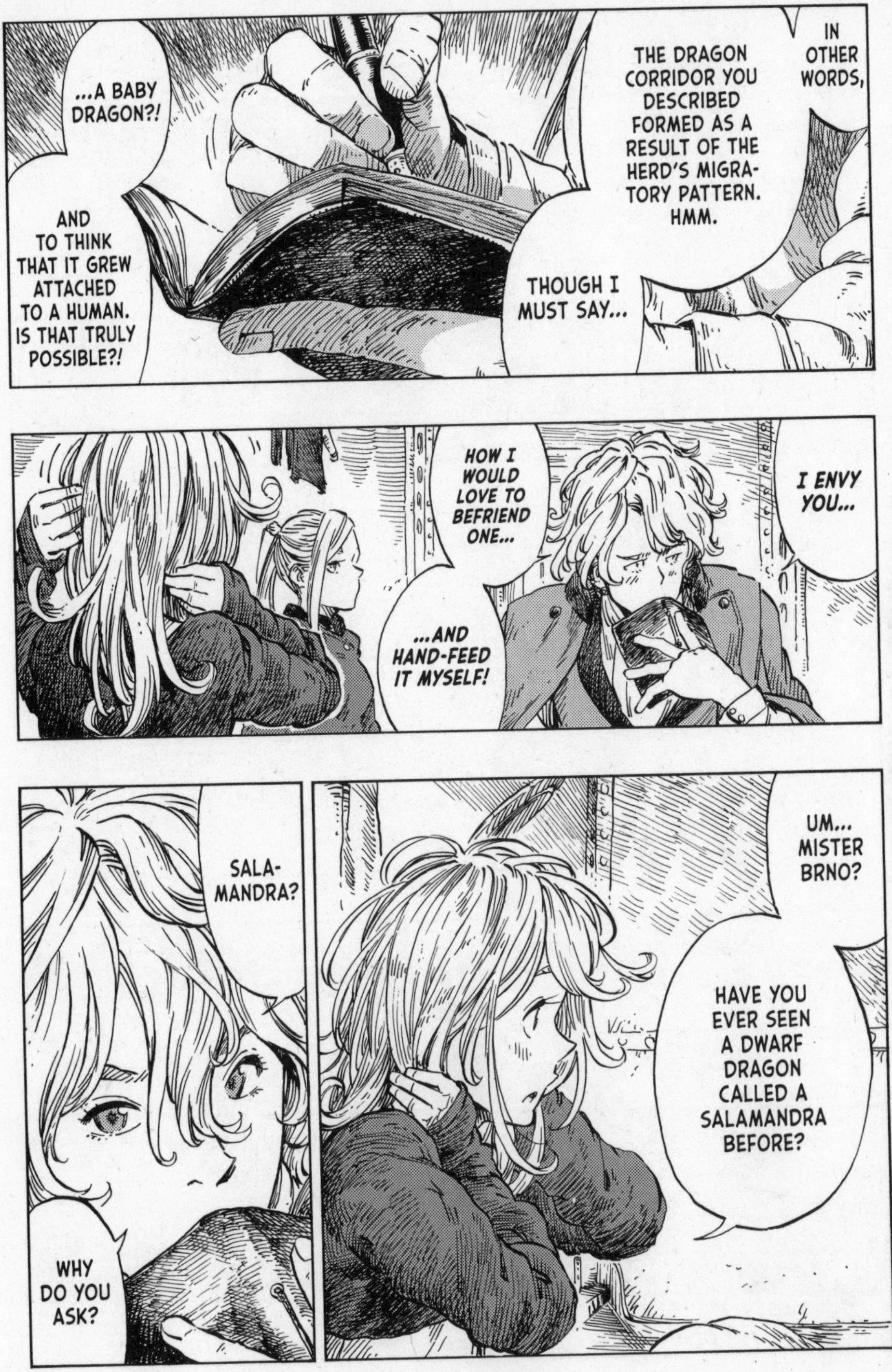
IN OTHER WORDS,
THE DRAGON CORRIDOR YOU DESCRIBED FORMED AS A RESULT OF THE HERD'S MIGRATORY PATTERN. HMM.
THOUGH I MUST SAY...
...A BABY DRAGON?!
AND TO THINK THAT IT GREW ATTACHED TO A HUMAN. IS THAT TRULY POSSIBLE?!
I ENVY YOU...
HOW I WOULD LOVE TO BEFRIEND ONE...
...AND HAND-FEED IT MYSELF!
UM... MISTER BRNO?
HAVE YOU EVER SEEN A DWARF DRAGON CALLED A SALAMANDRA BEFORE?
SALA-MANDRA?
WHY DO YOU ASK?

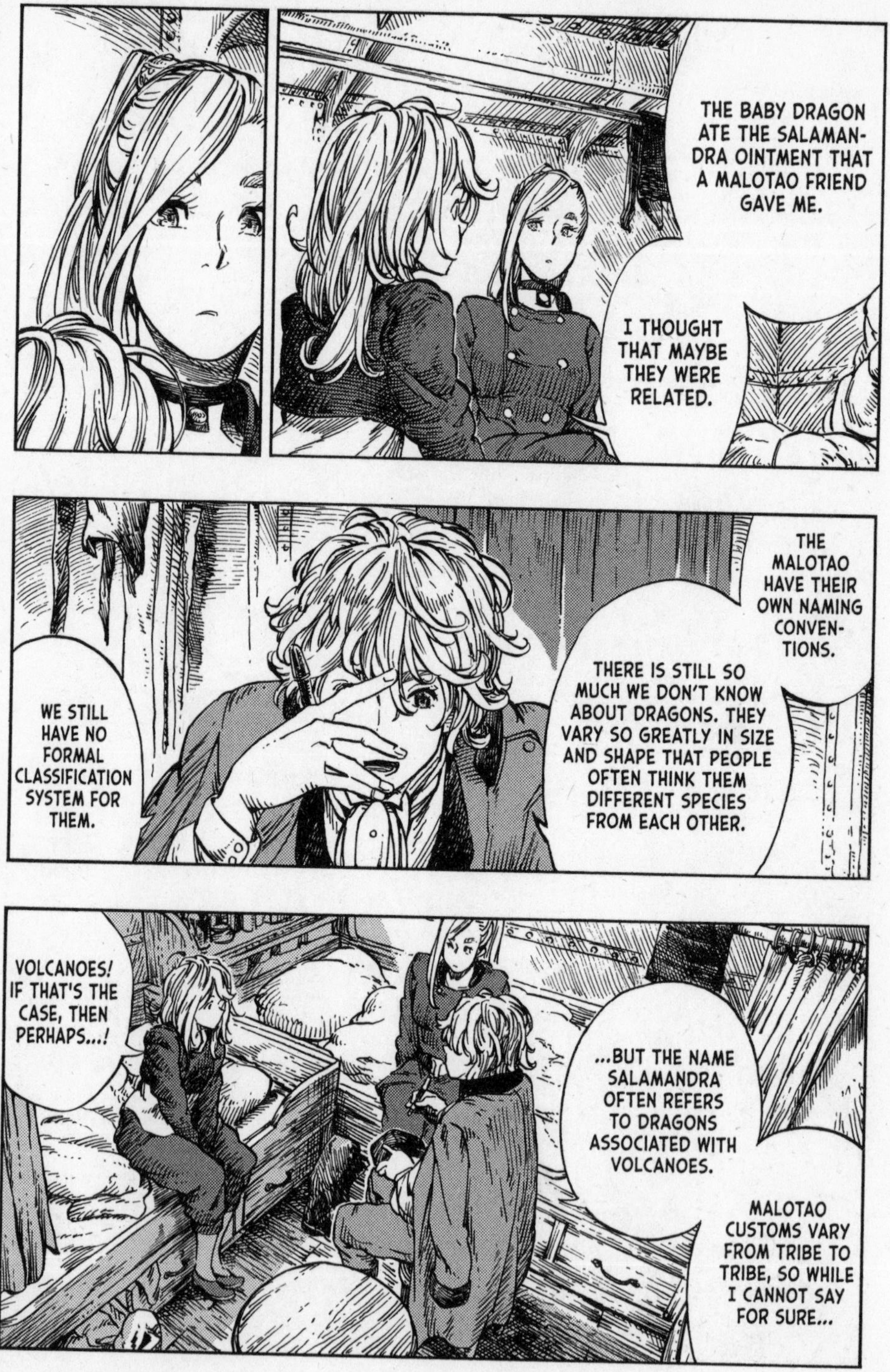
THE BABY DRAGON ATE THE SALAMANDRA OINTMENT THAT A MALOTAO FRIEND GAVE ME.
I THOUGHT THAT MAYBE THEY WERE RELATED.
THE MALOTAO HAVE THEIR OWN NAMING CONVENTIONS.
THERE IS STILL SO MUCH WE DON'T KNOW ABOUT DRAGONS. THEY VARY SO GREATLY IN SIZE AND SHAPE THAT PEOPLE OFTEN THINK THEM DIFFERENT SPECIES FROM EACH OTHER.
WE STILL HAVE NO FORMAL CLASSIFICATION SYSTEM FOR THEM.
MALOTAO CUSTOMS VARY FROM TRIBE TO TRIBE, SO WHILE I CANNOT SAY FOR SURE...
...BUT THE NAME SALAMANDRA OFTEN REFERS TO DRAGONS ASSOCIATED WITH VOLCANOES.
VOLCANOES! IF THAT'S THE CASE, THEN PERHAPS...!

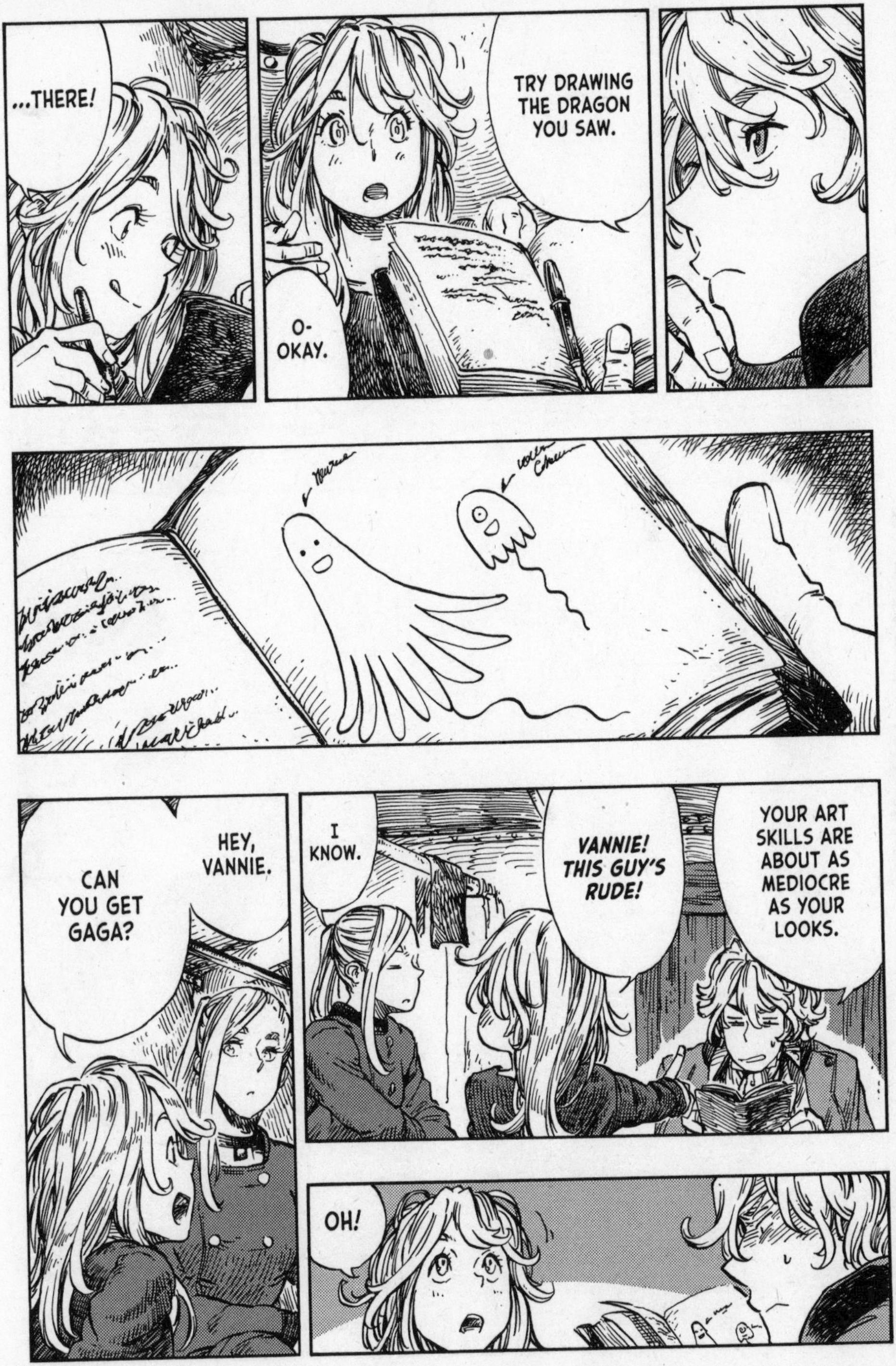
TRY DRAWING THE DRAGON YOU SAW.
O-OKAY.
...THERE!
YOUR ART SKILLS ARE ABOUT AS MEDIOCRE AS YOUR LOOKS.
VANNIE! THIS GUY'S RUDE!
I KNOW.
OH!
HEY, VANNIE.
CAN YOU GET GAGA?

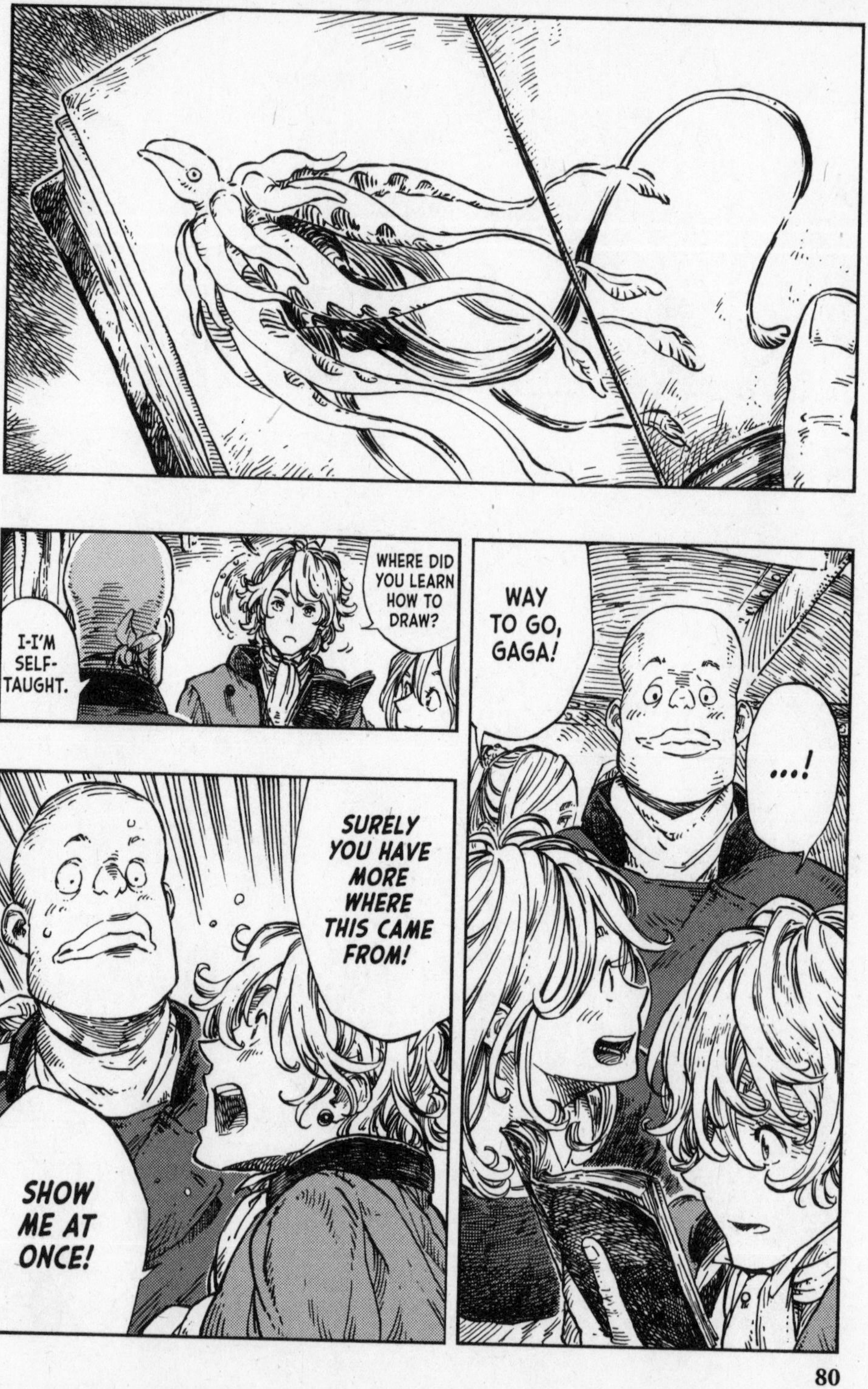
WAY TO GO, GAGA!
...!
WHERE DID YOU LEARN HOW TO DRAW?
I-I'M SELF-TAUGHT.
SURELY YOU HAVE MORE WHERE THIS CAME FROM!
SHOW ME AT ONCE!

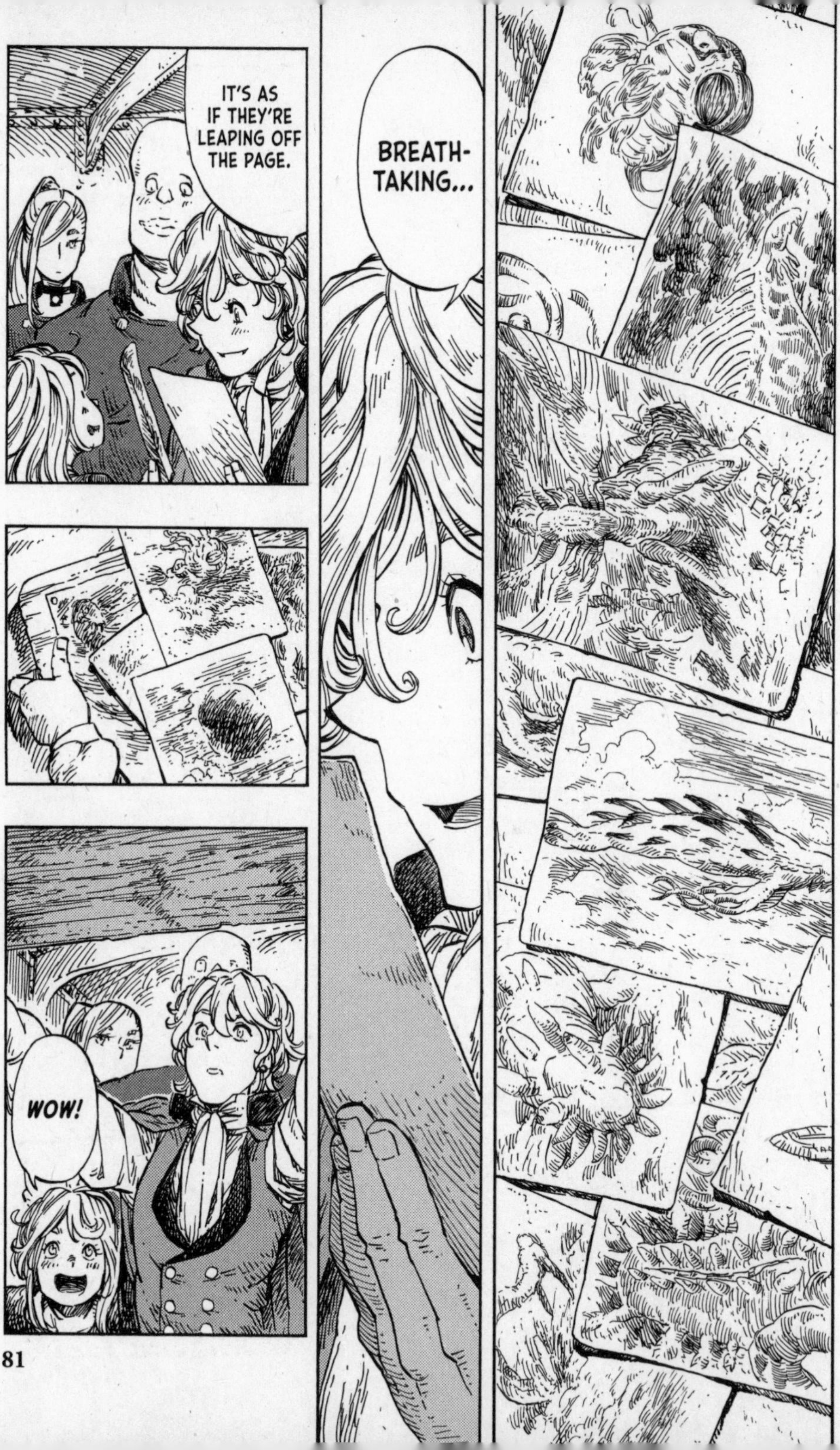
BREATH-TAKING...
IT'S AS IF THEY'RE LEAPING OFF THE PAGE.
WOW!

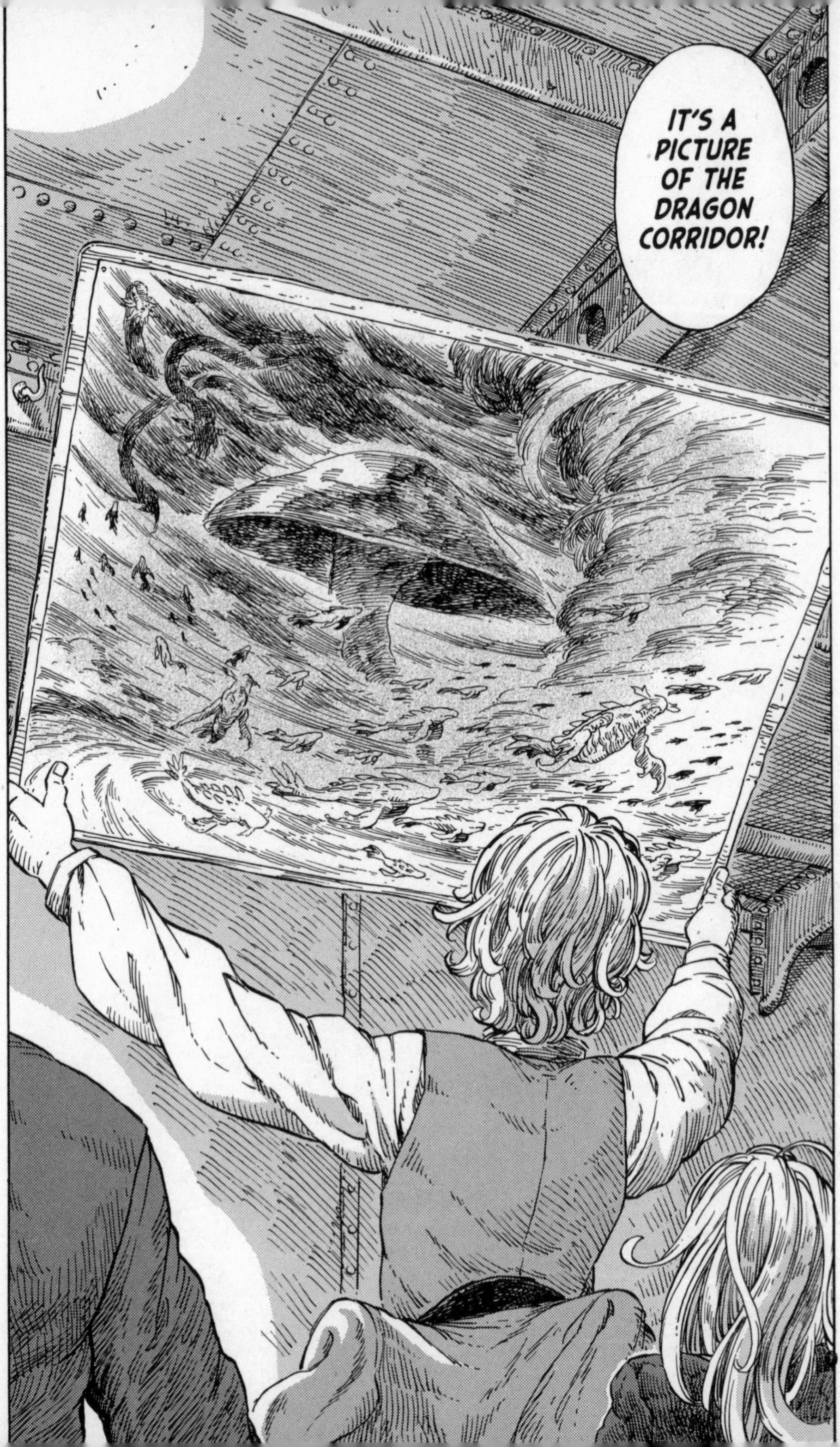
IT'S A PICTURE OF THE DRAGON CORRIDOR!

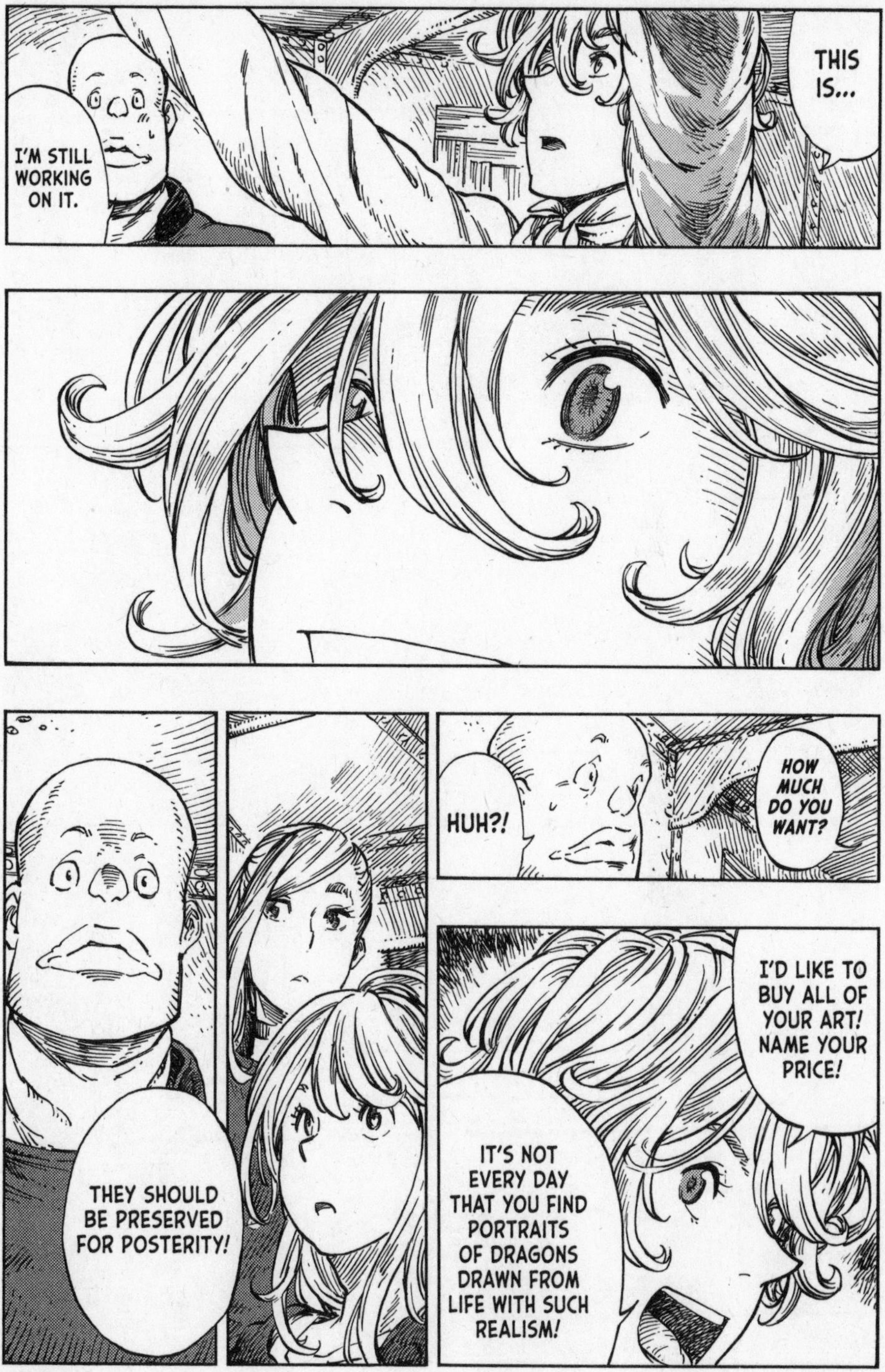
THIS IS...
I'M STILL WORKING ON IT.
HOW MUCH DO YOU WANT?
HUH?!
I'D LIKE TO BUY ALL OF YOUR ART! NAME YOUR PRICE!
IT'S NOT EVERY DAY THAT YOU FIND PORTRAITS OF DRAGONS DRAWN FROM LIFE WITH SUCH REALISM!
THEY SHOULD BE PRESERVED FOR POSTERITY!

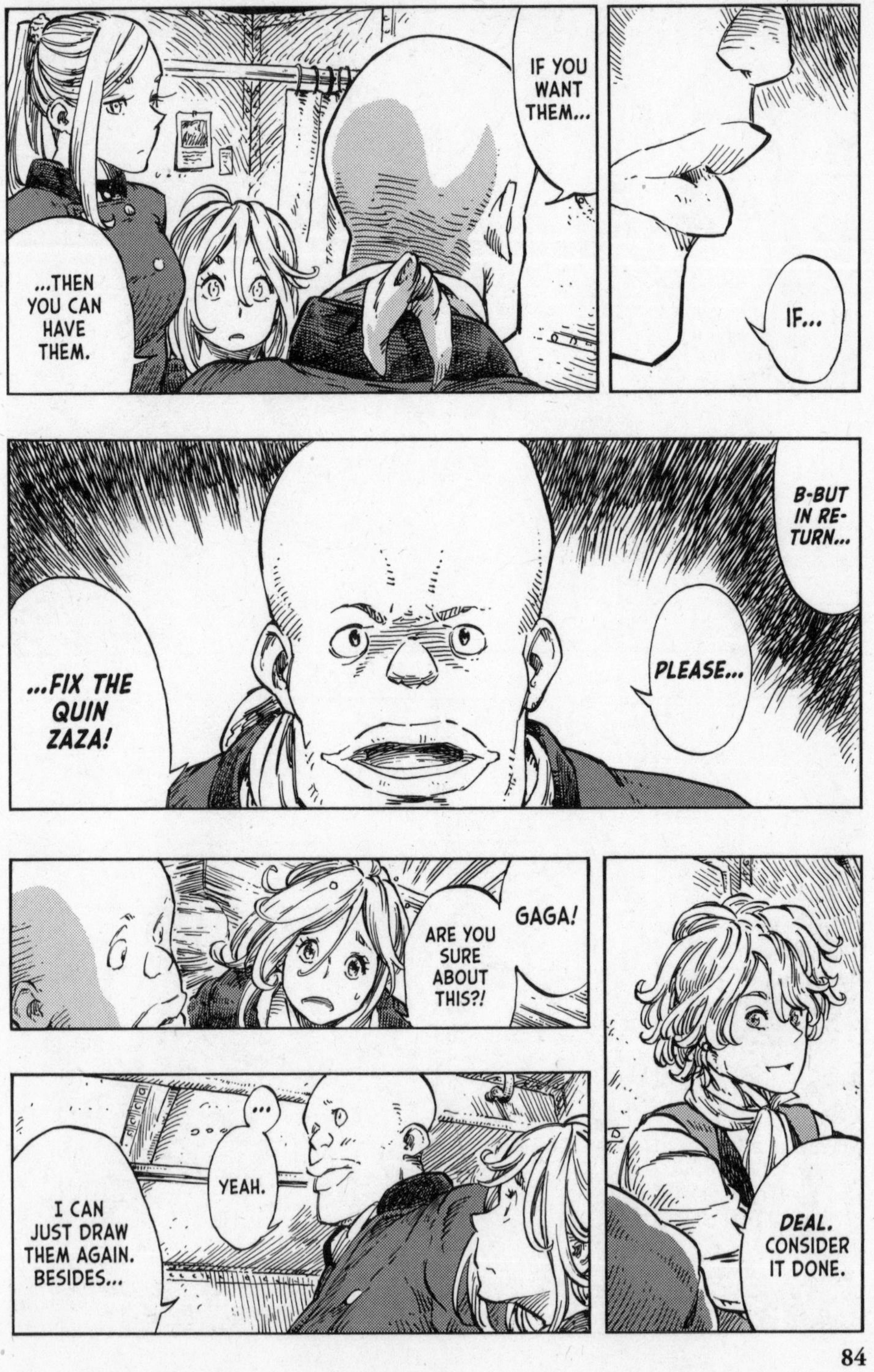
IF...
IF YOU WANT THEM...
...THEN YOU CAN HAVE THEM.
B-BUT IN RE-TURN...
PLEASE...
...FIX THE QUIN ZAZA!
DEAL. CONSIDER IT DONE.
GAGA!
ARE YOU SURE ABOUT THIS?!
...
YEAH.
I CAN JUST DRAW THEM AGAIN. BESIDES...

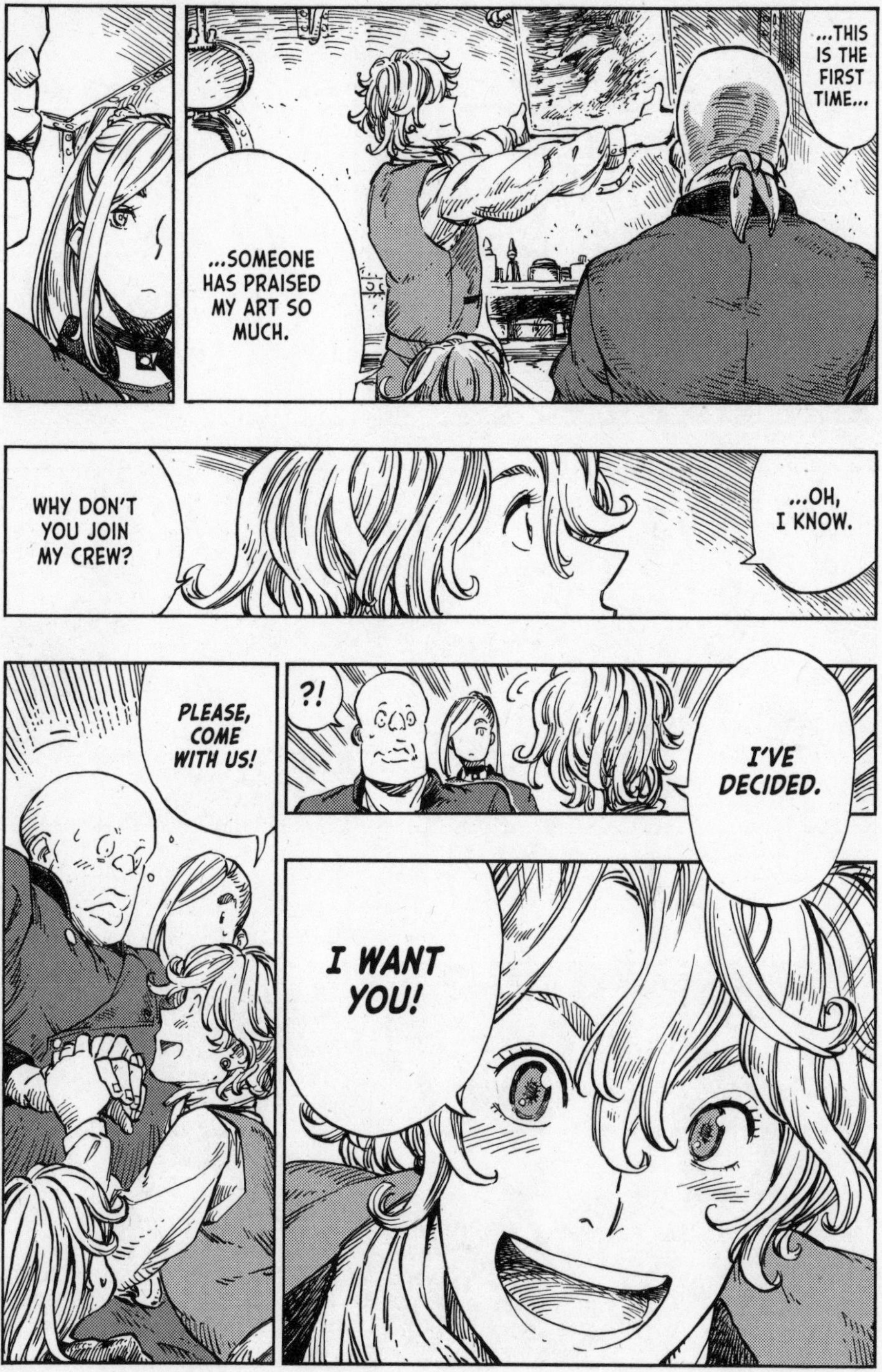
...THIS IS THE FIRST TIME...
...SOMEONE HAS PRAISED MY ART SO MUCH.
...OH, I KNOW.
WHY DON'T YOU JOIN MY CREW?
I'VE DECIDED.
?!
I WANT YOU!
PLEASE, COME WITH US!

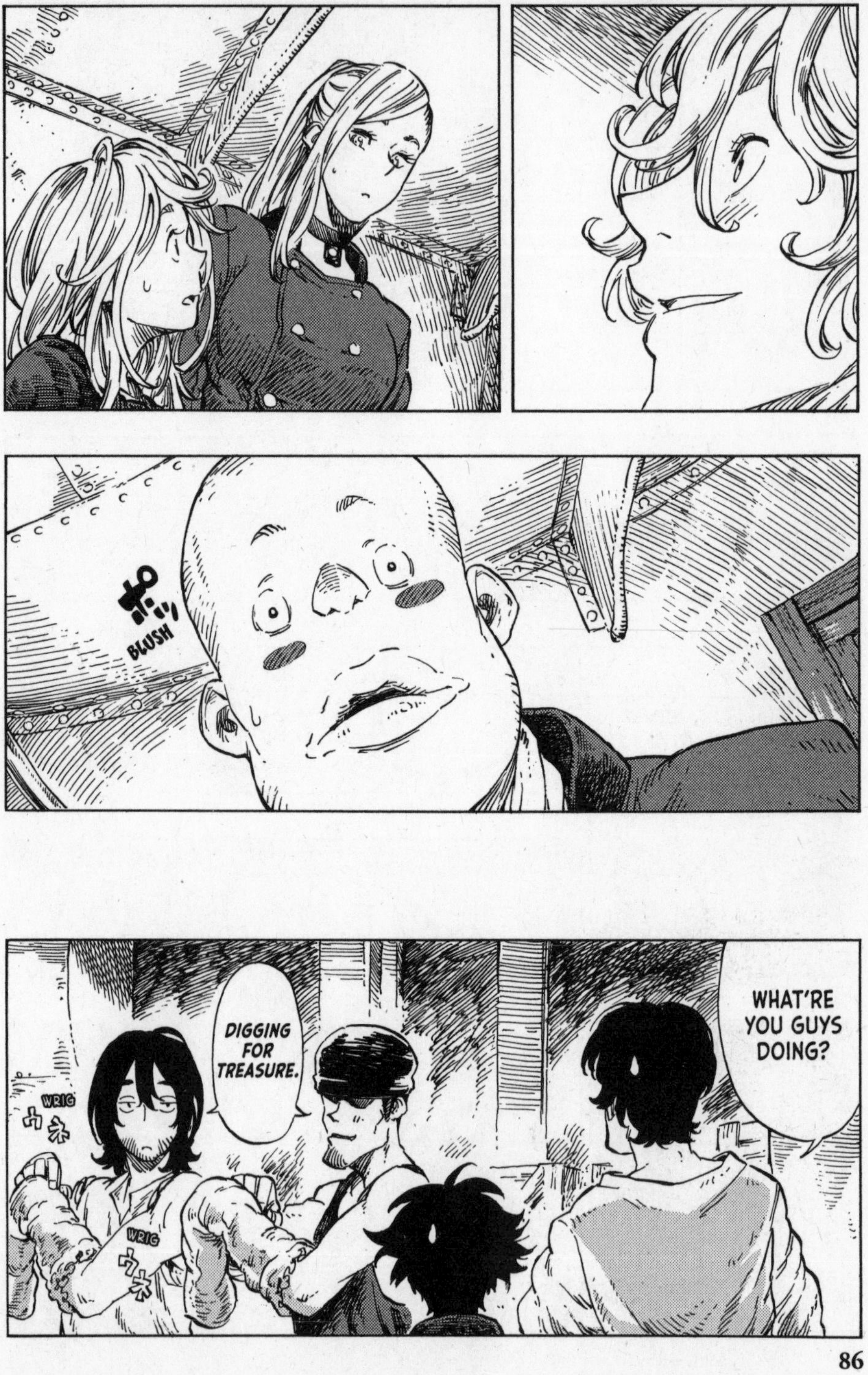
ポッ
BLUSH
WHAT'RE YOU GUYS DOING?
DIGGING FOR TREASURE.
ウネ
WRIG
ウネ
WRIG

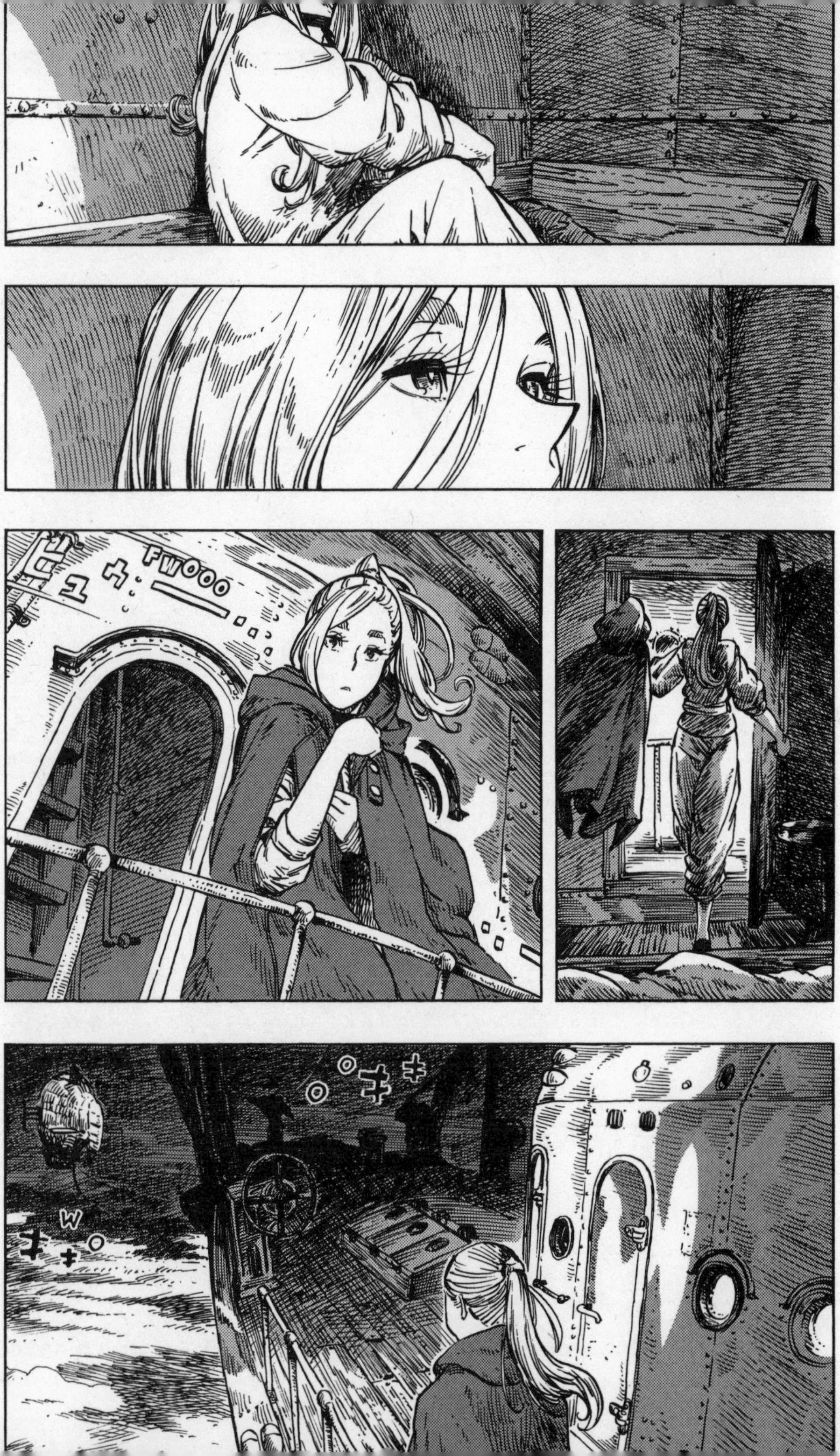
ヒュウ—
FWOOO

Flight 21 Panna Cotta & Hunt Order

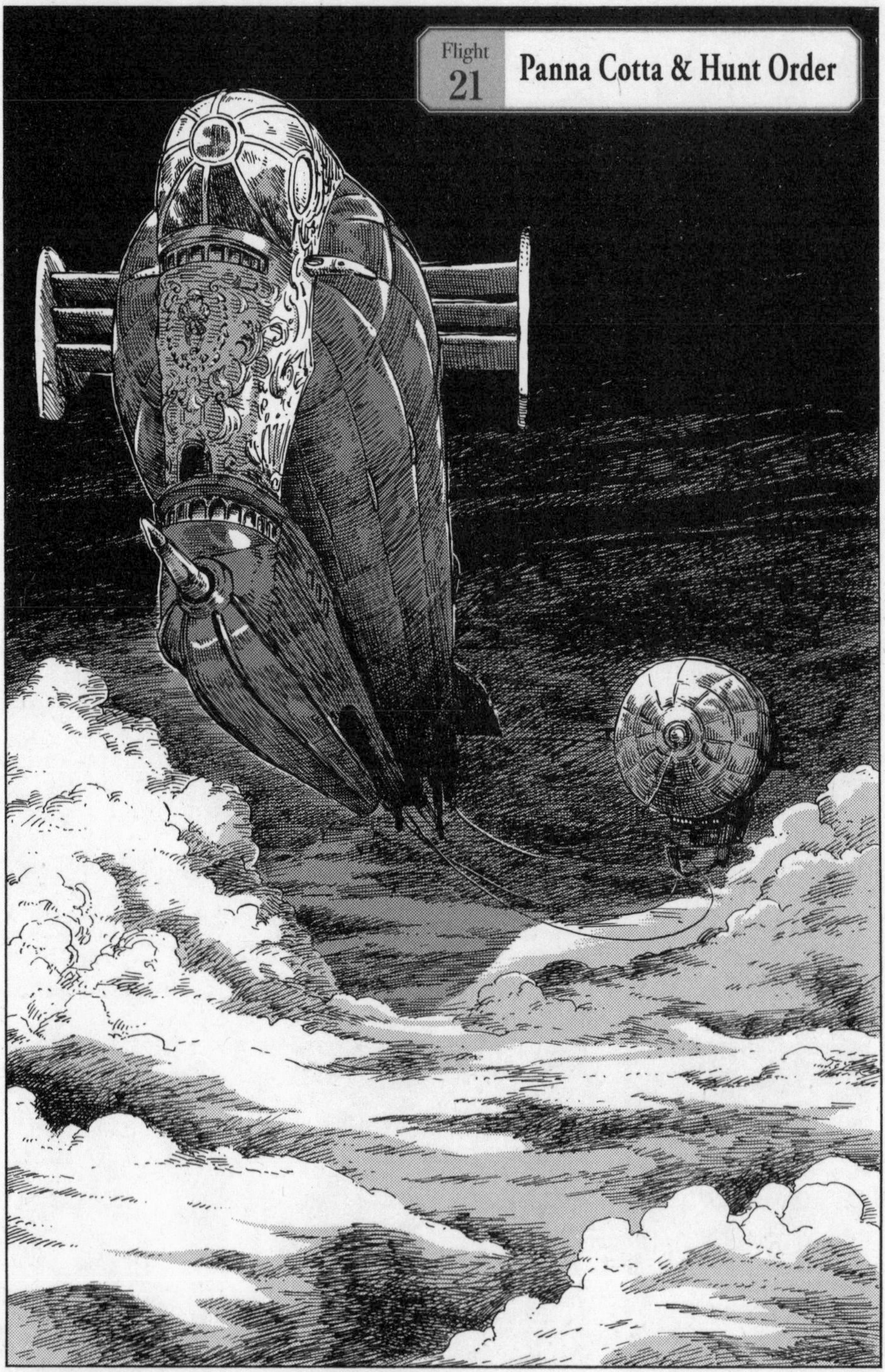

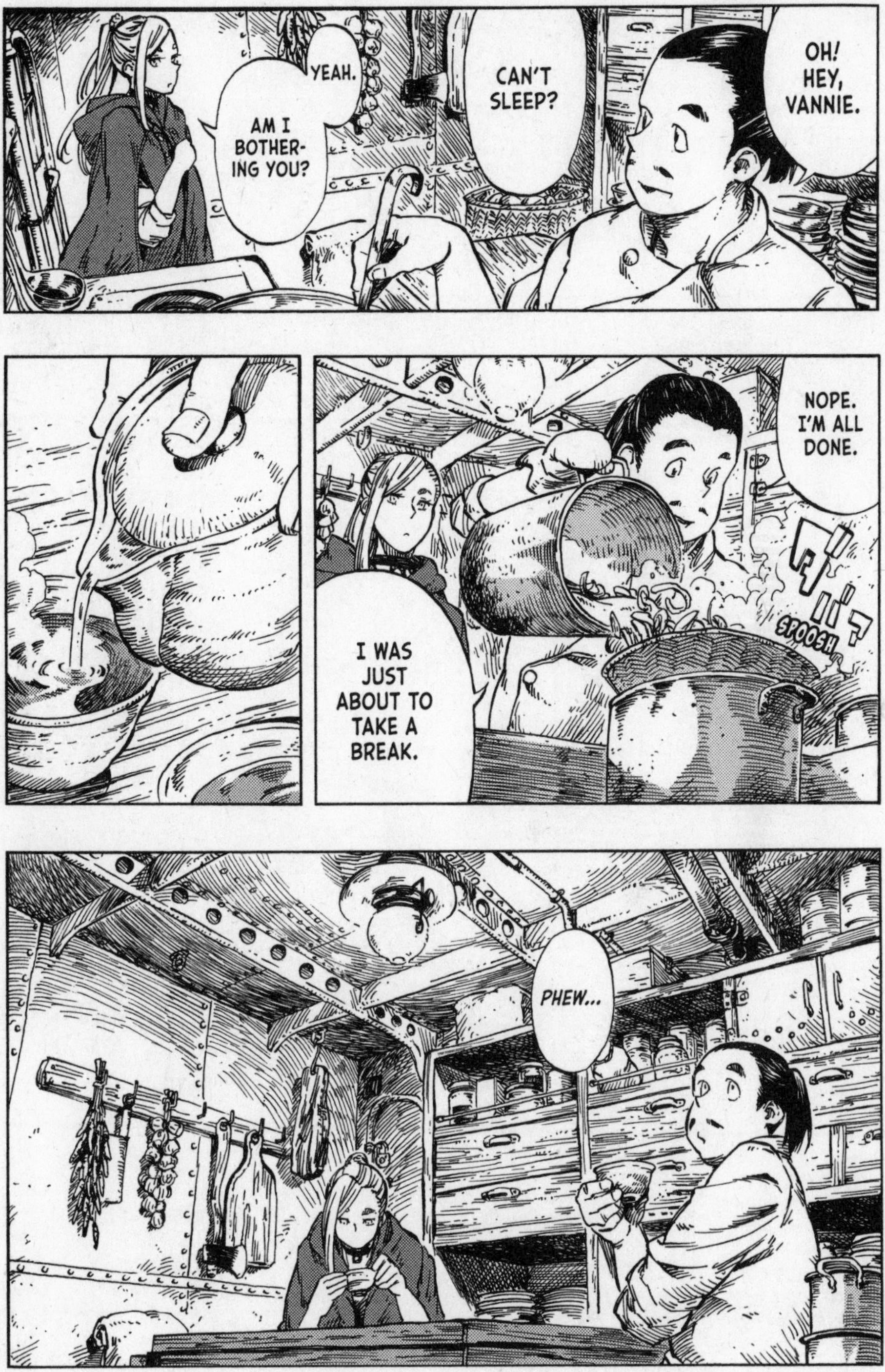
OH! HEY, VANNIE.
CAN'T SLEEP?
YEAH.
AM I BOTHERING YOU?
NOPE. I'M ALL DONE.
SPOOSH
I WAS JUST ABOUT TO TAKE A BREAK.
PHEW...

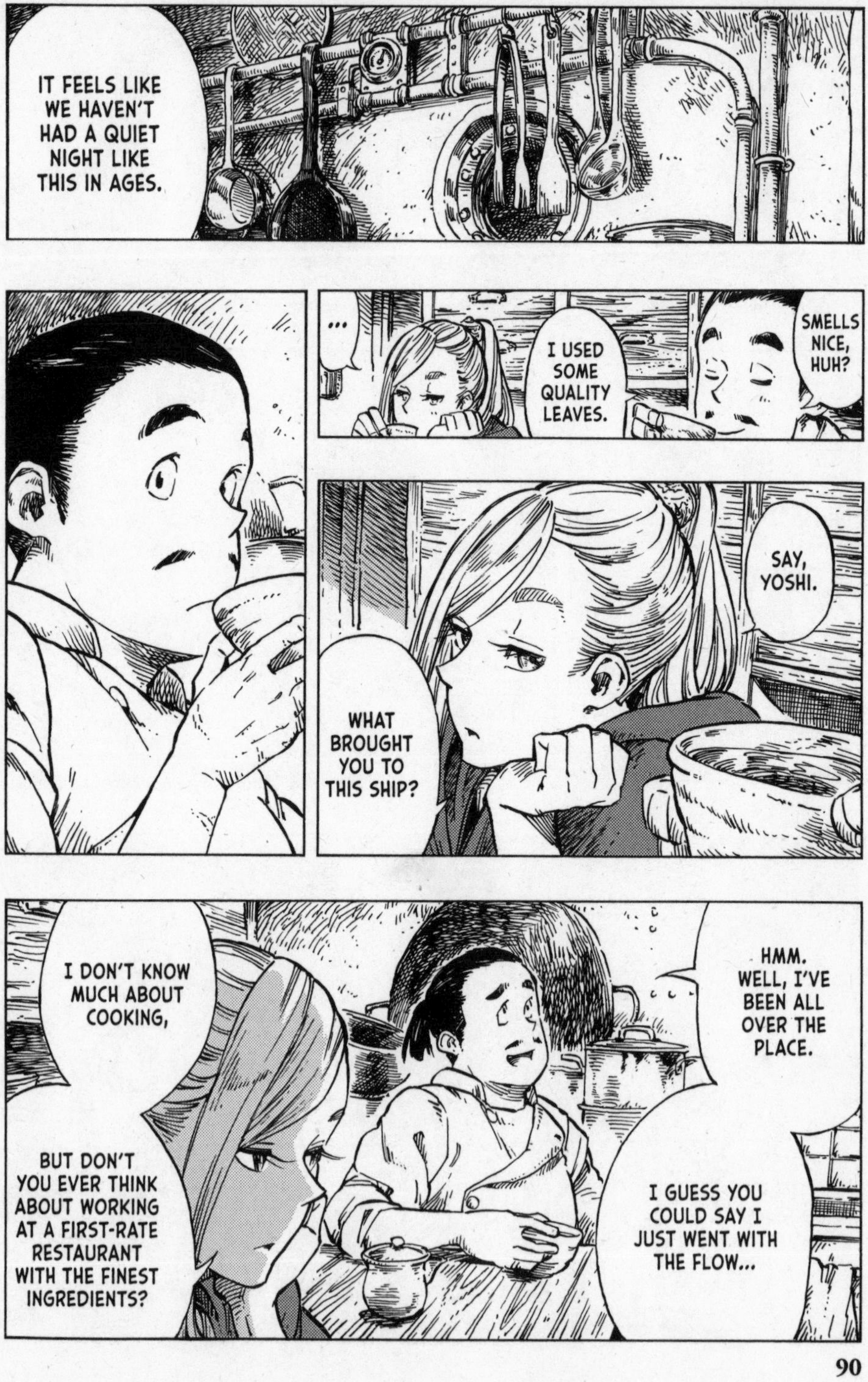
IT FEELS LIKE WE HAVEN'T HAD A QUIET NIGHT LIKE THIS IN AGES.
SMELLS NICE, HUH?
I USED SOME QUALITY LEAVES.
...
SAY, YOSHI.
WHAT BROUGHT YOU TO THIS SHIP?
HMM. WELL, I'VE BEEN ALL OVER THE PLACE.
I GUESS YOU COULD SAY I JUST WENT WITH THE FLOW...
I DON'T KNOW MUCH ABOUT COOKING,
BUT DON'T YOU EVER THINK ABOUT WORKING AT A FIRST-RATE RESTAURANT WITH THE FINEST INGREDIENTS?

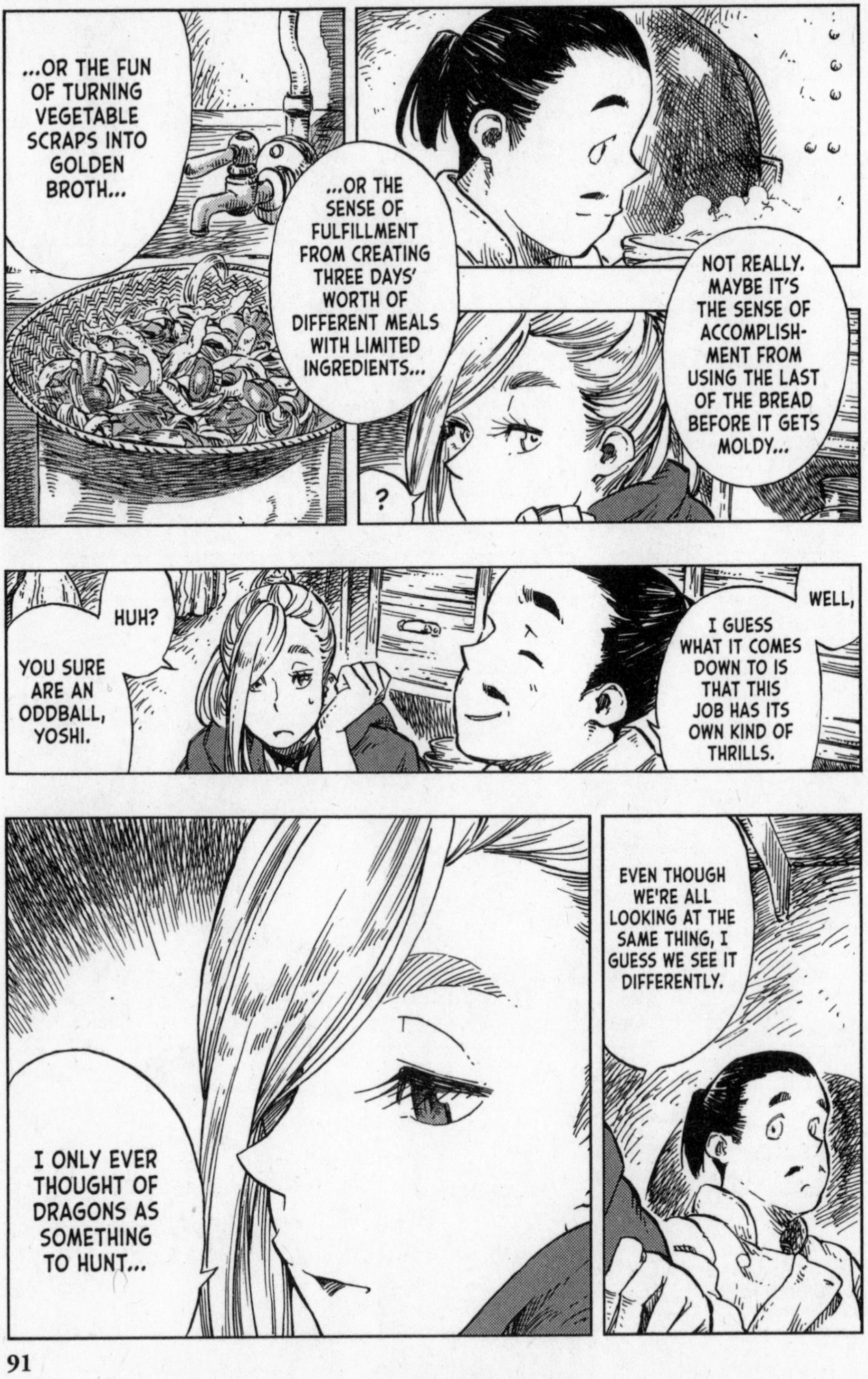
NOT REALLY. MAYBE IT'S THE SENSE OF ACCOMPLISHMENT FROM USING THE LAST OF THE BREAD BEFORE IT GETS MOLDY...
...OR THE SENSE OF FULFILLMENT FROM CREATING THREE DAYS' WORTH OF DIFFERENT MEALS WITH LIMITED INGREDIENTS...
?
...OR THE FUN OF TURNING VEGETABLE SCRAPS INTO GOLDEN BROTH...
WELL, I GUESS WHAT IT COMES DOWN TO IS THAT THIS JOB HAS ITS OWN KIND OF THRILLS.
HUH?
YOU SURE ARE AN ODDBALL, YOSHI.
EVEN THOUGH WE'RE ALL LOOKING AT THE SAME THING, I GUESS WE SEE IT DIFFERENTLY.
I ONLY EVER THOUGHT OF DRAGONS AS SOMETHING TO HUNT...

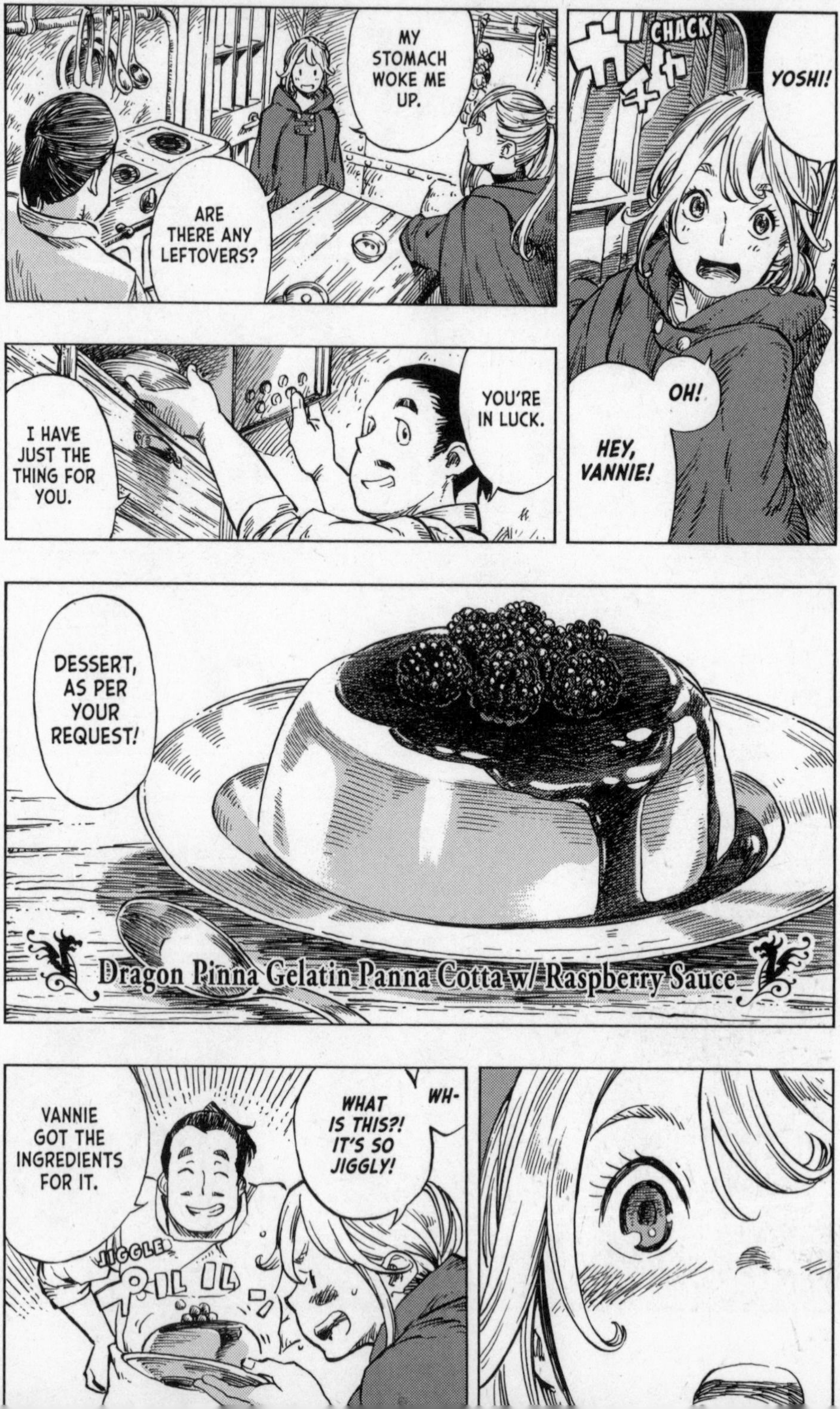
CHACK
YOSHI!
OH!
HEY, VANNIE!
MY STOMACH WOKE ME UP.
ARE THERE ANY LEFTOVERS?
YOU'RE IN LUCK.
I HAVE JUST THE THING FOR YOU.
DESSERT, AS PER YOUR REQUEST!
Dragon Pinna Gelatin Panna Cotta w/ Raspberry Sauce
WH-
WHAT IS THIS?! IT'S SO JIGGLY!
VANNIE GOT THE INGREDIENTS FOR IT.
JIGGLE

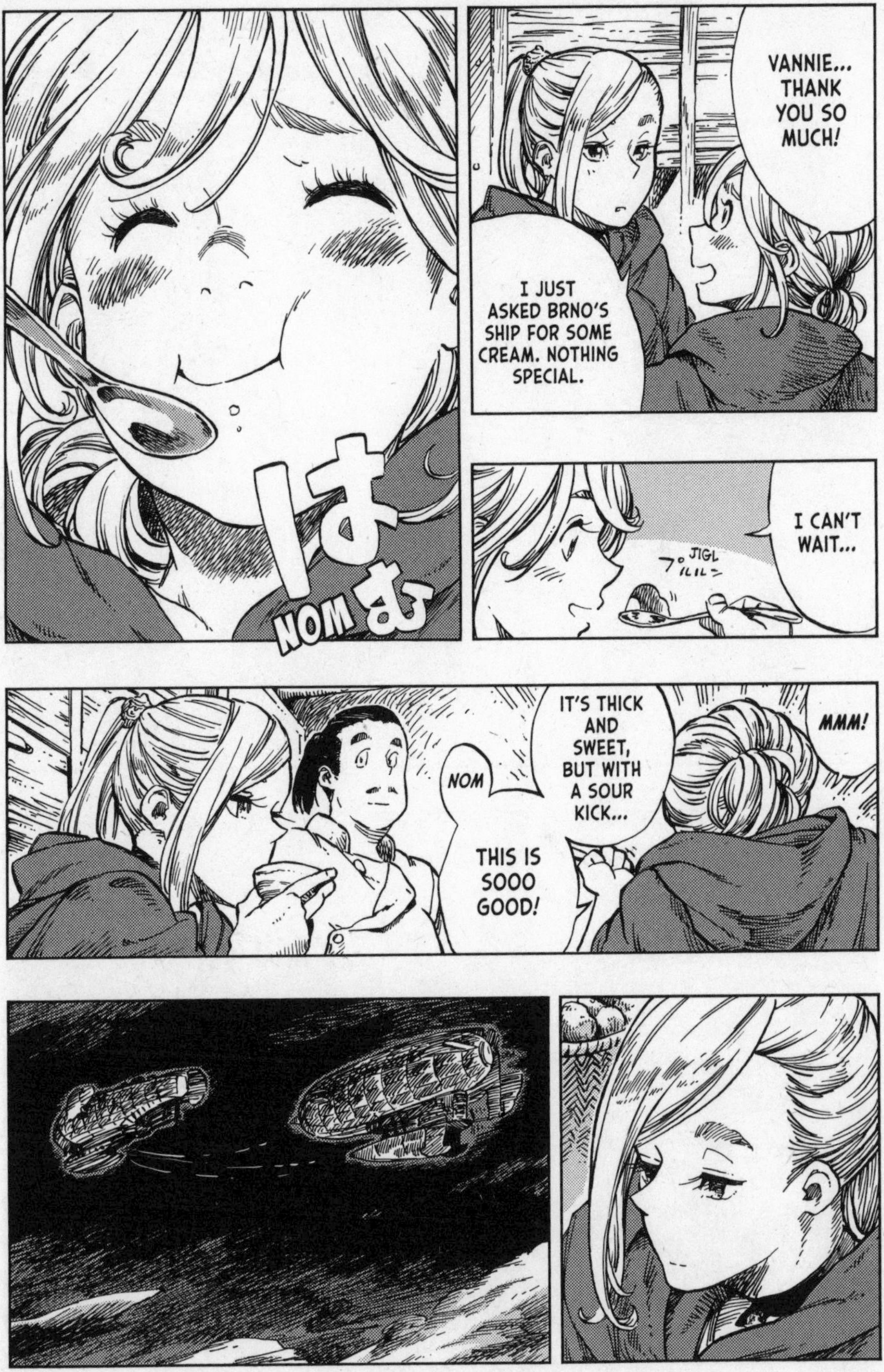
VANNIE... THANK YOU SO MUCH!
I JUST ASKED BRNO'S SHIP FOR SOME CREAM. NOTHING SPECIAL.
I CAN'T WAIT...
JIGL
はむ
NOM
MMM!
IT'S THICK AND SWEET, BUT WITH A SOUR KICK...
NOM
THIS IS SOOO GOOD!

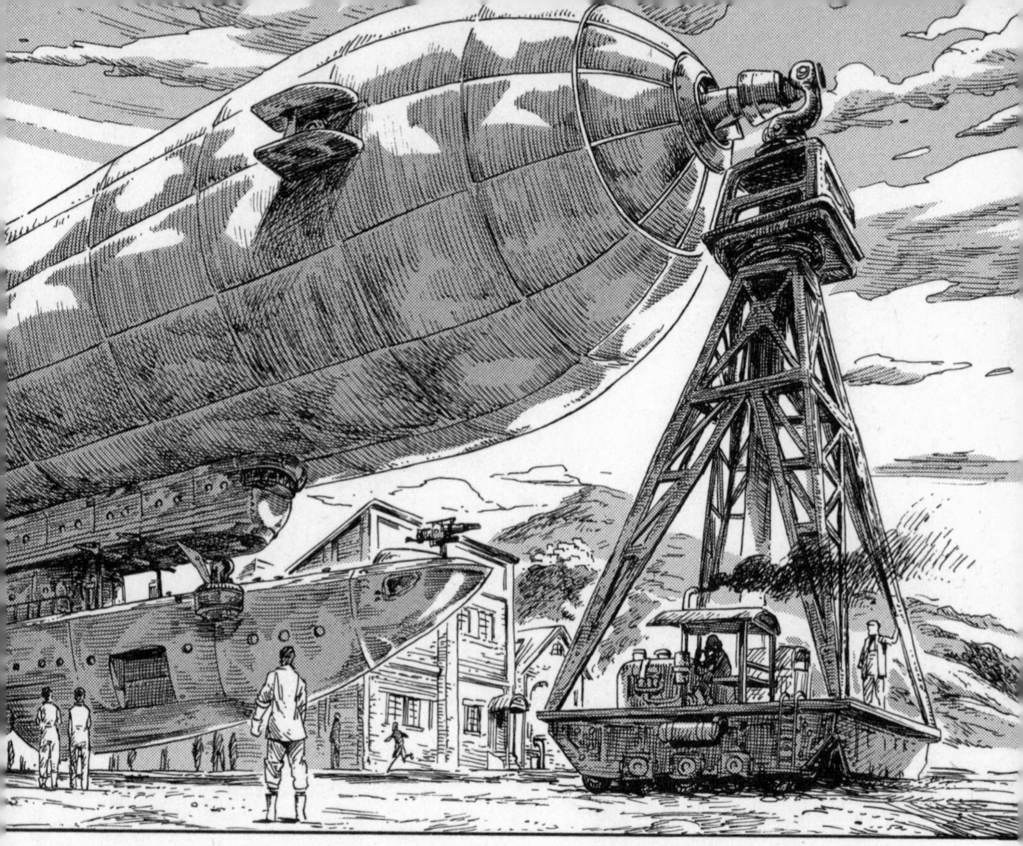
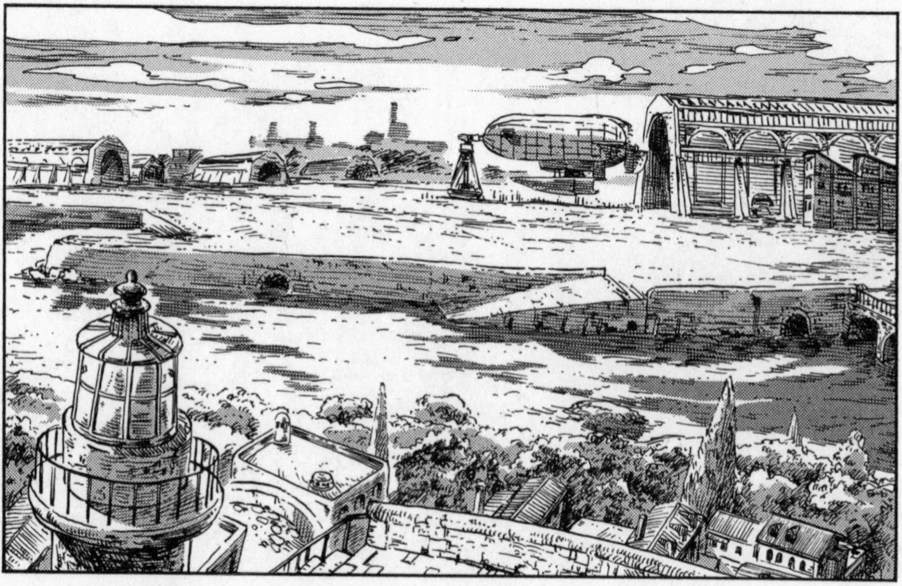

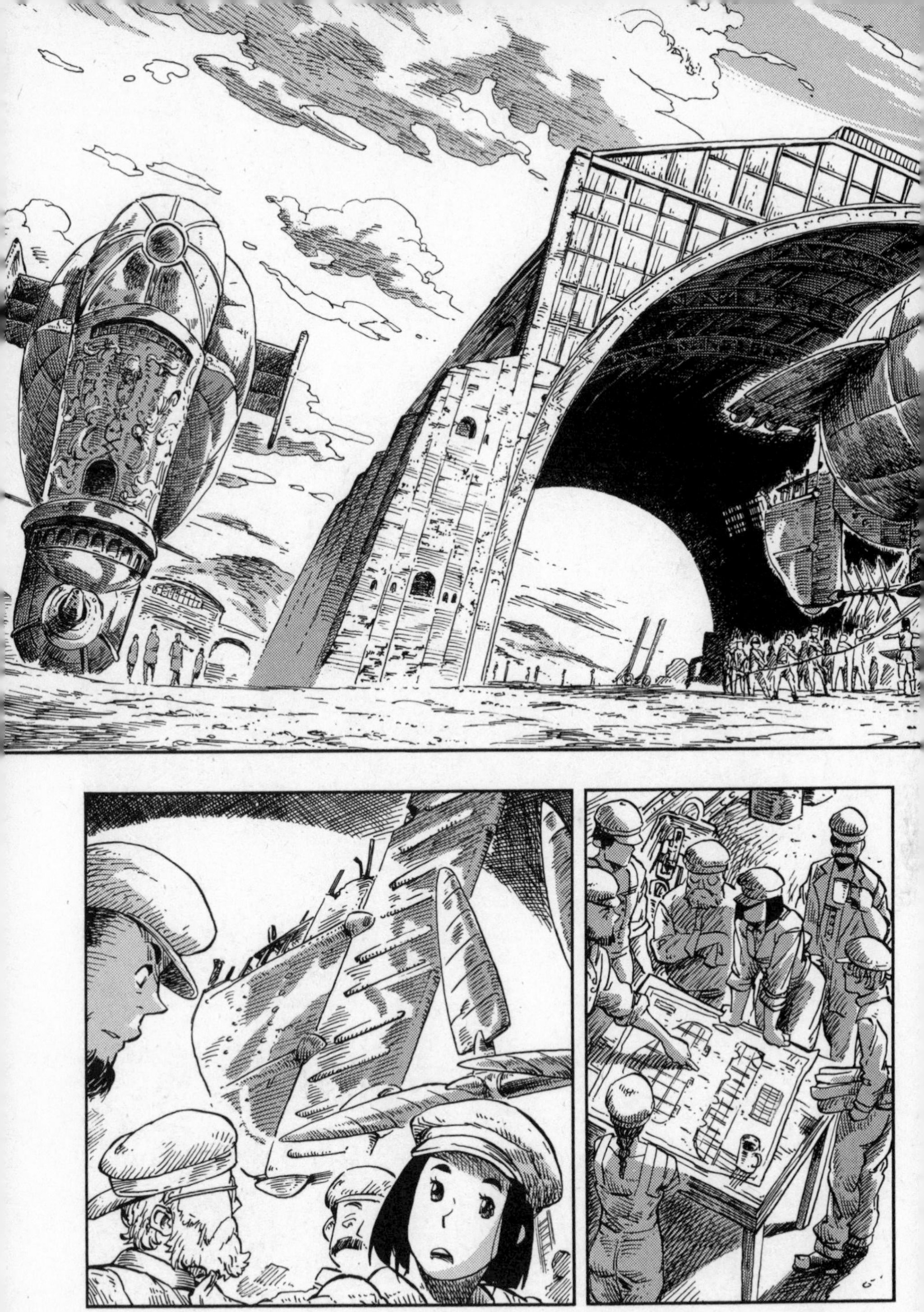

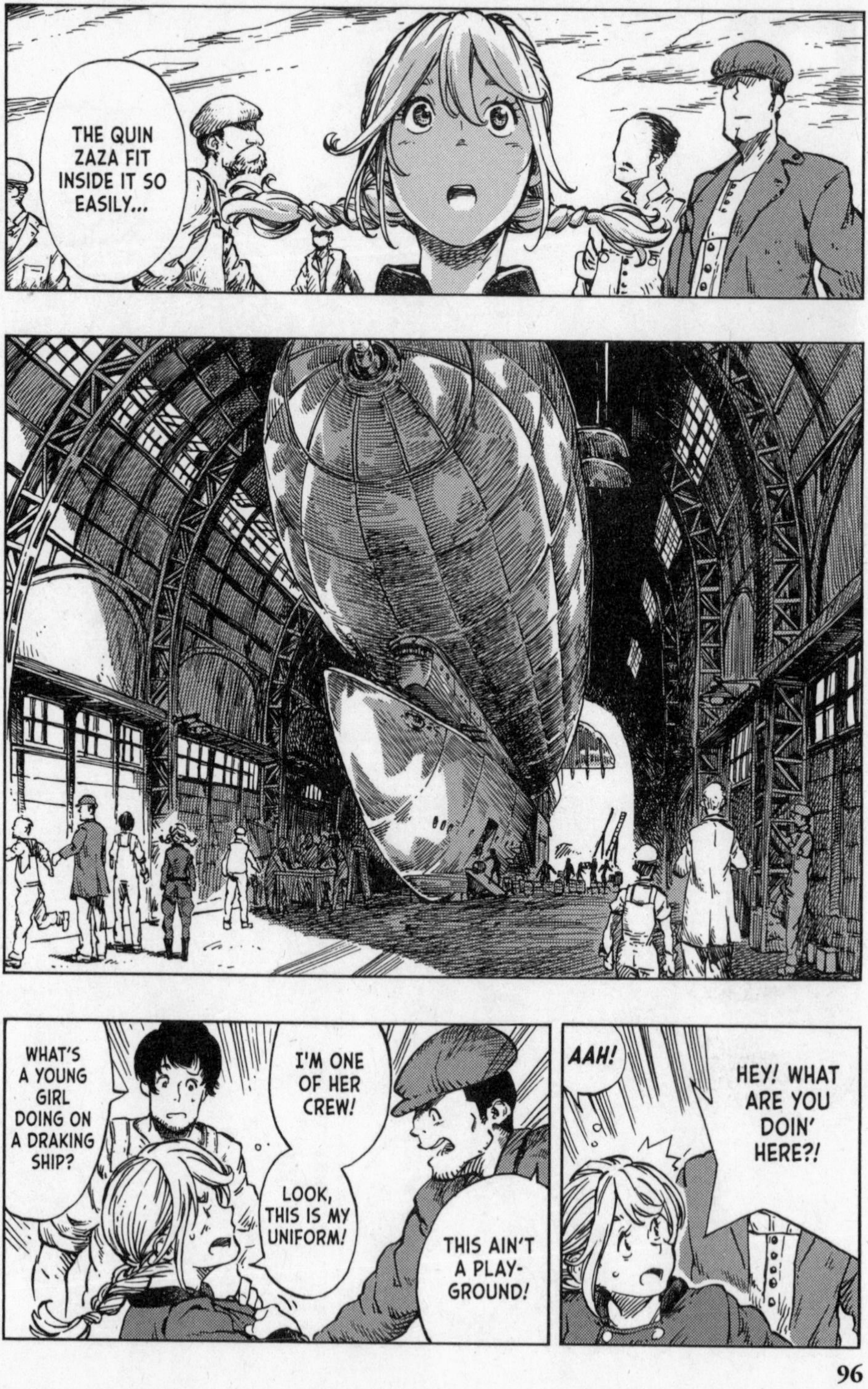
THE QUIN ZAZA FIT INSIDE IT SO EASILY...
AAH!
HEY! WHAT ARE YOU DOIN' HERE?!
THIS AIN'T A PLAY-GROUND!
I'M ONE OF HER CREW!
LOOK, THIS IS MY UNIFORM!
WHAT'S A YOUNG GIRL DOING ON A DRAKING SHIP?

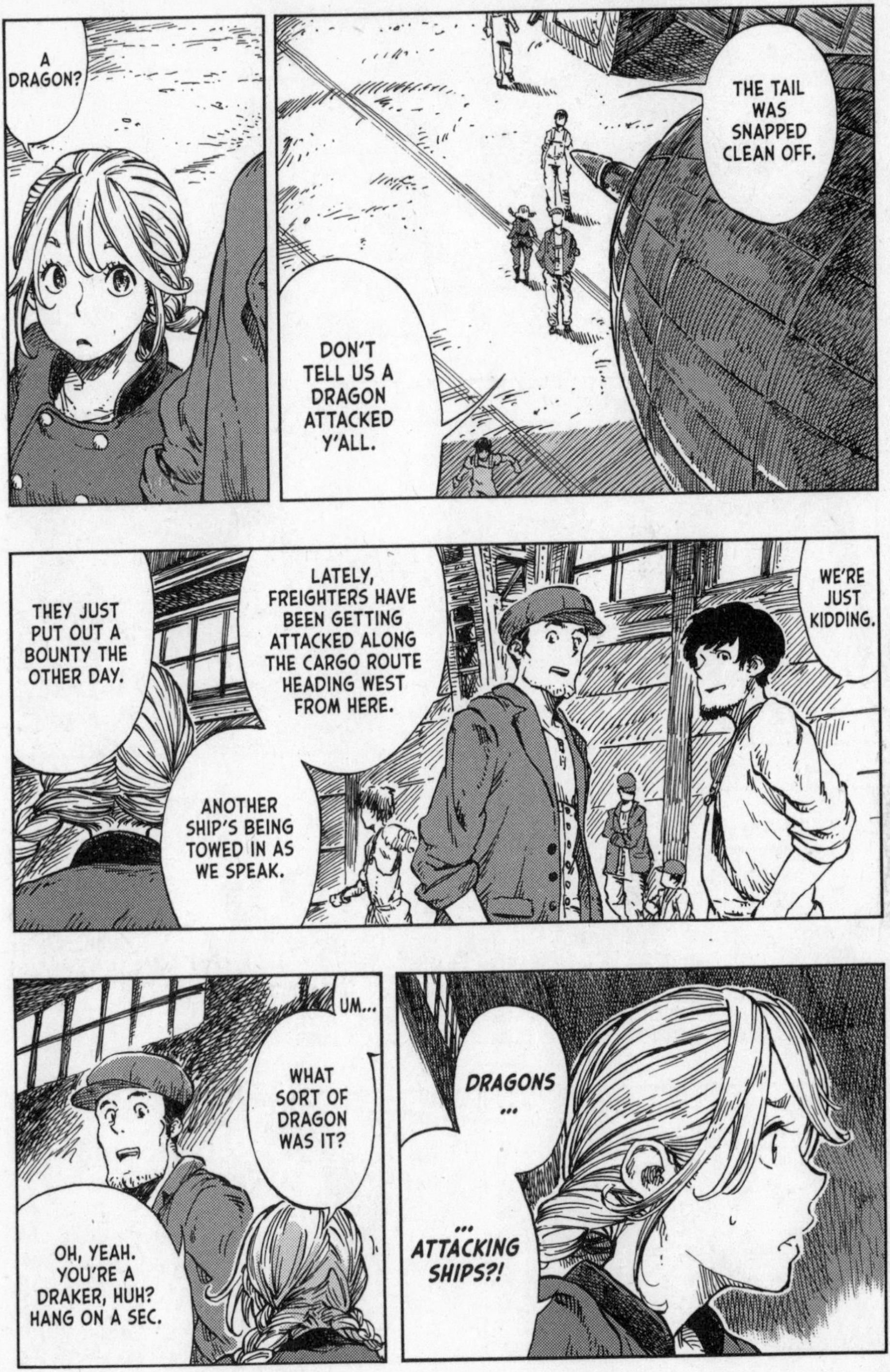
THE TAIL WAS SNAPPED CLEAN OFF.
DON'T TELL US A DRAGON ATTACKED Y'ALL.
A DRAGON?
WE'RE JUST KIDDING.
LATELY, FREIGHTERS HAVE BEEN GETTING ATTACKED ALONG THE CARGO ROUTE HEADING WEST FROM HERE.
THEY JUST PUT OUT A BOUNTY THE OTHER DAY.
ANOTHER SHIP'S BEING TOWED IN AS WE SPEAK.
DRAGONS ...
... *ATTACKING SHIPS?!*
UM...
WHAT SORT OF DRAGON WAS IT?
OH, YEAH. YOU'RE A DRAKER, HUH? HANG ON A SEC.

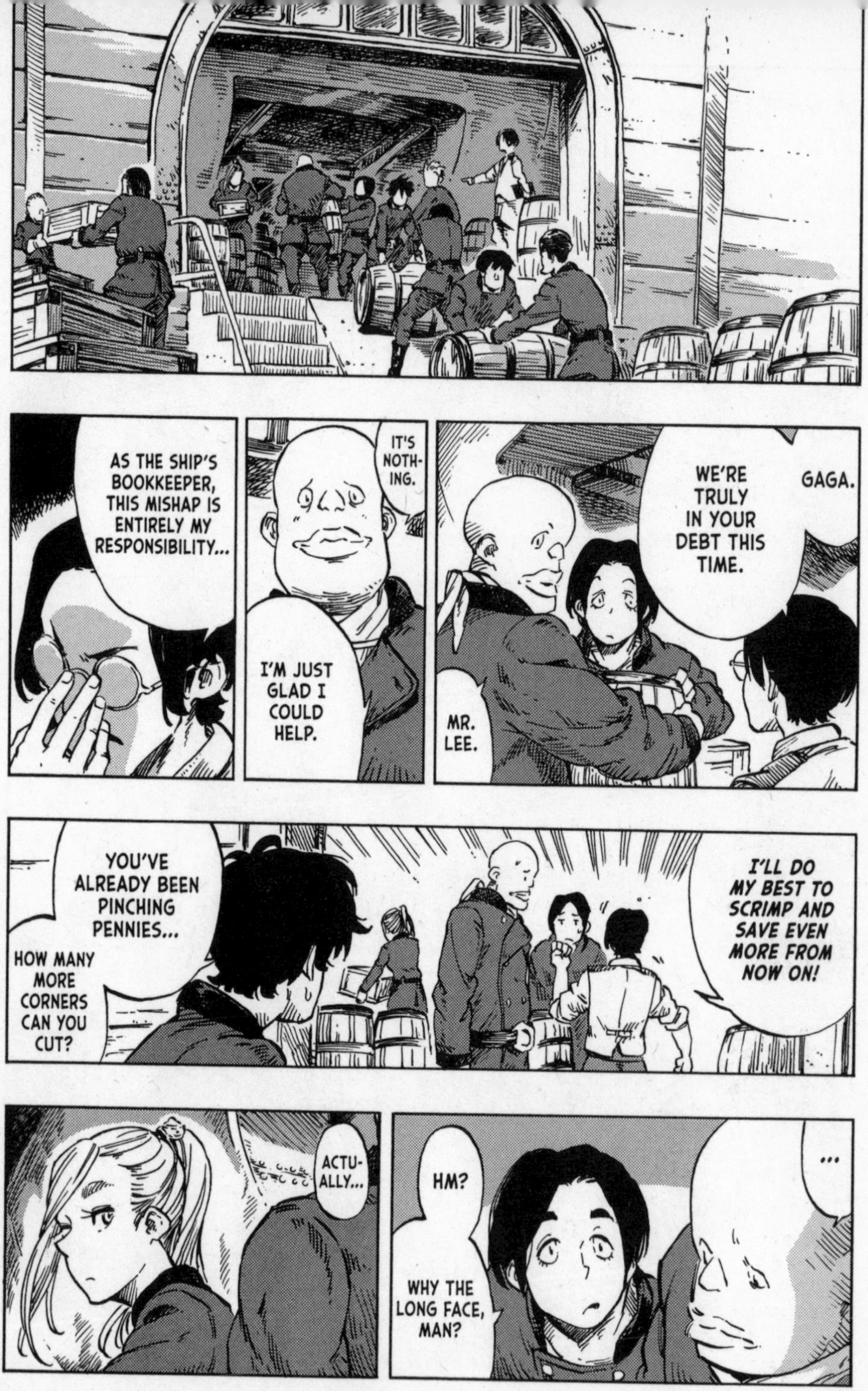
GAGA.
WE'RE TRULY IN YOUR DEBT THIS TIME.
MR. LEE.
IT'S NOTH-ING.
I'M JUST GLAD I COULD HELP.
AS THE SHIP'S BOOKKEEPER, THIS MISHAP IS ENTIRELY MY RESPONSIBILITY...
I'LL DO MY BEST TO SCRIMP AND SAVE EVEN MORE FROM NOW ON!
YOU'VE ALREADY BEEN PINCHING PENNIES...
HOW MANY MORE CORNERS CAN YOU CUT?
...
HM?
WHY THE LONG FACE, MAN?
ACTU-ALLY...

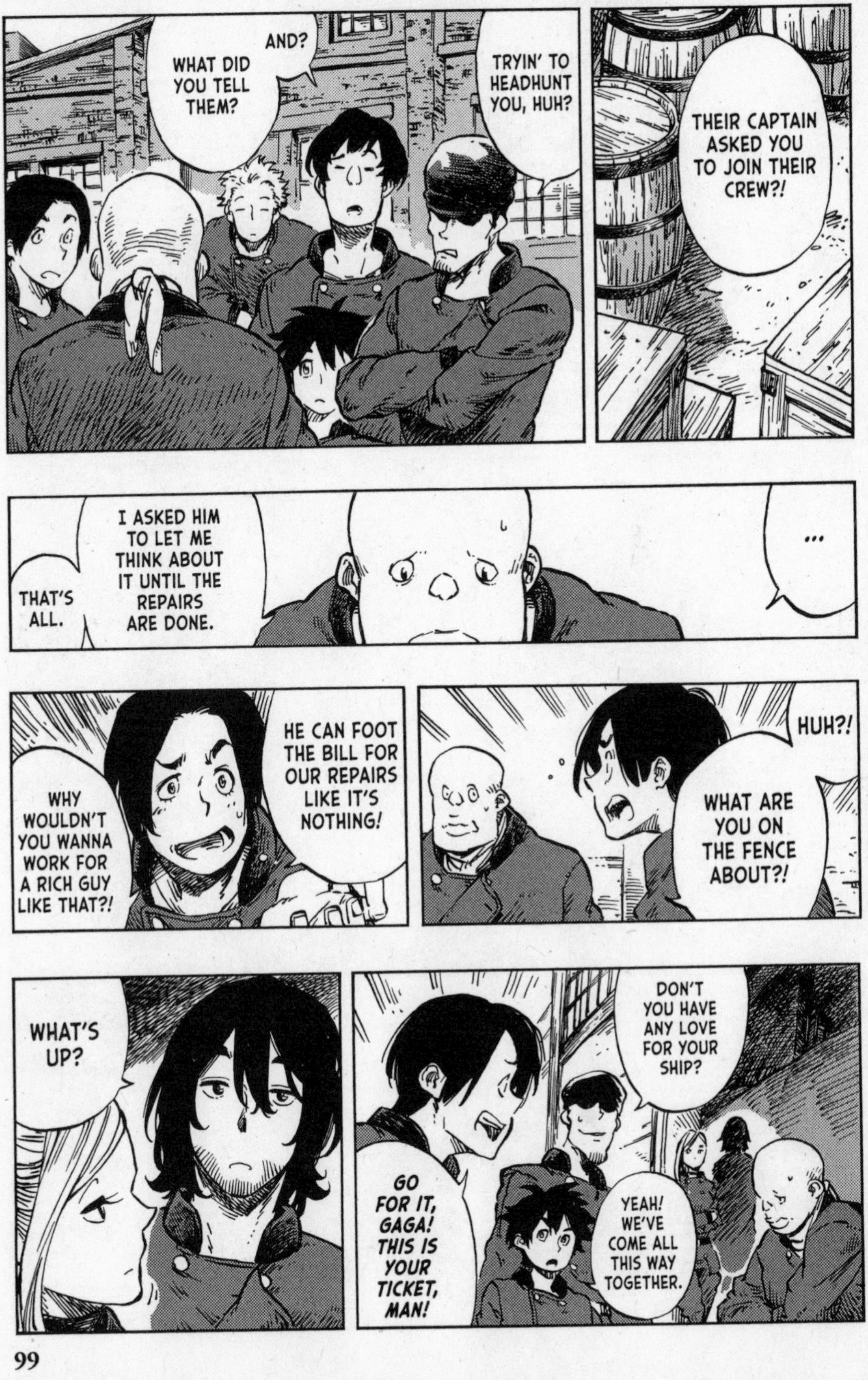
THEIR CAPTAIN ASKED YOU TO JOIN THEIR CREW?!
TRYIN' TO HEADHUNT YOU, HUH?
AND?
WHAT DID YOU TELL THEM?
...
I ASKED HIM TO LET ME THINK ABOUT IT UNTIL THE REPAIRS ARE DONE.
THAT'S ALL.
HUH?!
WHAT ARE YOU ON THE FENCE ABOUT?!
HE CAN FOOT THE BILL FOR OUR REPAIRS LIKE IT'S NOTHING!
WHY WOULDN'T YOU WANNA WORK FOR A RICH GUY LIKE THAT?!
DON'T YOU HAVE ANY LOVE FOR YOUR SHIP?
YEAH! WE'VE COME ALL THIS WAY TOGETHER.
GO FOR IT, GAGA! THIS IS YOUR TICKET, MAN!
WHAT'S UP?

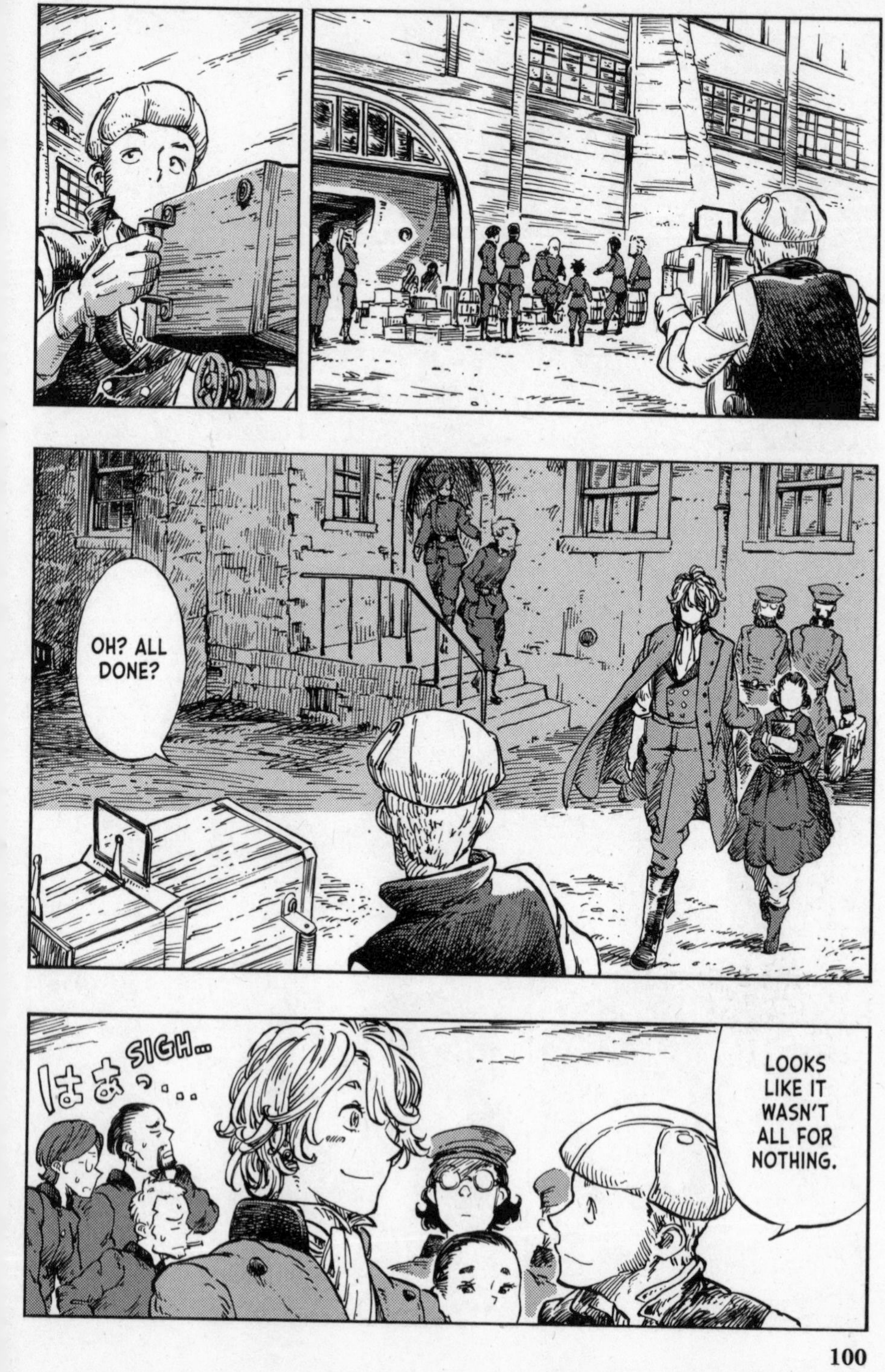
OH? ALL DONE?
LOOKS LIKE IT WASN'T ALL FOR NOTHING.
はあっ…
SIGH…

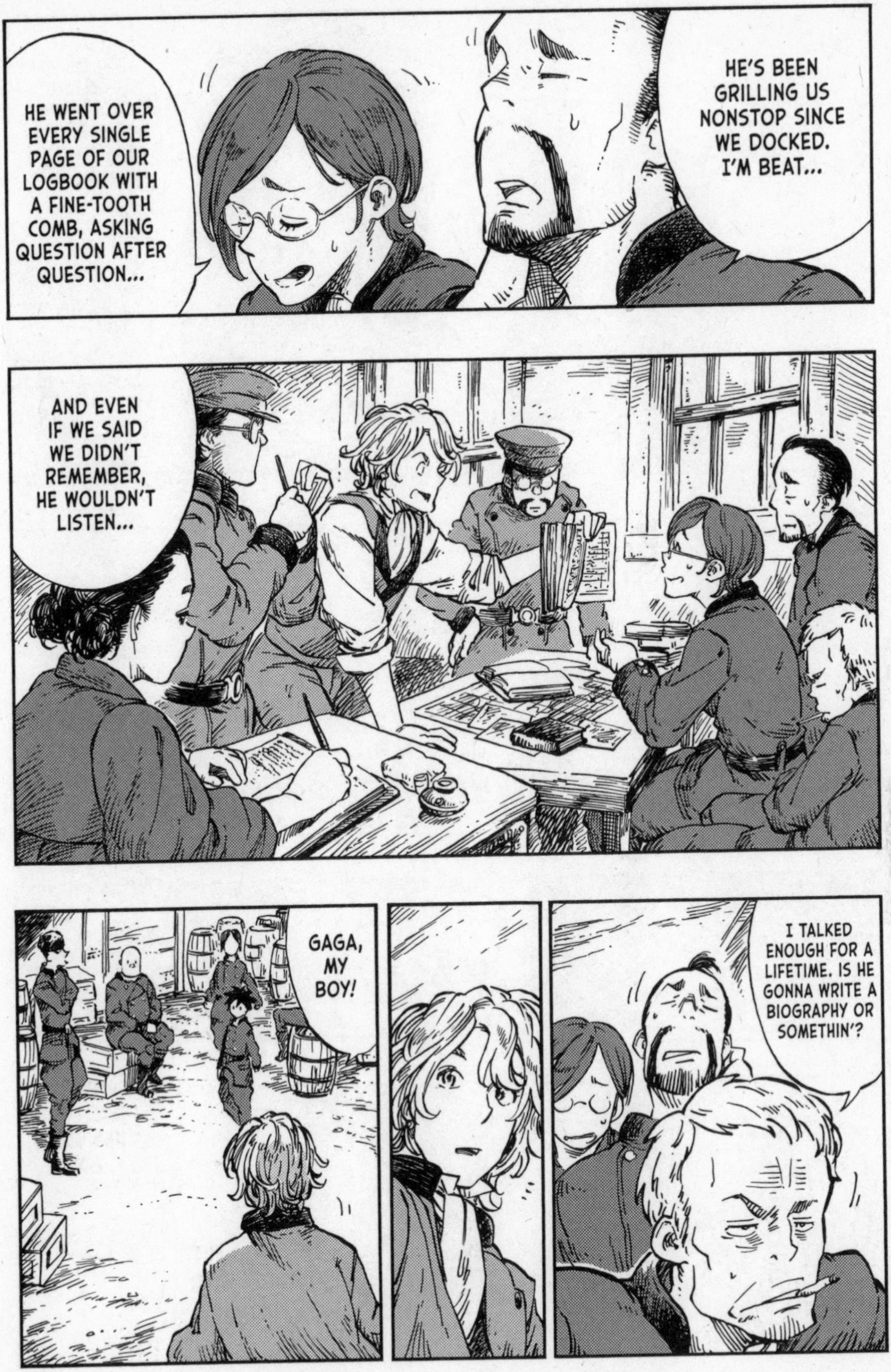
HE'S BEEN GRILLING US NONSTOP SINCE WE DOCKED. I'M BEAT...
HE WENT OVER EVERY SINGLE PAGE OF OUR LOGBOOK WITH A FINE-TOOTH COMB, ASKING QUESTION AFTER QUESTION...
AND EVEN IF WE SAID WE DIDN'T REMEMBER, HE WOULDN'T LISTEN...
I TALKED ENOUGH FOR A LIFETIME. IS HE GONNA WRITE A BIOGRAPHY OR SOMETHIN'?
GAGA, MY BOY!

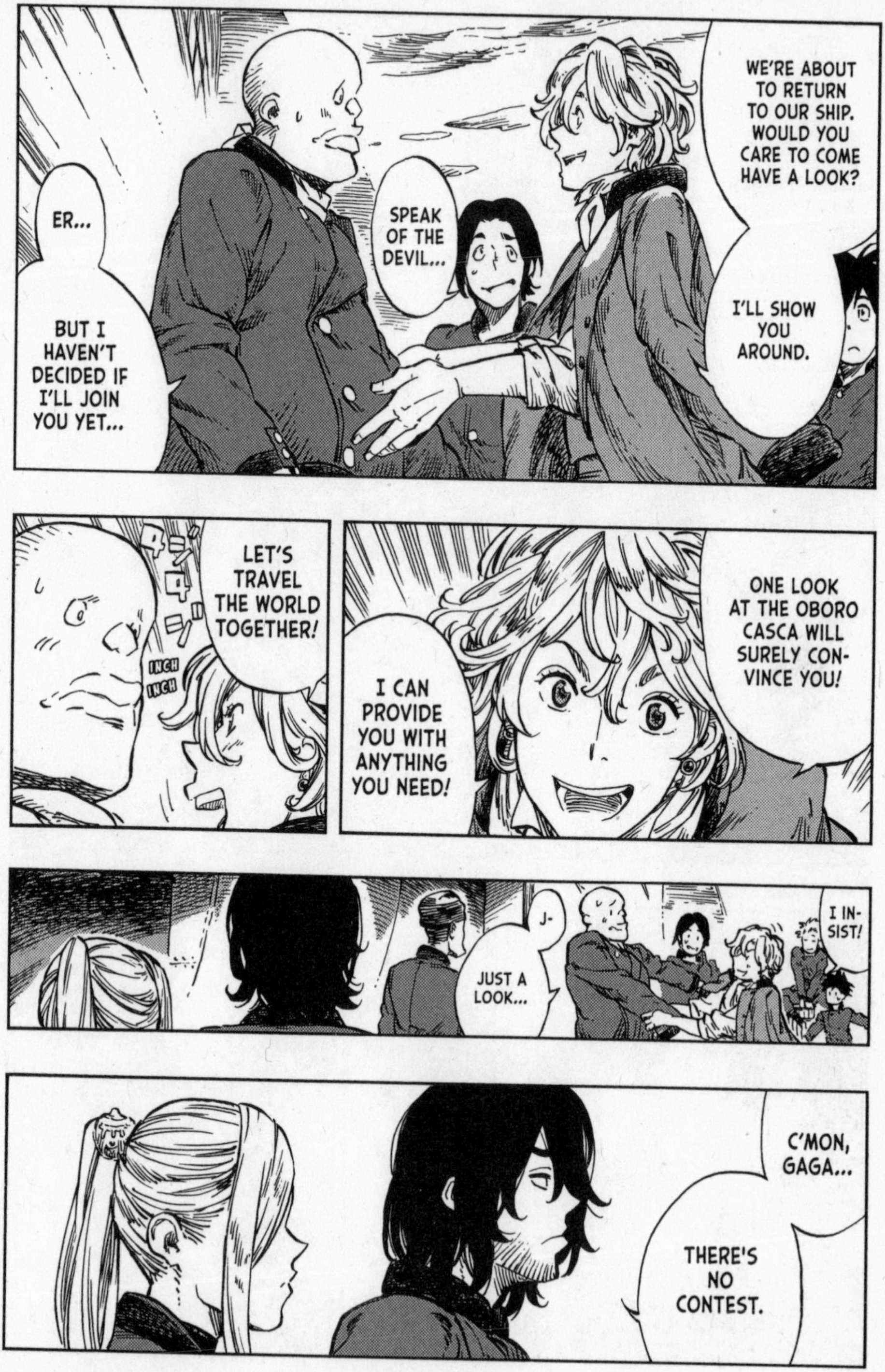
WE'RE ABOUT TO RETURN TO OUR SHIP. WOULD YOU CARE TO COME HAVE A LOOK?
I'LL SHOW YOU AROUND.
SPEAK OF THE DEVIL...
ER...
BUT I HAVEN'T DECIDED IF I'LL JOIN YOU YET...
ONE LOOK AT THE OBORO CASCA WILL SURELY CONVINCE YOU!
I CAN PROVIDE YOU WITH ANYTHING YOU NEED!
LET'S TRAVEL THE WORLD TOGETHER!
INCH
INCH
I INSIST!
J-
JUST A LOOK...
C'MON, GAGA...
THERE'S NO CONTEST.

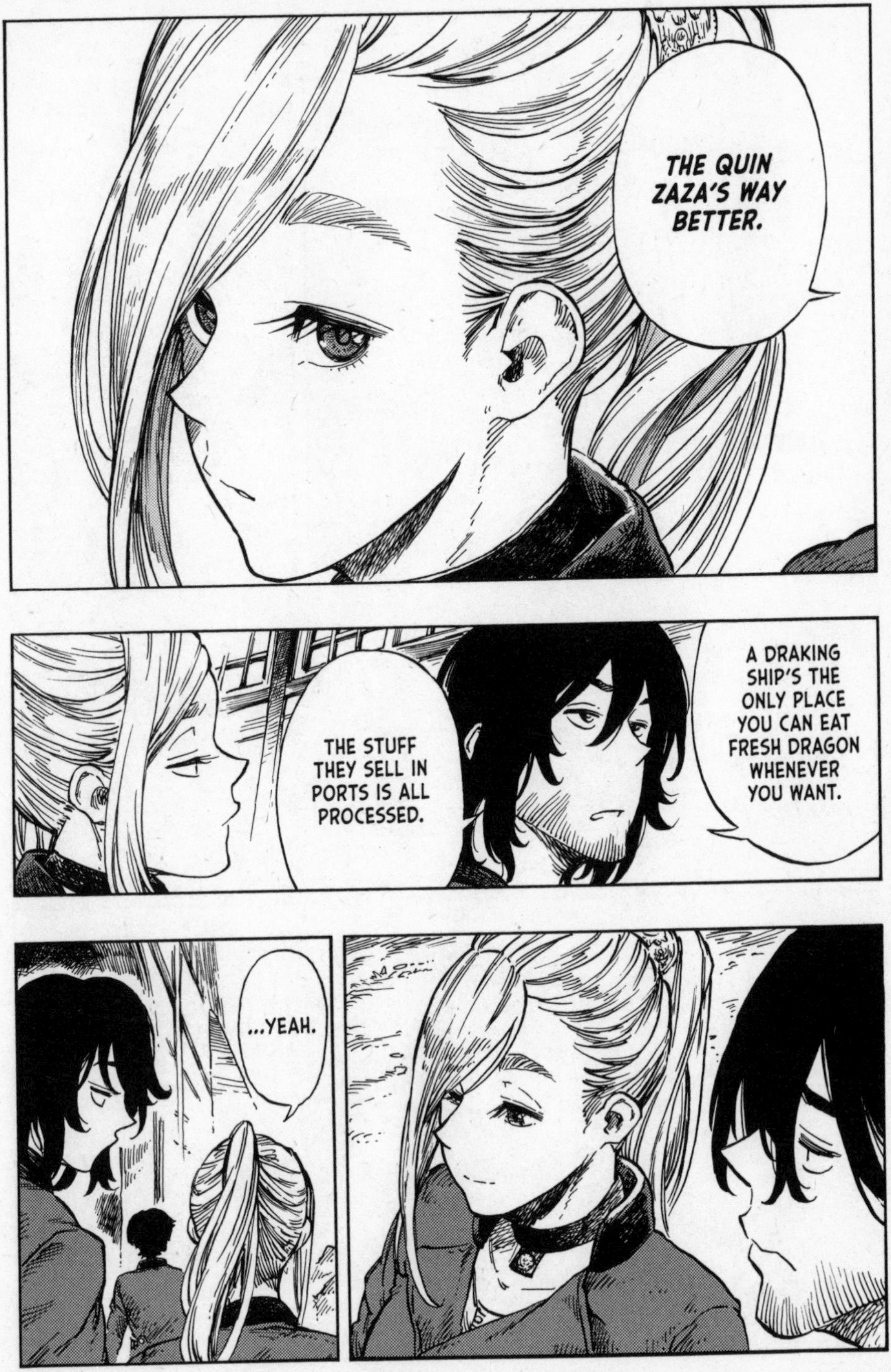
THE QUIN ZAZA'S WAY BETTER.
A DRAKING SHIP'S THE ONLY PLACE YOU CAN EAT FRESH DRAGON WHENEVER YOU WANT.
THE STUFF THEY SELL IN PORTS IS ALL PROCESSED.
...YEAH.

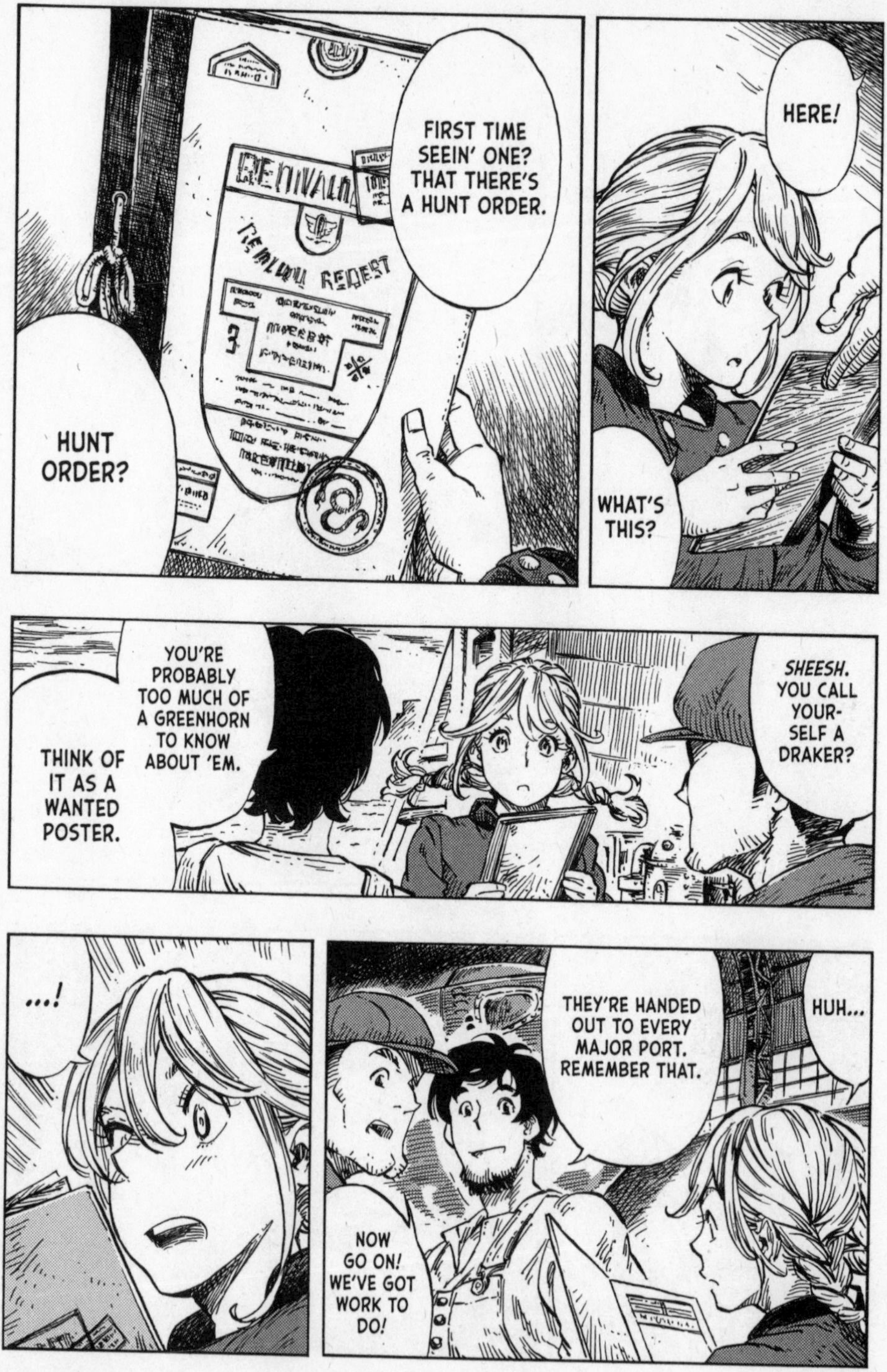
HERE!
WHAT'S THIS?
FIRST TIME SEEIN' ONE? THAT THERE'S A HUNT ORDER.
HUNT ORDER?
SHEESH. YOU CALL YOUR-SELF A DRAKER?
YOU'RE PROBABLY TOO MUCH OF A GREENHORN TO KNOW ABOUT 'EM.
THINK OF IT AS A WANTED POSTER.
HUH...
THEY'RE HANDED OUT TO EVERY MAJOR PORT. REMEMBER THAT.
NOW GO ON! WE'VE GOT WORK TO DO!
...!

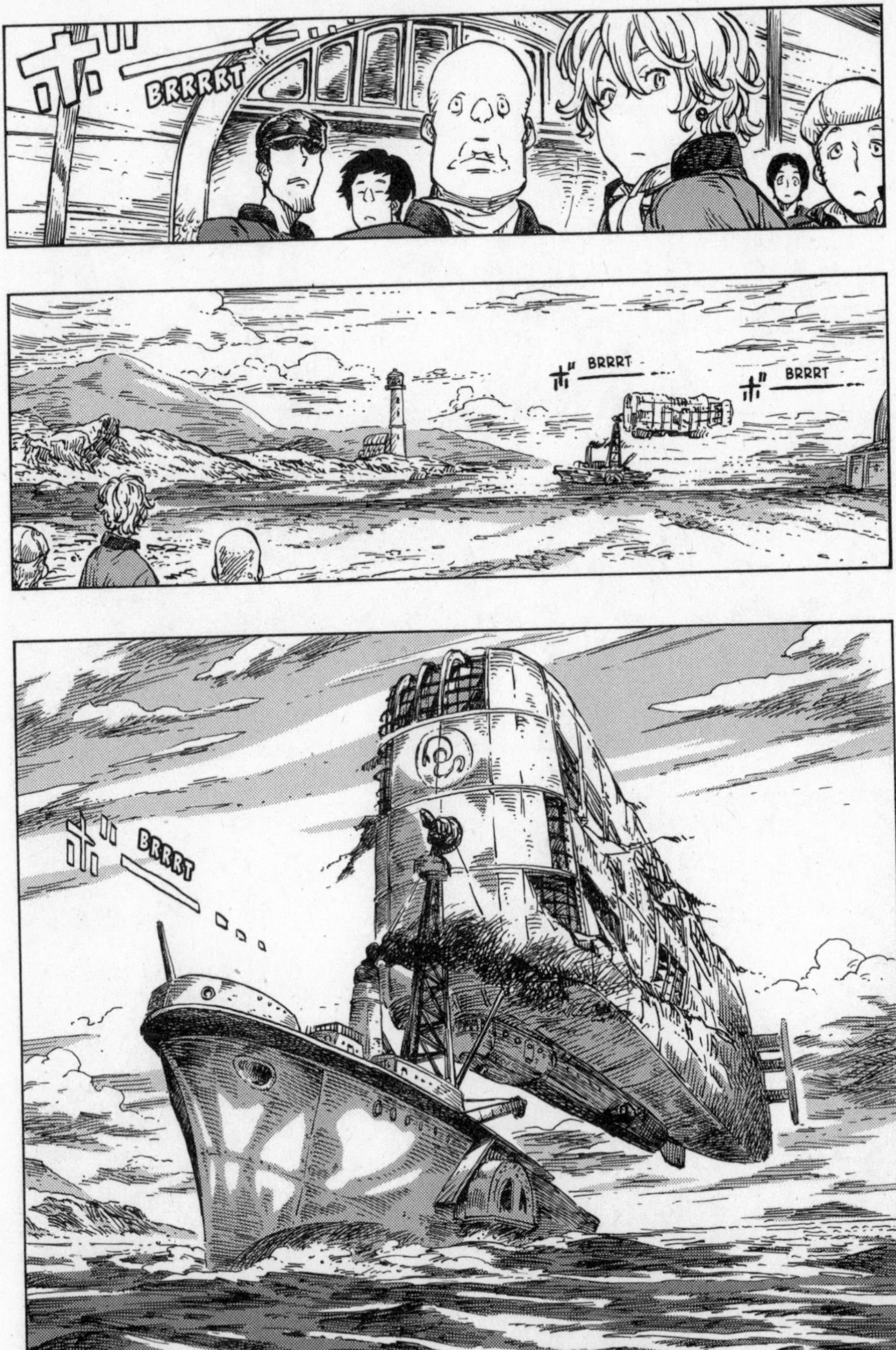
ボ
BRRRRT
ボ
BRRRT
ボ
BRRRT
ボ
BRRRT

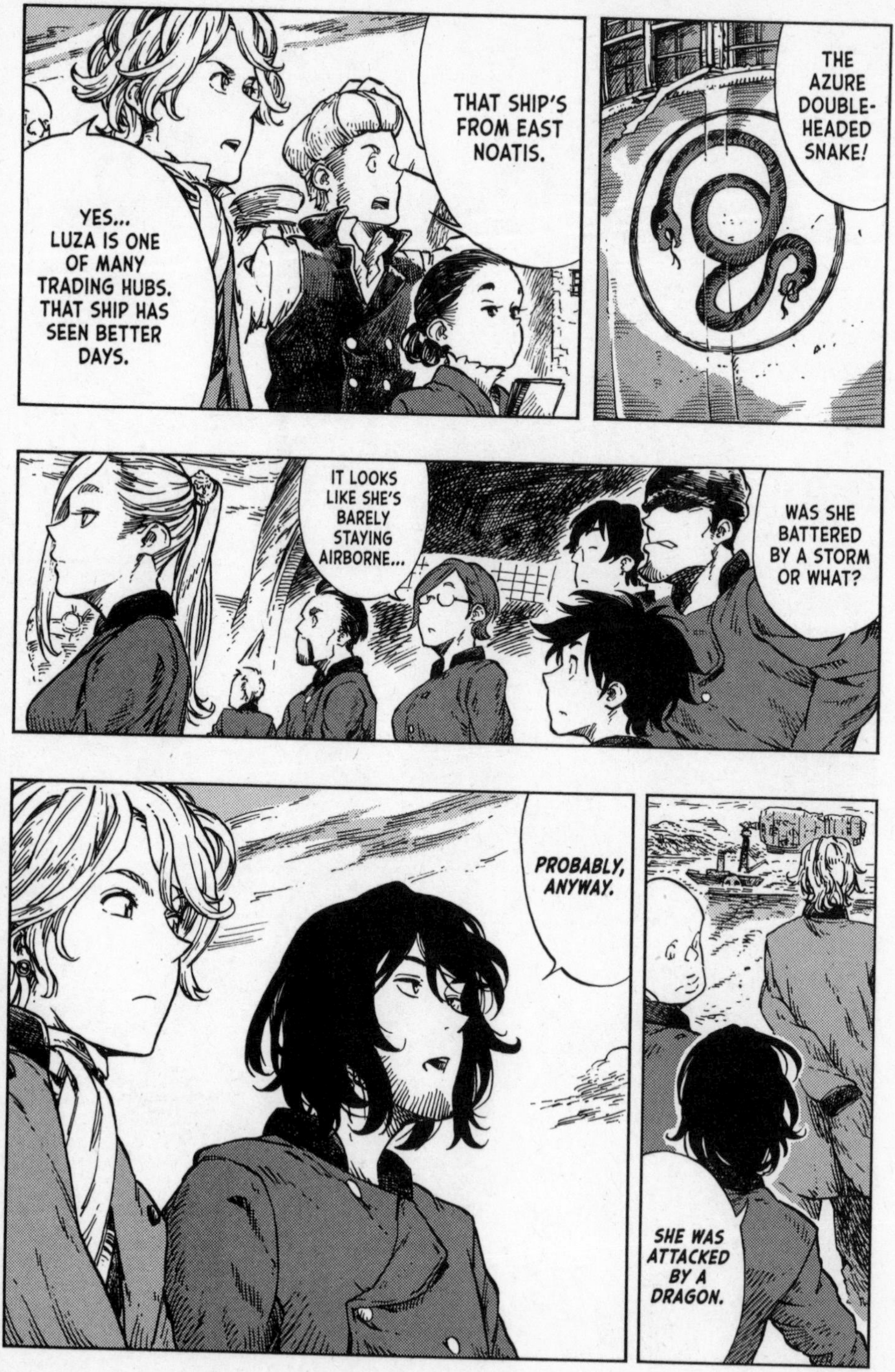
THE AZURE DOUBLE-HEADED SNAKE!
THAT SHIP'S FROM EAST NOATIS.
YES... LUZA IS ONE OF MANY TRADING HUBS. THAT SHIP HAS SEEN BETTER DAYS.
WAS SHE BATTERED BY A STORM OR WHAT?
IT LOOKS LIKE SHE'S BARELY STAYING AIRBORNE...
SHE WAS ATTACKED BY A DRAGON.
PROBABLY, ANYWAY.

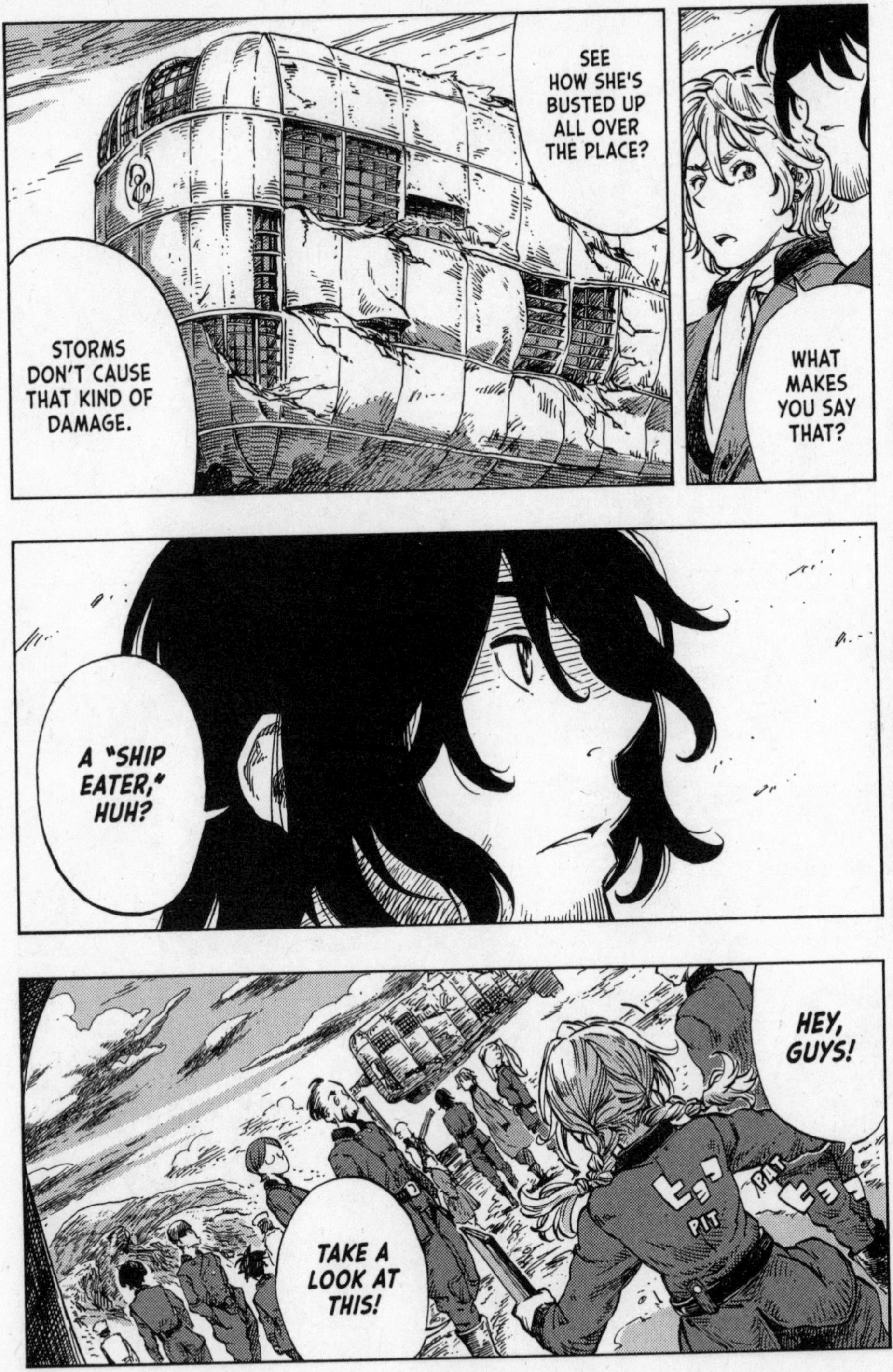
WHAT MAKES YOU SAY THAT?
SEE HOW SHE'S BUSTED UP ALL OVER THE PLACE?
STORMS DON'T CAUSE THAT KIND OF DAMAGE.
A "SHIP EATER," HUH?
HEY, GUYS!
PAT
PIT
TAKE A LOOK AT THIS!

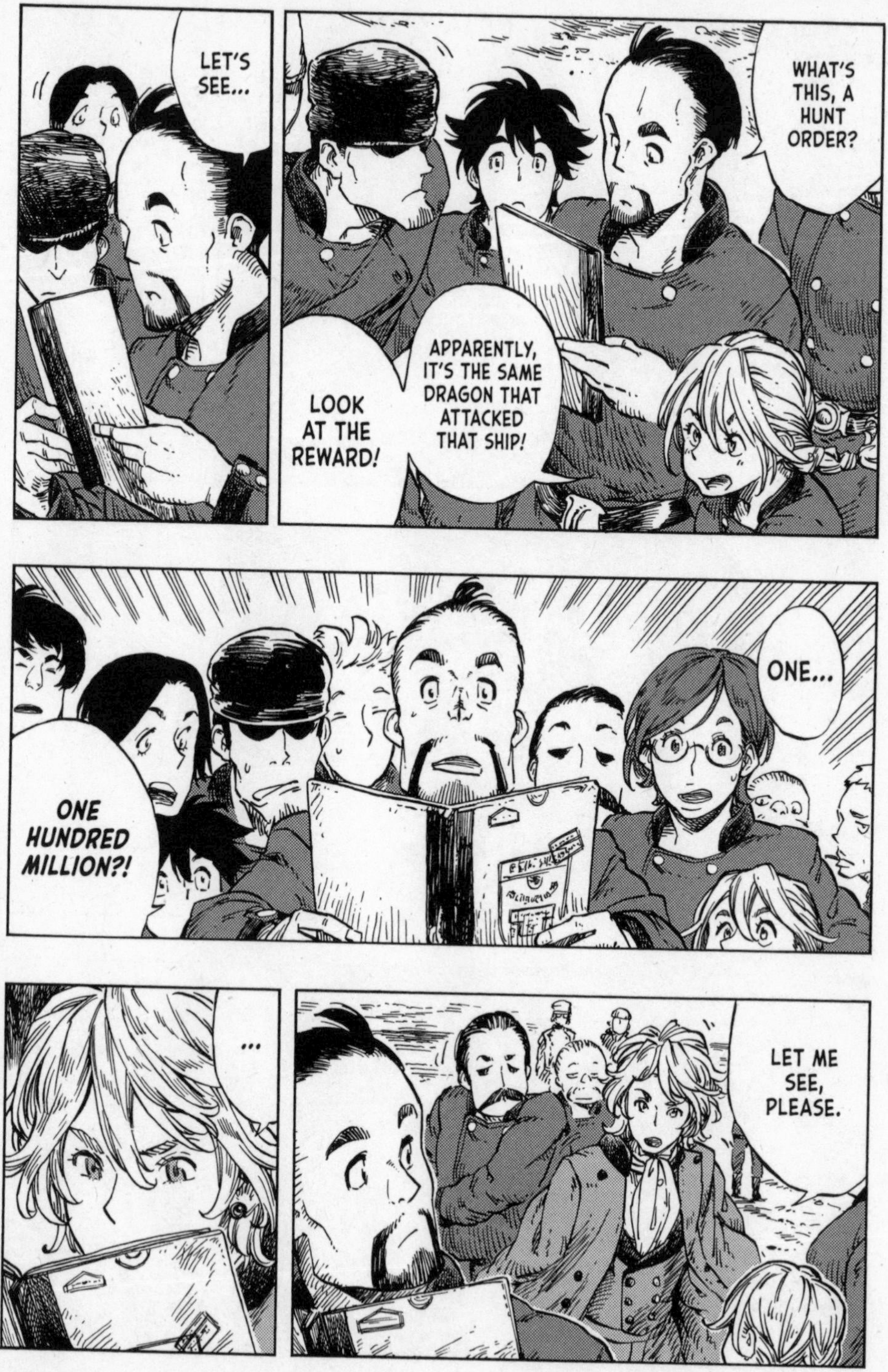
WHAT'S THIS, A HUNT ORDER?
APPARENTLY, IT'S THE SAME DRAGON THAT ATTACKED THAT SHIP!
LOOK AT THE REWARD!
LET'S SEE...
ONE...
ONE HUNDRED MILLION?!
LET ME SEE, PLEASE.
...

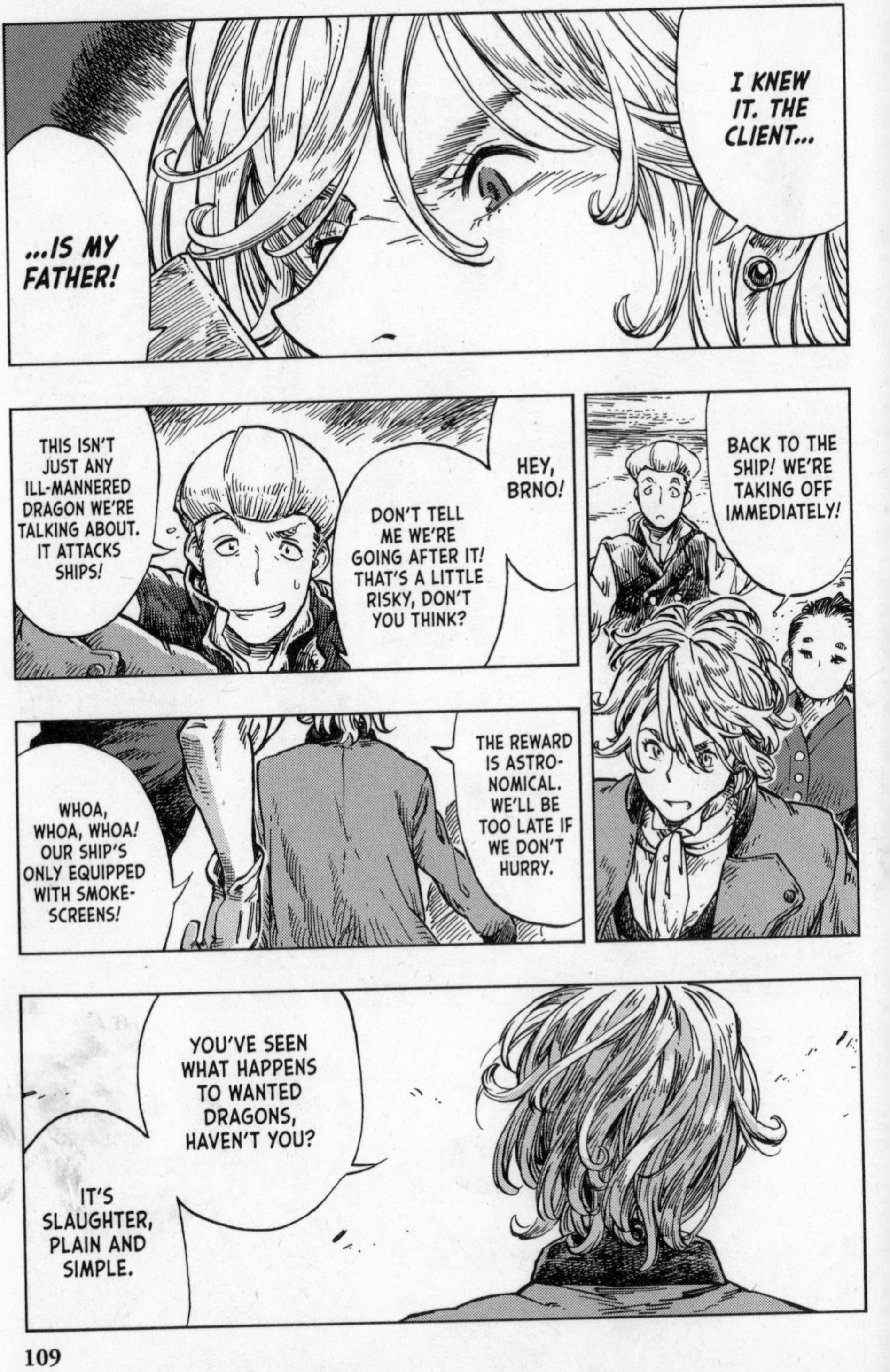
I KNEW IT. THE CLIENT...
...IS MY FATHER!
BACK TO THE SHIP! WE'RE TAKING OFF IMMEDIATELY!
HEY, BRNO!
DON'T TELL ME WE'RE GOING AFTER IT! THAT'S A LITTLE RISKY, DON'T YOU THINK?
THIS ISN'T JUST ANY ILL-MANNERED DRAGON WE'RE TALKING ABOUT. IT ATTACKS SHIPS!
THE REWARD IS ASTRONOMICAL. WE'LL BE TOO LATE IF WE DON'T HURRY.
WHOA, WHOA, WHOA! OUR SHIP'S ONLY EQUIPPED WITH SMOKE-SCREENS!
YOU'VE SEEN WHAT HAPPENS TO WANTED DRAGONS, HAVEN'T YOU?
IT'S SLAUGHTER, PLAIN AND SIMPLE.

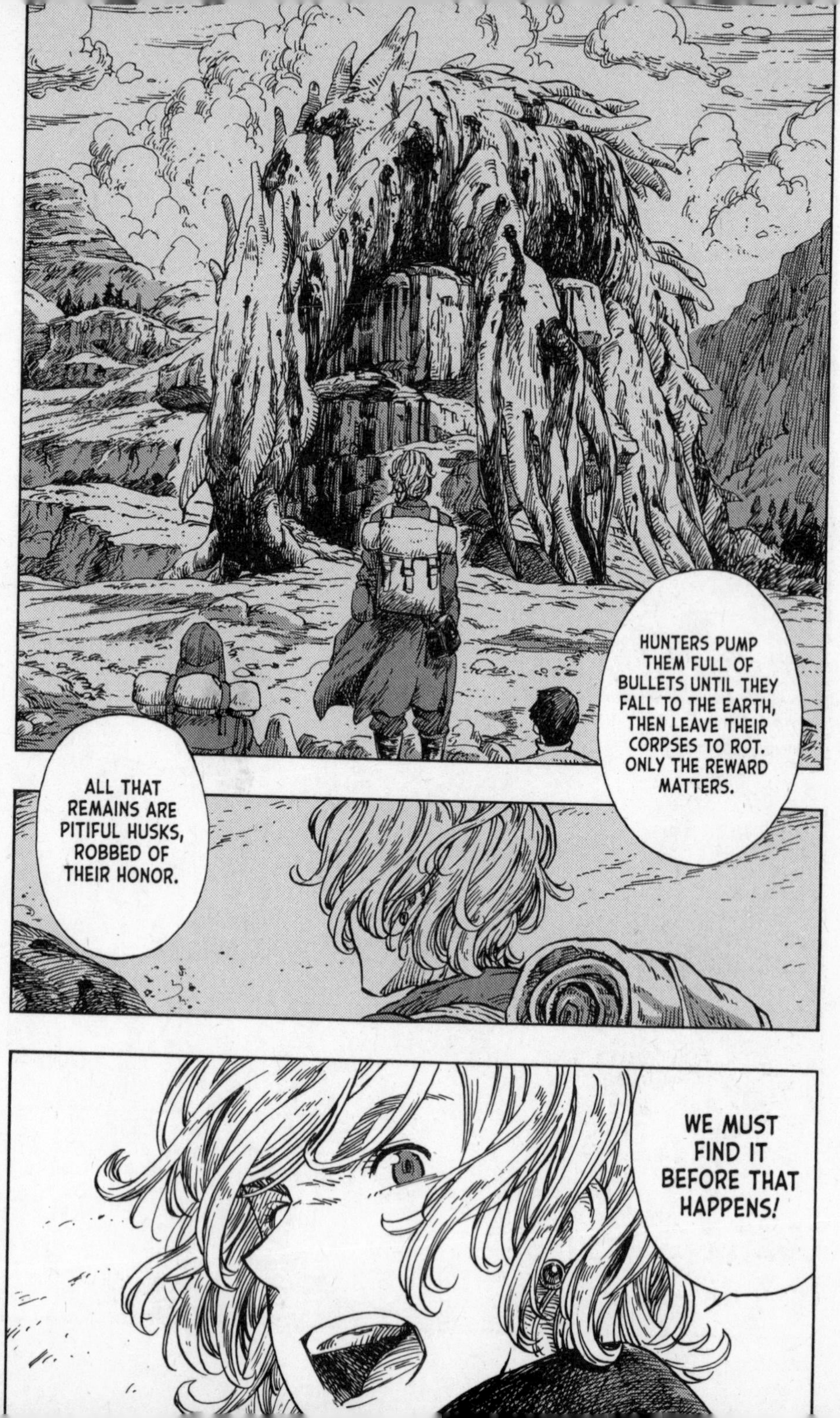
HUNTERS PUMP THEM FULL OF BULLETS UNTIL THEY FALL TO THE EARTH, THEN LEAVE THEIR CORPSES TO ROT. ONLY THE REWARD MATTERS.
ALL THAT REMAINS ARE PITIFUL HUSKS, ROBBED OF THEIR HONOR.
WE MUST FIND IT BEFORE THAT HAPPENS!

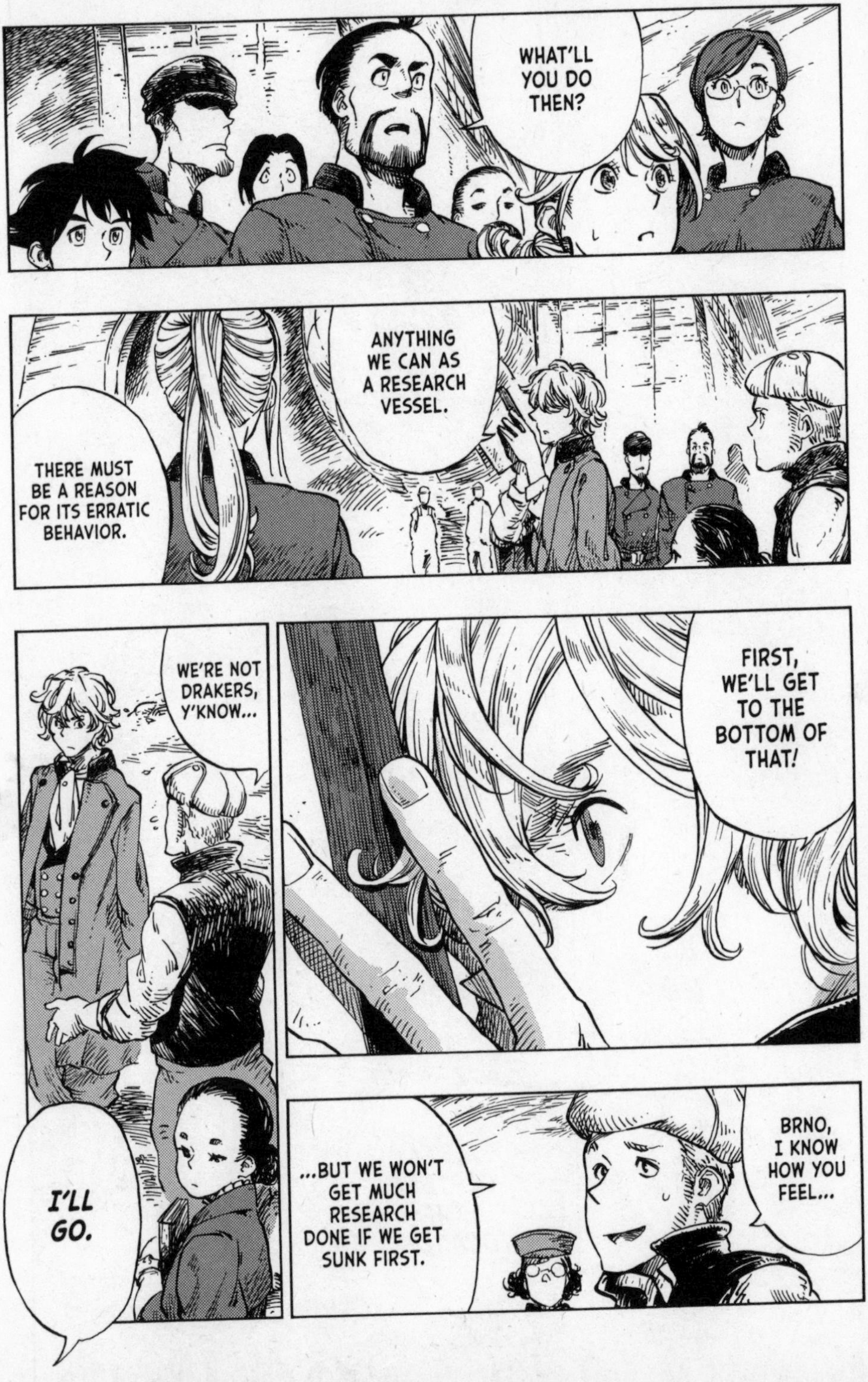
WHAT'LL YOU DO THEN?
ANYTHING WE CAN AS A RESEARCH VESSEL.
THERE MUST BE A REASON FOR ITS ERRATIC BEHAVIOR.
FIRST, WE'LL GET TO THE BOTTOM OF THAT!
BRNO, I KNOW HOW YOU FEEL...
...BUT WE WON'T GET MUCH RESEARCH DONE IF WE GET SUNK FIRST.
WE'RE NOT DRAKERS, Y'KNOW...
I'LL GO.

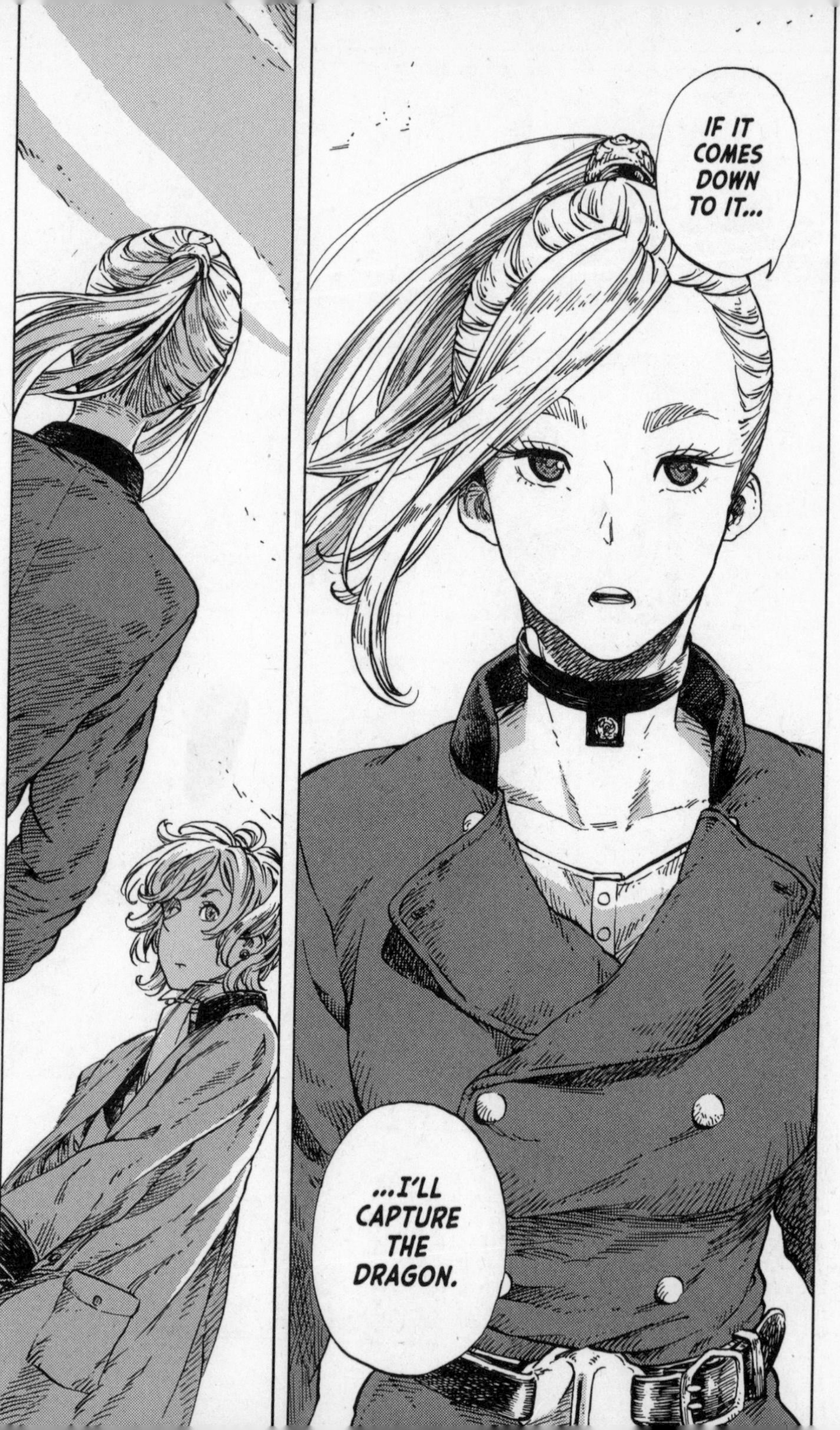
IF IT COMES DOWN TO IT...
...I'LL CAPTURE THE DRAGON.

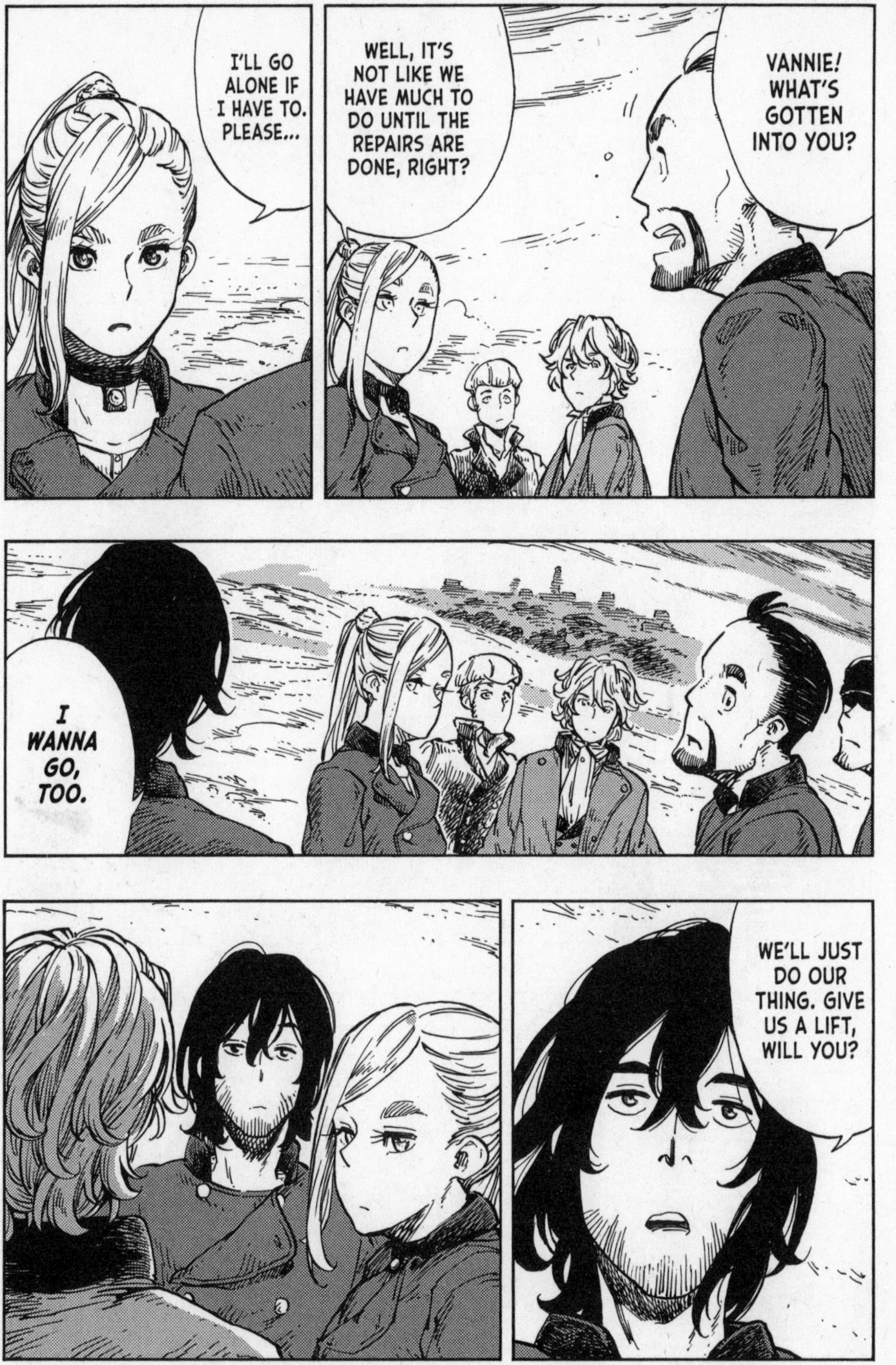
VANNIE! WHAT'S GOTTEN INTO YOU?
WELL, IT'S NOT LIKE WE HAVE MUCH TO DO UNTIL THE REPAIRS ARE DONE, RIGHT?
I'LL GO ALONE IF I HAVE TO. PLEASE...
I WANNA GO, TOO.
WE'LL JUST DO OUR THING. GIVE US A LIFT, WILL YOU?

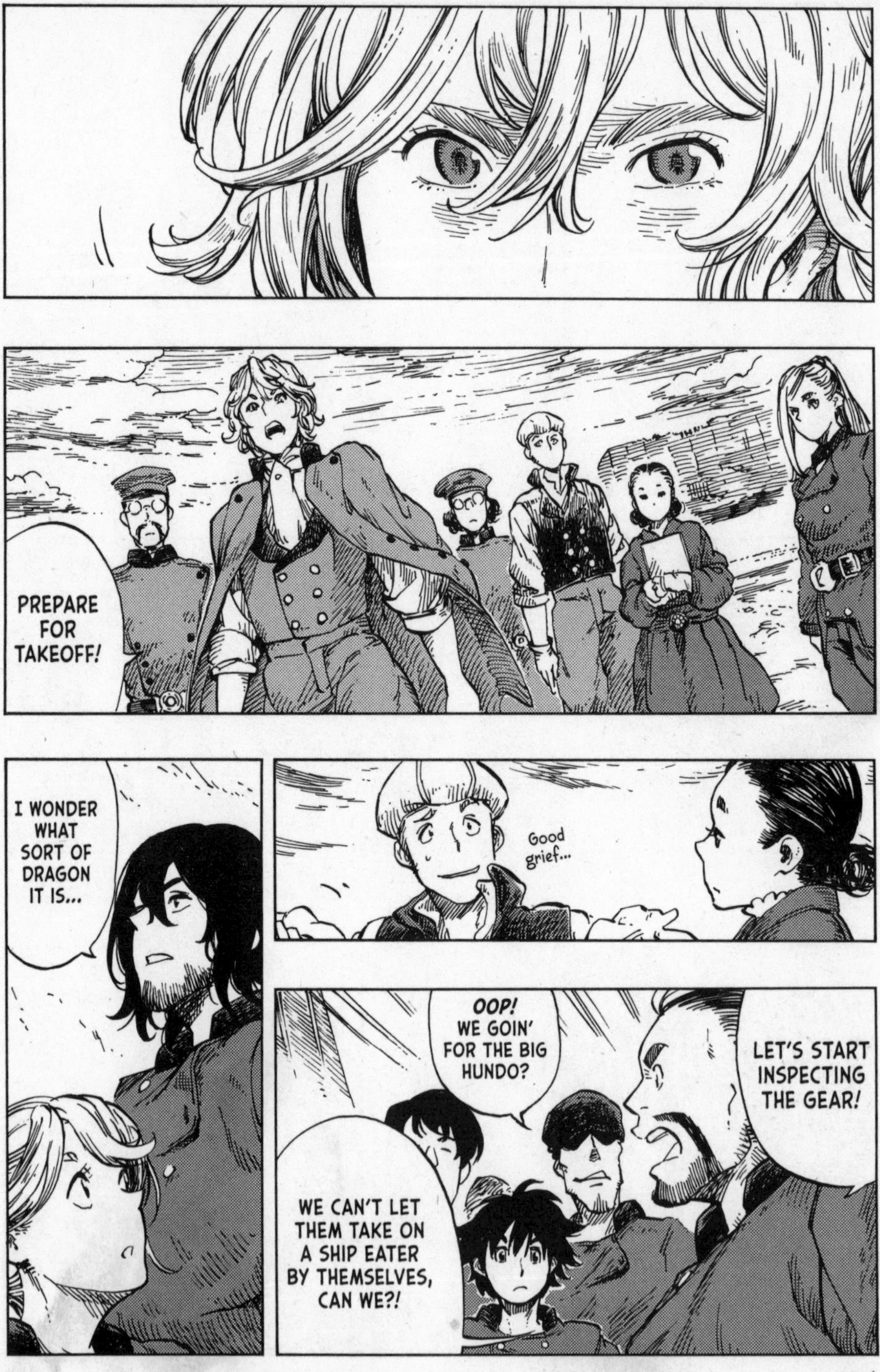
PREPARE FOR TAKEOFF!
Good grief...
LET'S START INSPECTING THE GEAR!
OOP! WE GOIN' FOR THE BIG HUNDO?
WE CAN'T LET THEM TAKE ON A SHIP EATER BY THEMSELVES, CAN WE?!
I WONDER WHAT SORT OF DRAGON IT IS...

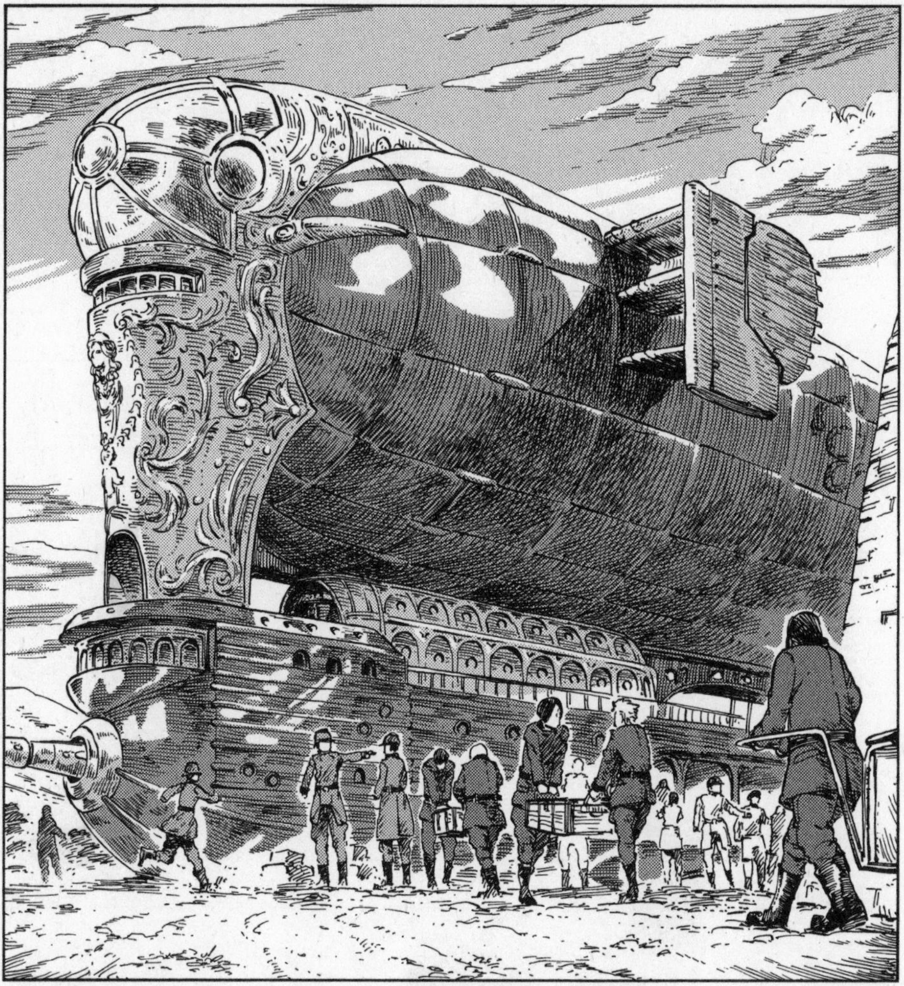
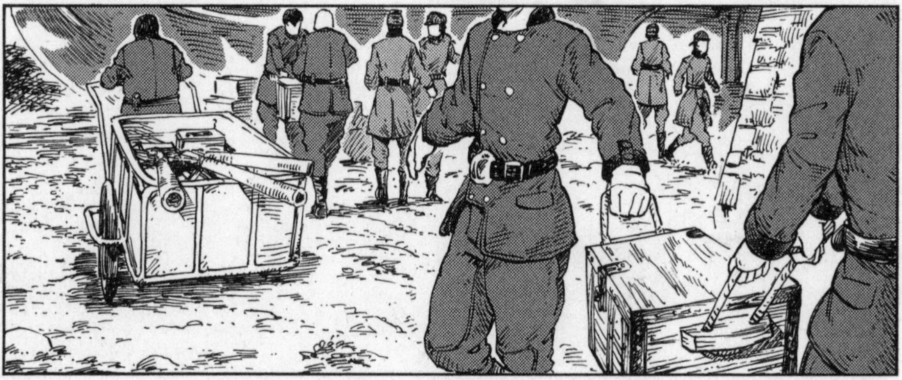

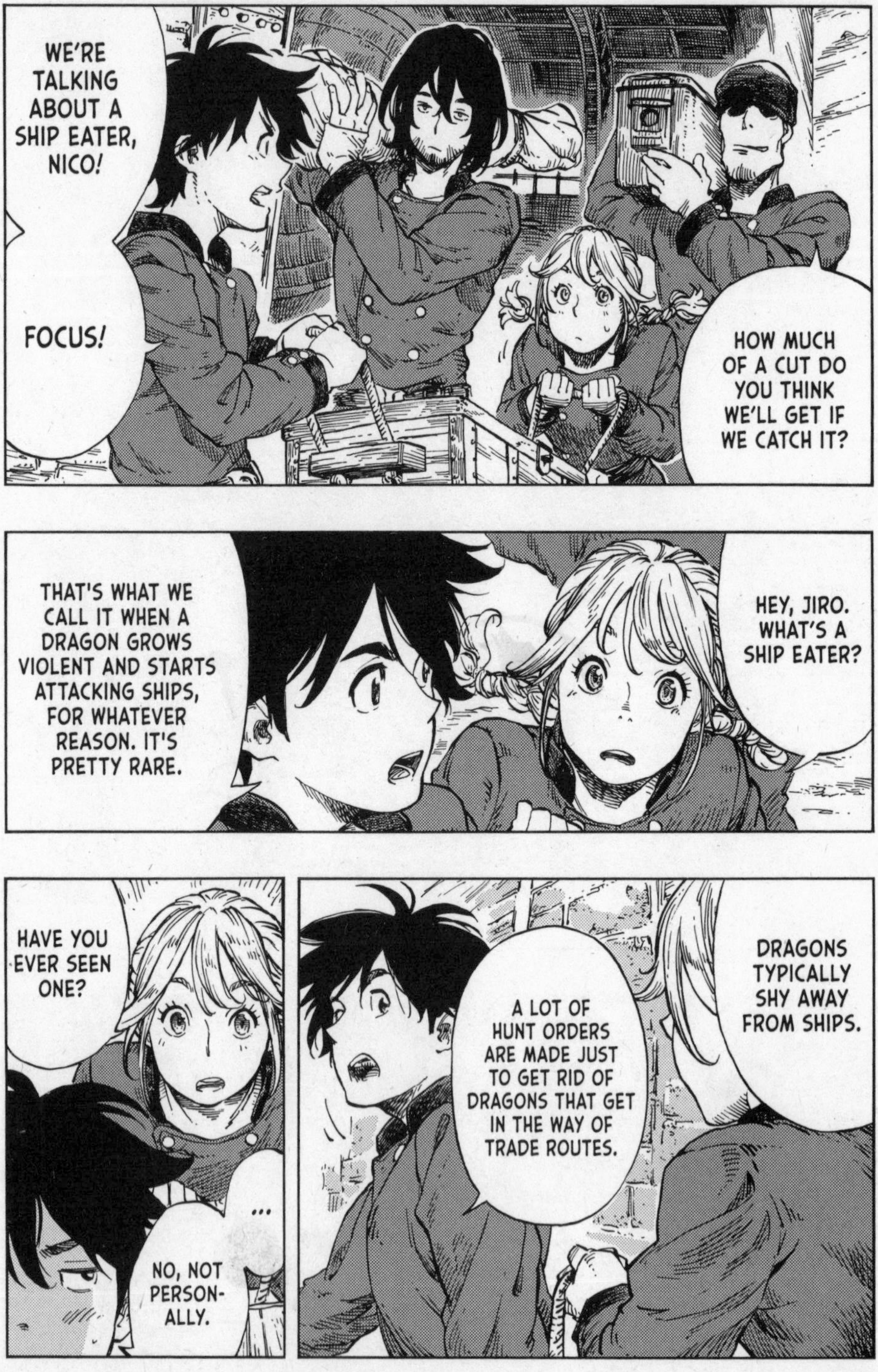
HOW MUCH OF A CUT DO YOU THINK WE'LL GET IF WE CATCH IT?
WE'RE TALKING ABOUT A SHIP EATER, NICO!
FOCUS!
HEY, JIRO. WHAT'S A SHIP EATER?
THAT'S WHAT WE CALL IT WHEN A DRAGON GROWS VIOLENT AND STARTS ATTACKING SHIPS, FOR WHATEVER REASON. IT'S PRETTY RARE.
DRAGONS TYPICALLY SHY AWAY FROM SHIPS.
A LOT OF HUNT ORDERS ARE MADE JUST TO GET RID OF DRAGONS THAT GET IN THE WAY OF TRADE ROUTES.
HAVE YOU EVER SEEN ONE?
...
NO, NOT PERSON-ALLY.

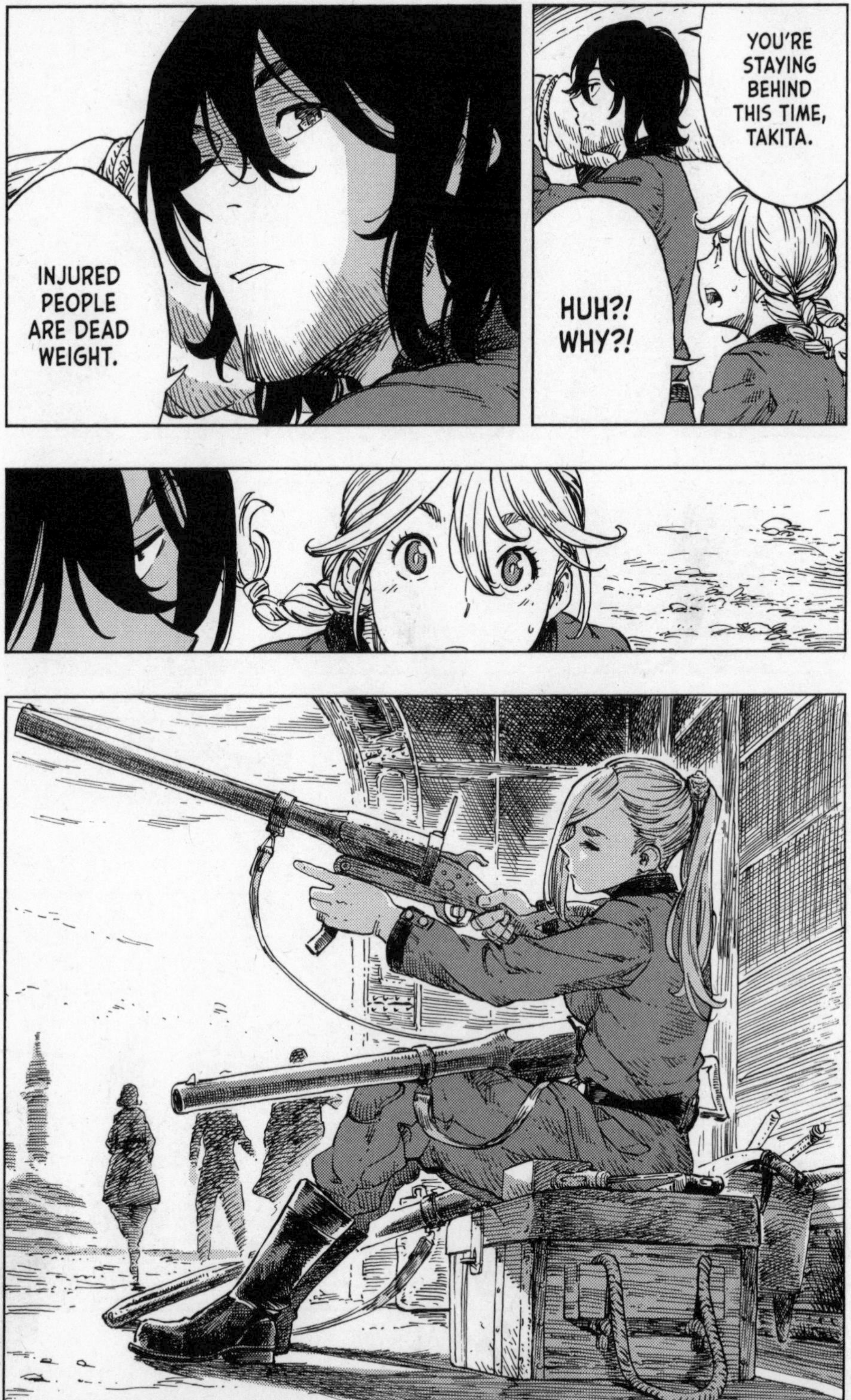
YOU'RE STAYING BEHIND THIS TIME, TAKITA.
HUH?! WHY?!
INJURED PEOPLE ARE DEAD WEIGHT.

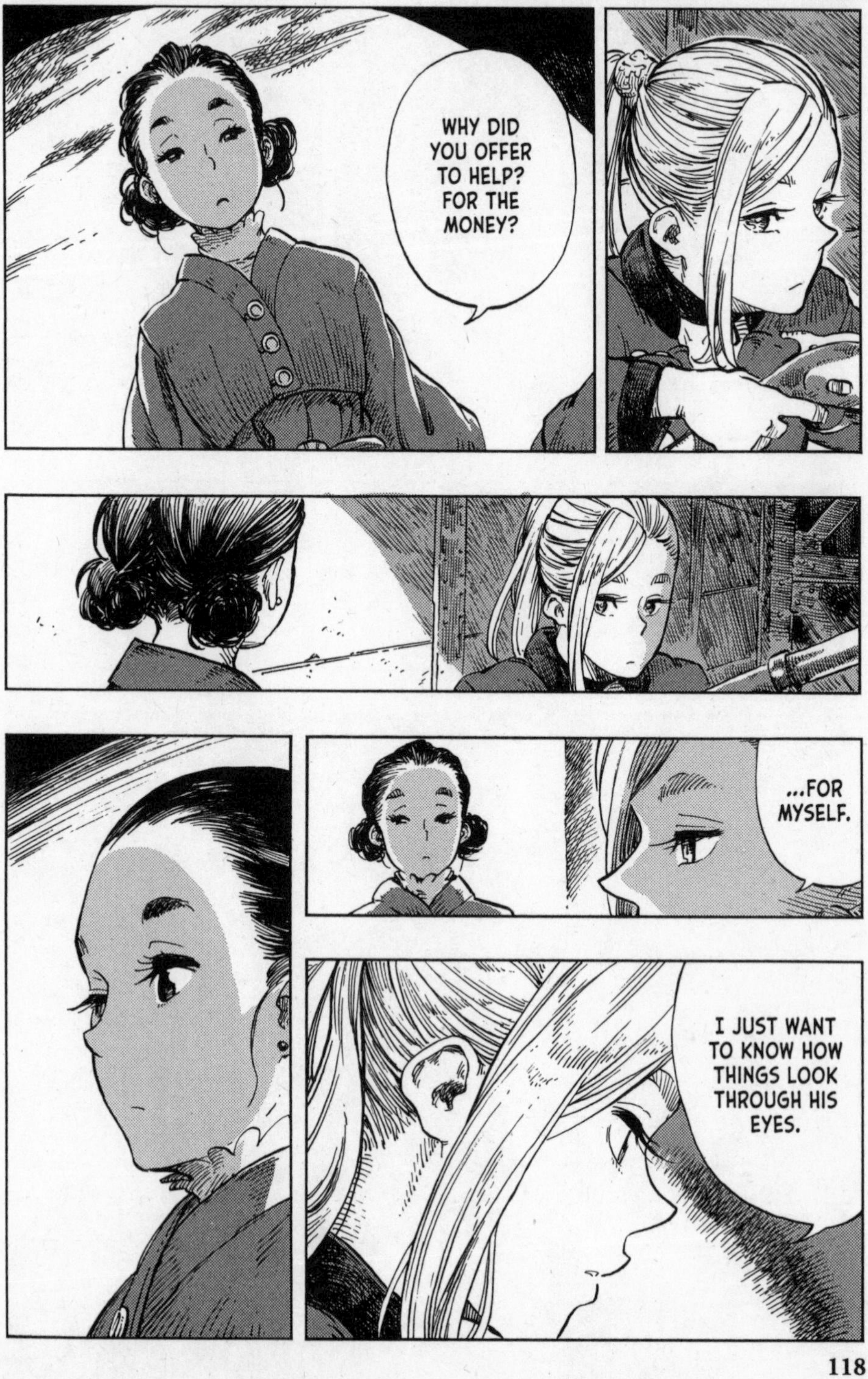
WHY DID YOU OFFER TO HELP? FOR THE MONEY?
...FOR MYSELF.
I JUST WANT TO KNOW HOW THINGS LOOK THROUGH HIS EYES.

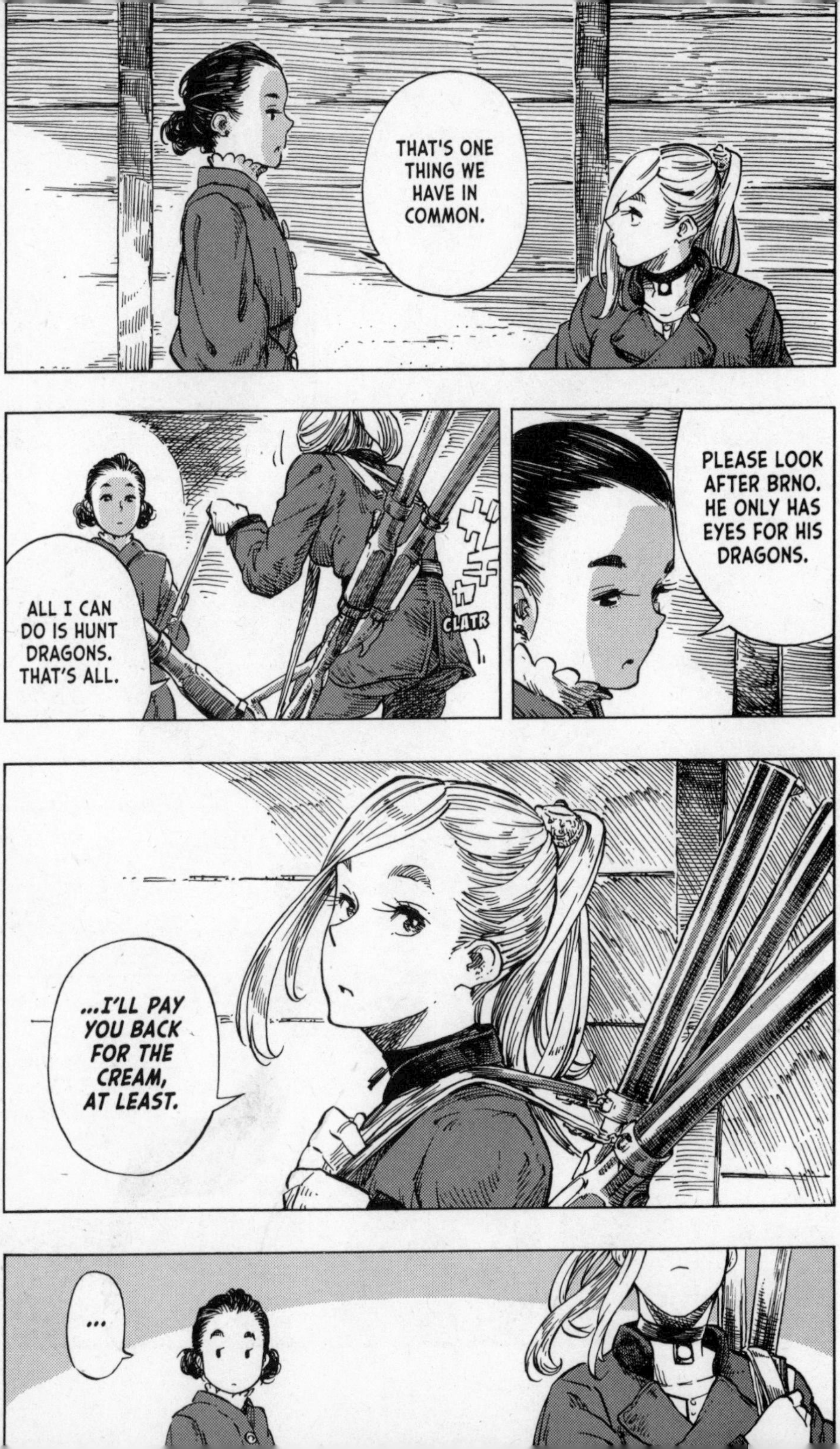
THAT'S ONE THING WE HAVE IN COMMON.
PLEASE LOOK AFTER BRNO. HE ONLY HAS EYES FOR HIS DRAGONS.
ALL I CAN DO IS HUNT DRAGONS. THAT'S ALL.
CLATR
...I'LL PAY YOU BACK FOR THE CREAM, AT LEAST.
...

MASTER BRNO. WE'RE READY FOR TAKEOFF.

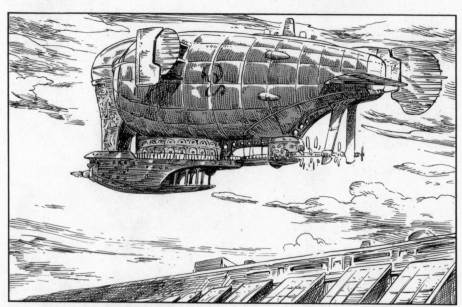

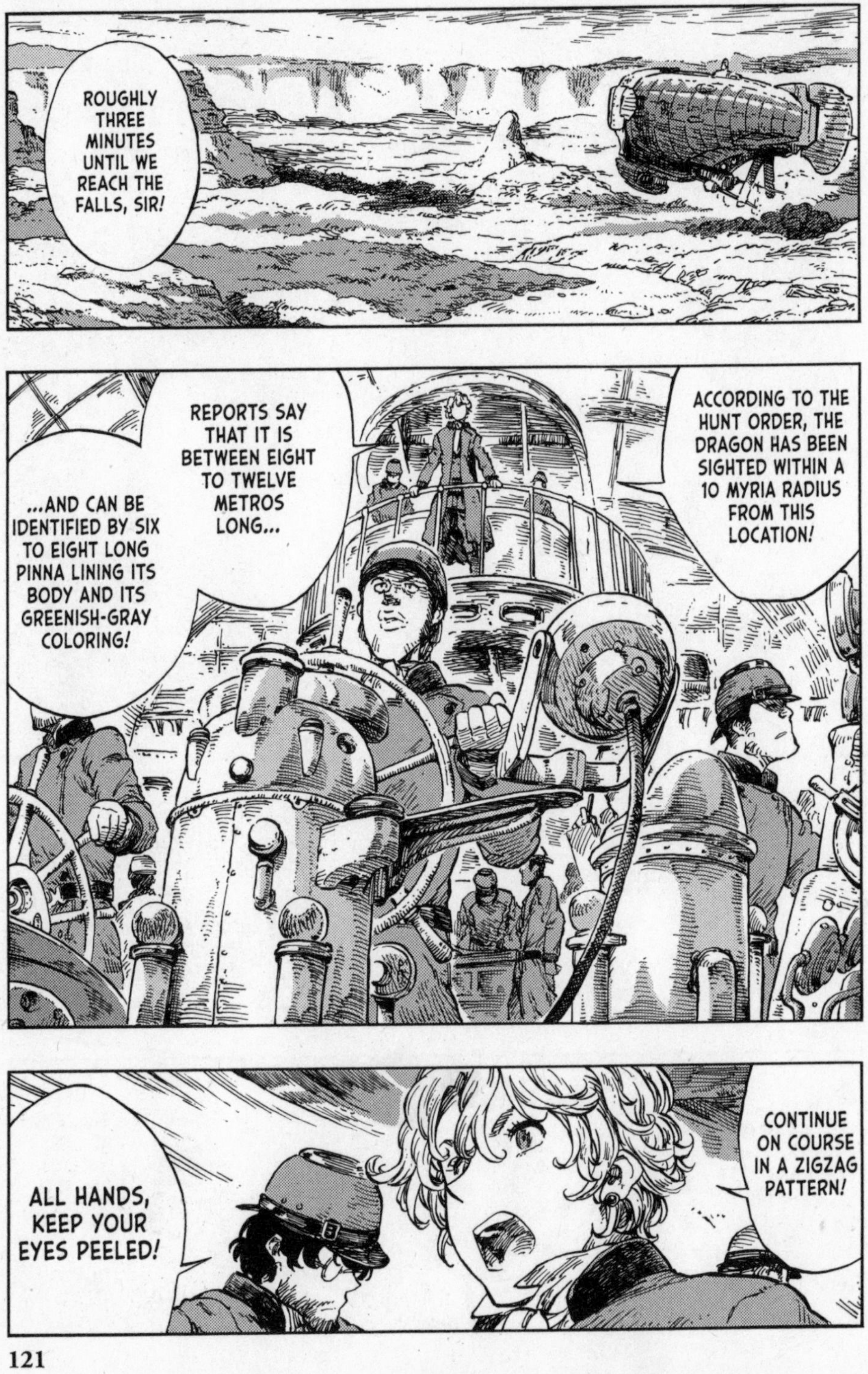
ROUGHLY THREE MINUTES UNTIL WE REACH THE FALLS, SIR!
ACCORDING TO THE HUNT ORDER, THE DRAGON HAS BEEN SIGHTED WITHIN A 10 MYRIA RADIUS FROM THIS LOCATION!
REPORTS SAY THAT IT IS BETWEEN EIGHT TO TWELVE METROS LONG...
...AND CAN BE IDENTIFIED BY SIX TO EIGHT LONG PINNA LINING ITS BODY AND ITS GREENISH-GRAY COLORING!
CONTINUE ON COURSE IN A ZIGZAG PATTERN!
ALL HANDS, KEEP YOUR EYES PEELED!

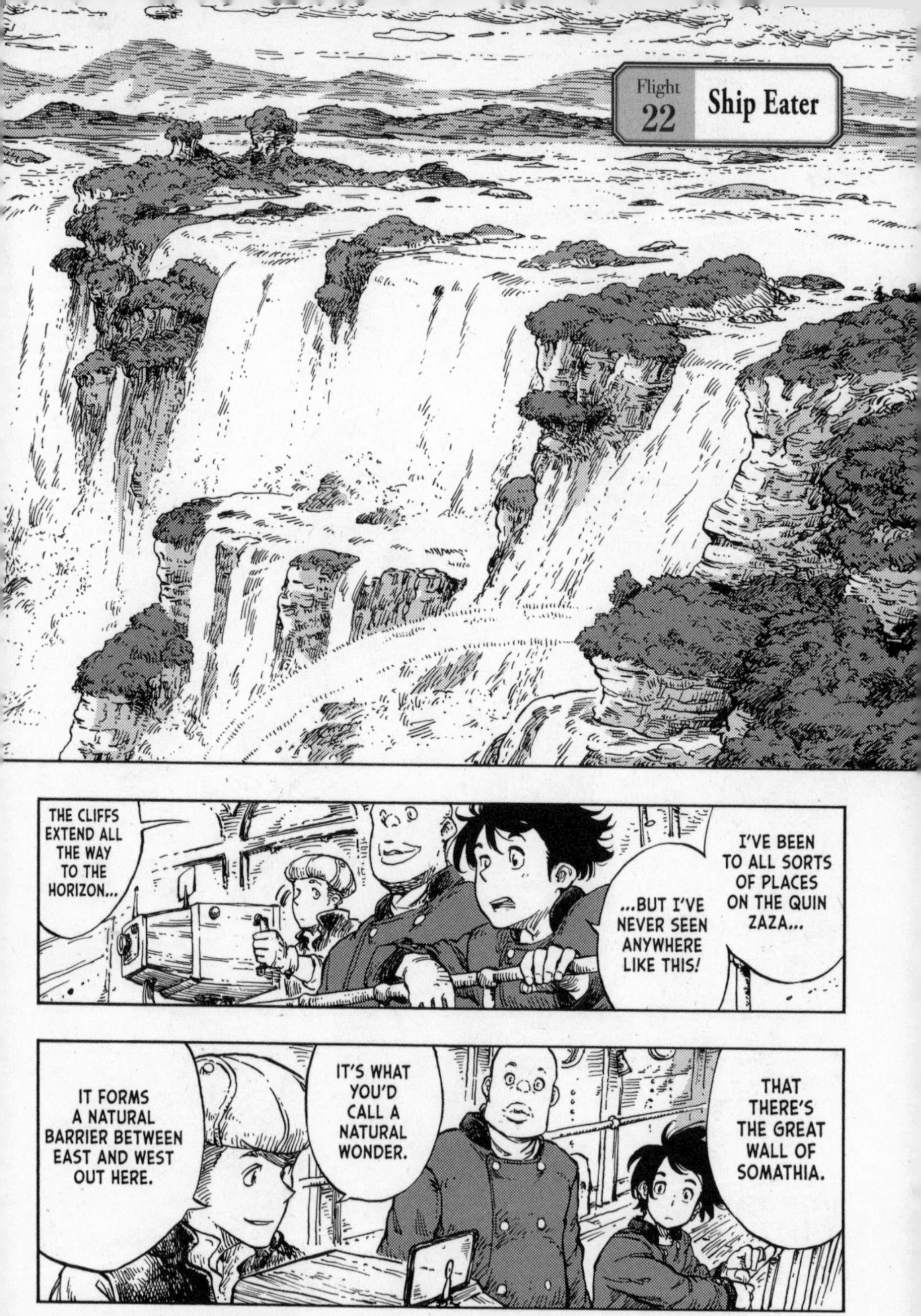
Flight 22
Ship Eater
I'VE BEEN TO ALL SORTS OF PLACES ON THE QUIN ZAZA...
...BUT I'VE NEVER SEEN ANYWHERE LIKE THIS!
THE CLIFFS EXTEND ALL THE WAY TO THE HORIZON...
THAT THERE'S THE GREAT WALL OF SOMATHIA.
IT'S WHAT YOU'D CALL A NATURAL WONDER.
IT FORMS A NATURAL BARRIER BETWEEN EAST AND WEST OUT HERE.

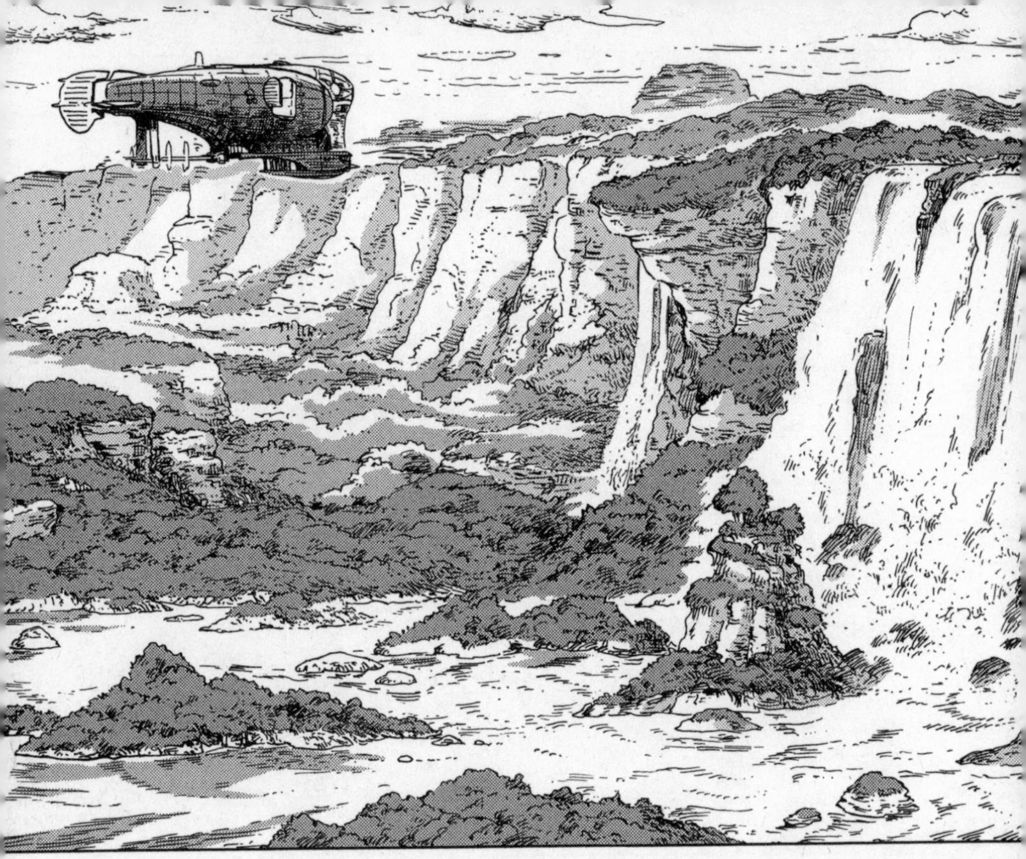

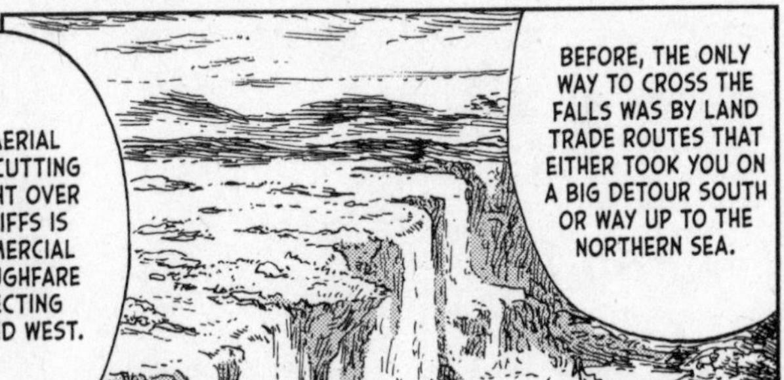
BEFORE, THE ONLY WAY TO CROSS THE FALLS WAS BY LAND TRADE ROUTES THAT EITHER TOOK YOU ON A BIG DETOUR SOUTH OR WAY UP TO THE NORTHERN SEA.

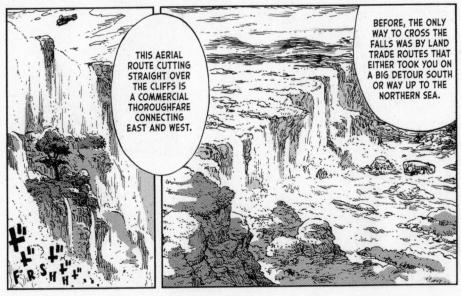

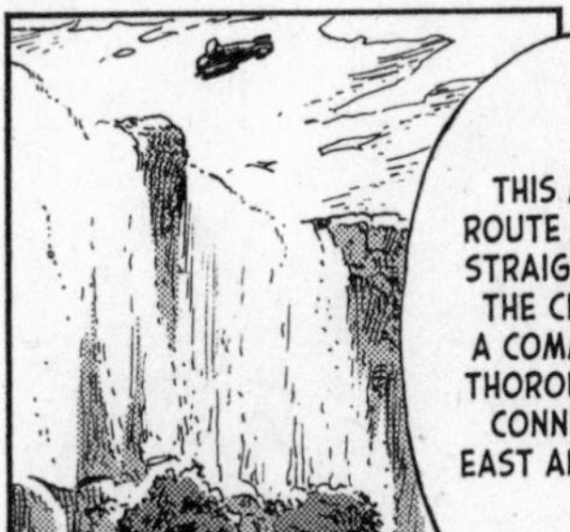
THIS AERIAL ROUTE CUTTING STRAIGHT OVER THE CLIFFS IS A COMMERCIAL THOROUGHFARE CONNECTING EAST AND WEST.
FRSHHH

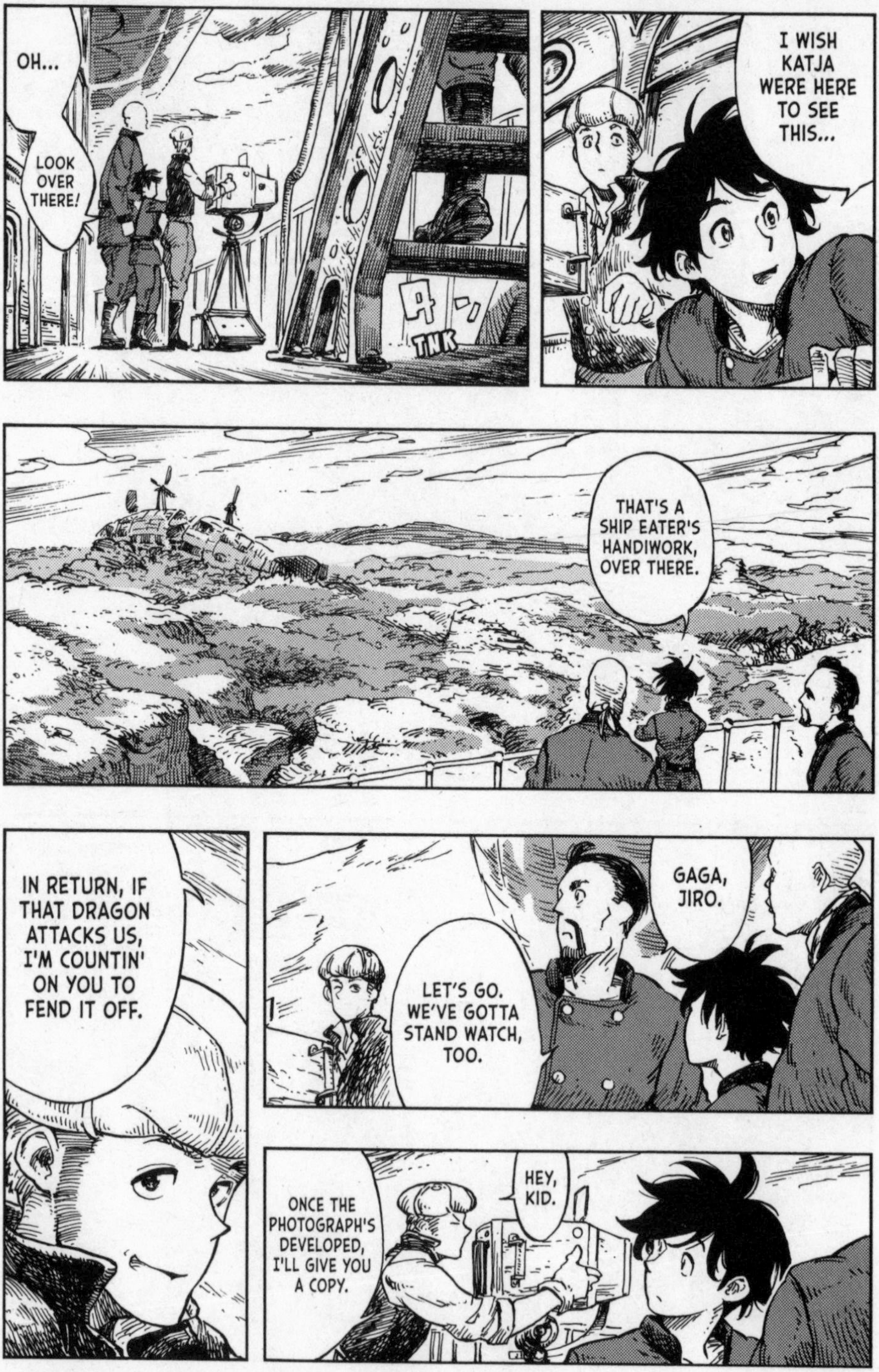
I WISH KATJA WERE HERE TO SEE THIS...
OH...
LOOK OVER THERE!
TNK
THAT'S A SHIP EATER'S HANDIWORK, OVER THERE.
GAGA, JIRO.
LET'S GO. WE'VE GOTTA STAND WATCH, TOO.
HEY, KID.
ONCE THE PHOTOGRAPH'S DEVELOPED, I'LL GIVE YOU A COPY.
IN RETURN, IF THAT DRAGON ATTACKS US, I'M COUNTIN' ON YOU TO FEND IT OFF.

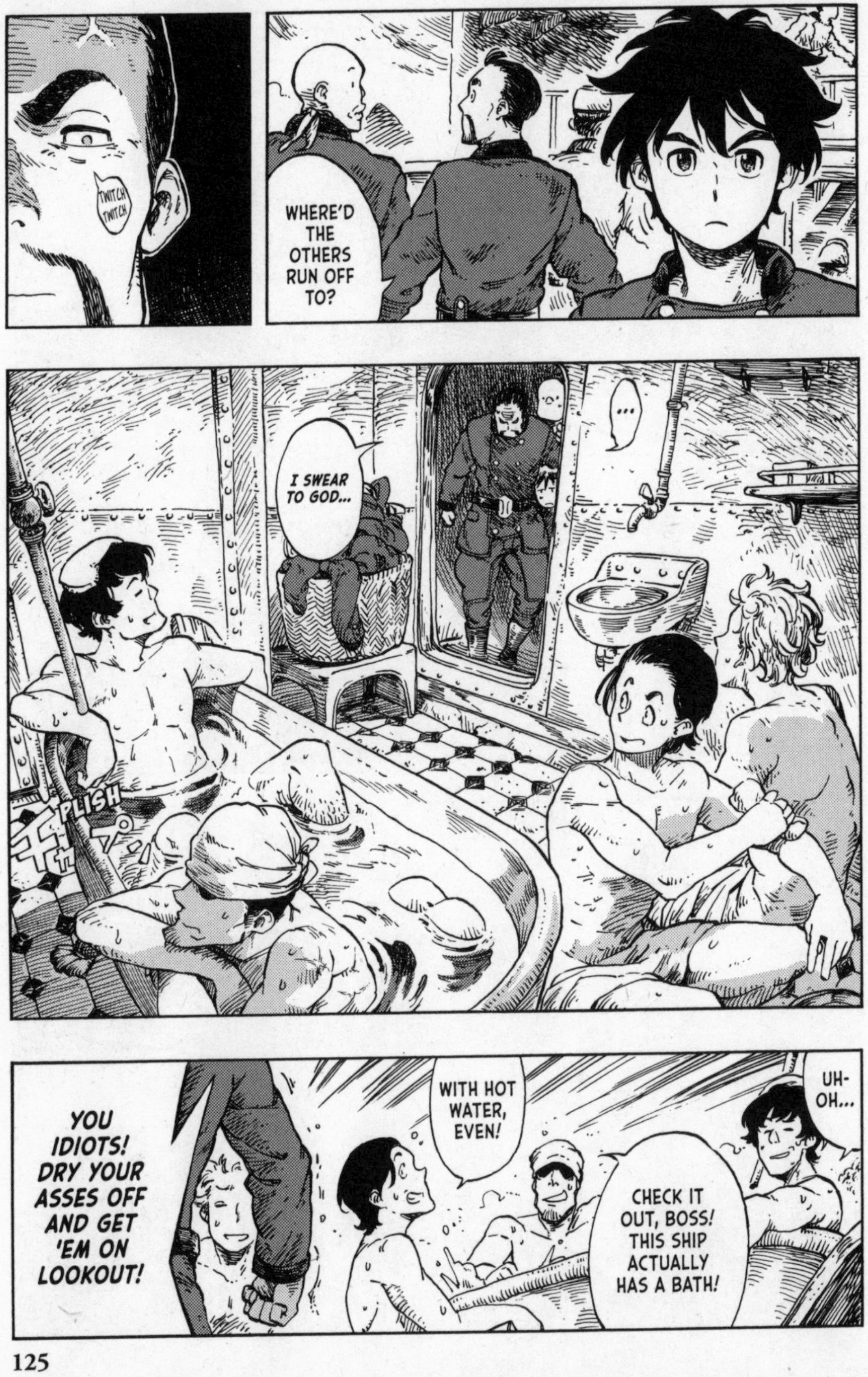
WHERE'D THE OTHERS RUN OFF TO?
TWITCH TWITCH
...
I SWEAR TO GOD...
PLISH
UH-OH...
CHECK IT OUT, BOSS! THIS SHIP ACTUALLY HAS A BATH!
WITH HOT WATER, EVEN!
YOU IDIOTS! DRY YOUR ASSES OFF AND GET 'EM ON LOOKOUT!

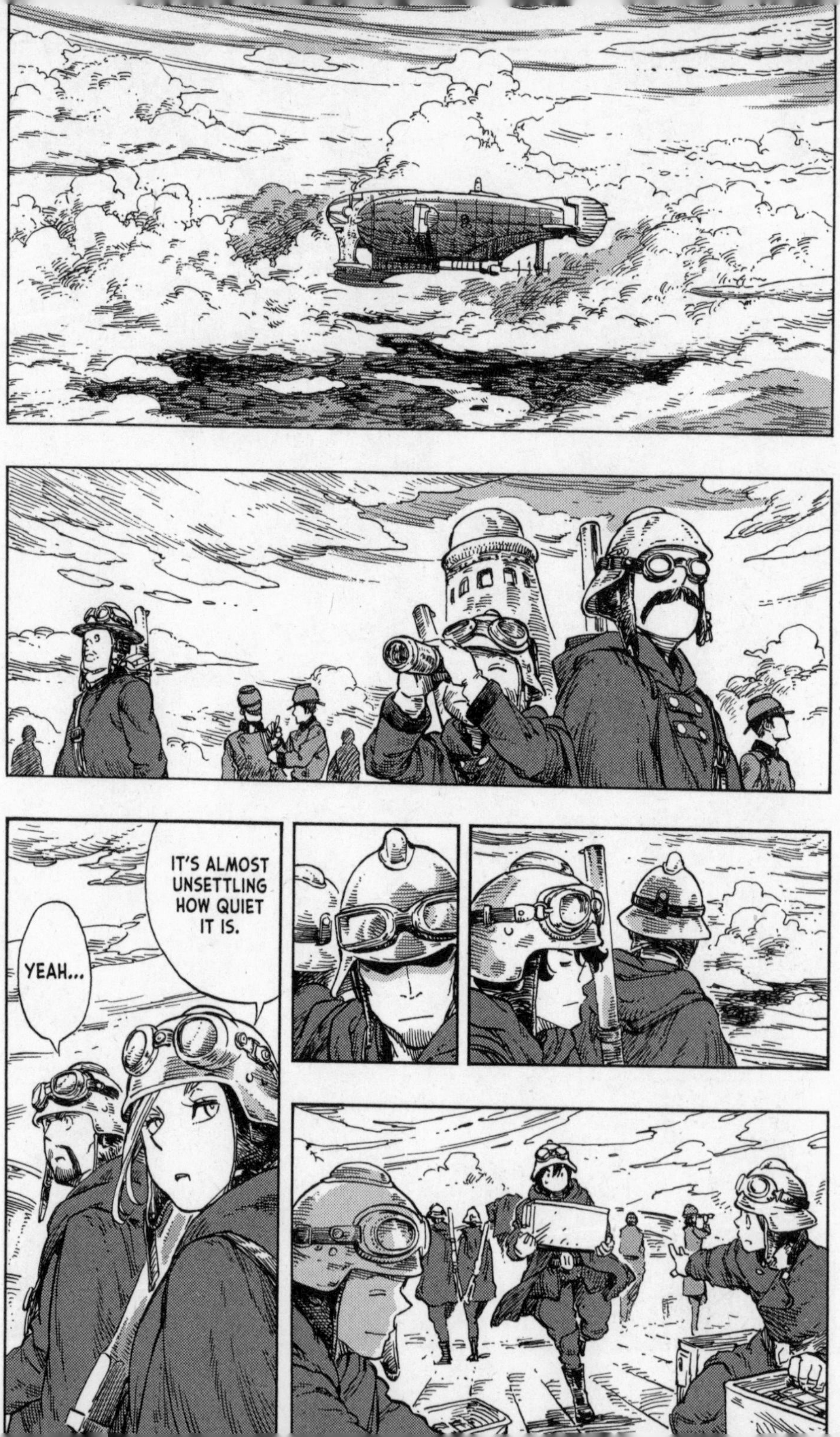
IT'S ALMOST UNSETTLING HOW QUIET IT IS.
YEAH...

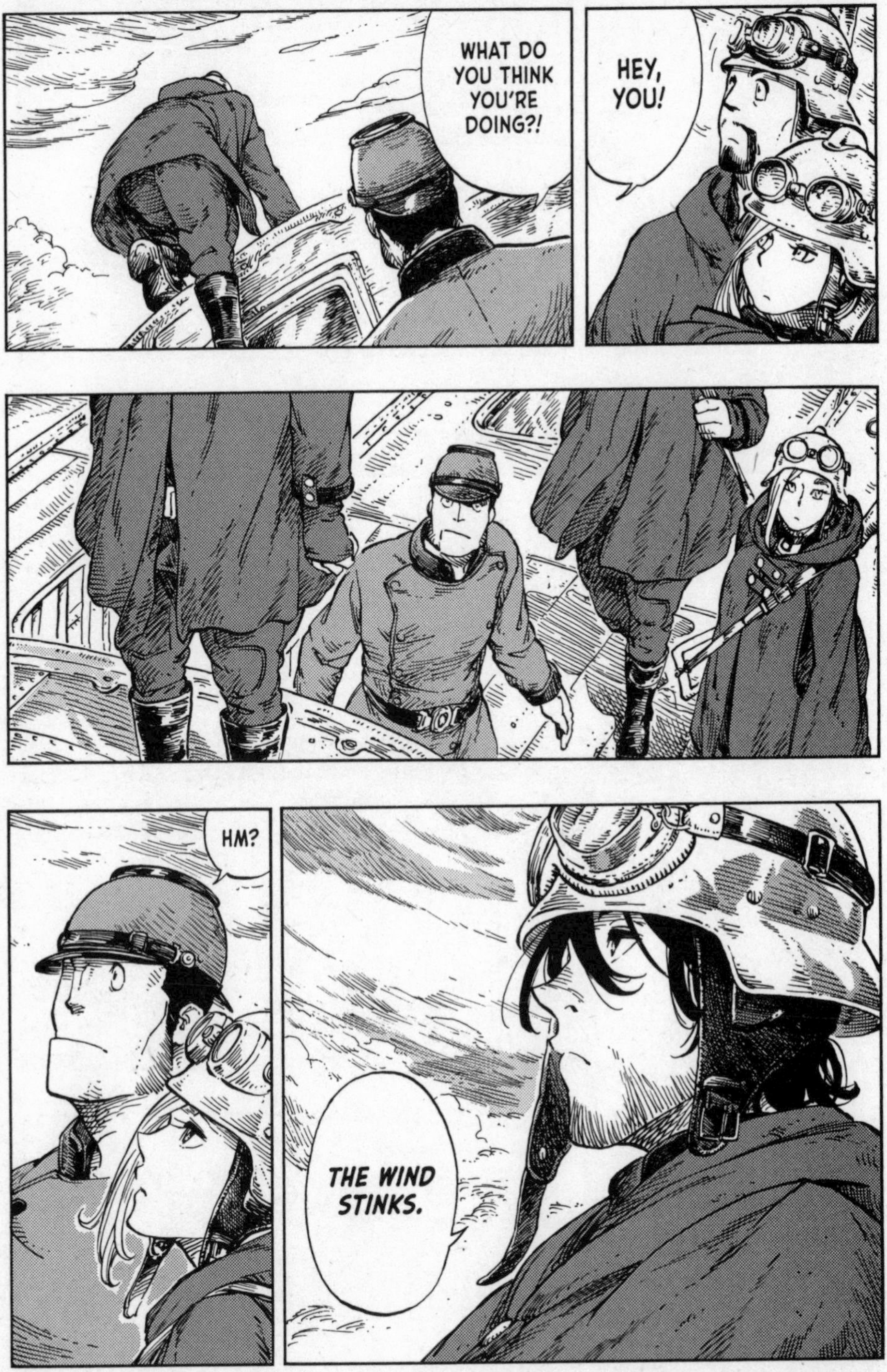
HEY, YOU!
WHAT DO YOU THINK YOU'RE DOING?!
THE WIND STINKS.
HM?

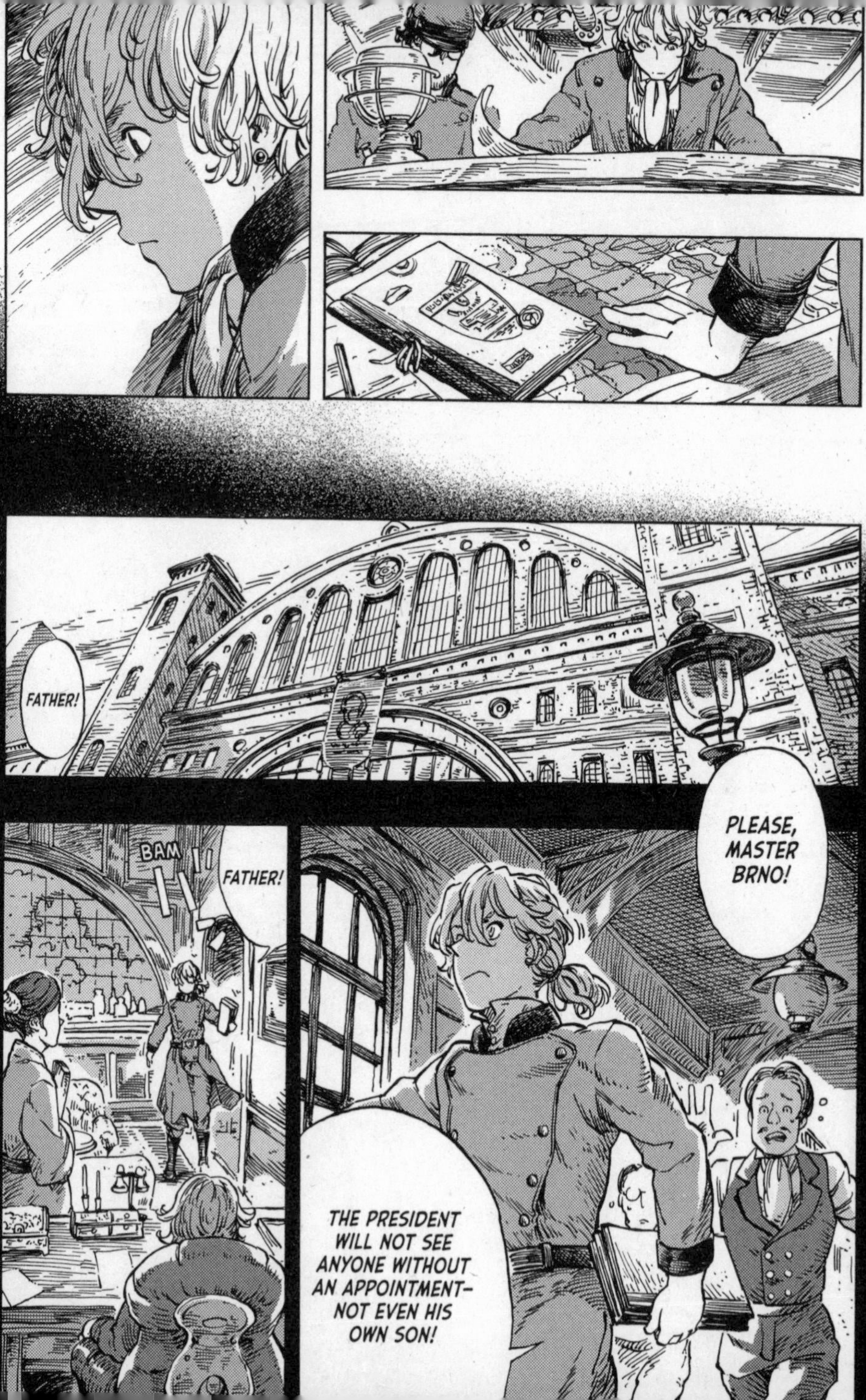
FATHER!
PLEASE, MASTER BRNO!
THE PRESIDENT WILL NOT SEE ANYONE WITHOUT AN APPOINTMENT—NOT EVEN HIS OWN SON!
BAM
FATHER!

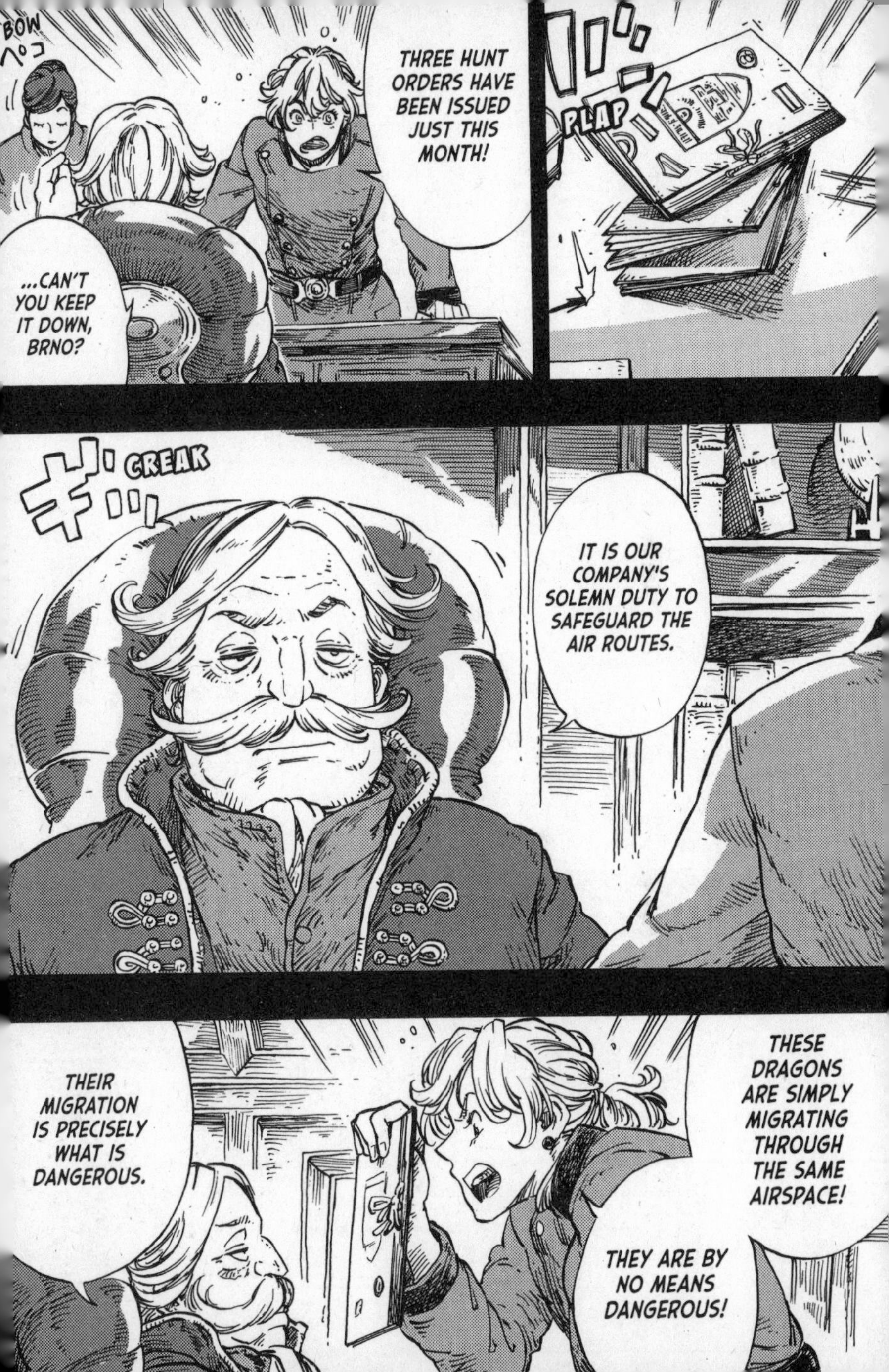
PLAP
THREE HUNT ORDERS HAVE BEEN ISSUED JUST THIS MONTH!
BOW
ペコ
...CAN'T YOU KEEP IT DOWN, BRNO?
CREAK
IT IS OUR COMPANY'S SOLEMN DUTY TO SAFEGUARD THE AIR ROUTES.
THESE DRAGONS ARE SIMPLY MIGRATING THROUGH THE SAME AIRSPACE!
THEY ARE BY NO MEANS DANGEROUS!
THEIR MIGRATION IS PRECISELY WHAT IS DANGEROUS.

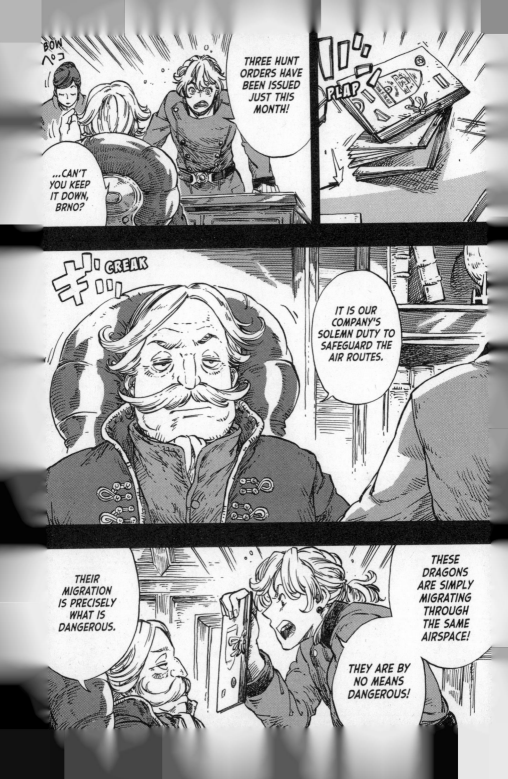

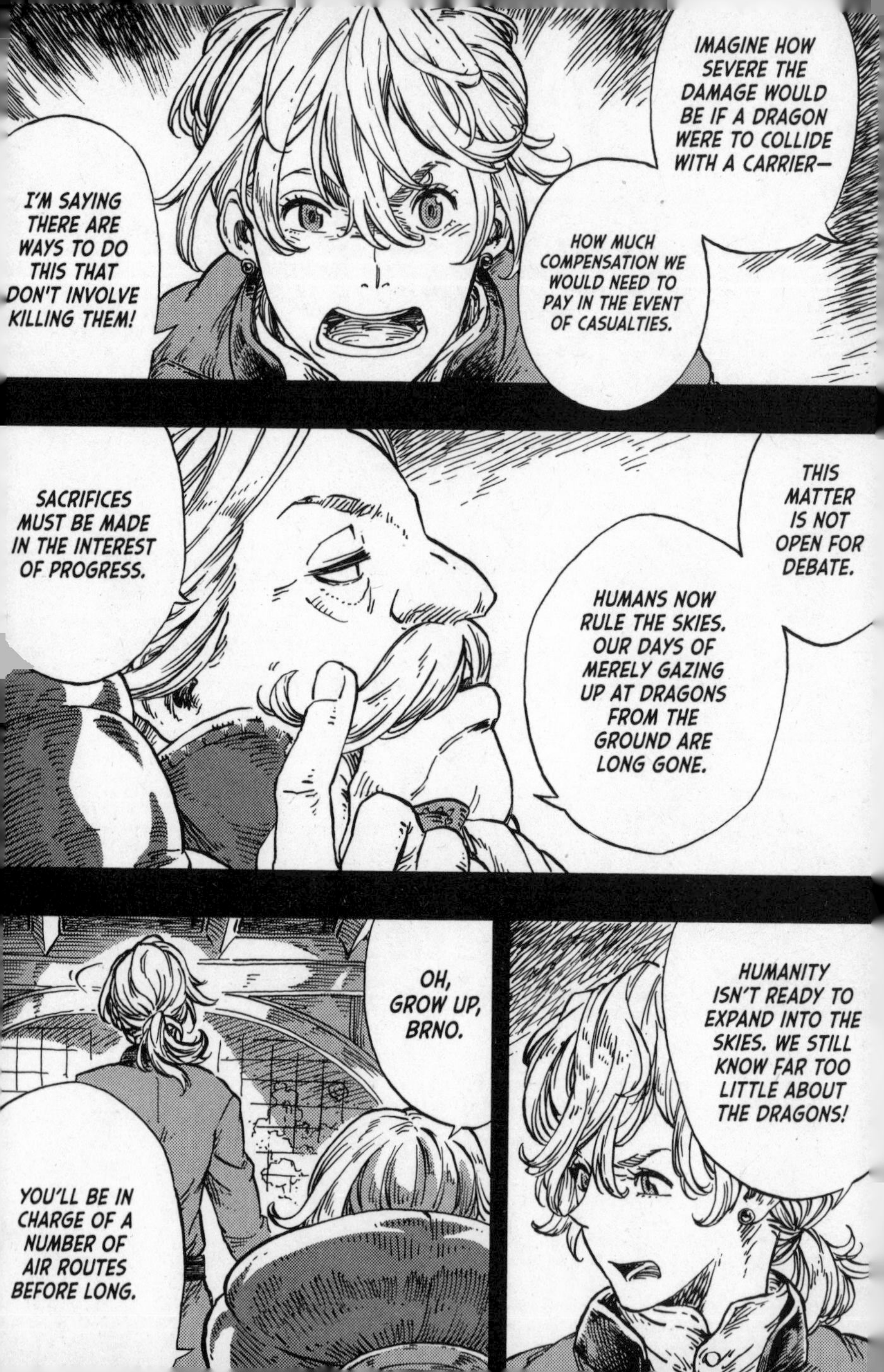
IMAGINE HOW SEVERE THE DAMAGE WOULD BE IF A DRAGON WERE TO COLLIDE WITH A CARRIER—
HOW MUCH COMPENSATION WE WOULD NEED TO PAY IN THE EVENT OF CASUALTIES.
I'M SAYING THERE ARE WAYS TO DO THIS THAT DON'T INVOLVE KILLING THEM!
THIS MATTER IS NOT OPEN FOR DEBATE.
HUMANS NOW RULE THE SKIES. OUR DAYS OF MERELY GAZING UP AT DRAGONS FROM THE GROUND ARE LONG GONE.
SACRIFICES MUST BE MADE IN THE INTEREST OF PROGRESS.
HUMANITY ISN'T READY TO EXPAND INTO THE SKIES. WE STILL KNOW FAR TOO LITTLE ABOUT THE DRAGONS!
OH, GROW UP, BRNO.
YOU'LL BE IN CHARGE OF A NUMBER OF AIR ROUTES BEFORE LONG.

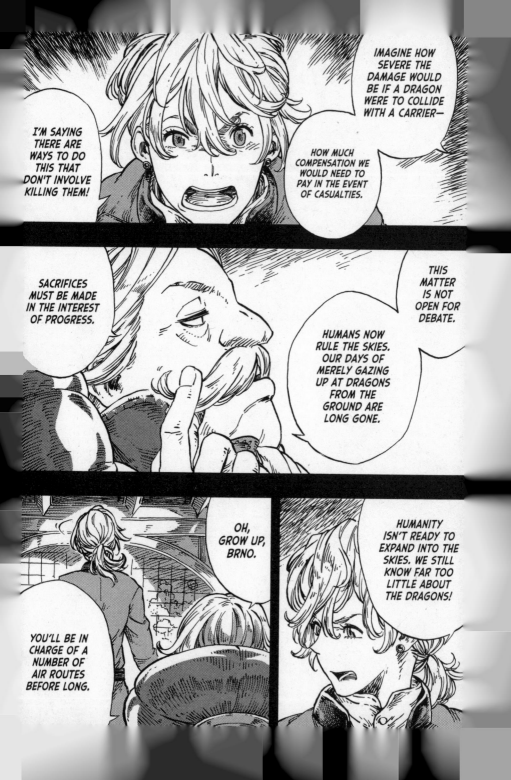

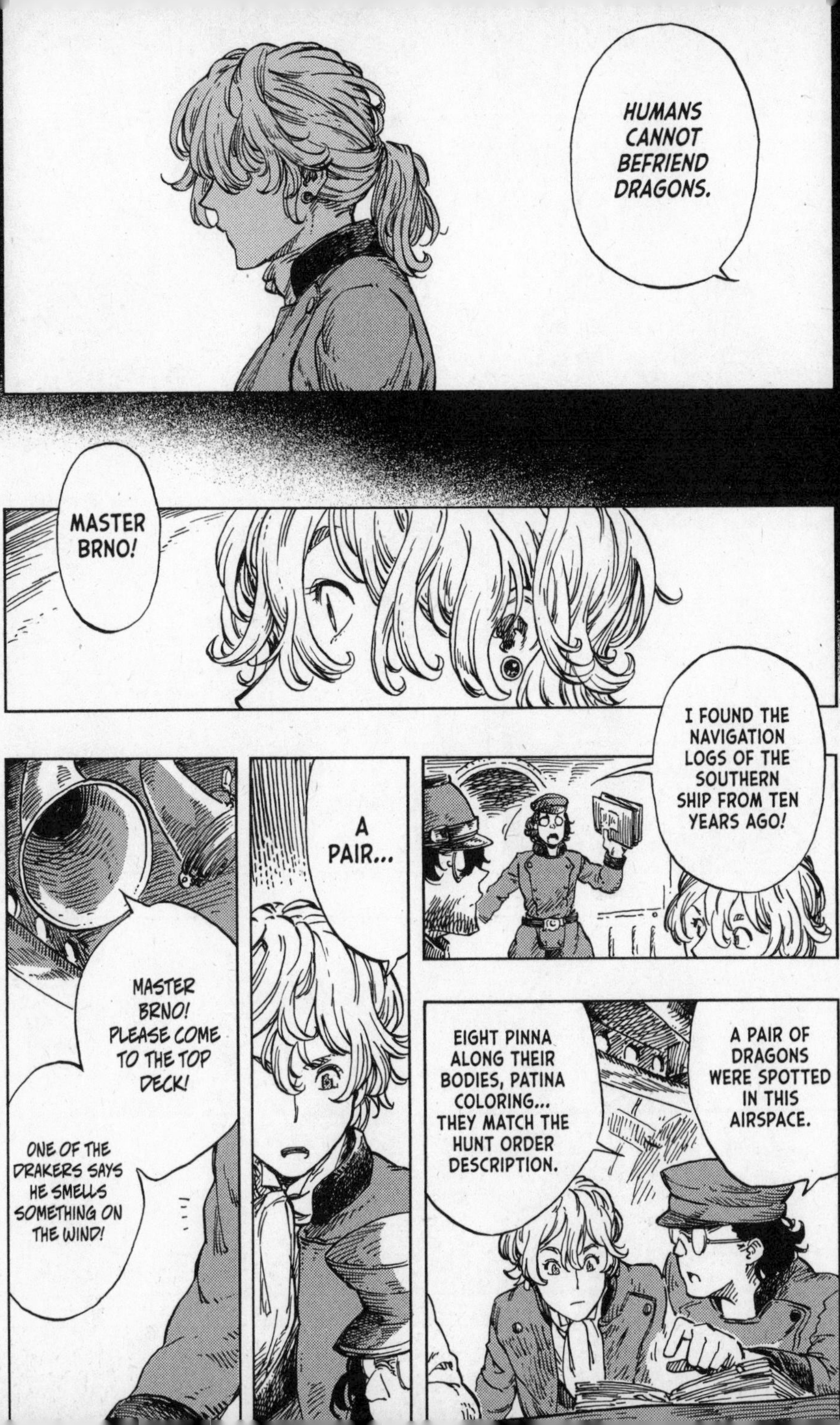
HUMANS CANNOT BEFRIEND DRAGONS.
MASTER BRNO!
I FOUND THE NAVIGATION LOGS OF THE SOUTHERN SHIP FROM TEN YEARS AGO!
A PAIR OF DRAGONS WERE SPOTTED IN THIS AIRSPACE.
EIGHT PINNA ALONG THEIR BODIES, PATINA COLORING... THEY MATCH THE HUNT ORDER DESCRIPTION.
A PAIR...
MASTER BRNO! PLEASE COME TO THE TOP DECK!
ONE OF THE DRAKERS SAYS HE SMELLS SOMETHING ON THE WIND!

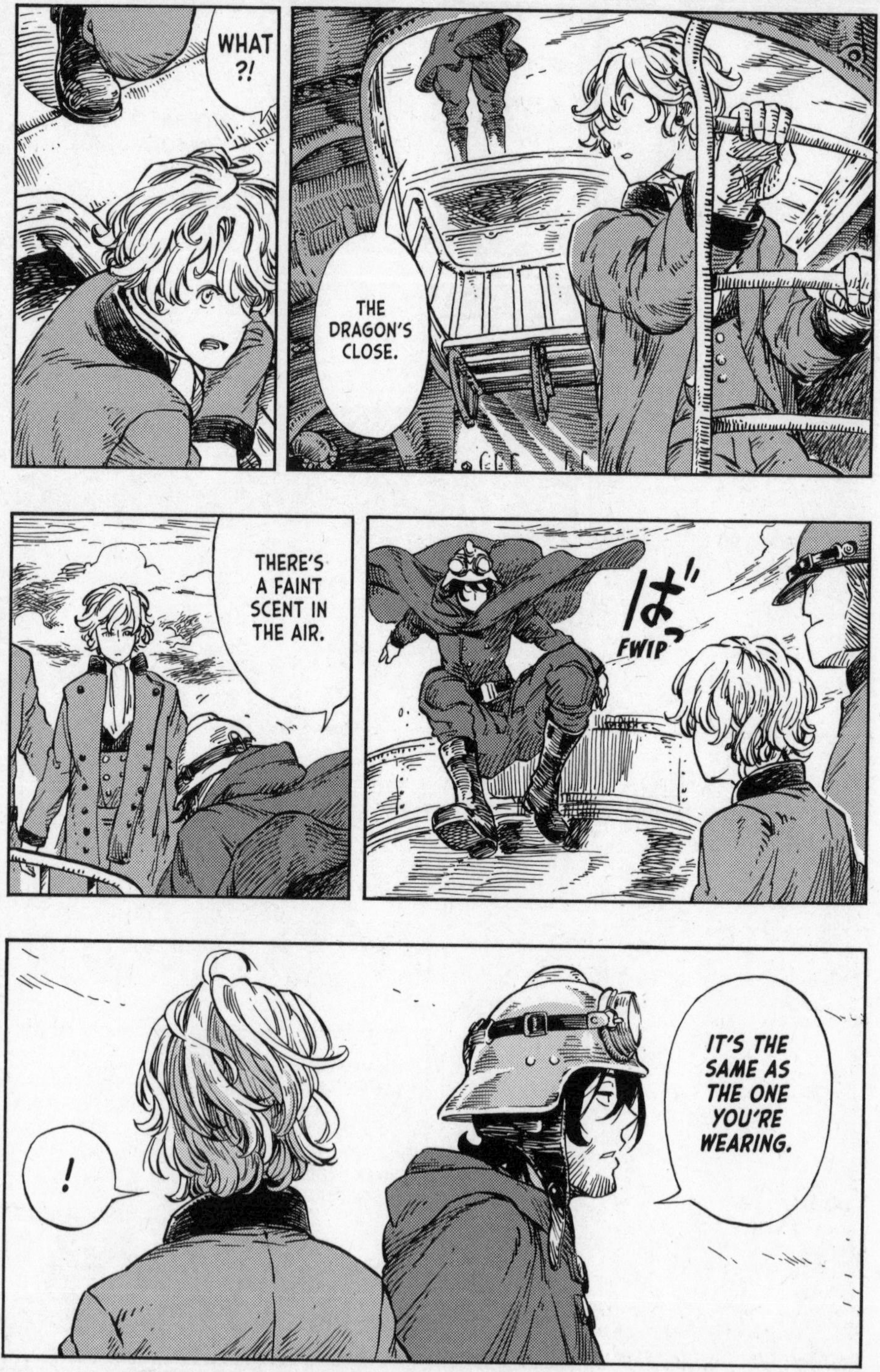
THE DRAGON'S CLOSE.
WHAT ?!
ばっ
FWIP
THERE'S A FAINT SCENT IN THE AIR.
IT'S THE SAME AS THE ONE YOU'RE WEARING.
!

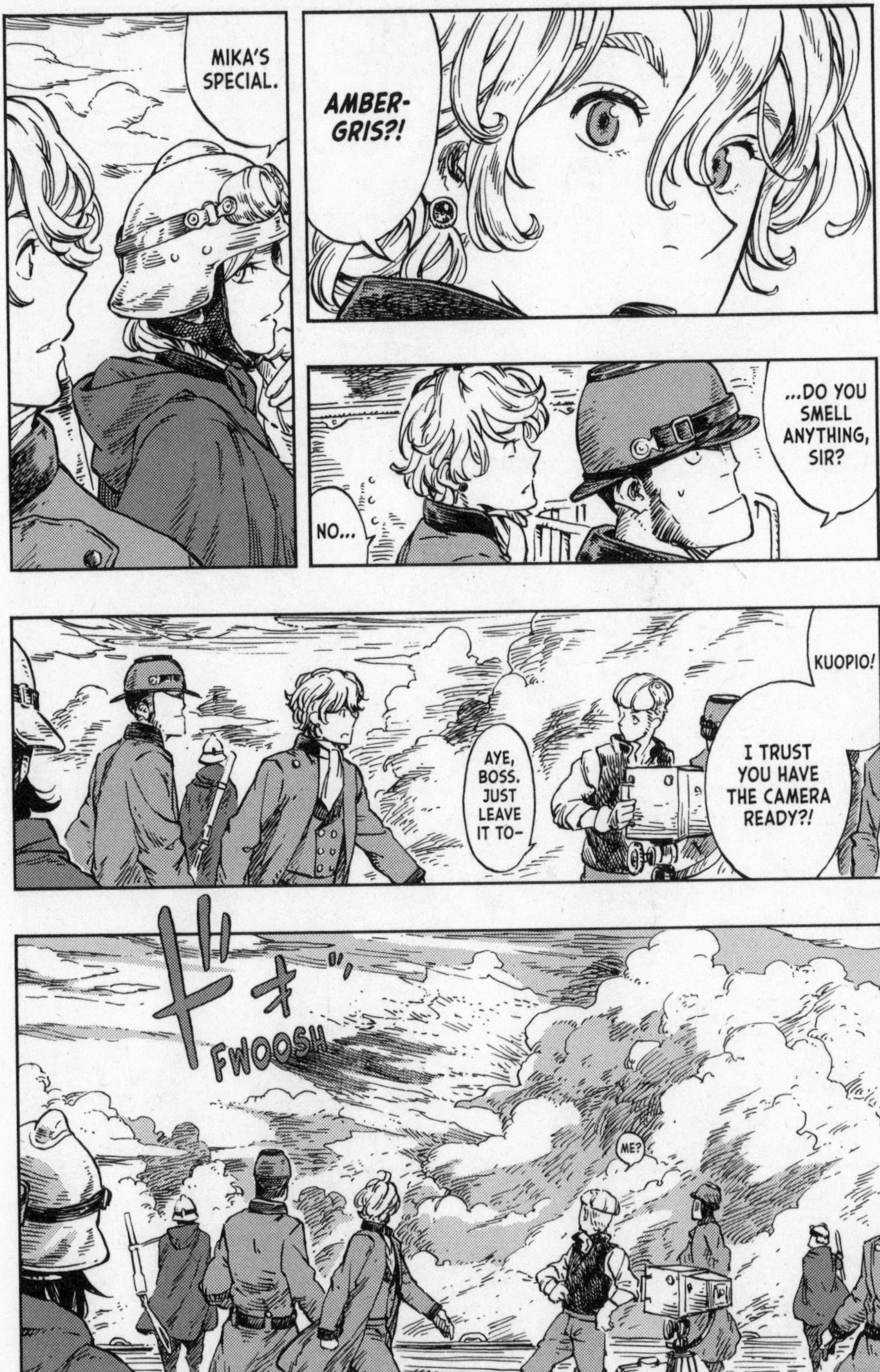
AMBER-GRIS?!
...DO YOU SMELL ANYTHING, SIR?
NO...
MIKA'S SPECIAL.
KUOPIO!
I TRUST YOU HAVE THE CAMERA READY?!
AYE, BOSS. JUST LEAVE IT TO-
FWOOSH
ME?

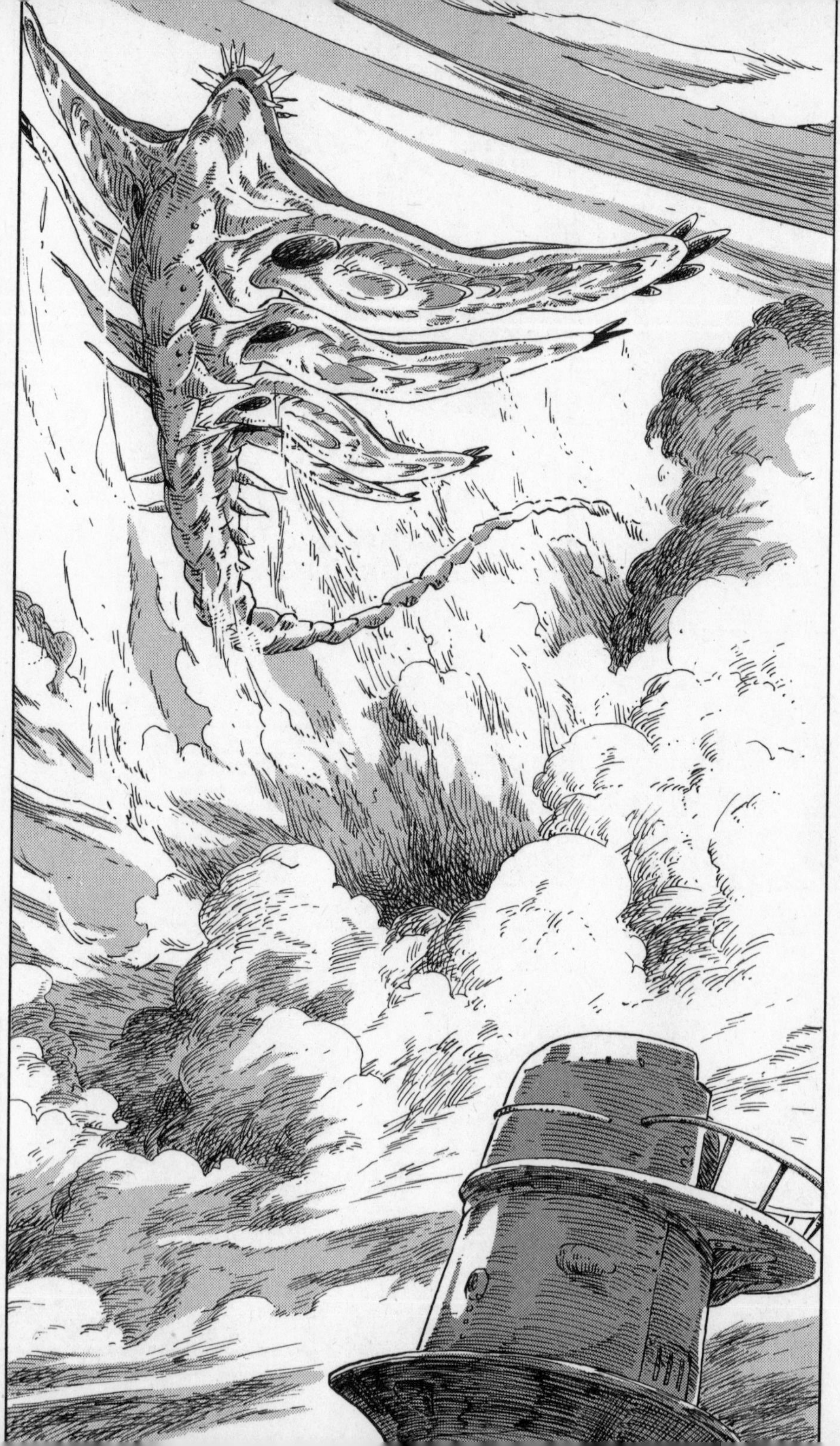

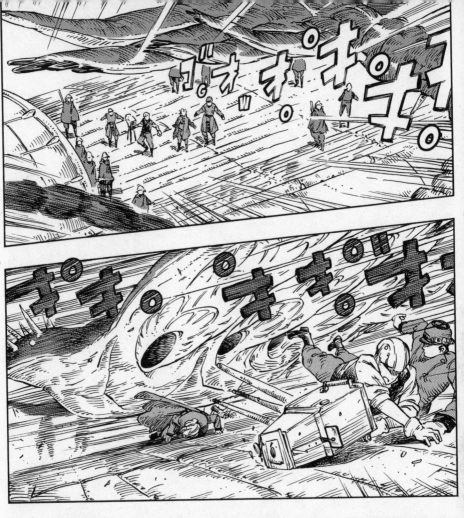

MASTER BRNO!

TCH....!

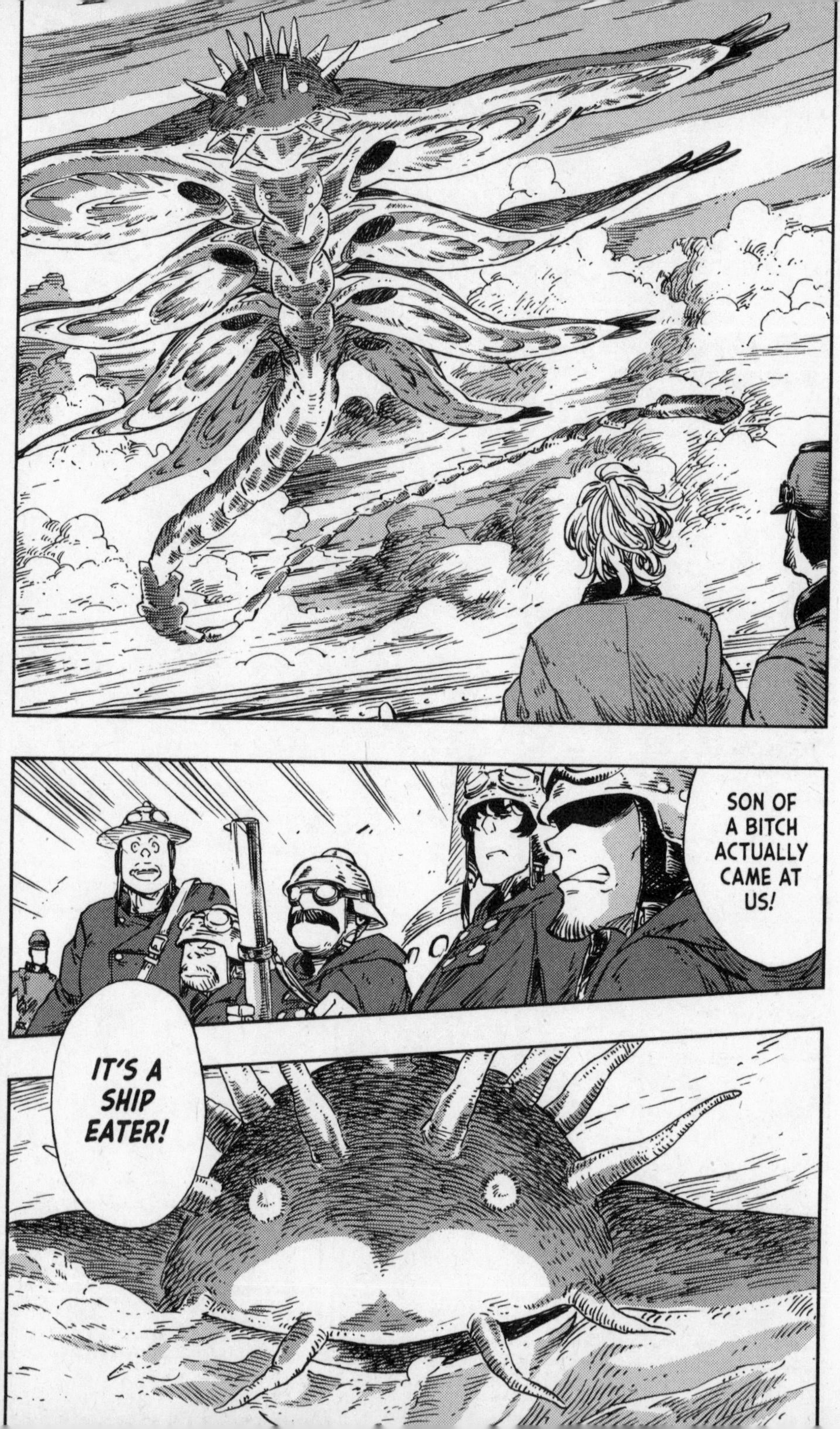
SON OF A BITCH ACTUALLY CAME AT US!
IT'S A SHIP EATER!

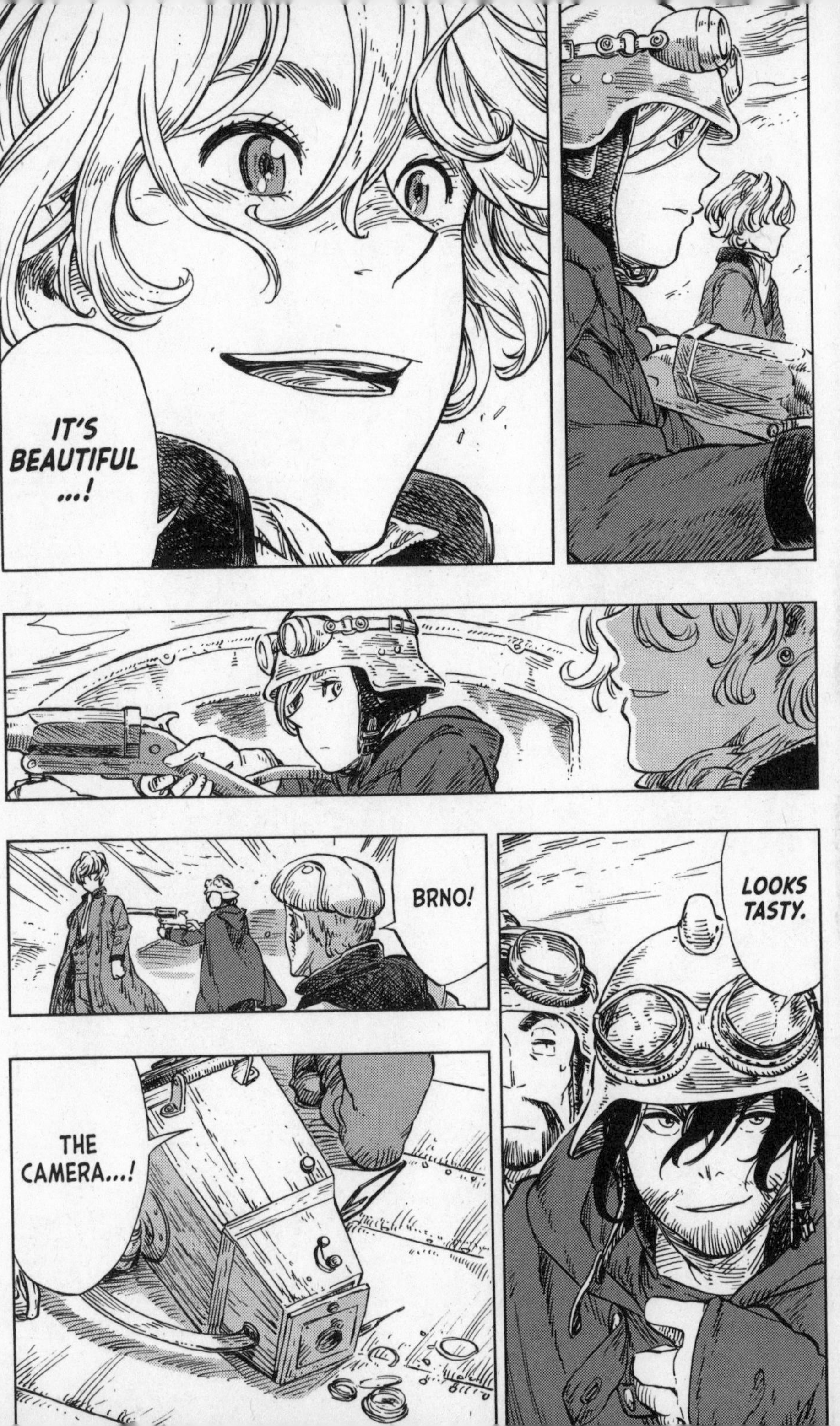
IT'S BEAUTIFUL ...!
LOOKS TASTY.
BRNO!
THE CAMERA...!

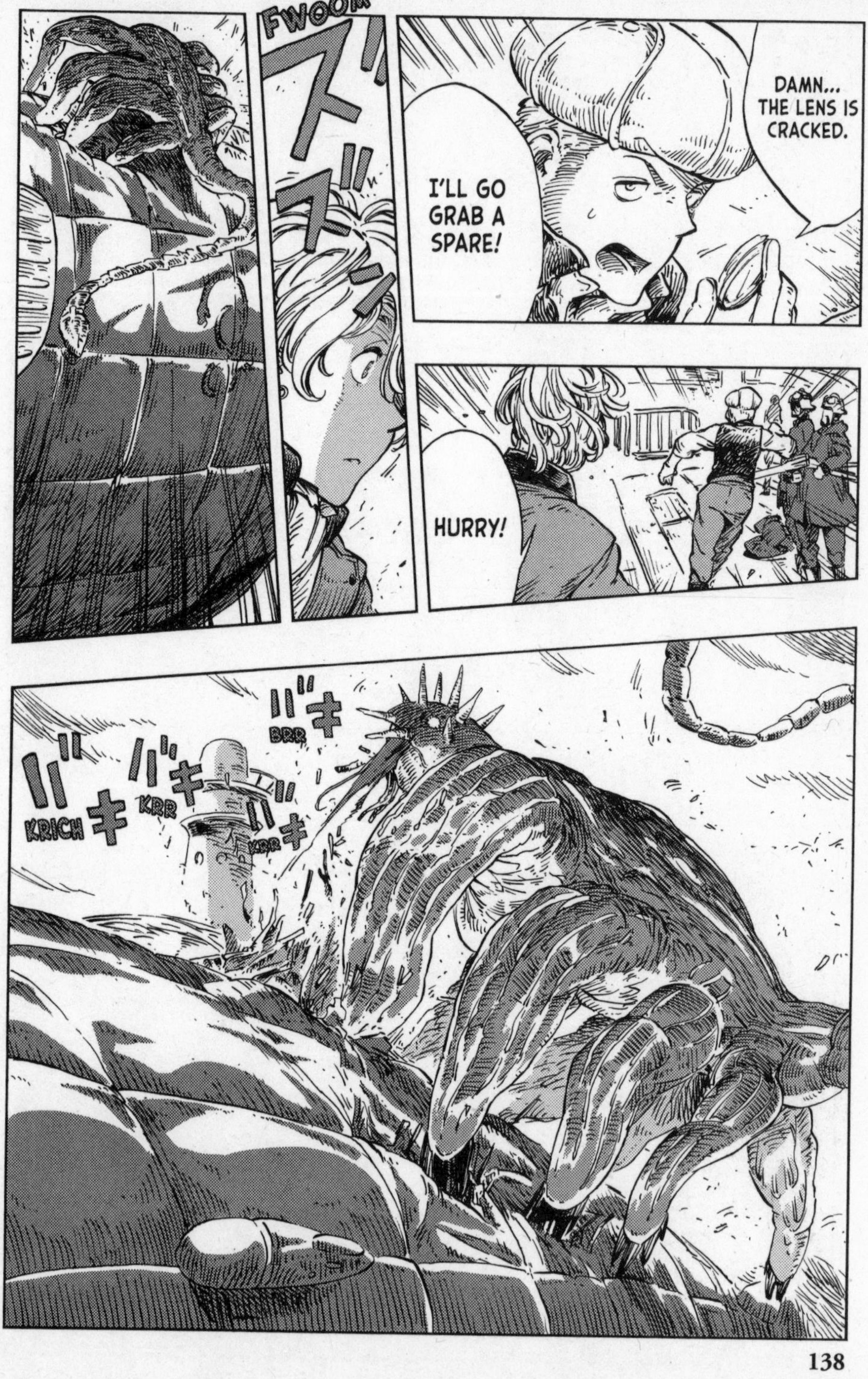

DAMN... THE LENS IS CRACKED.
I'LL GO GRAB A SPARE!
HURRY!
FWOOM
BRR
KRR
KRR
KRICH

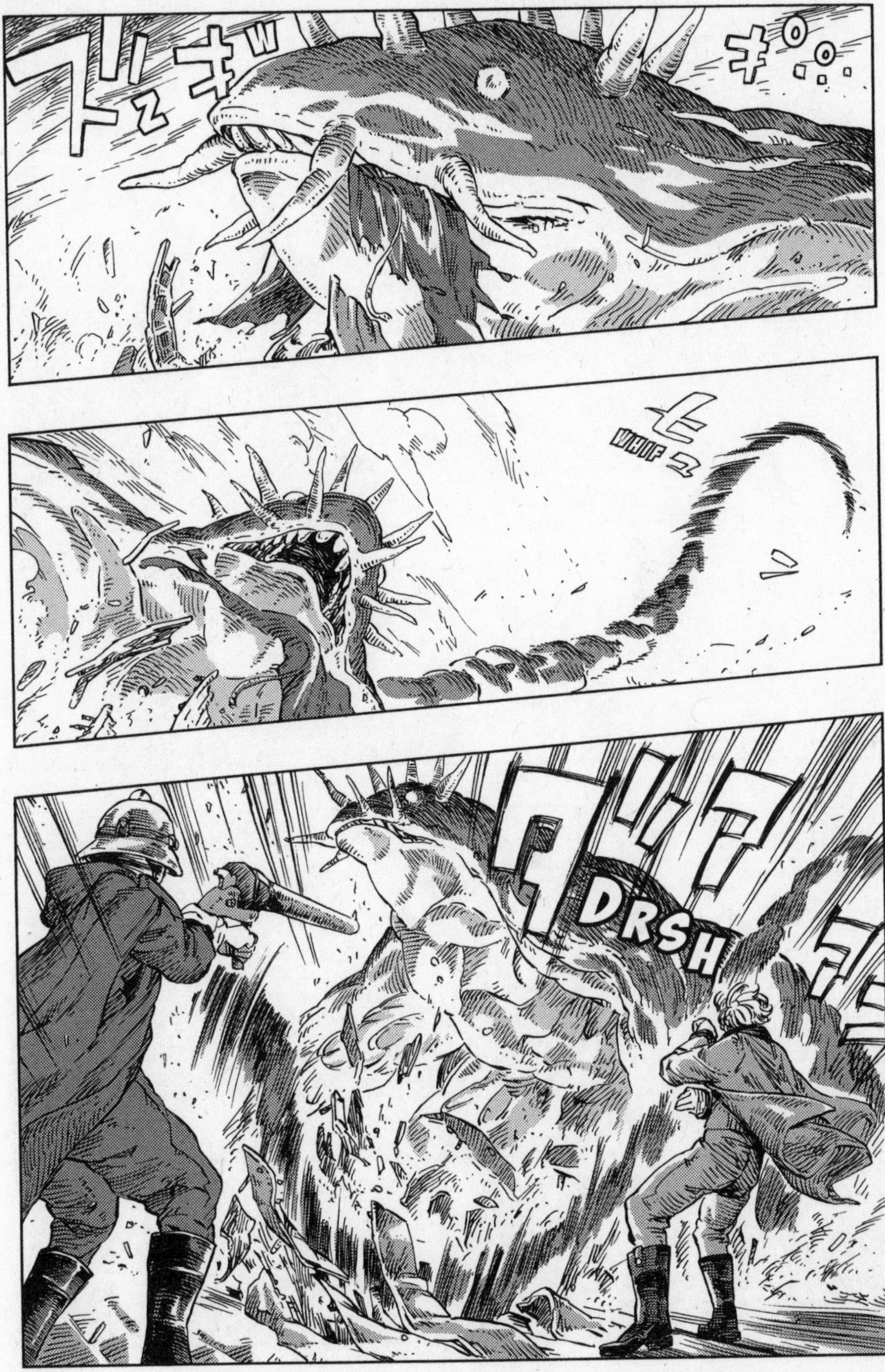
WHIF
DRSH

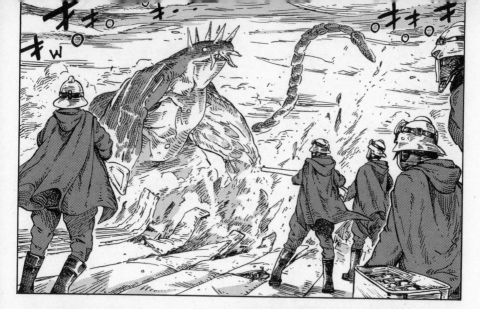

IT'S OUT OF ITS MIND!
WHAT'S WITH THIS SMELL?
IT'S SICKLY SWEET...
WE'RE GONNA HAVE TO TAKE IT DOWN!
FIRE!
HOLD YOUR FIRE!
SAY WHAT?!
BWAH

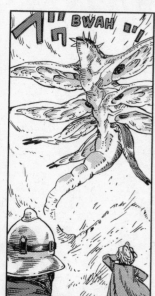

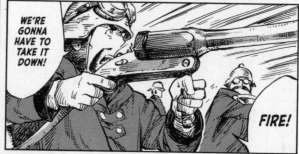

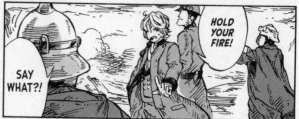

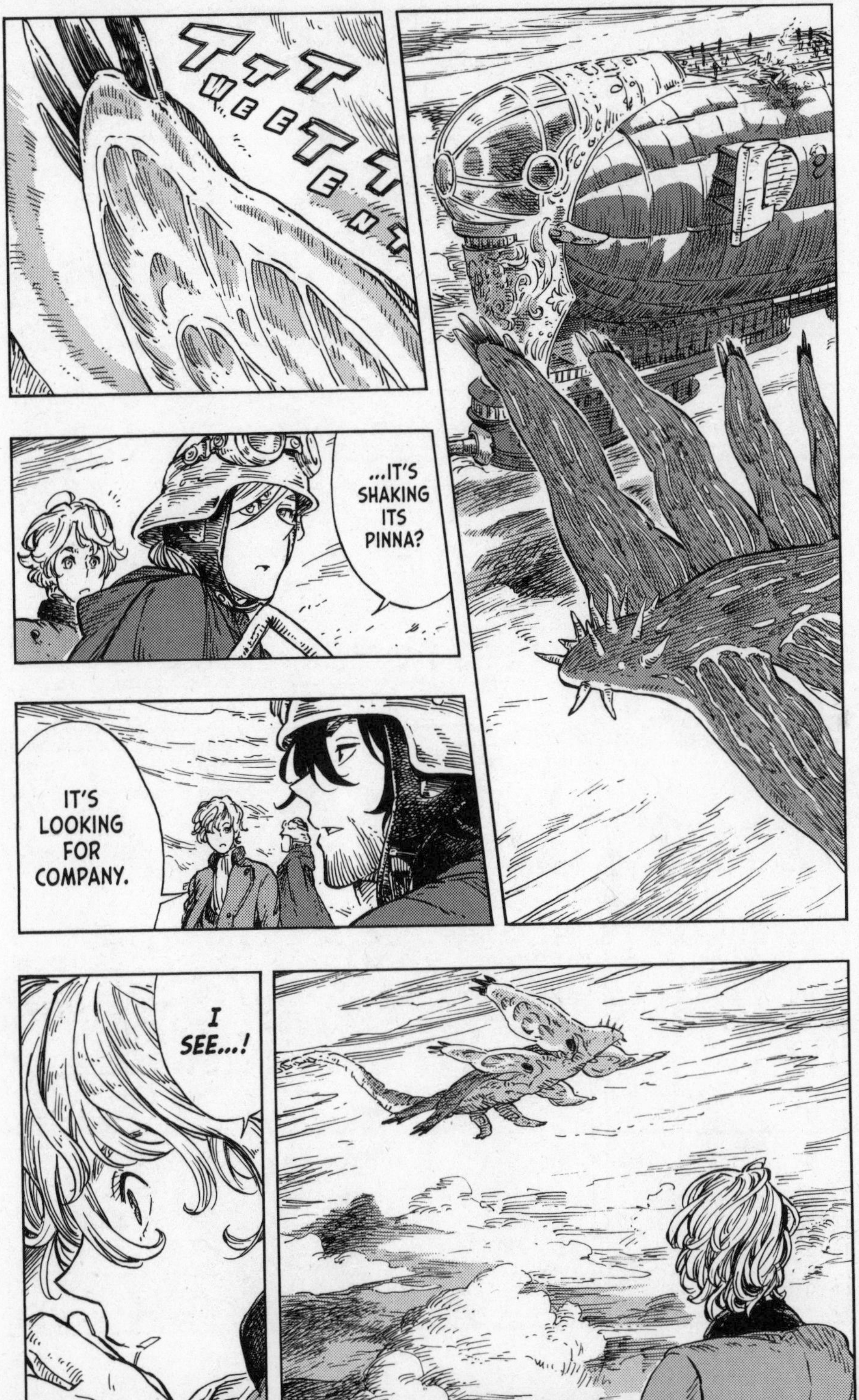
TTTWEETENT
...IT'S SHAKING ITS PINNA?
IT'S LOOKING FOR COMPANY.
I SEE...!

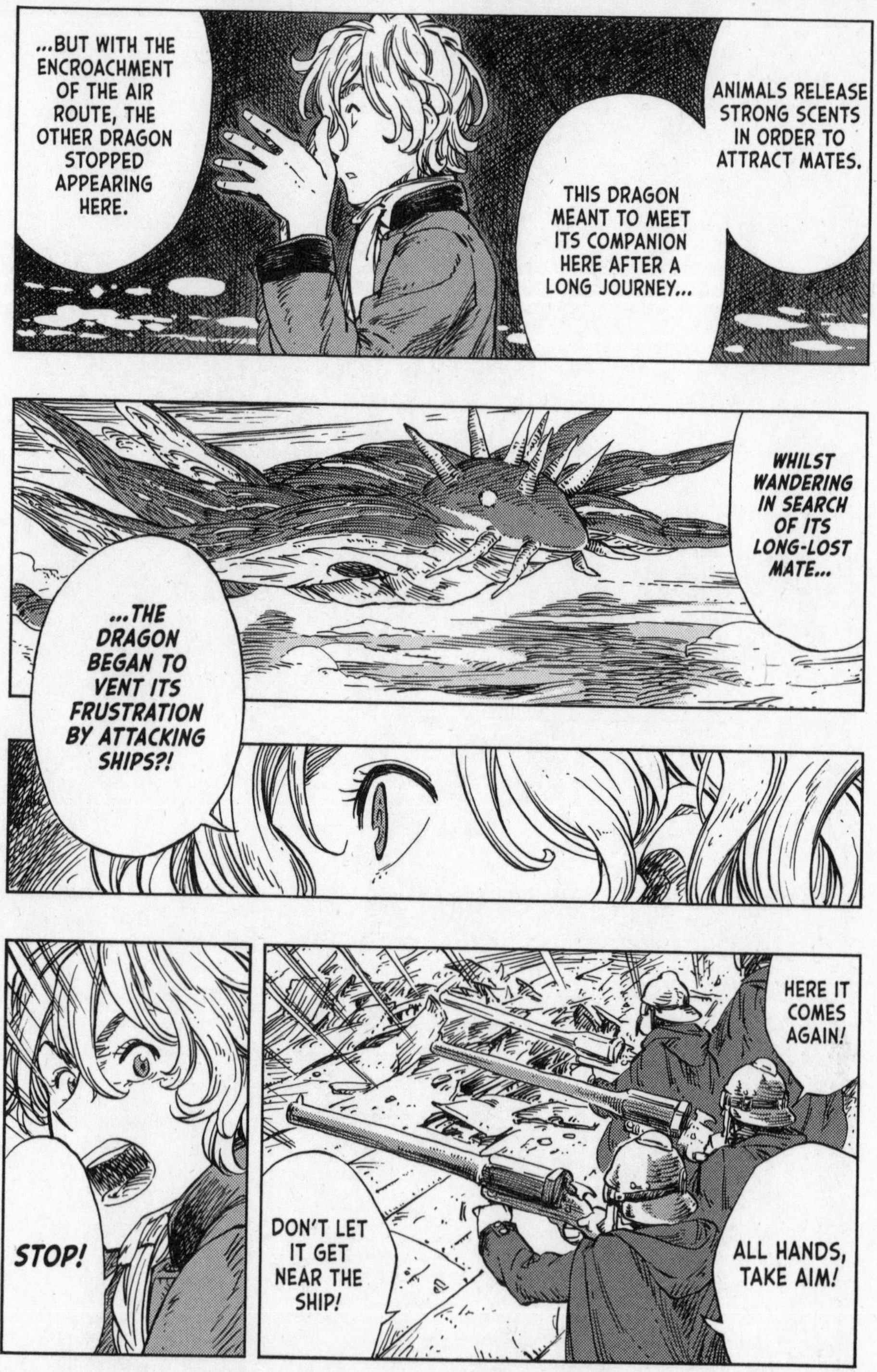
ANIMALS RELEASE STRONG SCENTS IN ORDER TO ATTRACT MATES.
THIS DRAGON MEANT TO MEET ITS COMPANION HERE AFTER A LONG JOURNEY...
...BUT WITH THE ENCROACHMENT OF THE AIR ROUTE, THE OTHER DRAGON STOPPED APPEARING HERE.
WHILST WANDERING IN SEARCH OF ITS LONG-LOST MATE...
...THE DRAGON BEGAN TO VENT ITS FRUSTRATION BY ATTACKING SHIPS?!
HERE IT COMES AGAIN!
ALL HANDS, TAKE AIM!
DON'T LET IT GET NEAR THE SHIP!
STOP!

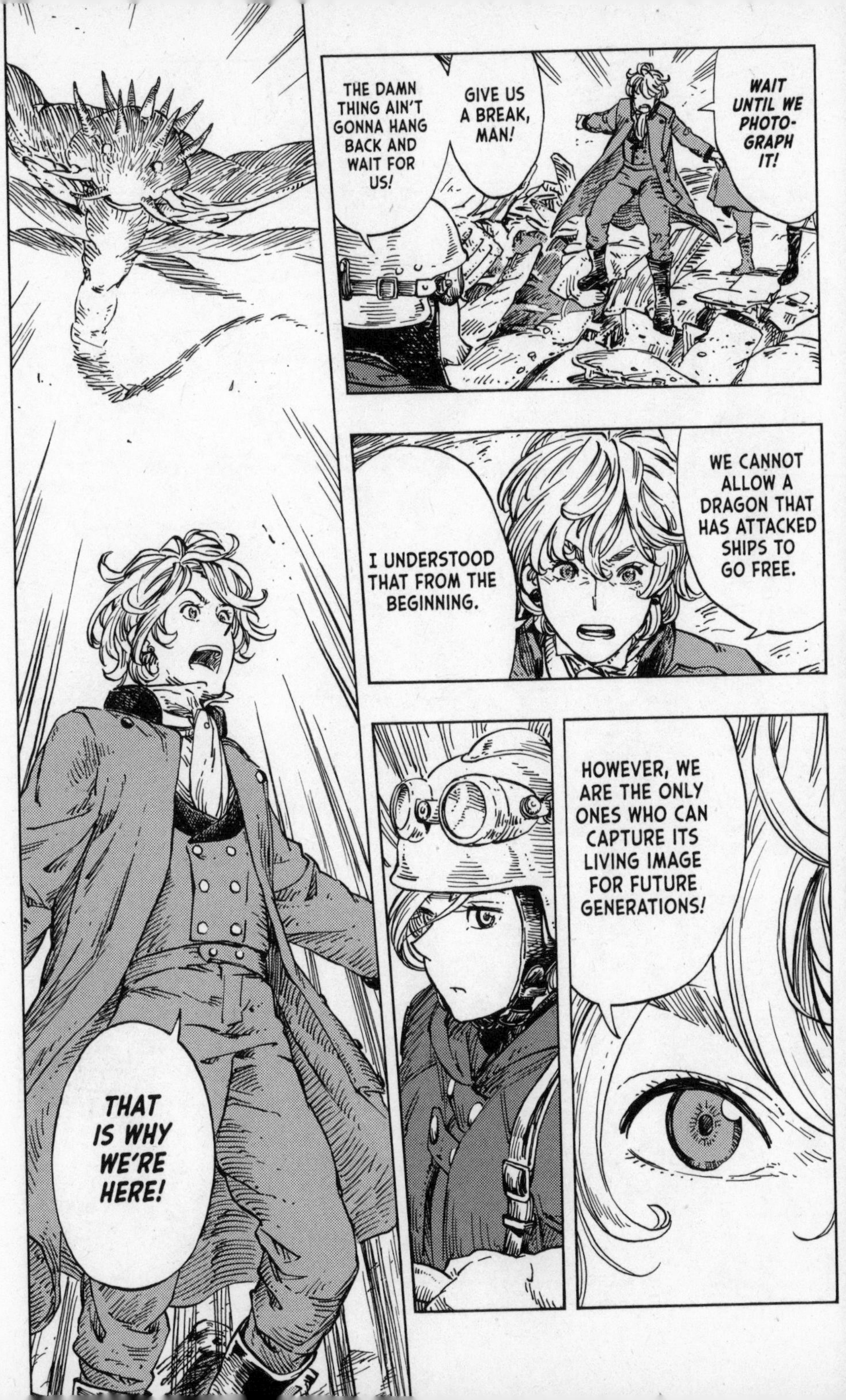
WAIT UNTIL WE PHOTOGRAPH IT!
GIVE US A BREAK, MAN!
THE DAMN THING AIN'T GONNA HANG BACK AND WAIT FOR US!
WE CANNOT ALLOW A DRAGON THAT HAS ATTACKED SHIPS TO GO FREE.
I UNDERSTOOD THAT FROM THE BEGINNING.
HOWEVER, WE ARE THE ONLY ONES WHO CAN CAPTURE ITS LIVING IMAGE FOR FUTURE GENERATIONS!
THAT IS WHY WE'RE HERE!

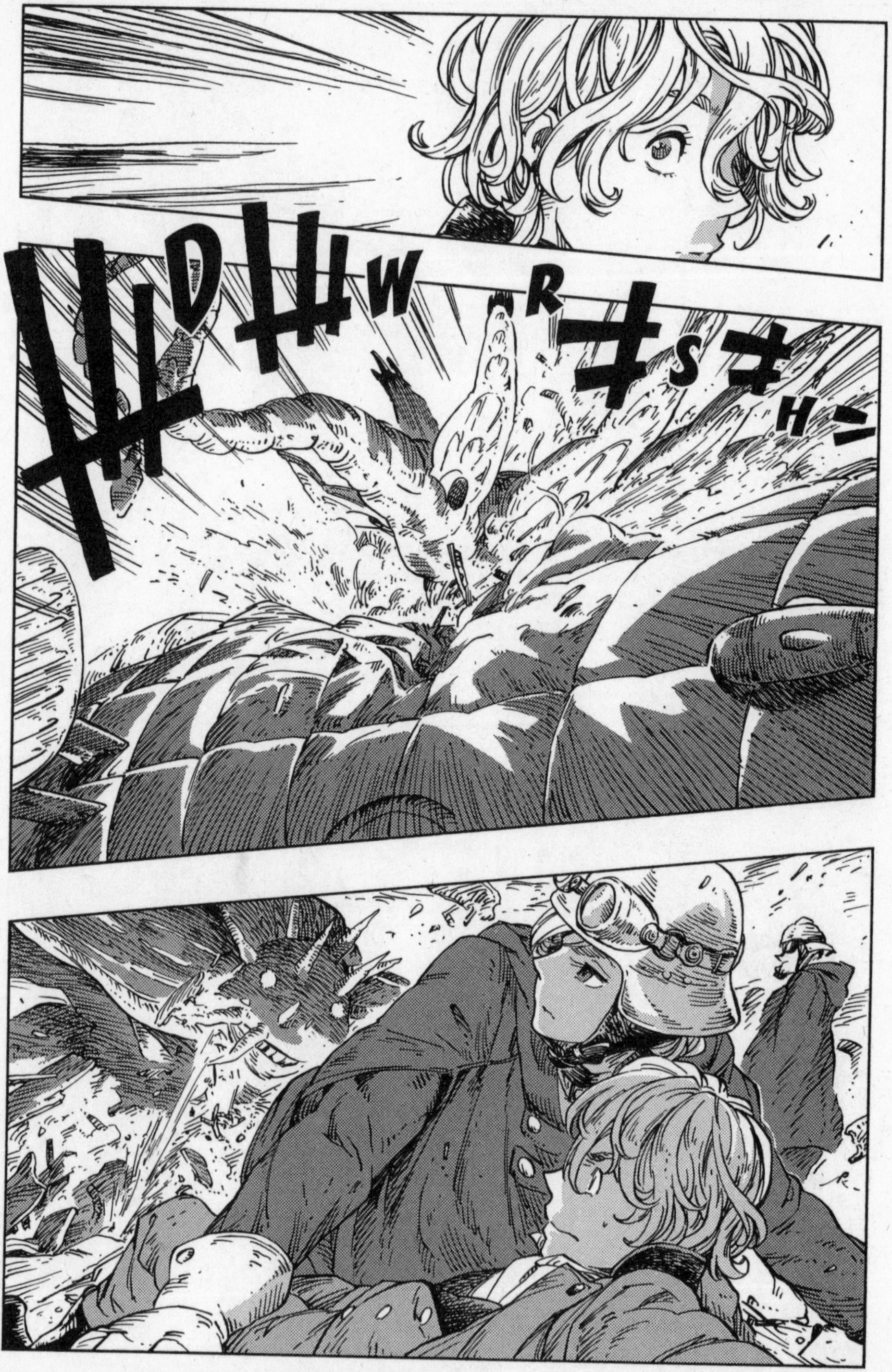
DWRSH

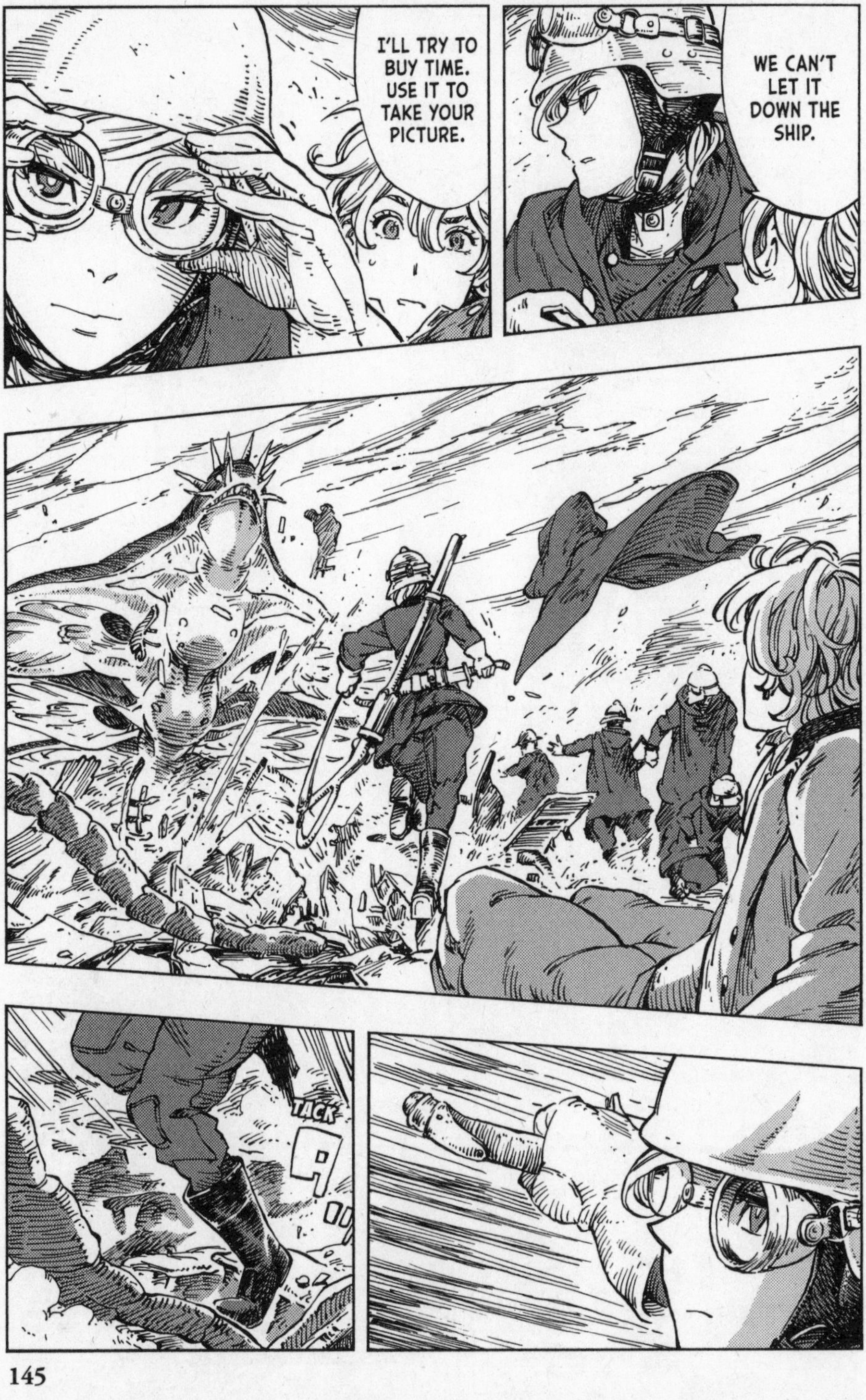
WE CAN'T LET IT DOWN THE SHIP.
I'LL TRY TO BUY TIME. USE IT TO TAKE YOUR PICTURE.
TACK

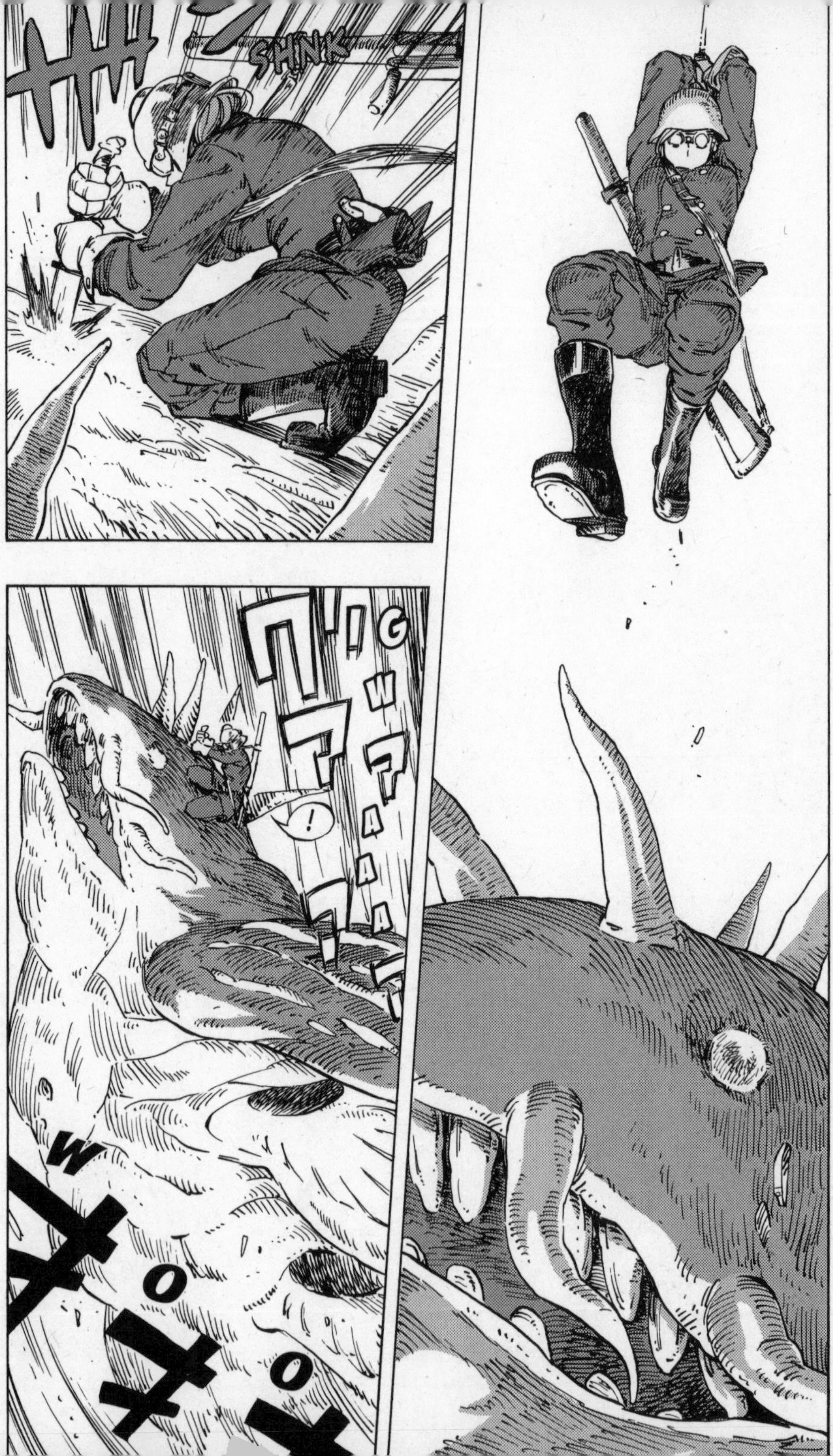
SHINK
GWAAA
!
WOO

THE HELL'S SHE DOING?!

CLATR

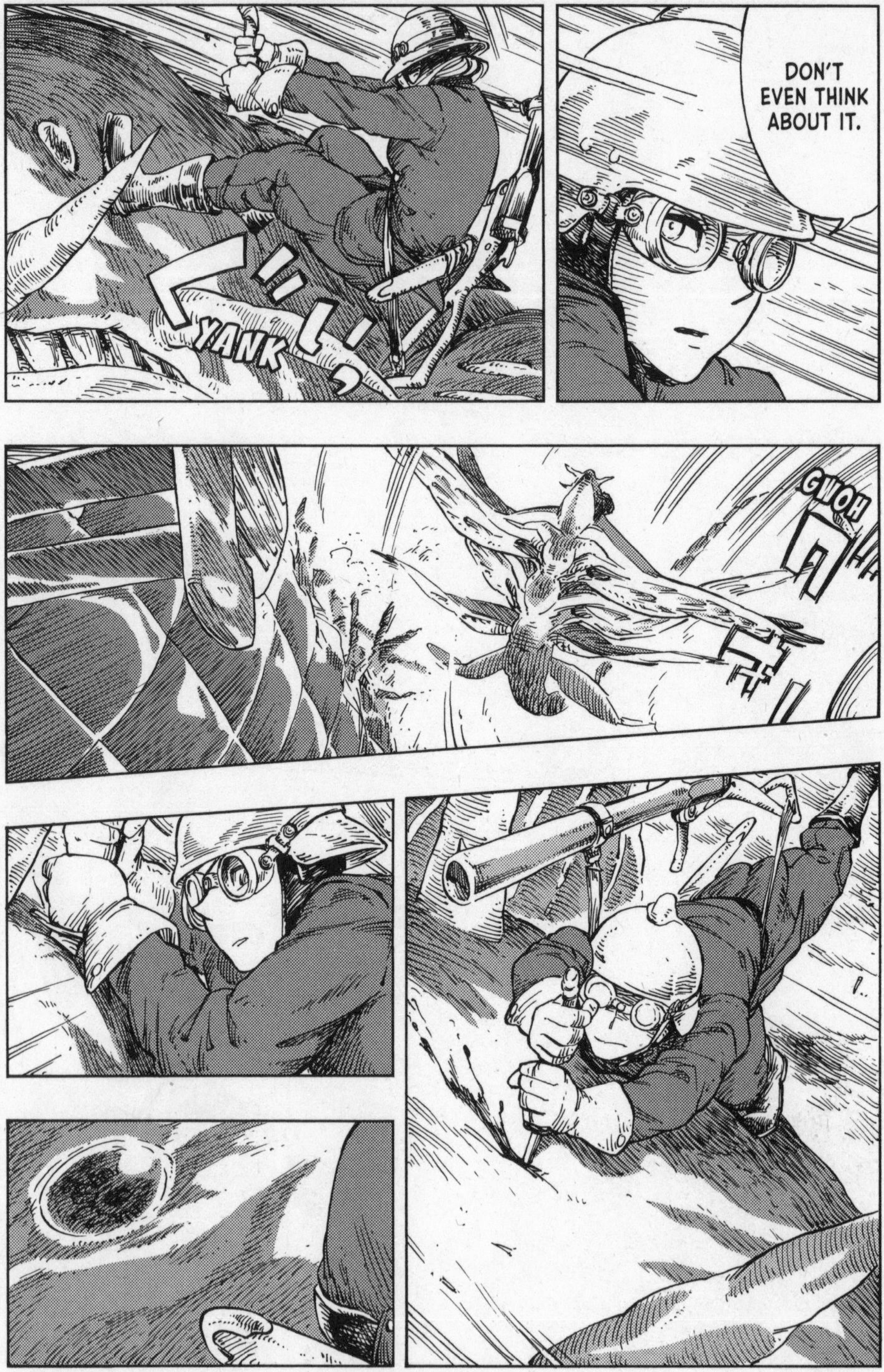
DON'T
EVEN THINK
ABOUT IT.
YANK
GWOH

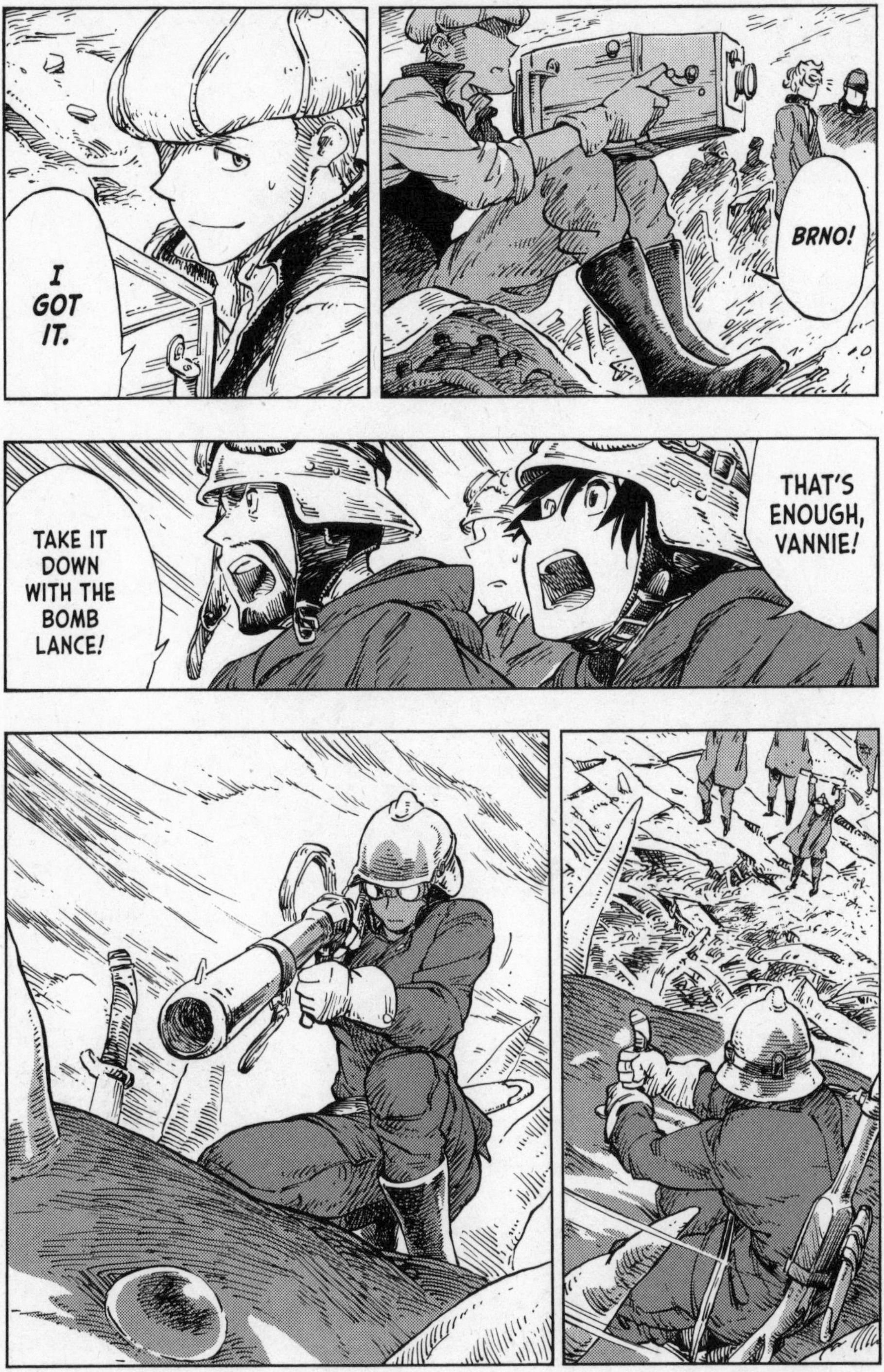
BRNO!
I GOT IT.
THAT'S ENOUGH, VANNIE!
TAKE IT DOWN WITH THE BOMB LANCE!

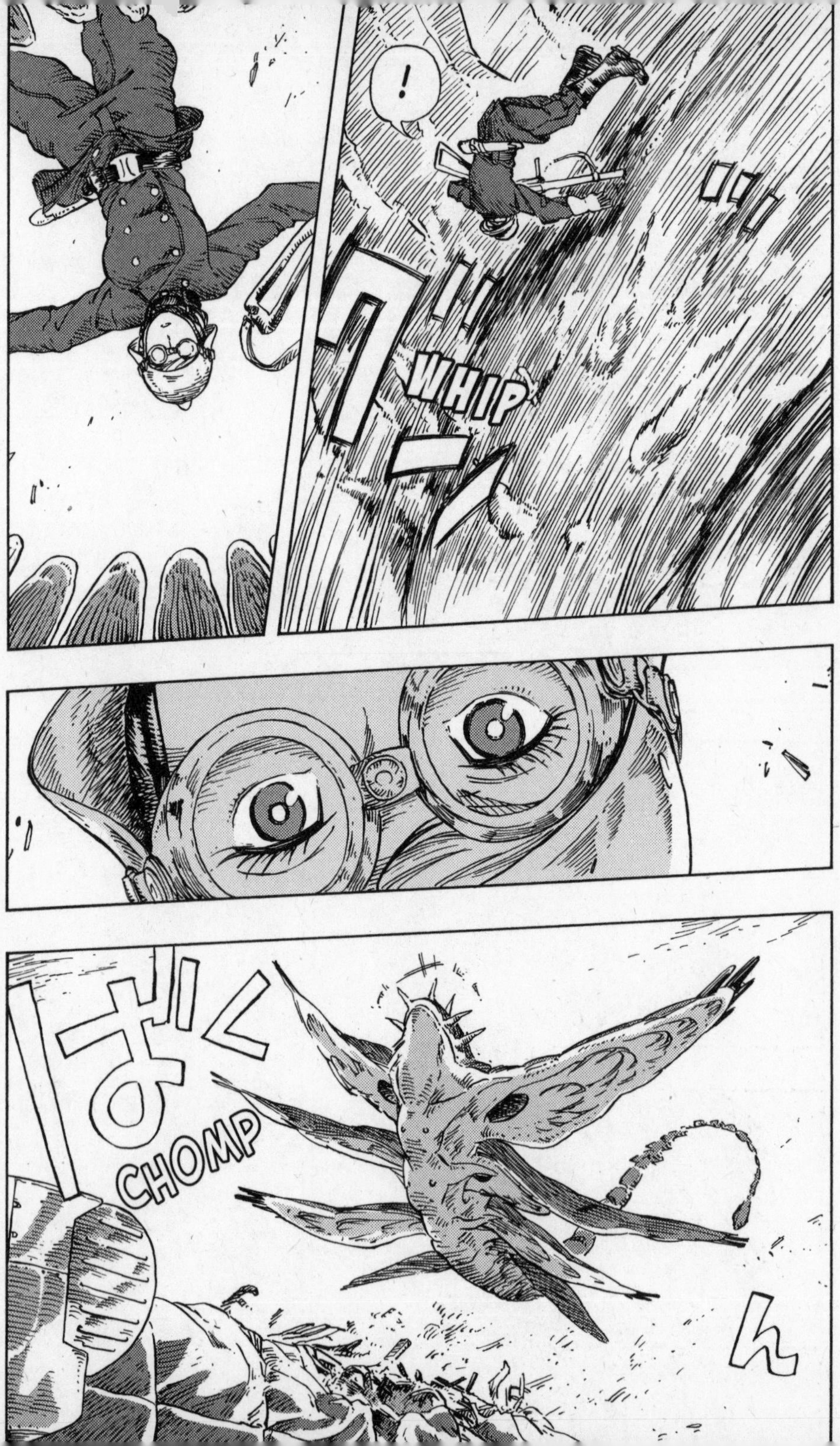
!
WHIP
CHOMP

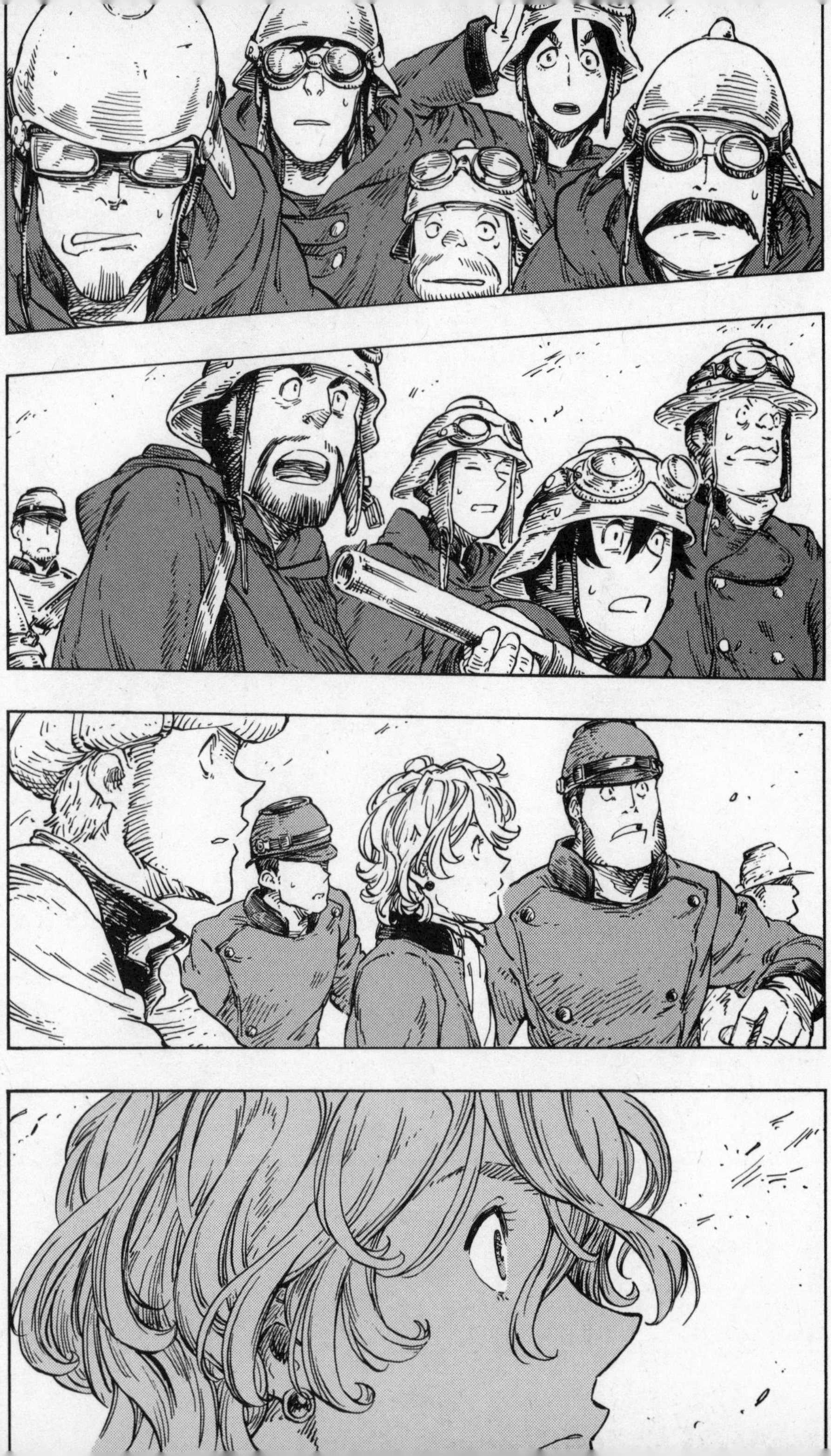

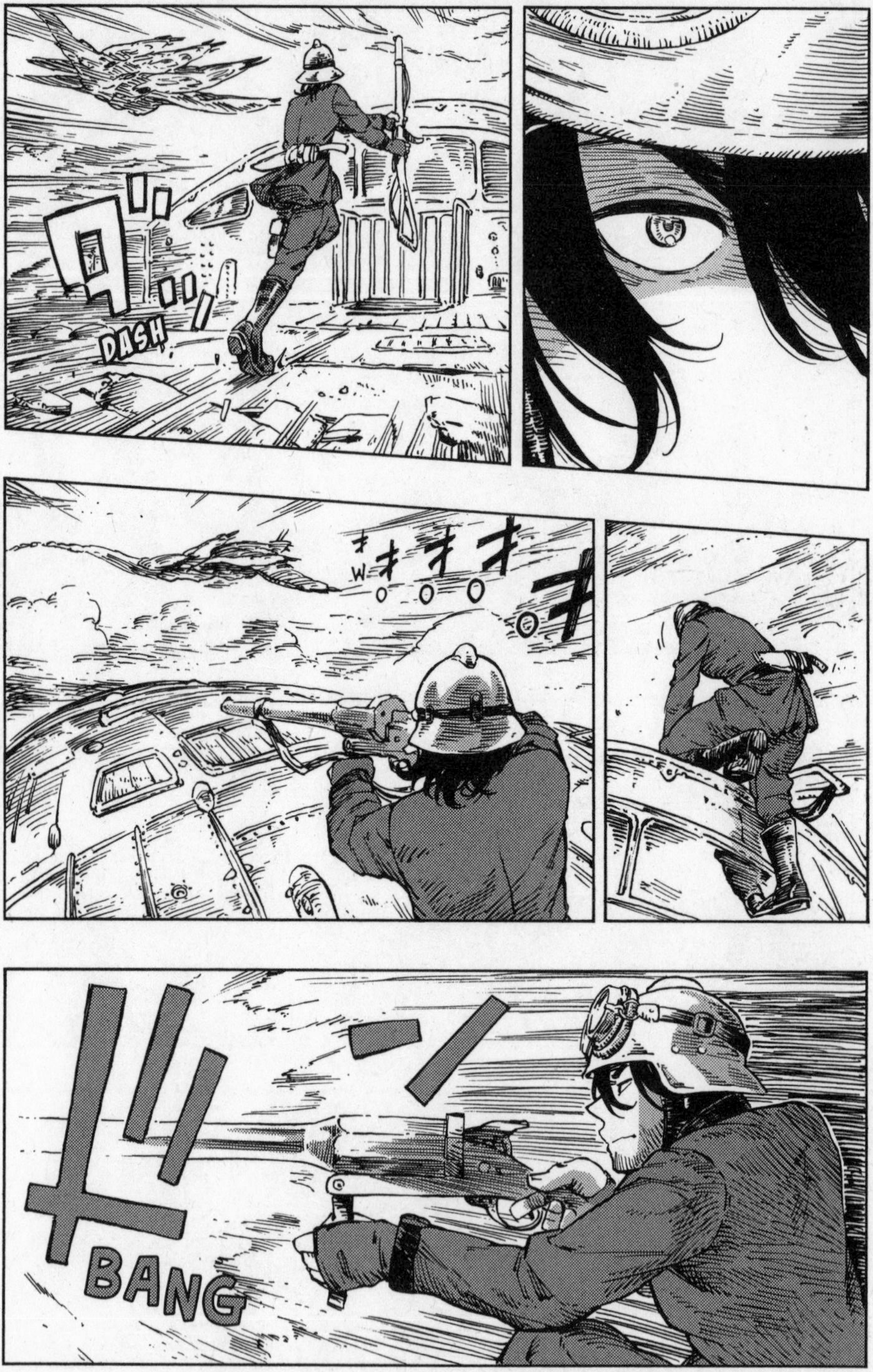
DASH
BANG

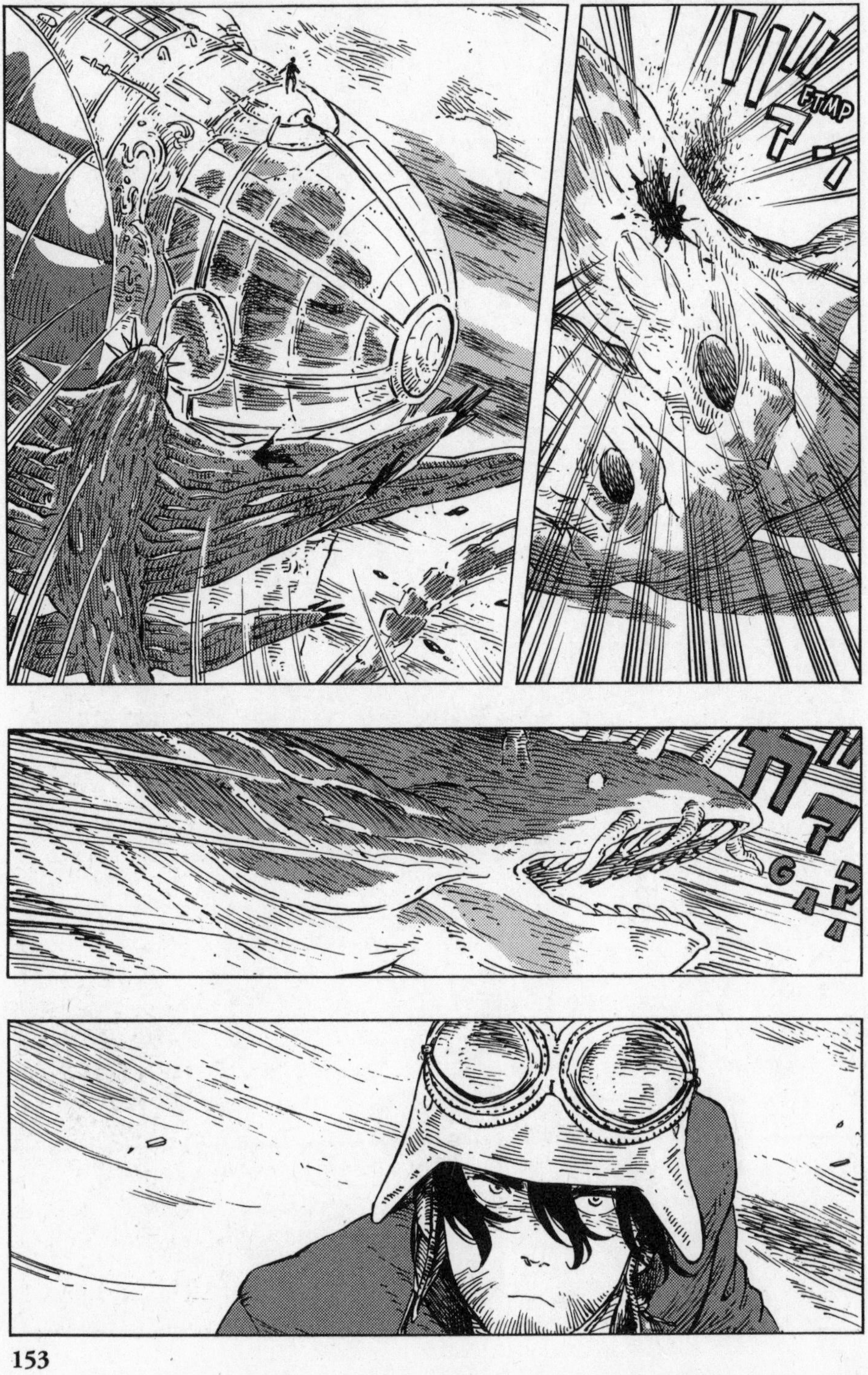
FTMP
GA

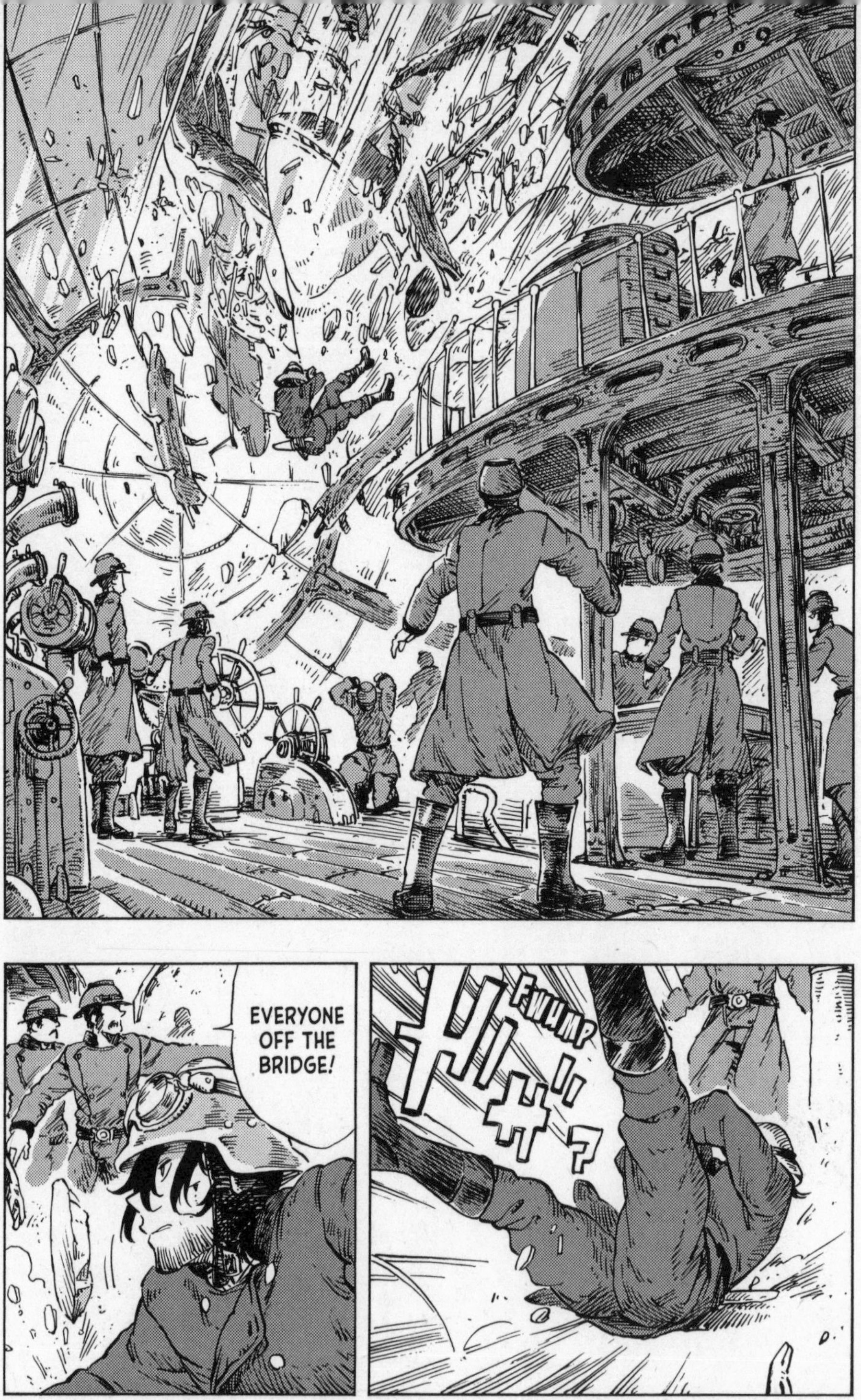
FWUMP
EVERYONE OFF THE BRIDGE!

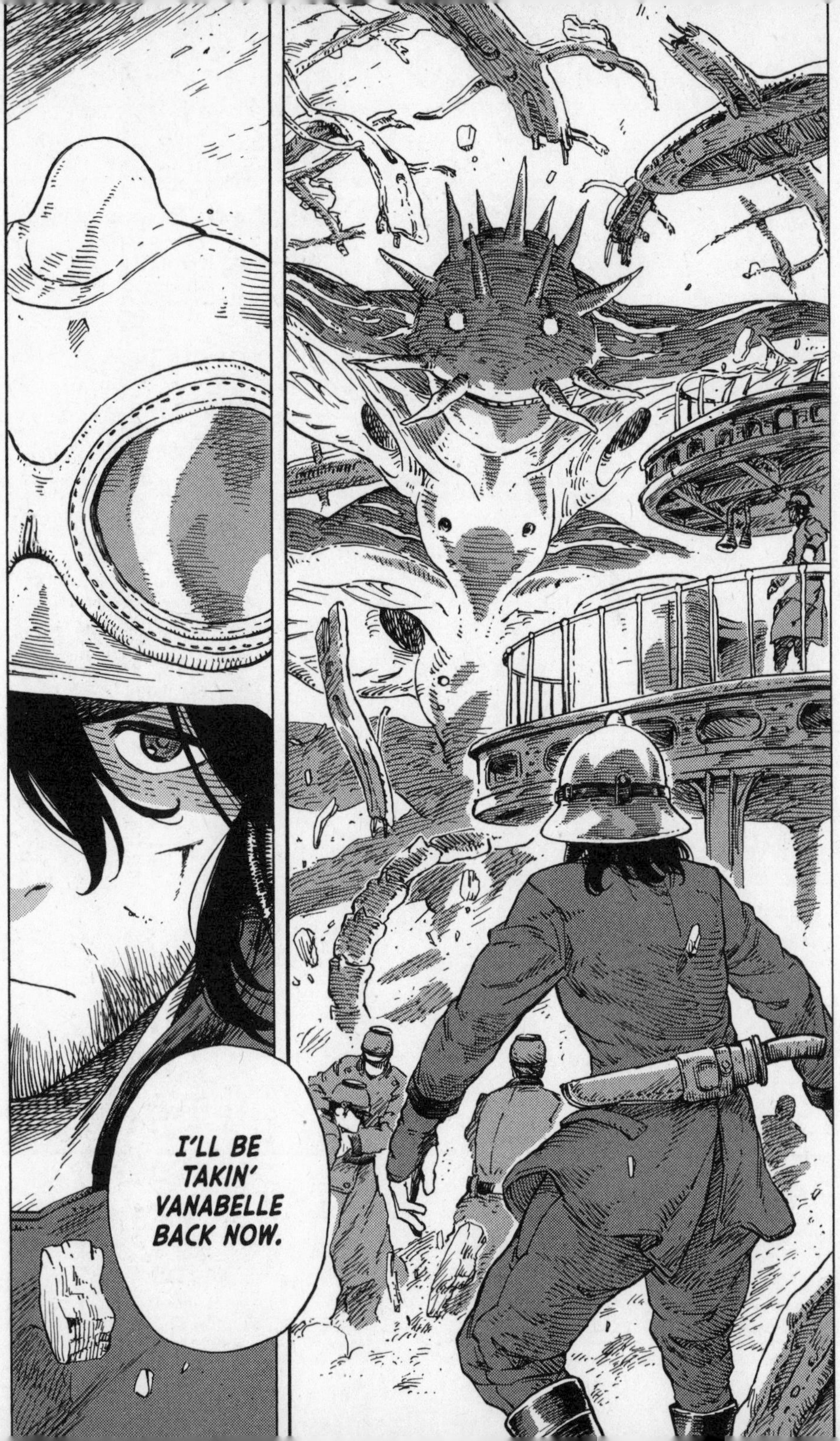
I'LL BE TAKIN' VANABELLE BACK NOW.

Dragon Pinna Gelatin Panna Cotta

Ingredients (Serves 2-3)

✦ 50 ml of dragon pinna liquid gelatin

✦ 200 ml of cream

✦ A dash of vanilla extract

✦ 2 Tbsp of sugar

01
Remove the skin and fat from the dragon pinna.

02
Boil pinna in a pot with ash for about 20 minutes. Remove and wash under water thoroughly, removing leftover bits of fat and meat.

03
Thinly slice pinna and place slices in a pot with just enough water to cover. Simmer gently without bringing to boil for 1-2 hours.

04
Remove pinna from the pot and continue to reduce on low heat until the liquid gelatin thickens further.

05
Put cream, vanilla extract, and sugar in a separate pot and warm on low heat.

06
Once warm, mix in liquid gelatin.

07
Wet the inside of a container with water or rum and gently pour the mixture in to prevent the formation of bubbles.

08
Chill in a cool, dark place for 5 hours before serving.

REPLACING THE CREAM WITH MILK AND EGGS WILL TURN THIS INTO A CUSTARD PUDDING.

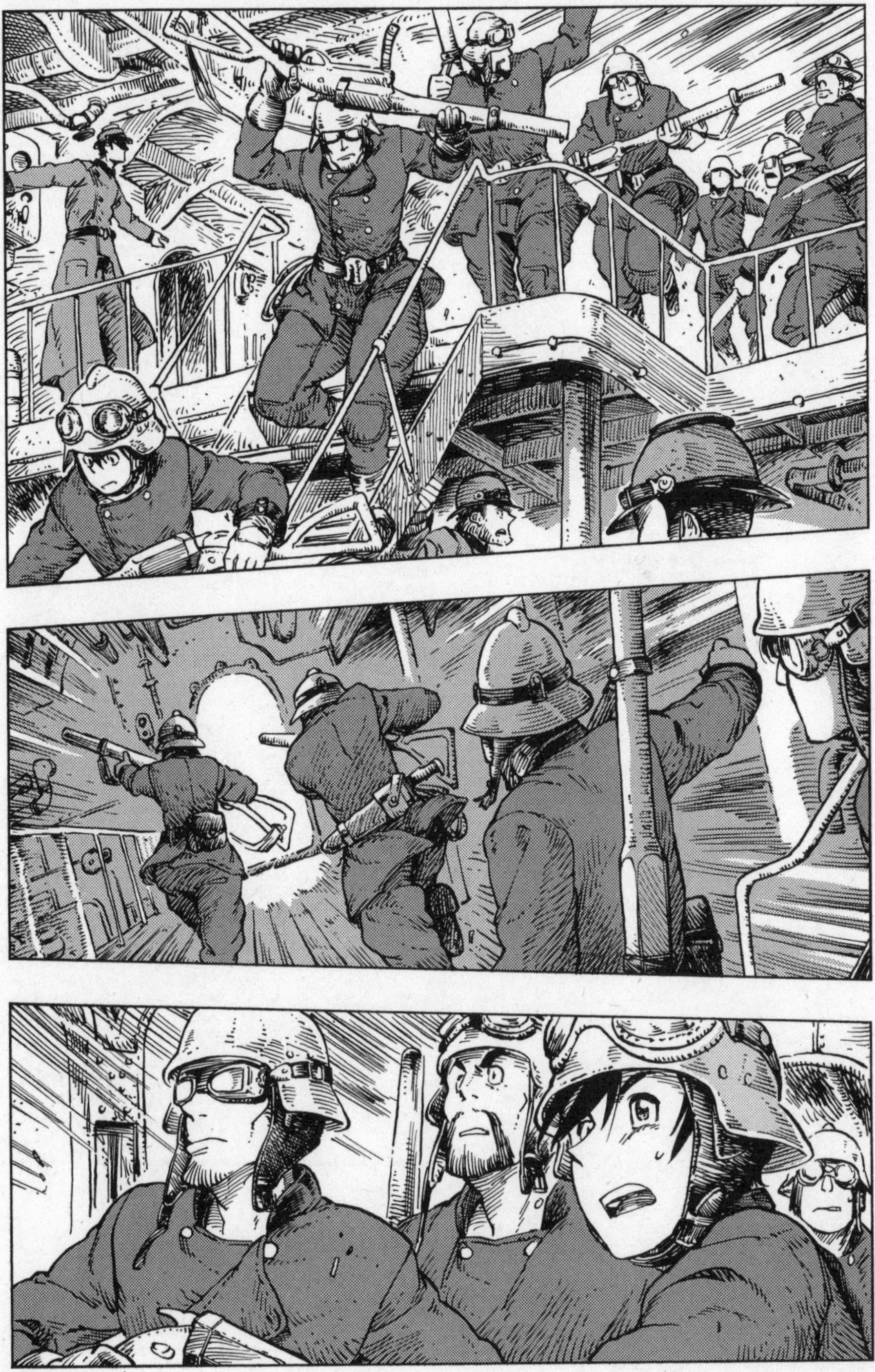

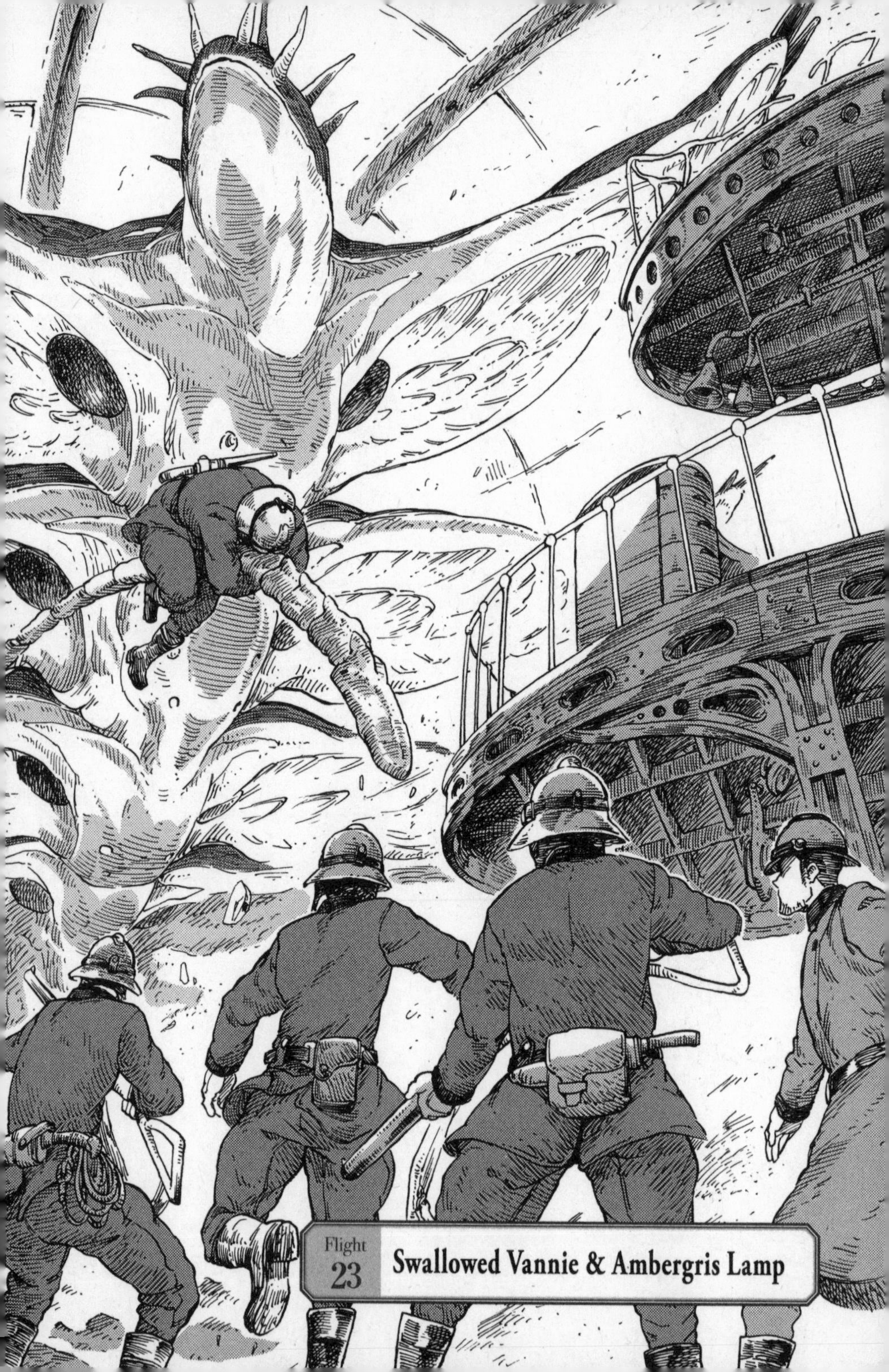
Flight
23
Swallowed Vannie & Ambergris Lamp

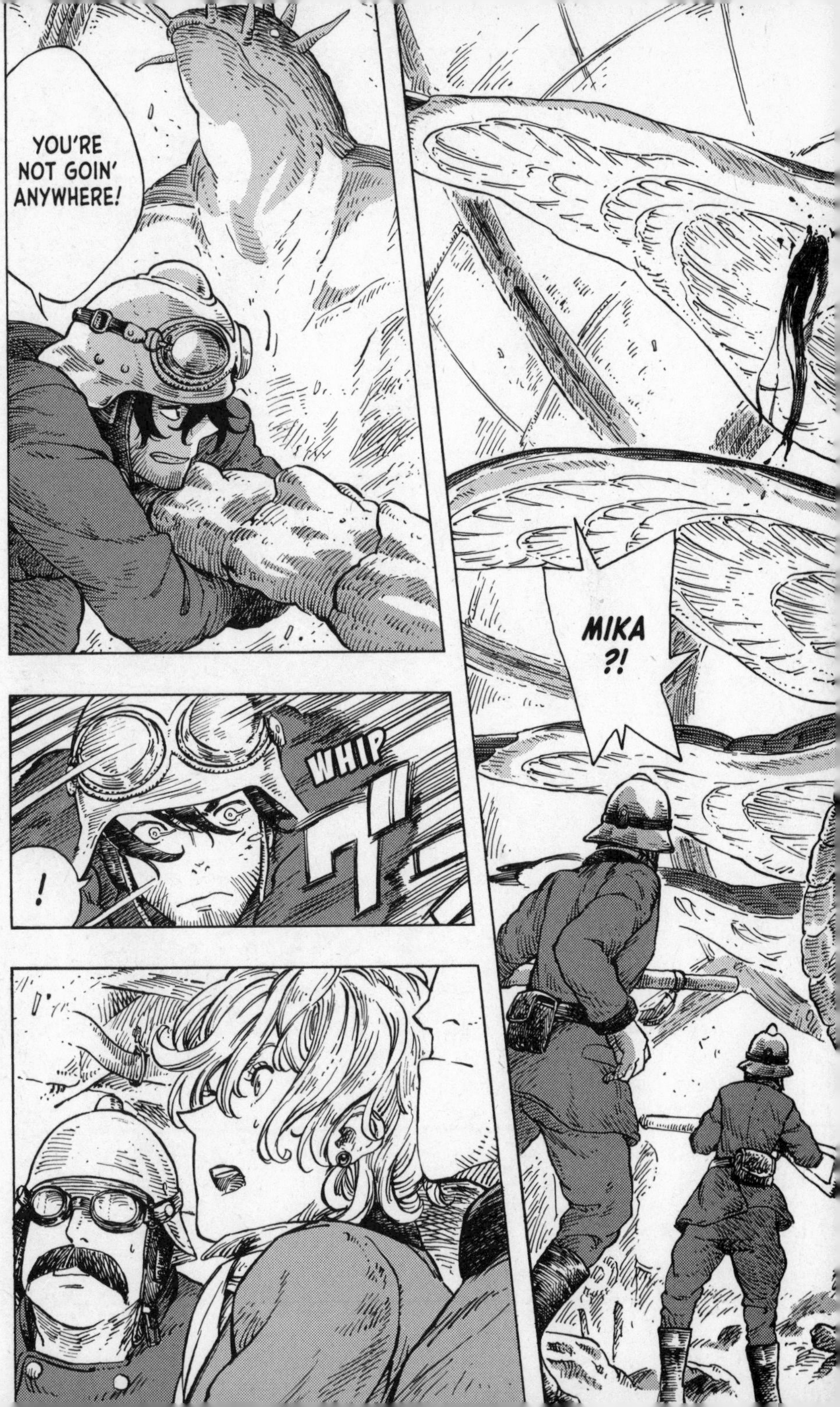
MIKA ?!
YOU'RE NOT GOIN' ANYWHERE!
WHIP
!

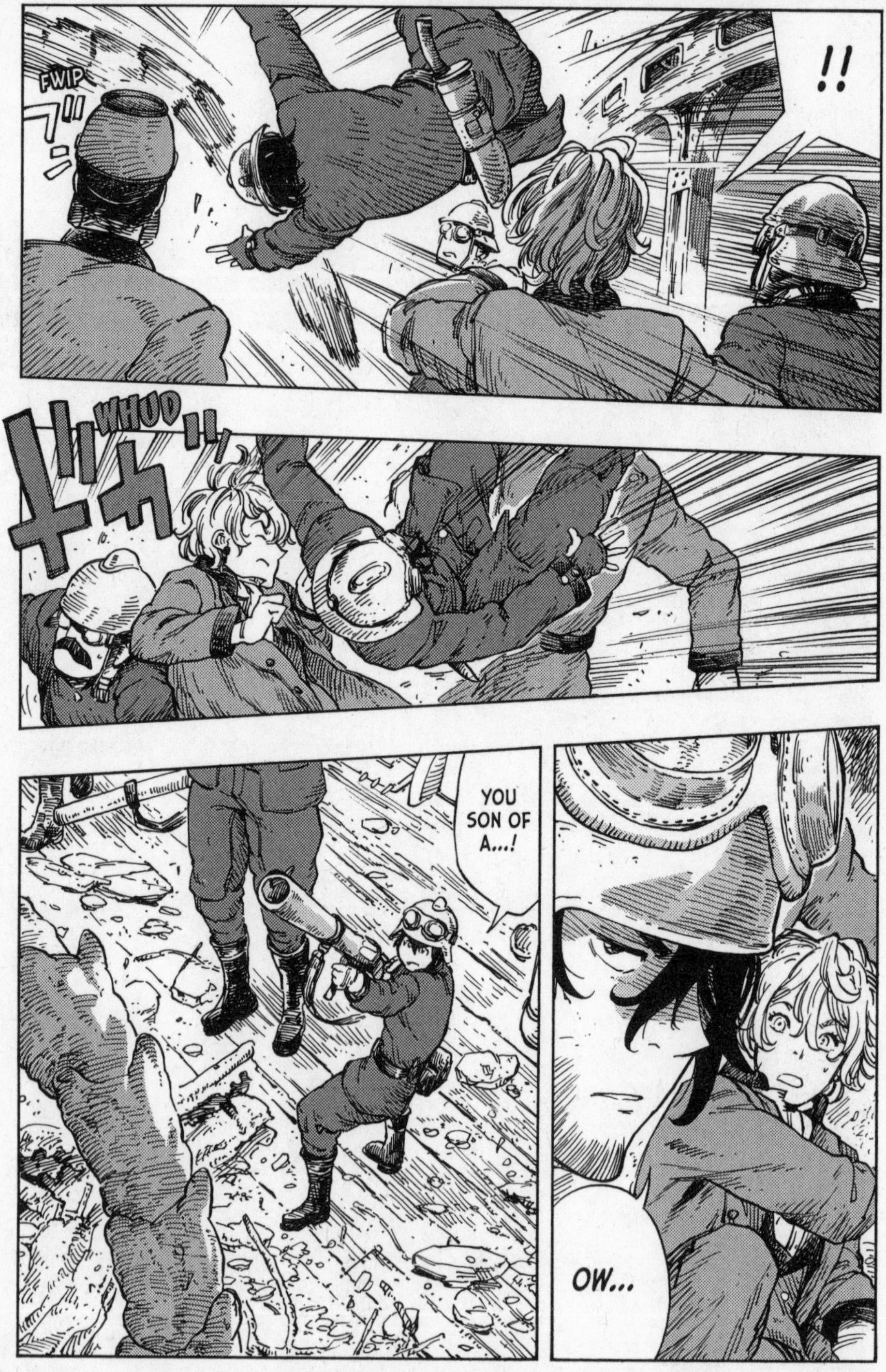
!!
FWIP
WHUD
OW...
YOU SON OF A...!

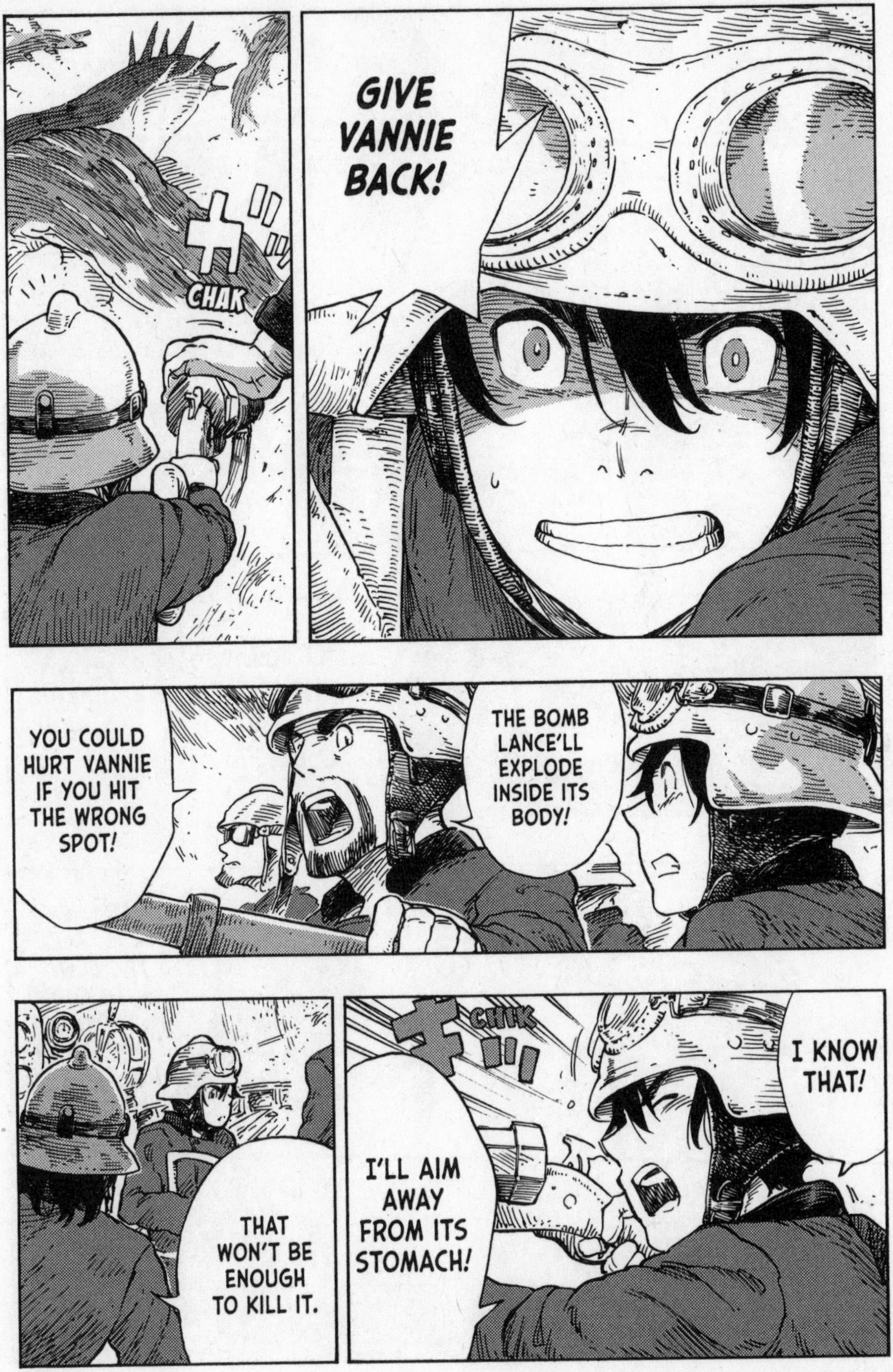
GIVE VANNIE BACK!
CHAK
THE BOMB LANCE'LL EXPLODE INSIDE ITS BODY!
YOU COULD HURT VANNIE IF YOU HIT THE WRONG SPOT!
CHIK
I KNOW THAT!
I'LL AIM AWAY FROM ITS STOMACH!
THAT WON'T BE ENOUGH TO KILL IT.

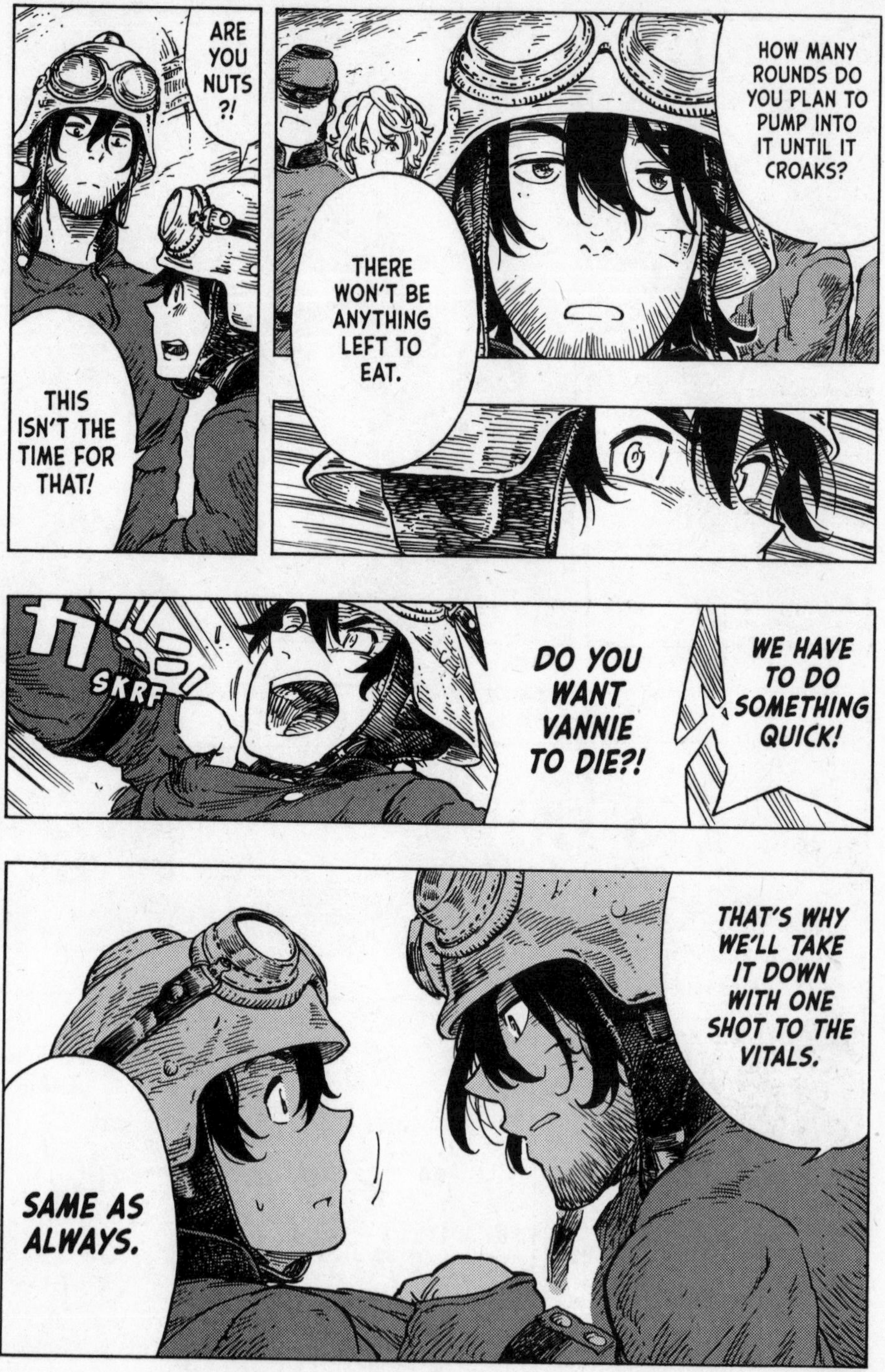
HOW MANY ROUNDS DO YOU PLAN TO PUMP INTO IT UNTIL IT CROAKS?
THERE WON'T BE ANYTHING LEFT TO EAT.
ARE YOU NUTS ?!
THIS ISN'T THE TIME FOR THAT!
WE HAVE TO DO SOMETHING QUICK!
DO YOU WANT VANNIE TO DIE?!
SKRF
THAT'S WHY WE'LL TAKE IT DOWN WITH ONE SHOT TO THE VITALS.
SAME AS ALWAYS.

HURRY!

BRING ME MY PILE LANCE.

KRRK

BRAK

CHIK

BANG

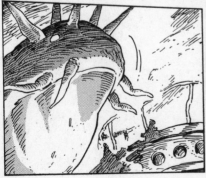

CLANG

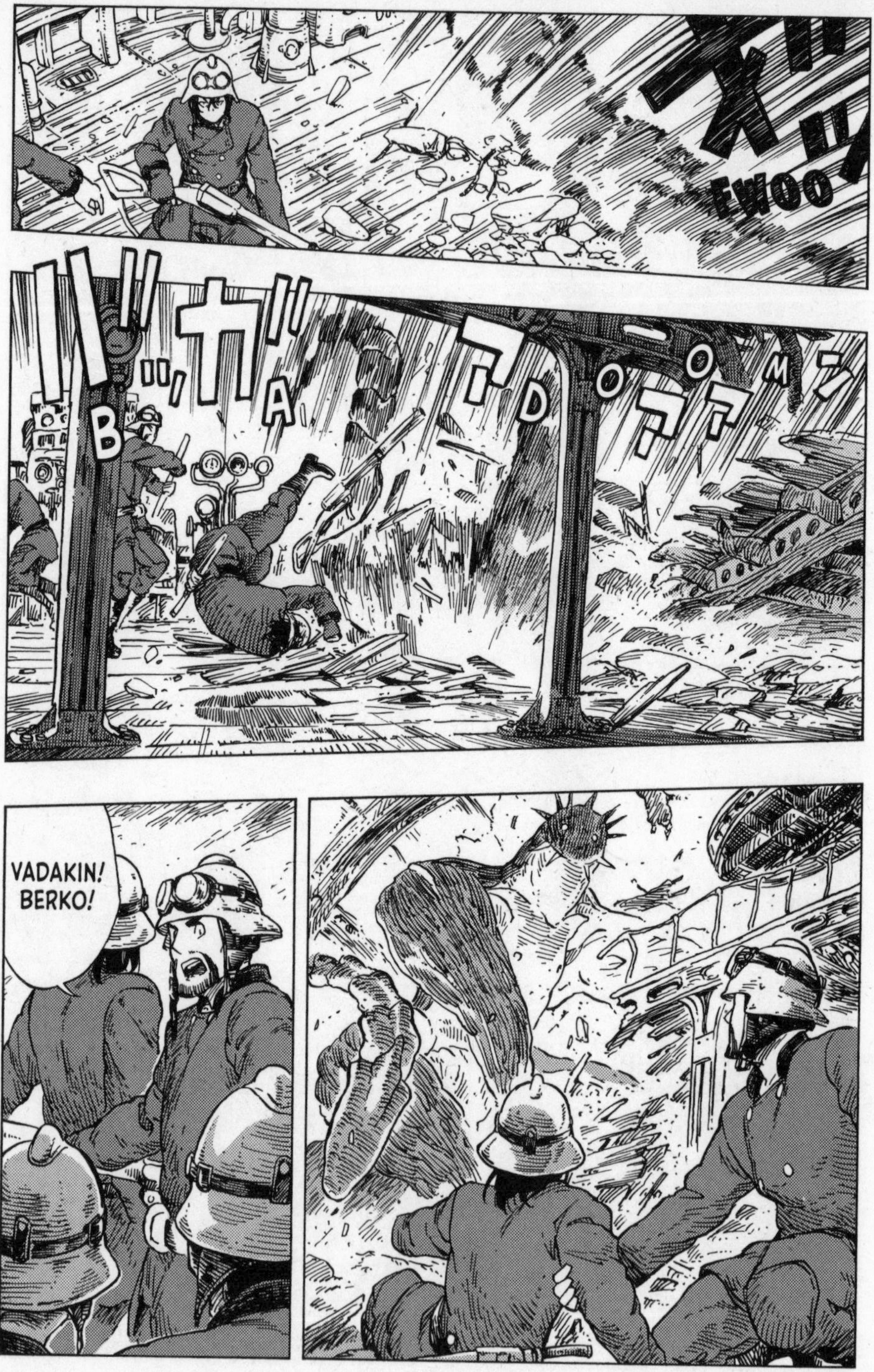
EWOO
BADOOM
VADAKIN! BERKO!

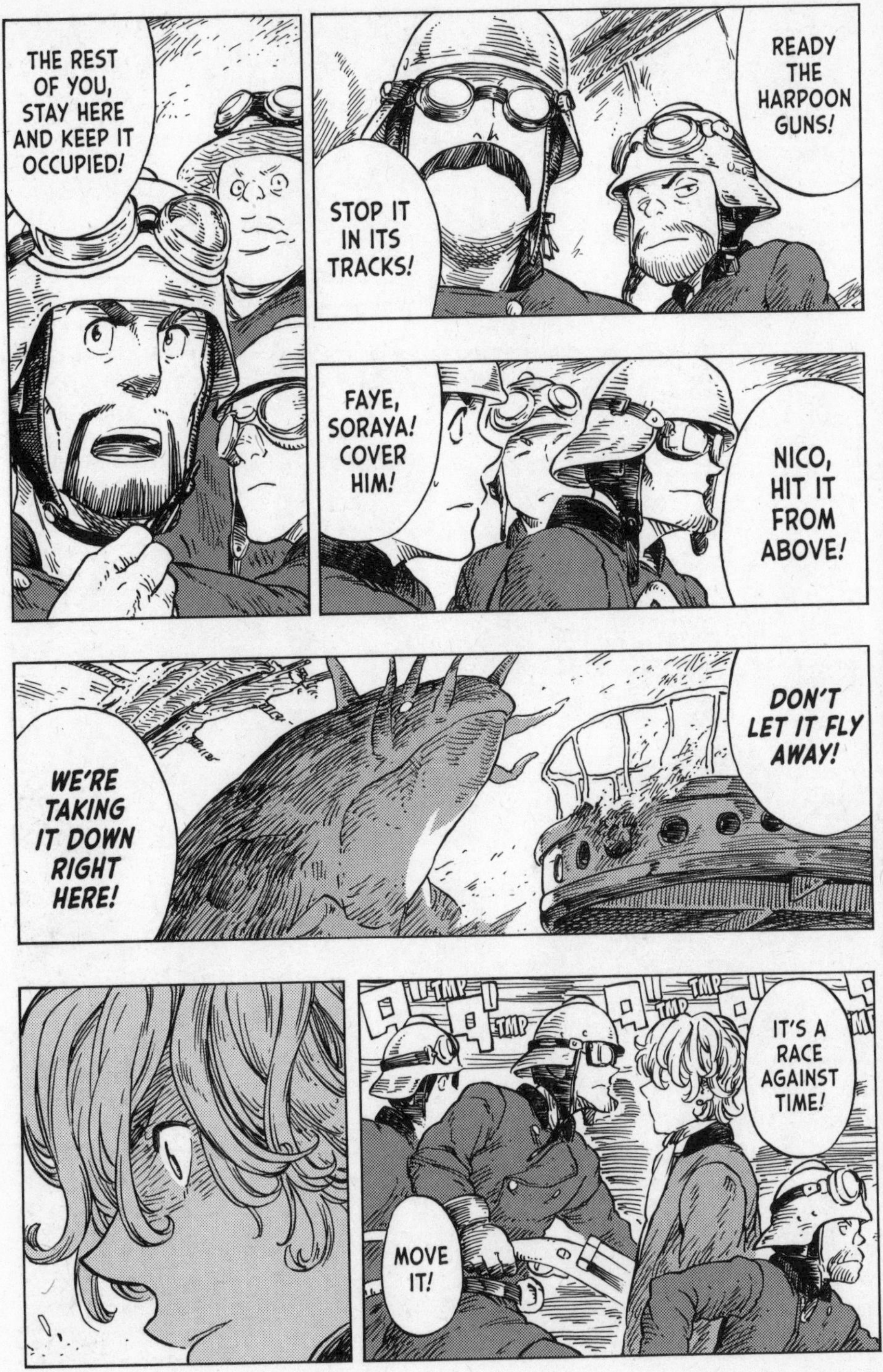
READY THE HARPOON GUNS!
STOP IT IN ITS TRACKS!
NICO, HIT IT FROM ABOVE!
FAYE, SORAYA! COVER HIM!
THE REST OF YOU, STAY HERE AND KEEP IT OCCUPIED!
DON'T LET IT FLY AWAY!
WE'RE TAKING IT DOWN RIGHT HERE!
TMP TMP TMP TMP
IT'S A RACE AGAINST TIME!
MOVE IT!

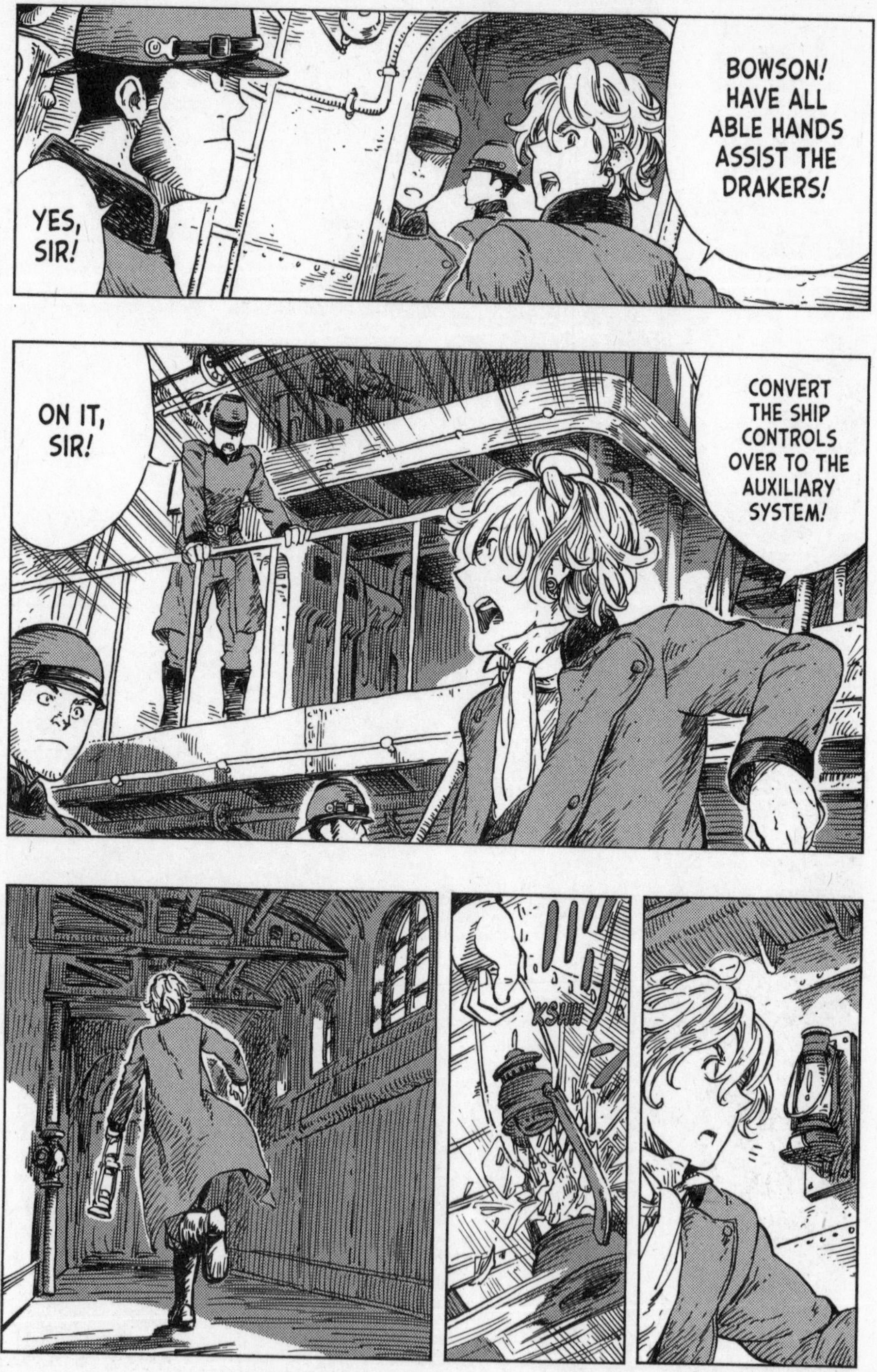
BOWSON! HAVE ALL ABLE HANDS ASSIST THE DRAKERS!
YES, SIR!
CONVERT THE SHIP CONTROLS OVER TO THE AUXILIARY SYSTEM!
ON IT, SIR!
KSHH

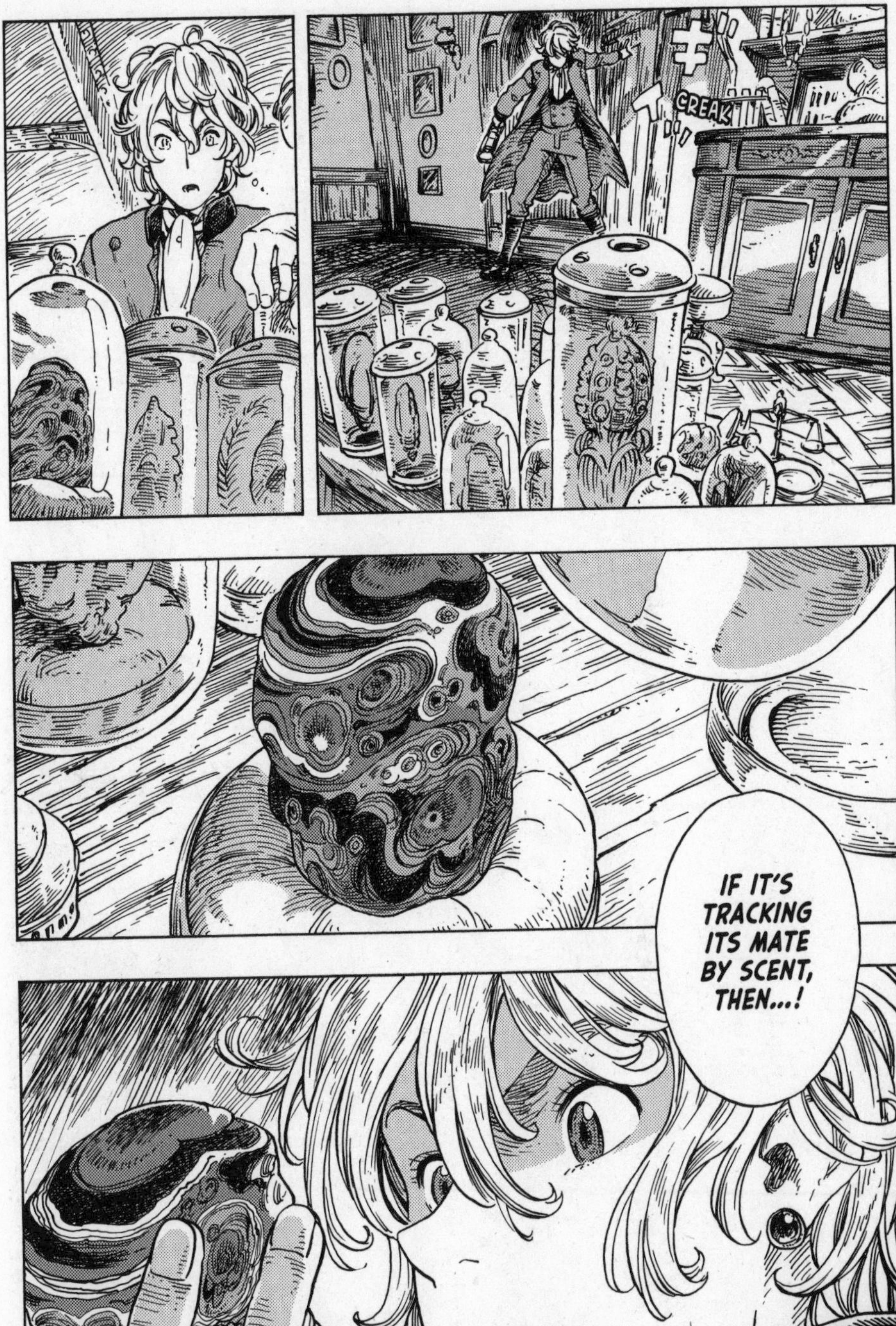
CREAK
IF IT'S TRACKING ITS MATE BY SCENT, THEN...!

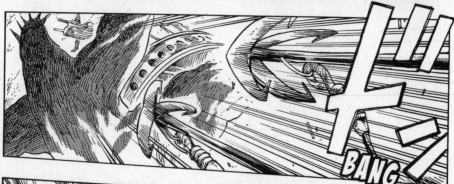

BANG

PULL!

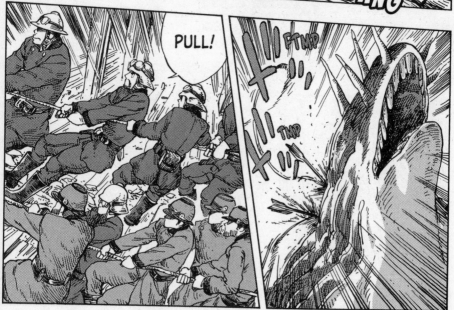

FTMP

TMP

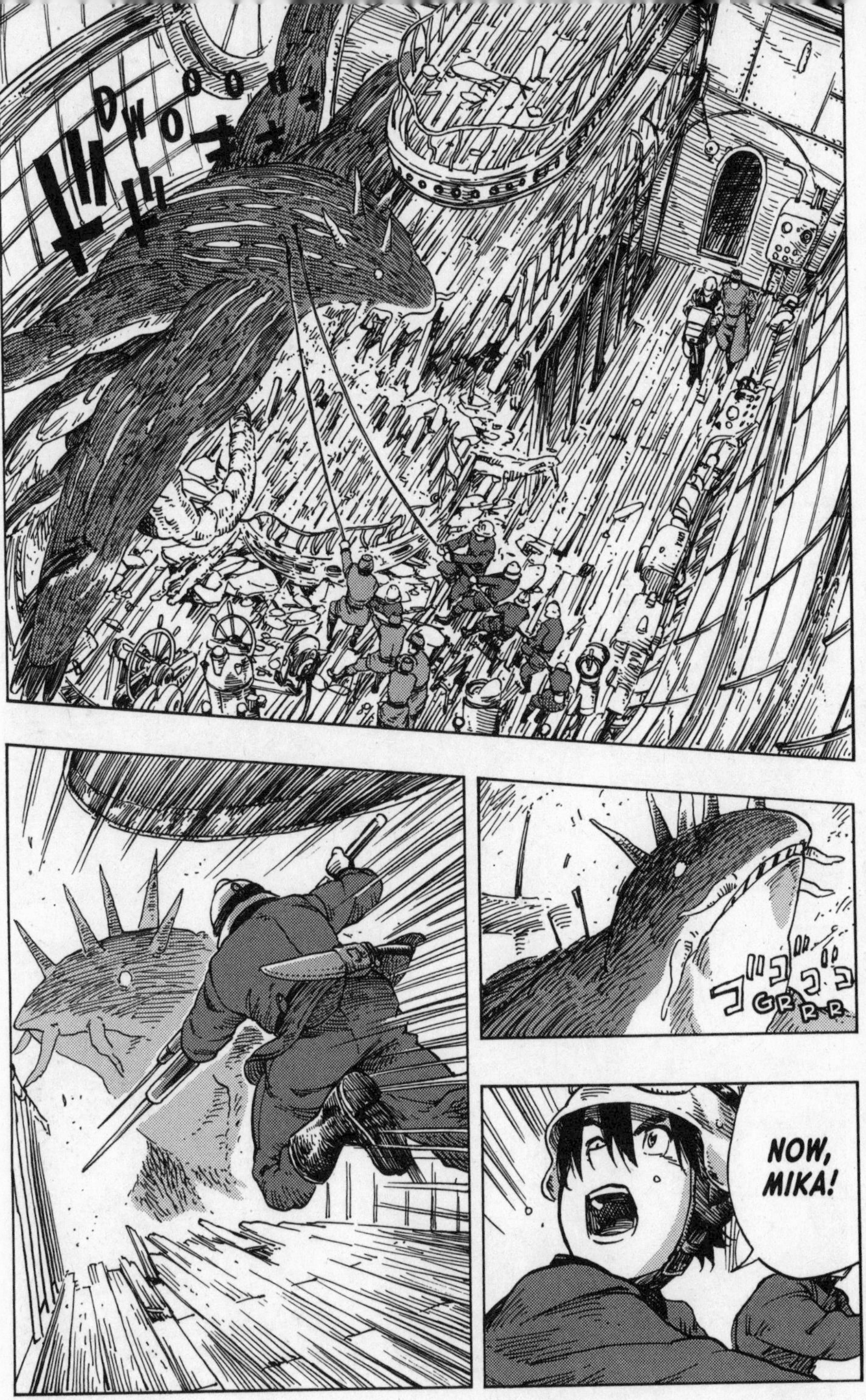
DWOOOO
GRRR
NOW, MIKA!

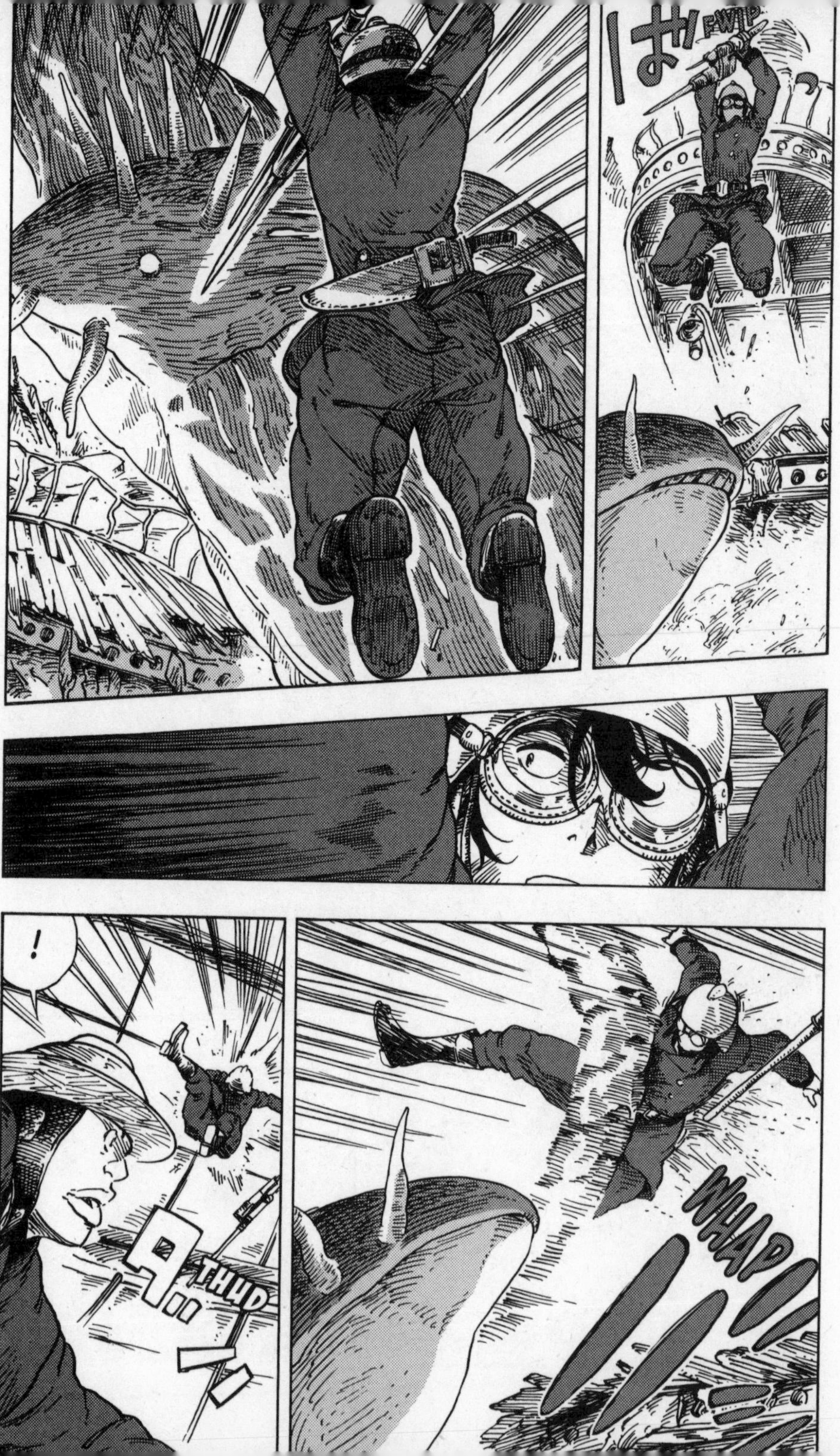

FWIP
WHAP
!
THUD

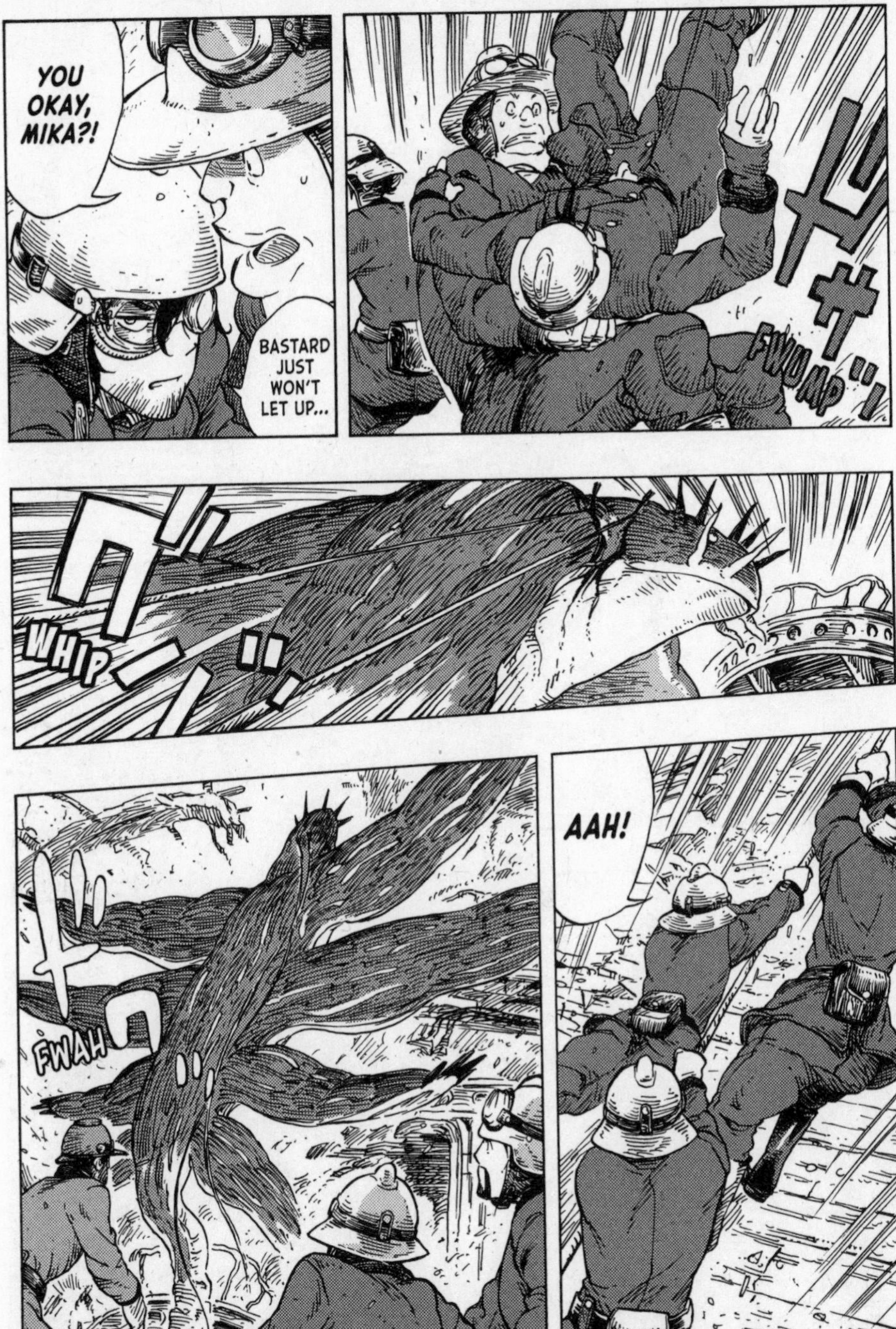
FWUMP
YOU OKAY, MIKA?!
BASTARD JUST WON'T LET UP...
WHIP
AAH!
FWAH

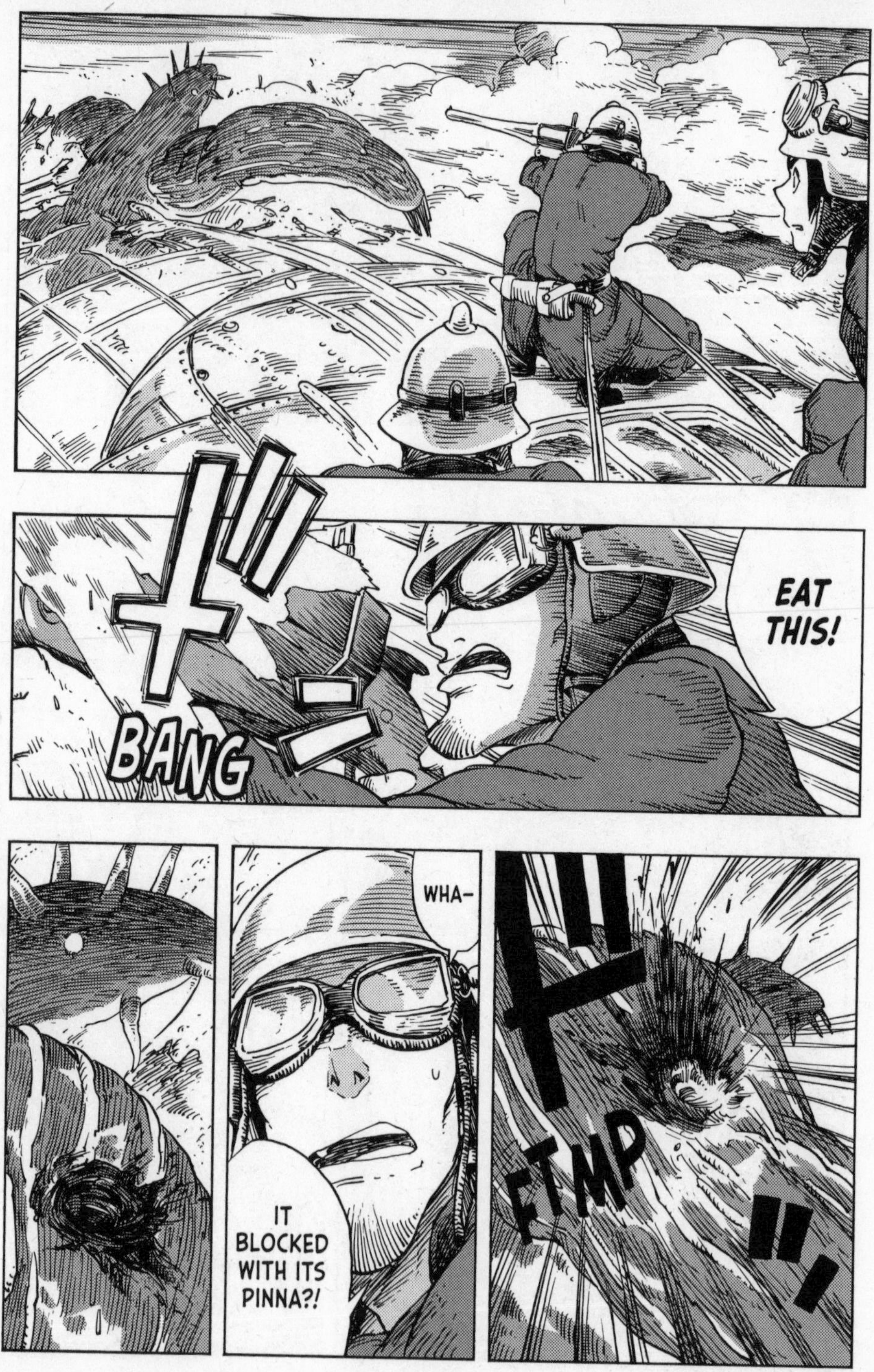
EAT THIS!
BANG
FTMP
WHA-
IT BLOCKED WITH ITS PINNA?!

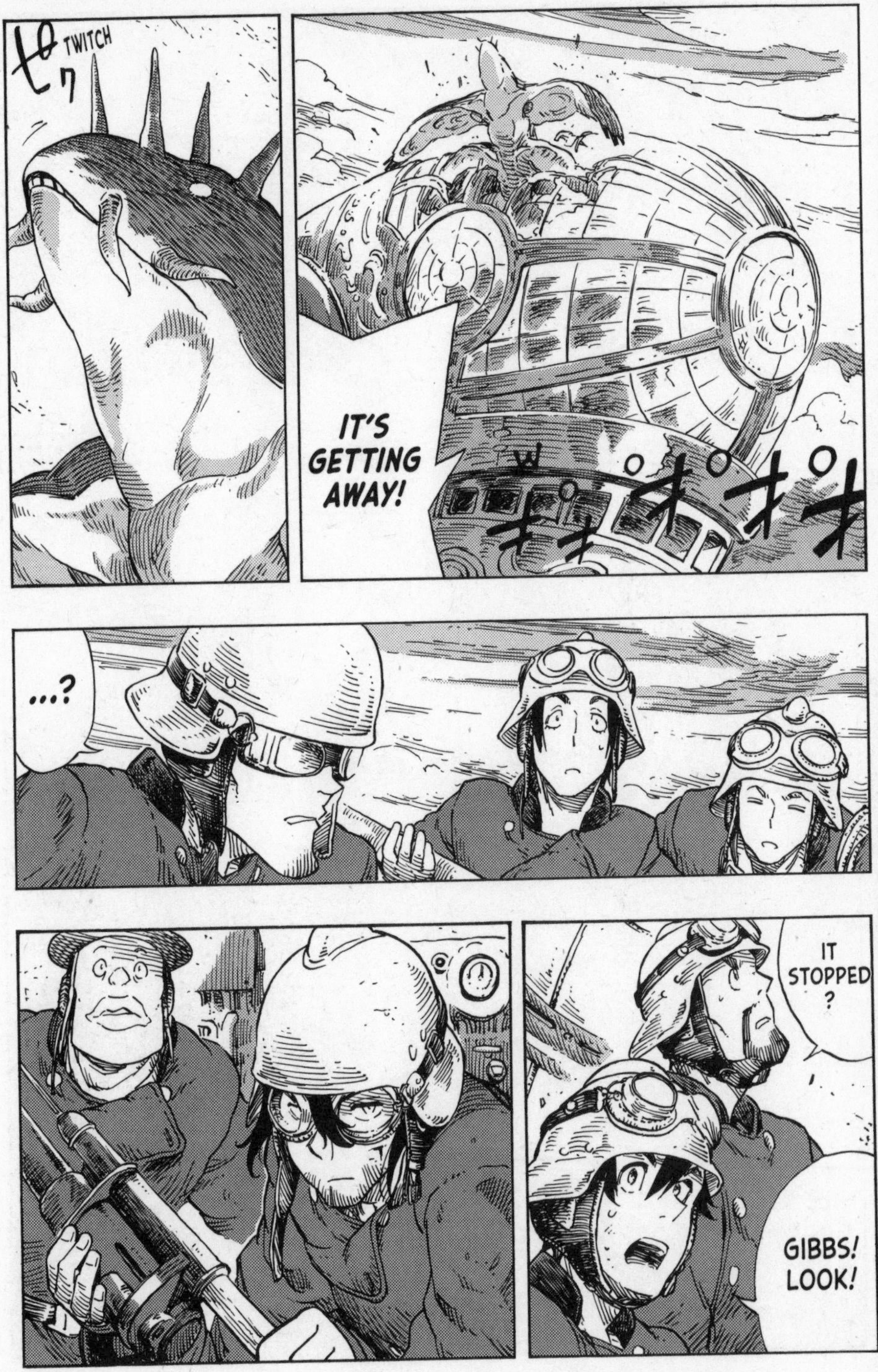
IT'S GETTING AWAY!
TWITCH
...?
IT STOPPED?
GIBBS! LOOK!

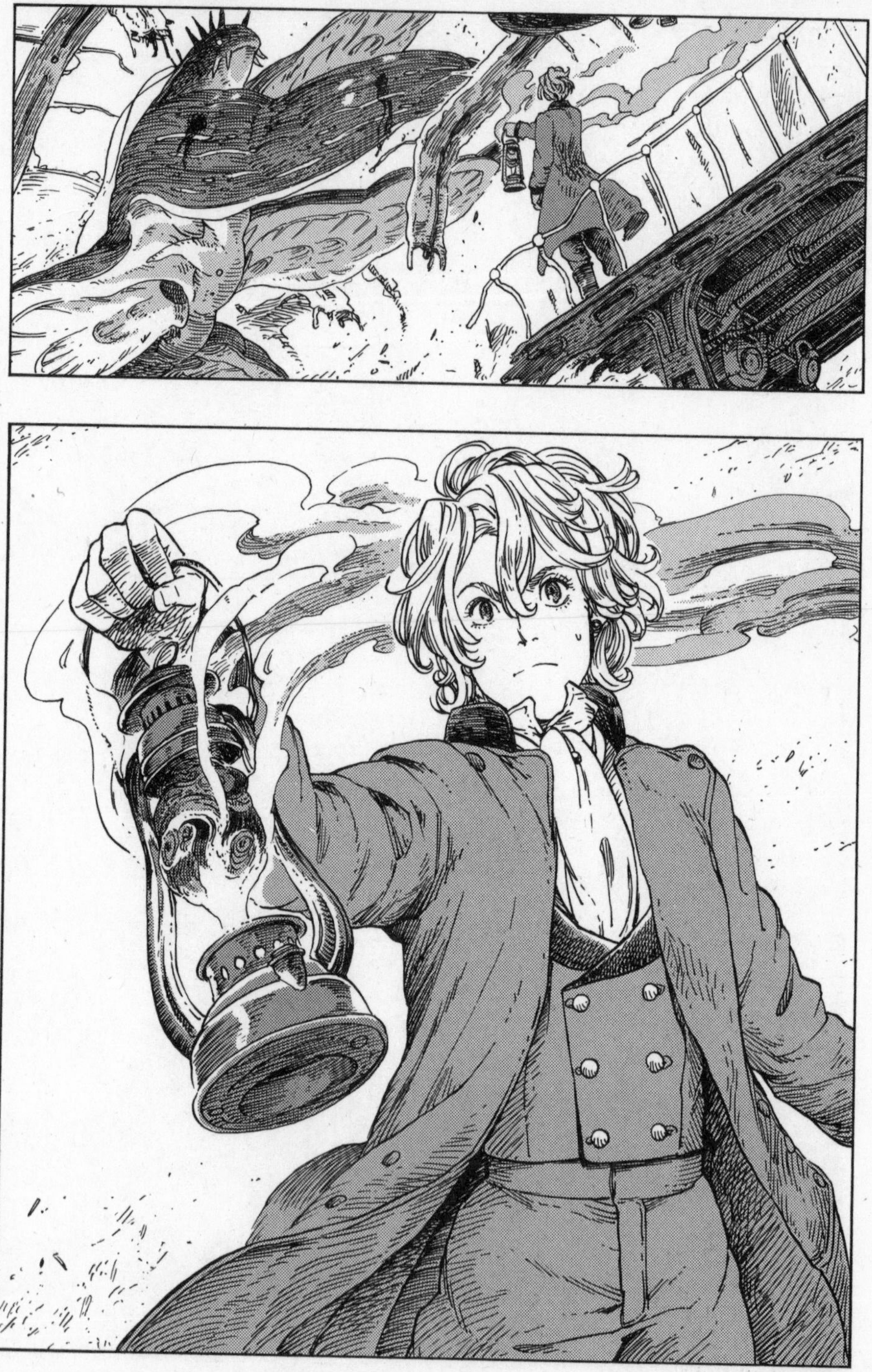

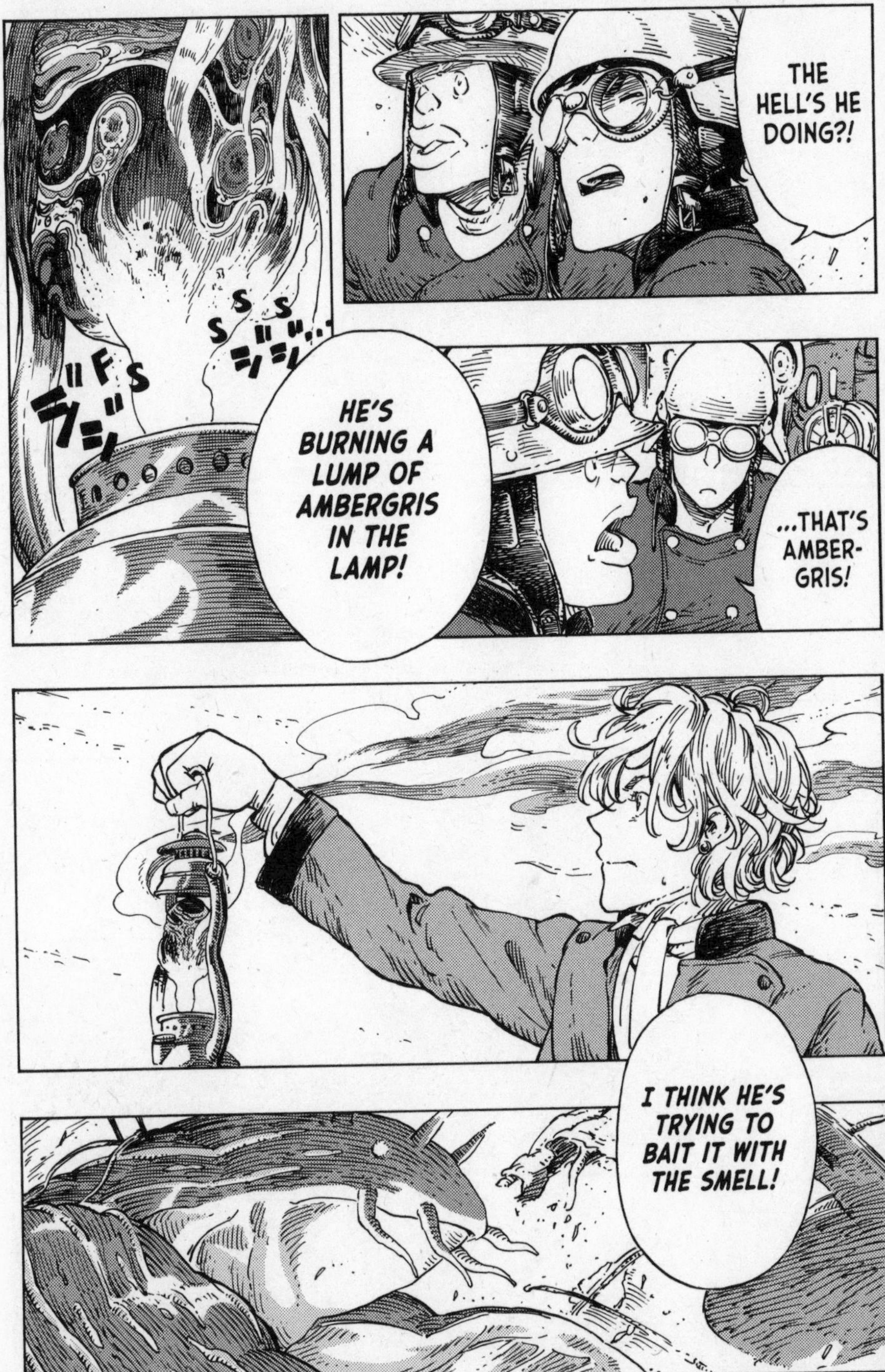
THE HELL'S HE DOING?!
...THAT'S AMBER-GRIS!
HE'S BURNING A LUMP OF AMBERGRIS IN THE LAMP!
FS
SSS
I THINK HE'S TRYING TO BAIT IT WITH THE SMELL!

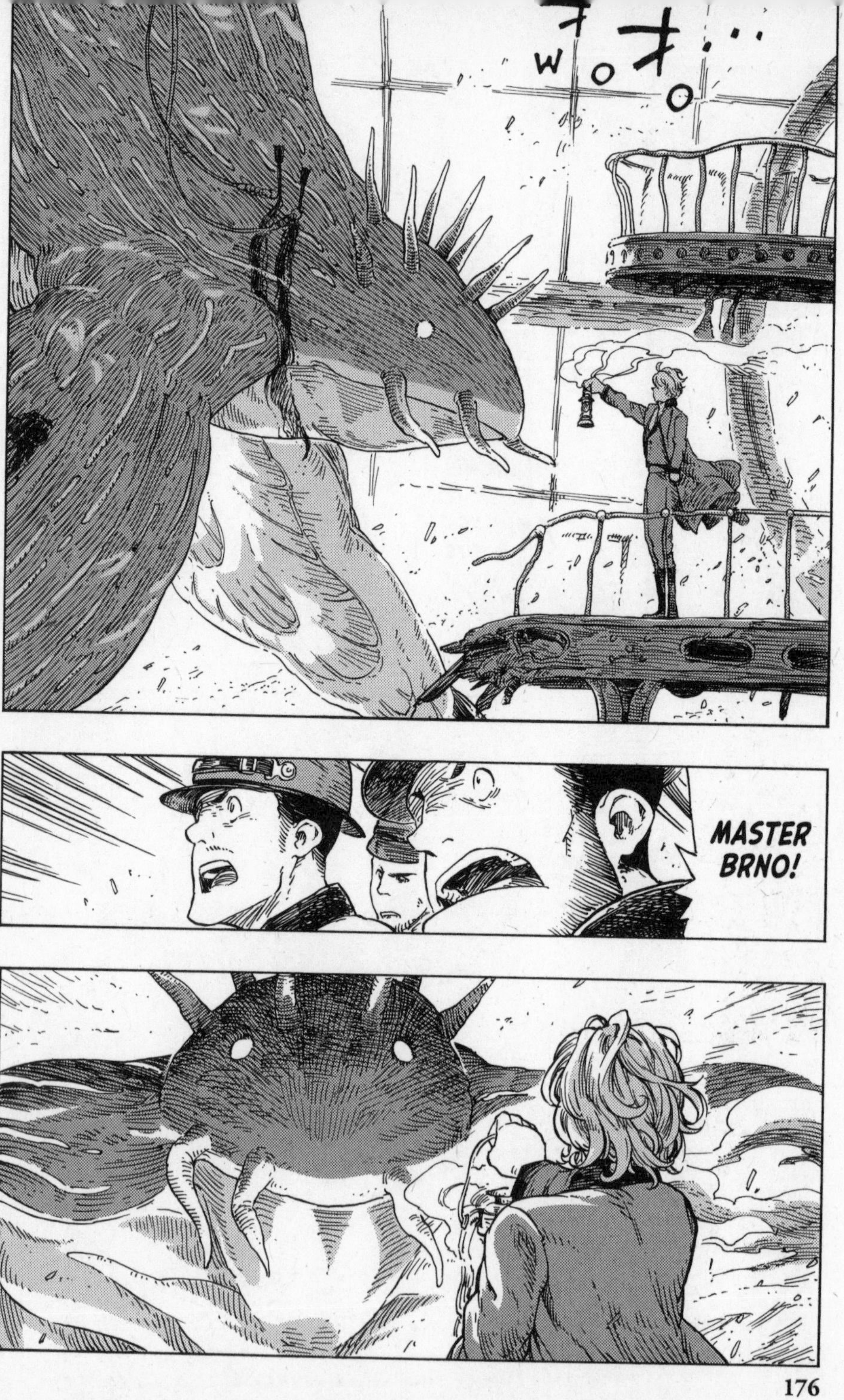
WOO
MASTER BRNO!

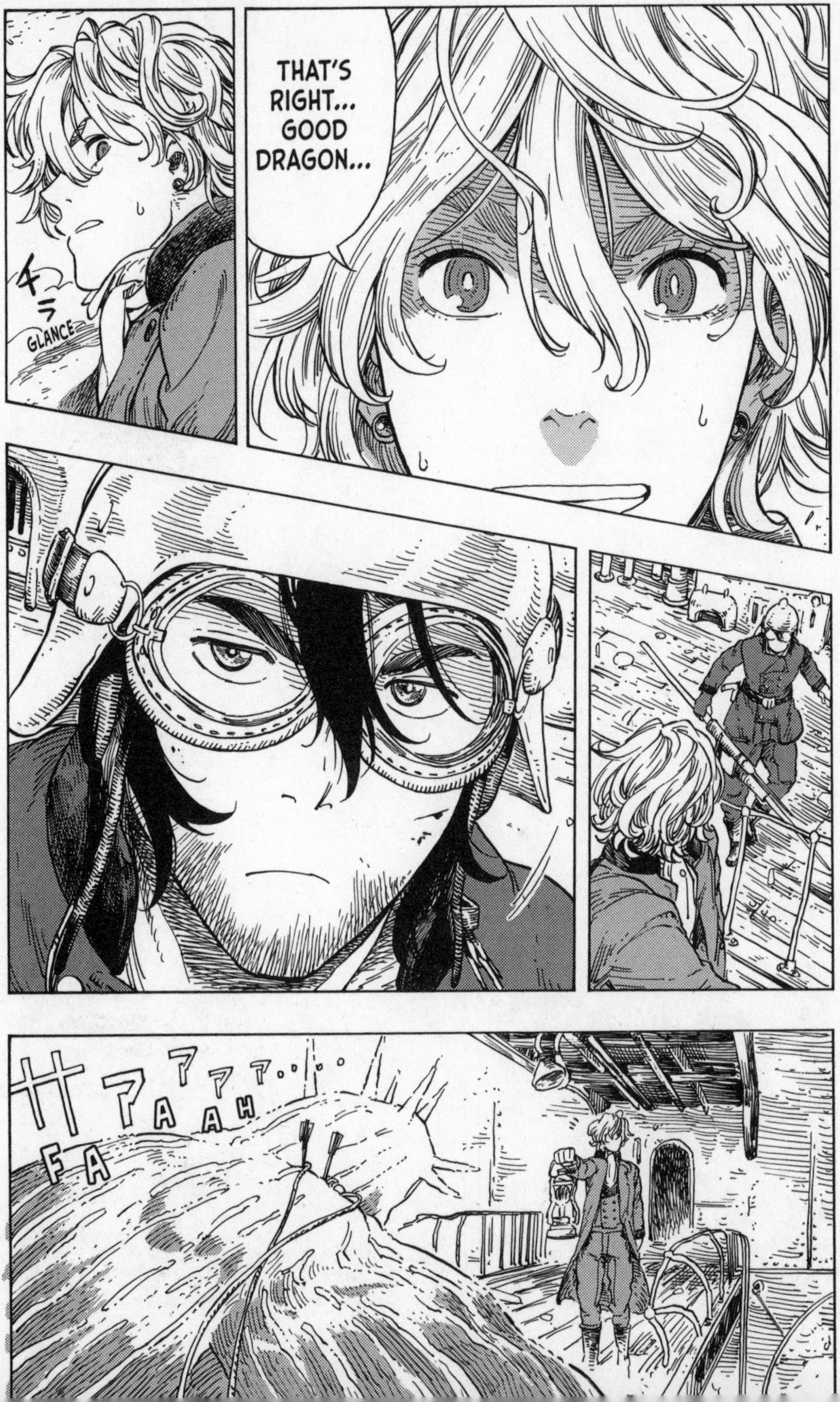
THAT'S RIGHT... GOOD DRAGON...
チラ
GLANCE
サァァァ…
FA A AH

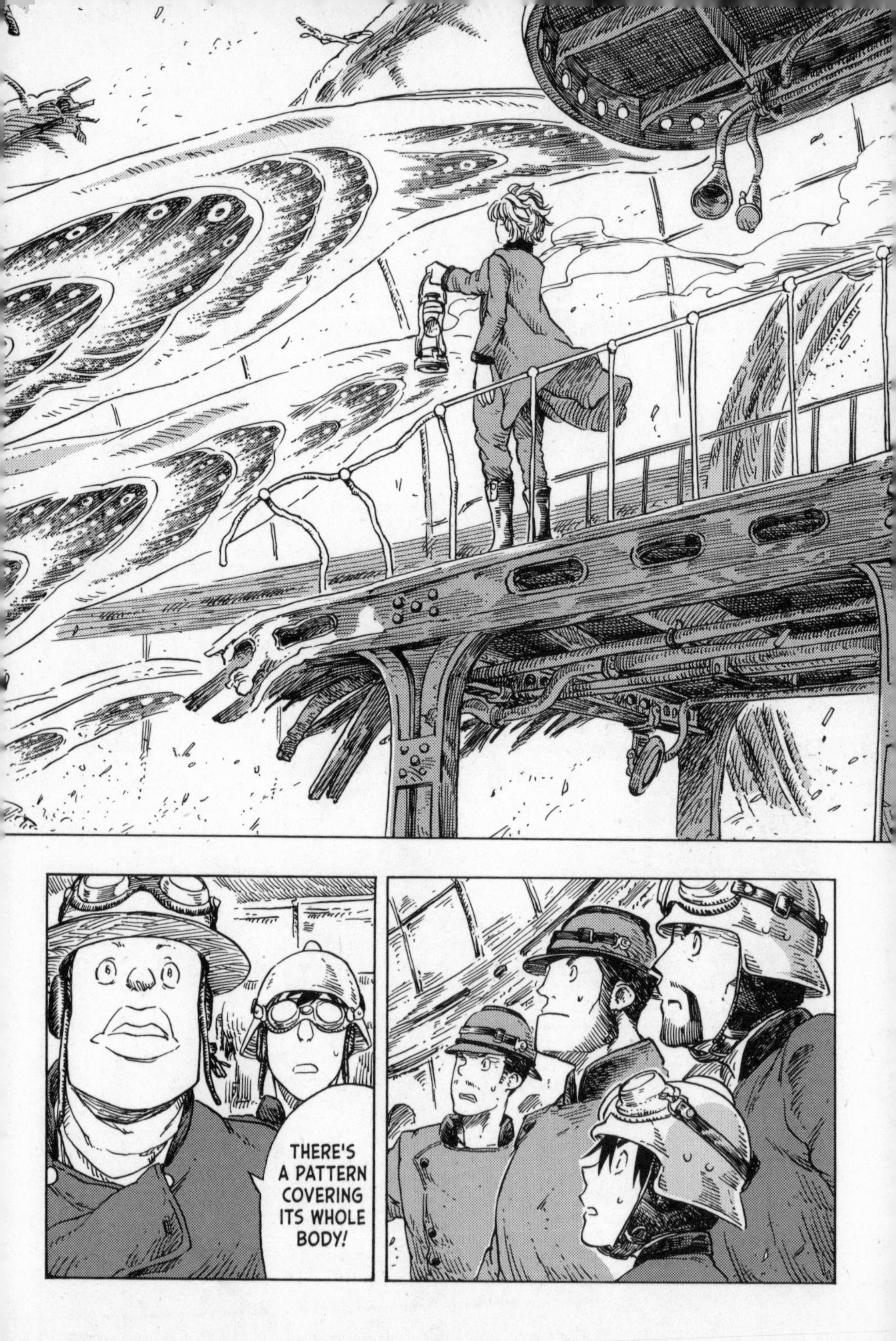
THERE'S A PATTERN COVERING ITS WHOLE BODY!

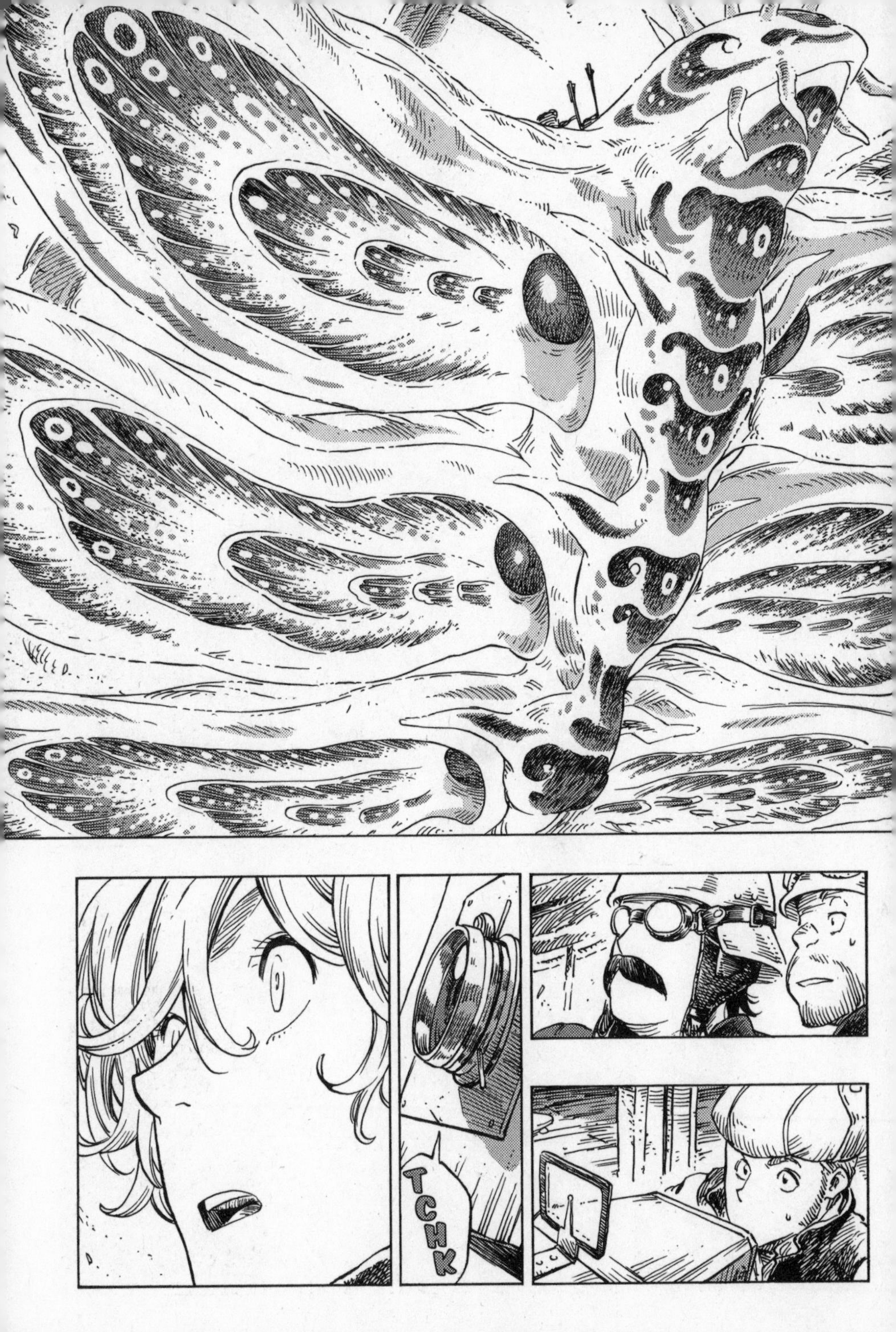
TCHK

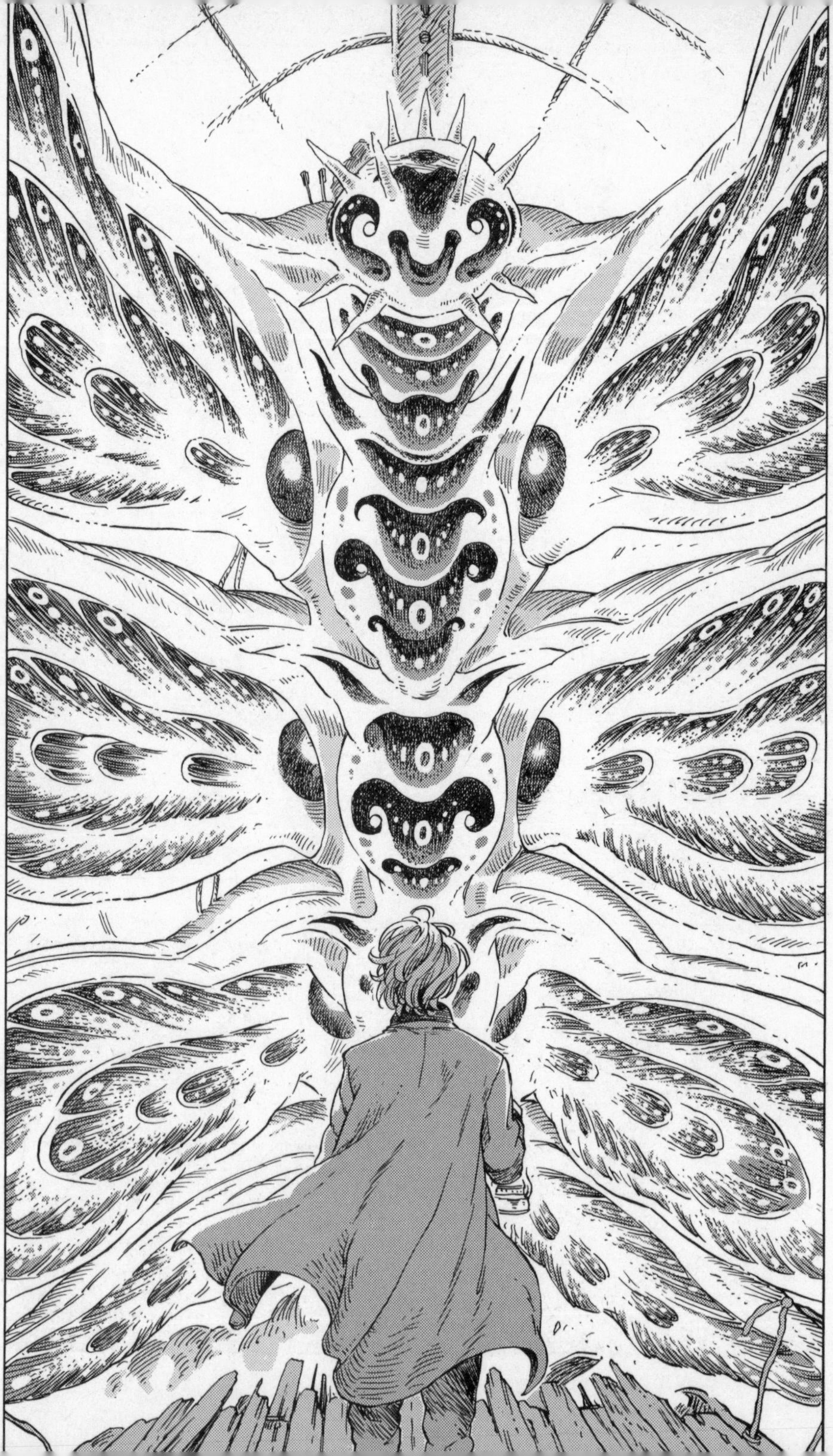

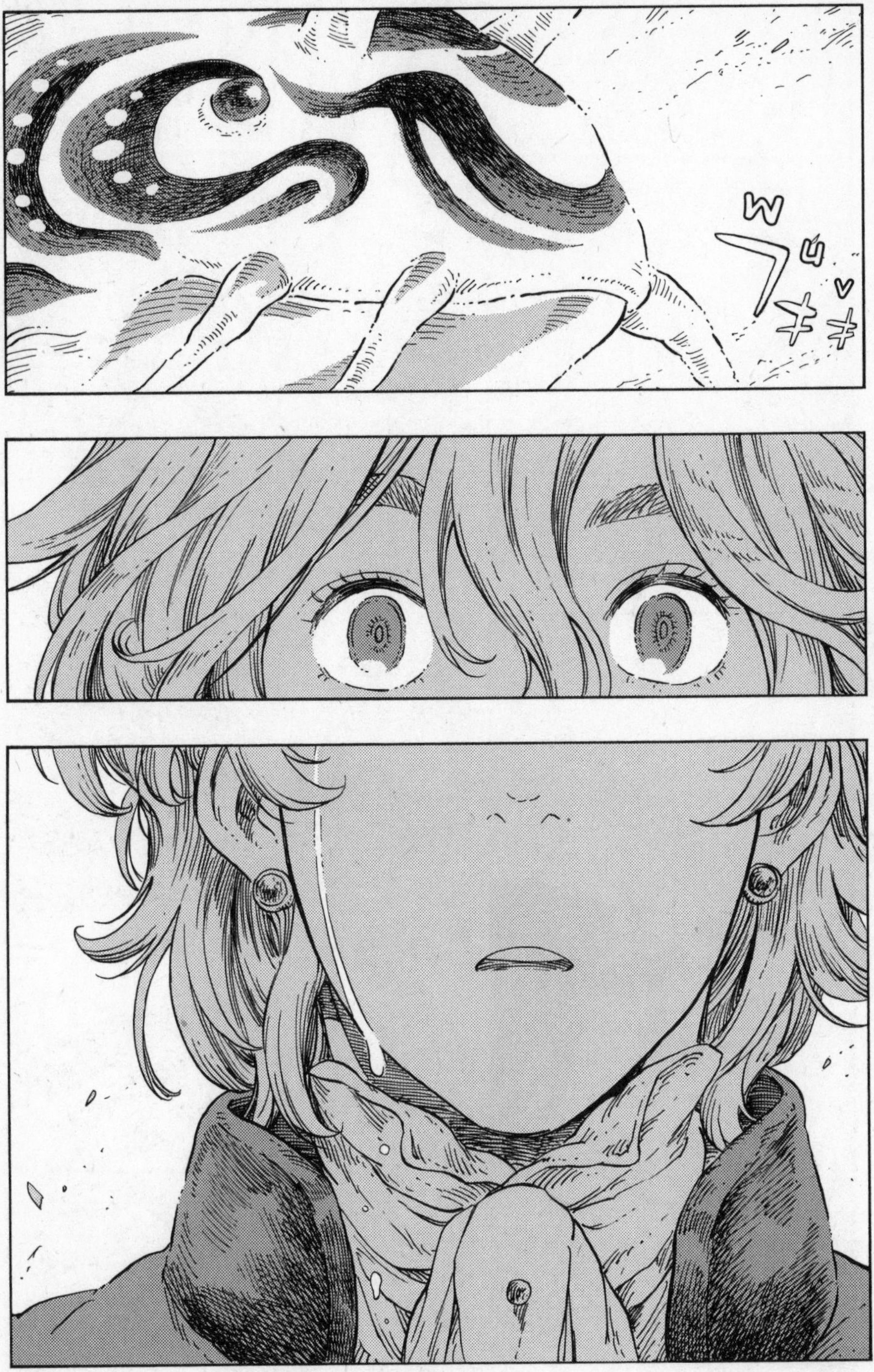
ギキュ～ッ

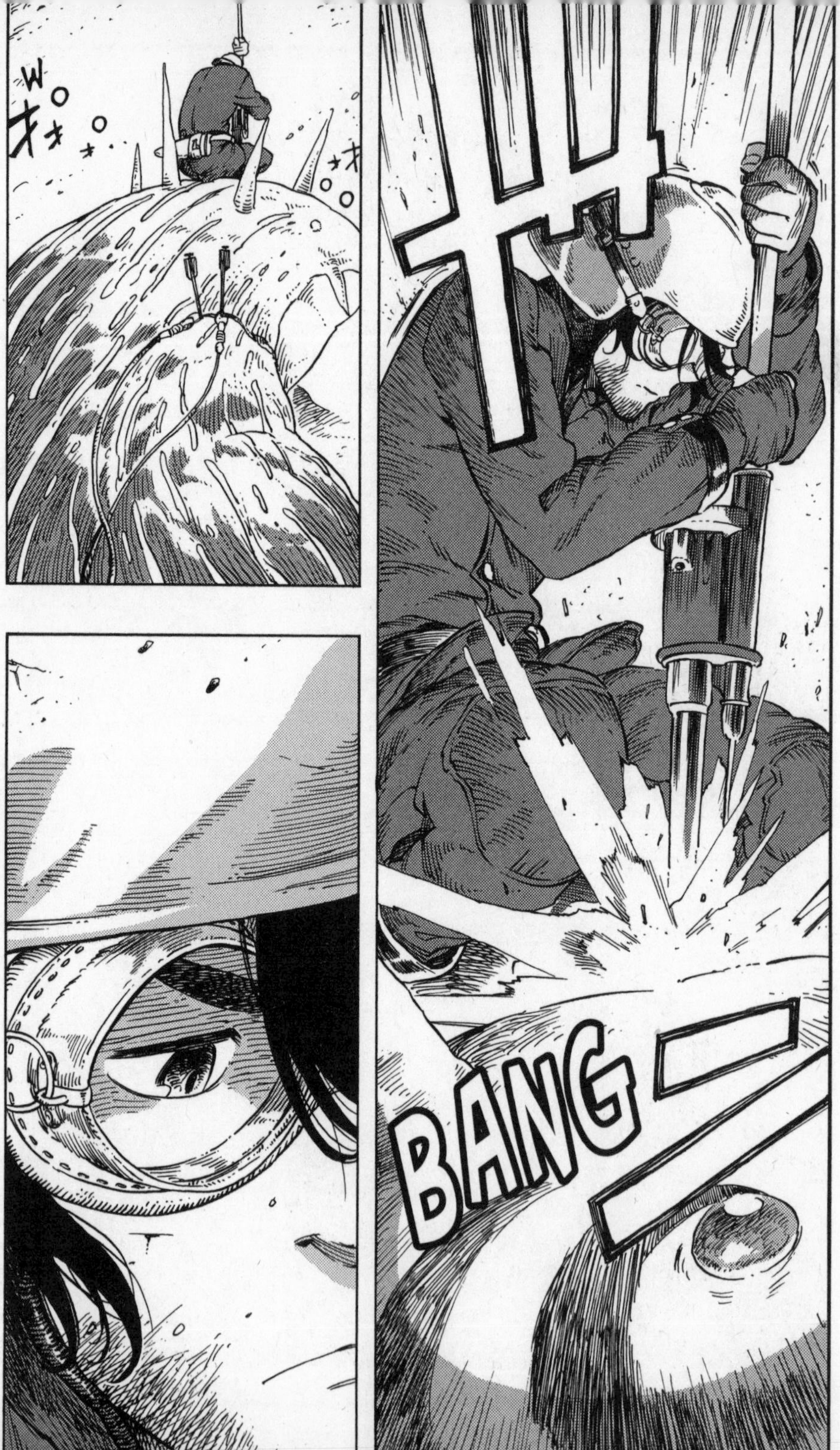
BANG
WOOO

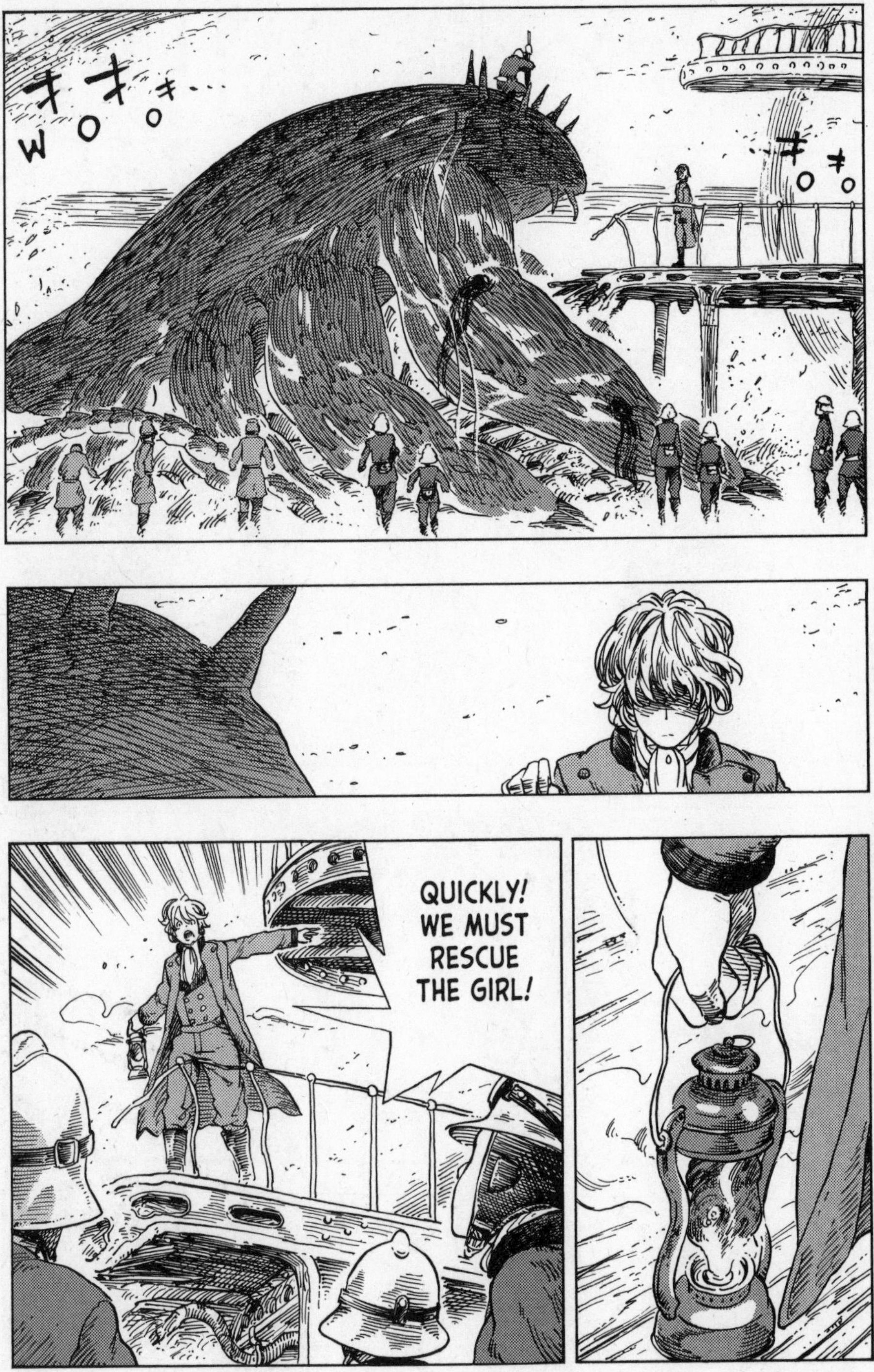
オオォ…
WOo
オォ
Oo
QUICKLY! WE MUST RESCUE THE GIRL!

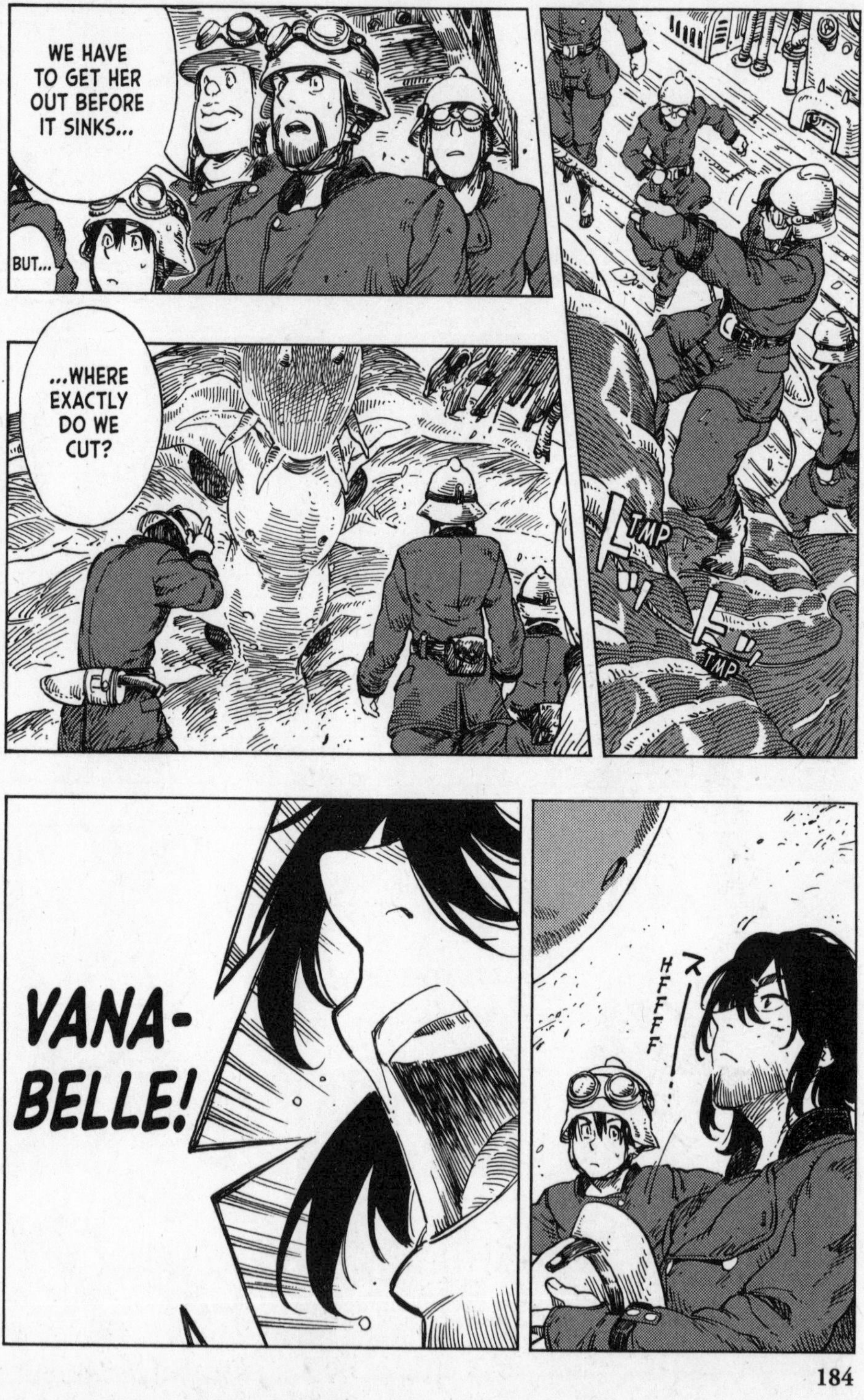
TMP
TMP
WE HAVE TO GET HER OUT BEFORE IT SINKS...
BUT...
...WHERE EXACTLY DO WE CUT?
HFFFFF
VANA-BELLE!

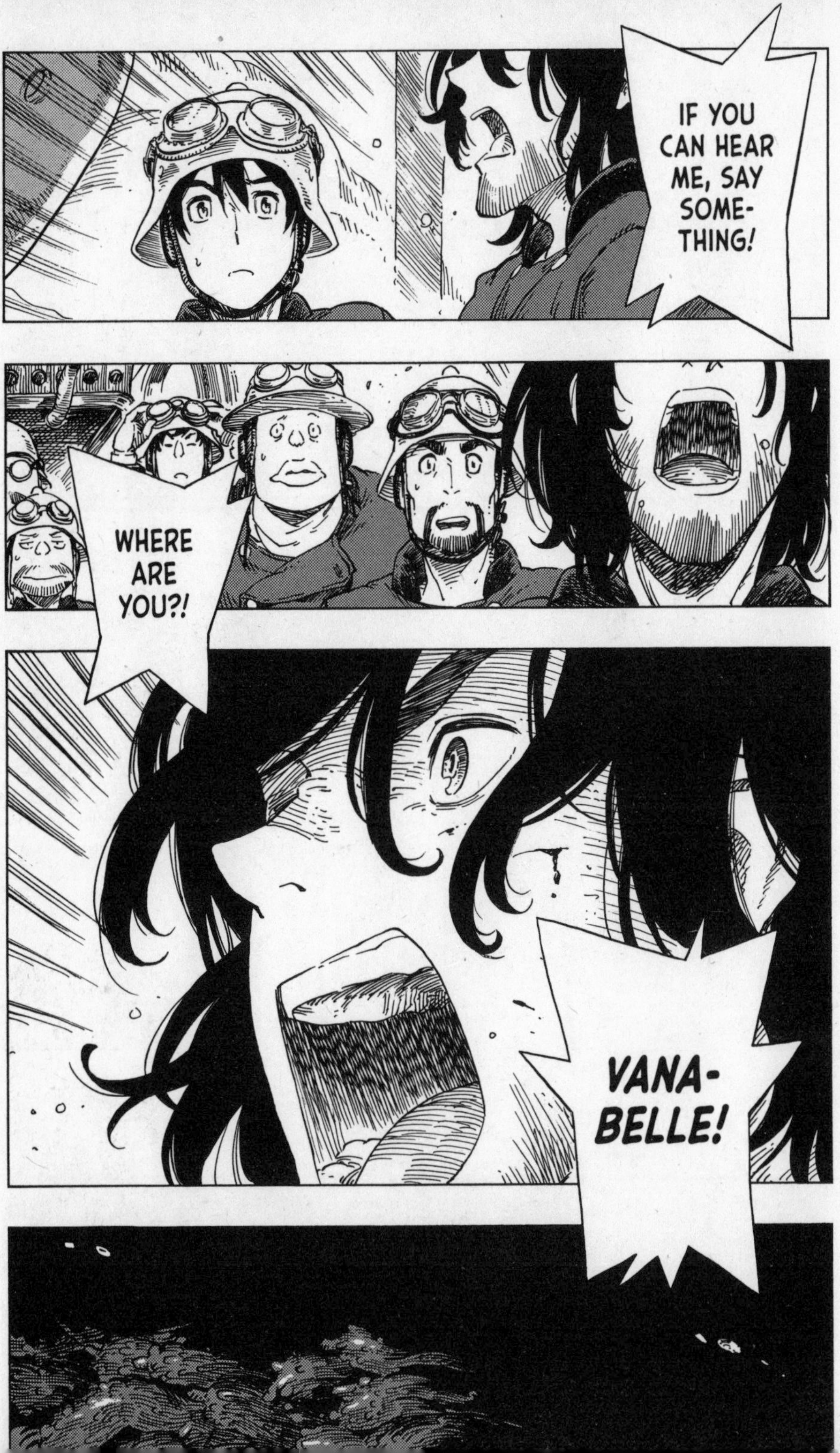
IF YOU CAN HEAR ME, SAY SOME- THING!
WHERE ARE YOU?!
VANA- BELLE!

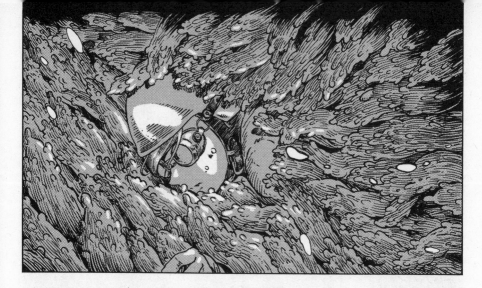

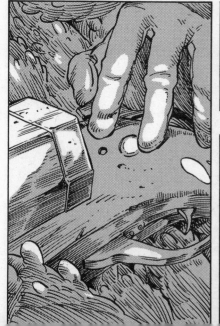

TWITCH

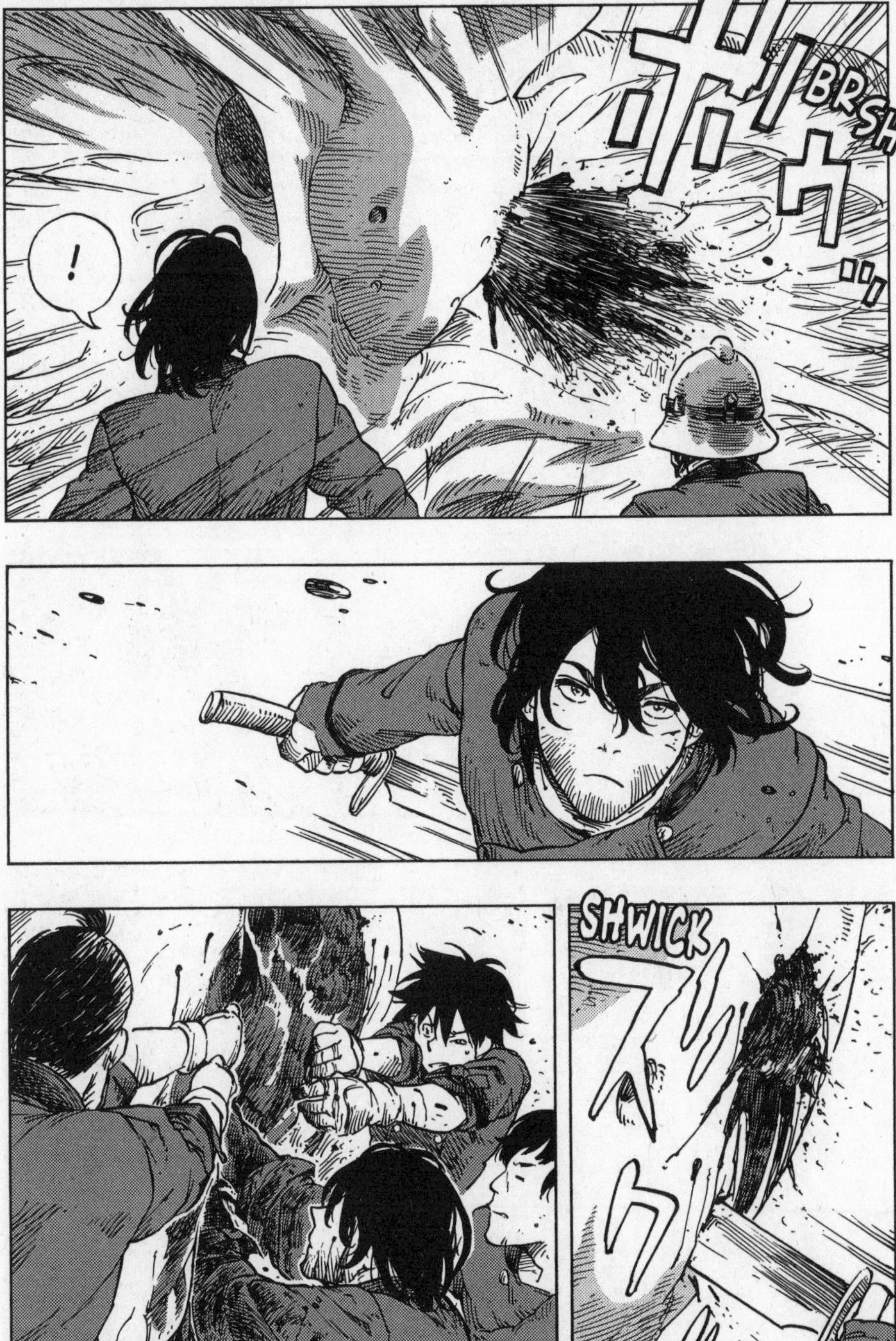
BRSH
!
SHWICK

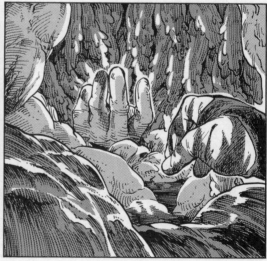

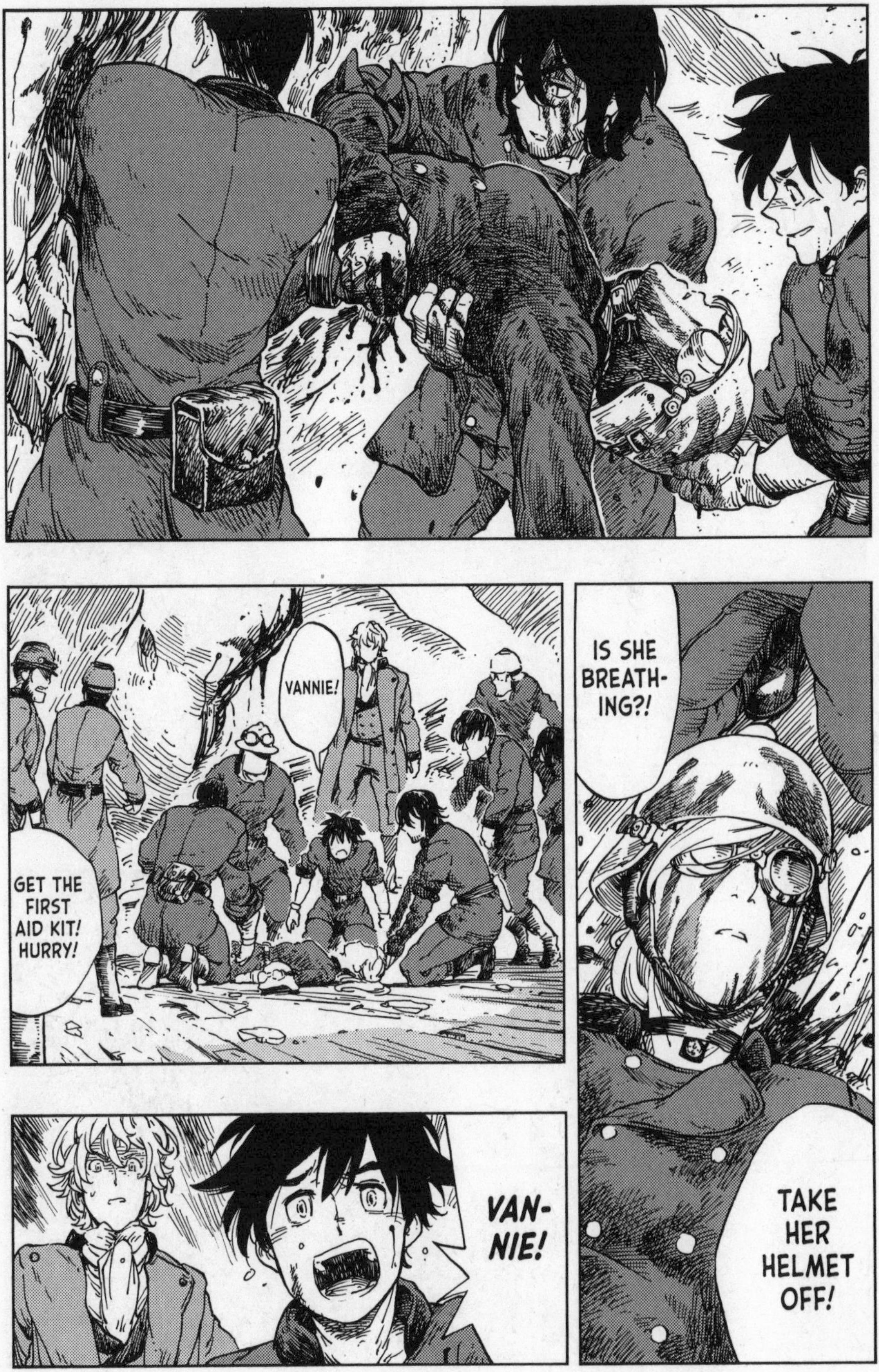
IS SHE BREATH-ING?!
TAKE HER HELMET OFF!
VANNIE!
GET THE FIRST AID KIT! HURRY!
VAN-NIE!

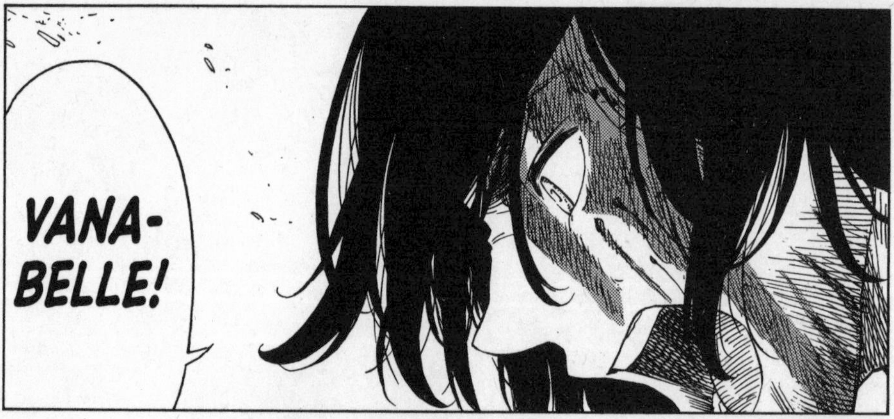
VANA-BELLE!
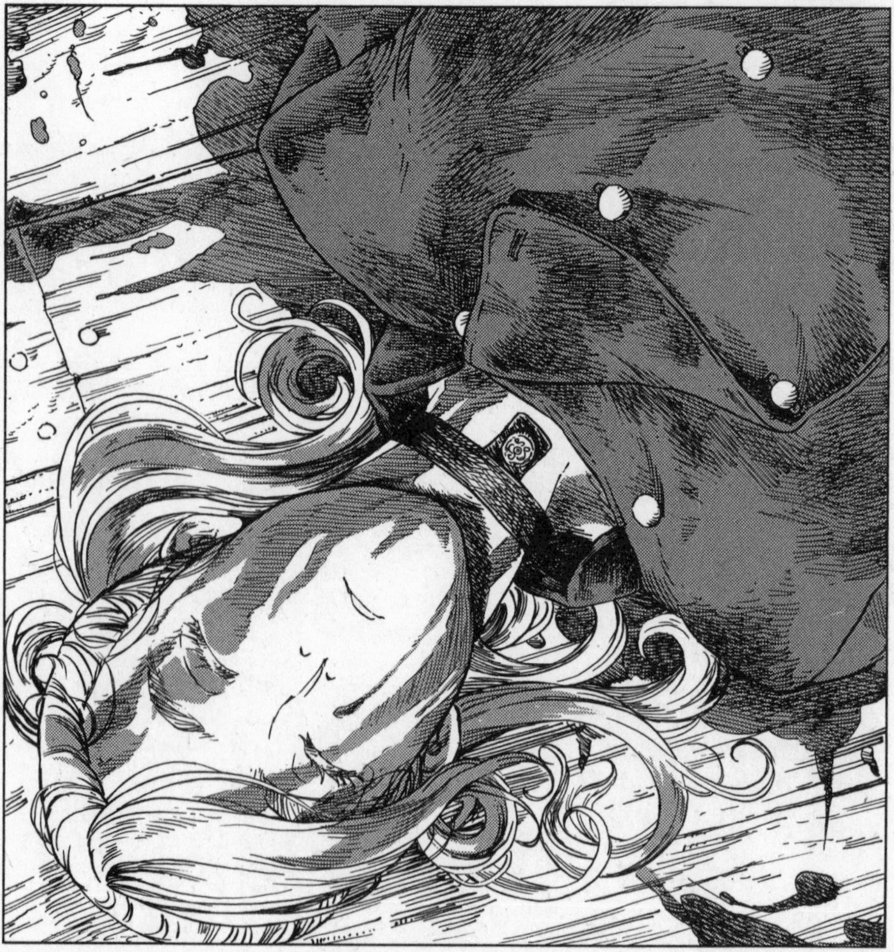

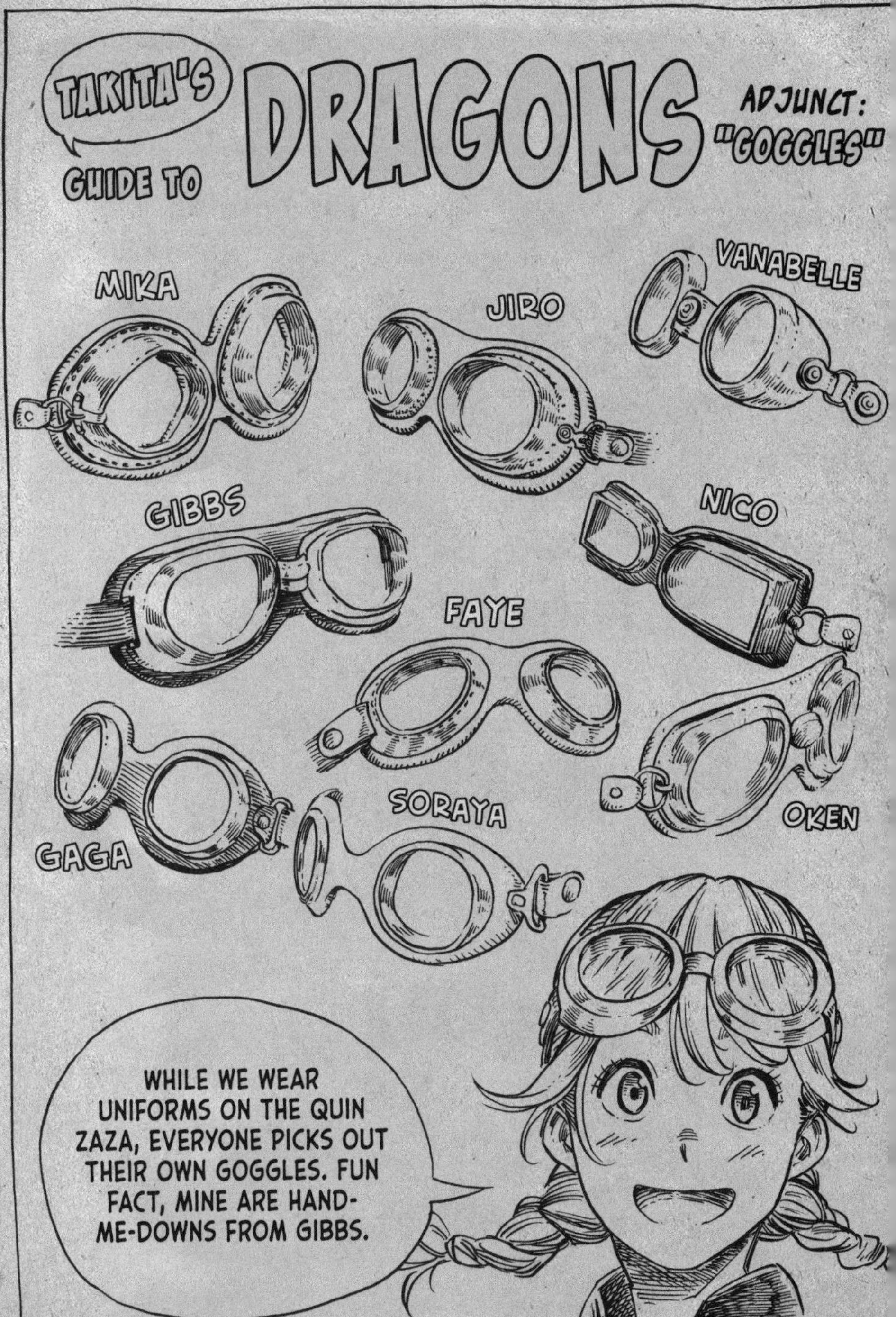
TAKITA'S GUIDE TO DRAGONS
ADJUNCT: "GOGGLES"
VANABELLE
JIRO
MIKA
NICO
GIBBS
FAYE
OKEN
SORAYA
GAGA
WHILE WE WEAR UNIFORMS ON THE QUIN ZAZA, EVERYONE PICKS OUT THEIR OWN GOGGLES. FUN FACT, MINE ARE HAND-ME-DOWNS FROM GIBBS.

A Kodansha Comics Trade Paperback Original
Drifting Dragons 4 copyright © 2018 Taku Kuwabara
English translation copyright © 2020 Taku Kuwabara

All rights reserved.

Published in the United States by Kodansha Comics, an imprint of Kodansha USA Publishing, LLC, New York.

Publication rights for this English edition arranged through Kodansha Ltd., Tokyo.

First published in Japan in 2018 by Kodansha Ltd., Tokyo as *Kuutei Doragonzu*, volume 4.

ISBN 978-1-63236-951-2

Original cover design by Miki Kawano

Printed in the United States of America.

www.kodanshacomics.com

9 8 7 6 5 4 3 2 1
Translation: Adam Hirsch
Lettering: Thea Willis
Editing: Sara Tilson & Ajani Oloye
Proofreading: Jacob Friedman
Kodansha Comics edition cover design by Phil Balsman

Publisher: Kiichiro Sugawara
Managing editor: Maya Rosewood
Vice president of marketing & publicity: Naho Yamada

Director of publishing services: Ben Applegate
Associate director of operations: Stephen Pakula
Publishing services managing editor: Noelle Webster
Assistant production manager: Emi Lotto